RAPTORS
OF NORTH AMERICA

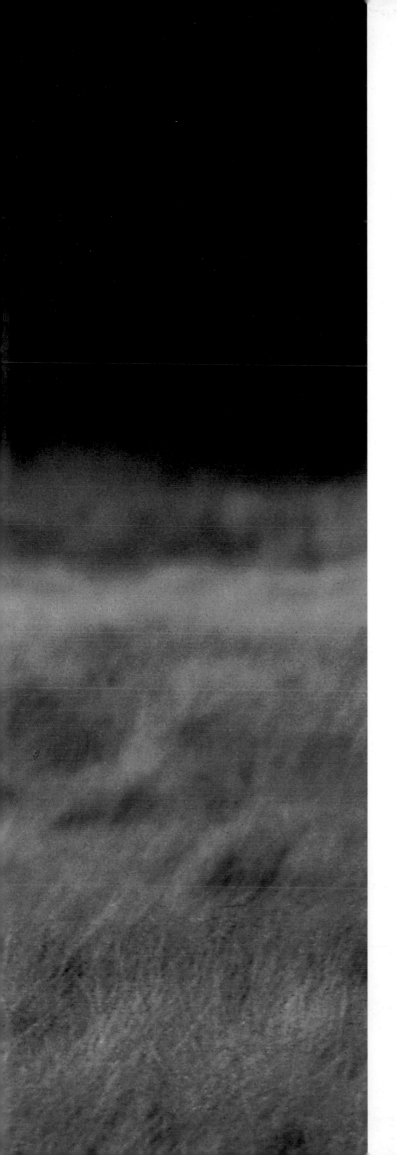

RAPTORS
OF NORTH AMERICA
NATURAL HISTORY AND CONSERVATION

NOEL AND HELEN SNYDER

Voyageur Press

To Chan Robbins and Brooke Meanley for early and enduring inspiration

Front cover photograph © Henry H. Holdsworth

Frontis: A Peregrine Falcon prepares to launch into flight in pursuit of
nearby waterfowl.

Title Page: A Short-eared Owl forages close to the ground with deep
slow wing beats.

Title Page inset: A male adult Cooper's Hawk stretches his wings and tail.

Table of Contents: The Great Gray Owl's piercing yellow eyes differ
strikingly from the dark eyes of its close relatives, the Barred Owl and
the Spotted Owl. Most owls have large eyes capable of detecting prey
in dim lighting, but some species with highly refined hearing, including
the Great Gray Owl, can also capture prey in total darkness.

Library of Congress Cataloging-in-Publication Data

Snyder, Noel F. R.
  Raptors of North America : natural history and conservation /
Noel and Helen Snyder.
     p. cm.
  Includes bibliographical references (p. 315) and index.
  ISBN-13: 978-0-7603-2582-7 (alk. paper)
  ISBN-10: 0-7603-2582-0 (alk. paper)
  1. Birds of prey—North America. 2. Birds—Conservation—North
America. I. Snyder, Helen, 1942– II. Title.
  QL696.F3S6784 2006   598.9097—dc22   006000011

Edited by Gretchen Bratvold
Jacket designed by Maria Friedrich
Interior designed by Brenda C. Canales

Printed in China

Carrying a branch to fortify her nest, a Golden Eagle lands next to her well-grown nestling in central Alaska. Fed a diet mainly of arctic ground squirrels, the nestling did not fledge until midsummer and likely remained dependent on his parents into the fall migration. As is true of most raptor species, Golden Eagles have time for only a single nesting effort per year.

Contents

Acknowledgments   9
Introduction   11
The Major Groups of North American Raptors   15
Observing and Studying Raptors   21

DIURNAL RAPTORS

Vultures
California Condor (*Gymnogyps californianus*)   29
Turkey Vulture (*Cathartes aura*)   40
Black Vulture (*Coragyps atratus*)   45

Kites
White-tailed Kite (*Elanus leucurus*)   51
Everglade (Snail) Kite (*Rostrhamus sociabilis*)   55
Hook-billed Kite (*Chondrohierax uncinatus*)   62
Mississippi Kite (*Ictinia mississippiensis*)   68
Swallow-tailed Kite (*Elanoides forficatus*)   74

Harriers
Northern Harrier (*Circus cyaneus*)   81

Accipiters
Northern Goshawk (*Accipiter gentilis*)   87
Cooper's Hawk (*Accipiter cooperii*)   94
Sharp-shinned Hawk (*Accipiter striatus*)   99

Buteos and Allies
Broad-winged Hawk (*Buteo platypterus*)   105
Red-tailed Hawk (*Buteo jamaicensis*)   109
Red-shouldered Hawk (*Buteo lineatus*)   114
Gray Hawk (*Asturina nitida*)   118
Short-tailed Hawk (*Buteo brachyurus*)   122
Swainson's Hawk (*Buteo swainsoni*)   127
Rough-legged Hawk (*Buteo lagopus*)   132
Ferruginous Hawk (*Buteo regalis*)   139
White-tailed Hawk (*Buteo albicaudatus*)   143
Zone-tailed Hawk (*Buteo albonotatus*)   146
Common Black Hawk (*Buteogallus anthracinus*)   150
Bay-winged (Harris's) Hawk (*Parabuteo unicinctus*)   155

Ospreys
Osprey (*Pandion haliaetus*)   161

Eagles
Golden Eagle (*Aquila chrysaetos*)   167
Bald Eagle (*Haliaeetus leucocephalus*)   173

Falcons and Caracaras
Gyrfalcon (*Falco rusticolus*)   181
Peregrine Falcon (*Falco peregrinus*)   184
Prairie Falcon (*Falco mexicanus*)   188
Aplomado Falcon (*Falco femoralis*)   193
Merlin (*Falco columbarius*)   198
American Kestrel (*Falco sparverius*)   202
Crested Caracara (*Caracara cheriway*)   206

NOCTURNAL RAPTORS

Barn Owls
Barn Owl (*Tyto alba*)   215

Eagle, Snowy, Wood, Eared, and Screech Owls
Great Horned Owl (*Bubo virginianus*)   221
Snowy Owl (*Nyctea scandiaca*)   225
Great Gray Owl (*Strix nebulosa*)   230
Barred Owl (*Strix varia*)   236
Spotted Owl (*Strix occidentalis*)   242
Short-eared Owl (*Asio flammeus*)   248
Long-eared Owl (*Asio otus*)   254
Eastern Screech Owl (*Otus asio*)   259
Western Screech Owl (*Otus kennicottii*)   263
Whiskered Screech Owl (*Otus trichopsis*)   268
Flammulated Owl (*Otus flammeolus*)   273

Burrowing, Boreal, Saw-whet, Hawk, Pygmy, and Elf Owls
Burrowing Owl (*Athene cunicularia* or *Speotyto cunicularia*)   281
Boreal Owl (*Aegolius funereus*)   286
Northern Saw-whet Owl (*Aegolius acadicus*)   291
Northern Hawk Owl (*Surnia ulula*)   295
Northern Pygmy Owl (*Glaucidium gnoma*)   299
Ferruginous Pygmy Owl (*Glaucidium brasilianum*)   304
Elf Owl (*Micrathene whitneyi*)   308

Suggested Further Readings   315
Index   316
About the Authors   320

Only female Sharp-shinned Hawks incubate eggs and brood young, although males often stand guard at nests while their mates feed on prey. Females are larger than males, following the usual pattern in raptors, and in this species weigh almost twice as much as their mates.

Acknowledgments

THE ASSEMBLY OF THIS BOOK has been a part-time effort for more than fifty years and has been aided by many individuals. We are especially indebted to associates who have collaborated in observations of various species in the wild and to an army of admirable raptor biologists, many of whom we have never met, who have conducted crucial research on various species over the years and whose publications have provided a foundation of knowledge of these birds. We can only begin to recognize all these individuals here and will focus on people we have worked with most closely in the field.

In studies of various vulture species, especially the California Condor, we worked with more than a hundred other individuals in the 1980s, and wish especially to acknowledge the contributions of Eric Johnson, Dave Clendenen, Dave Ledig, Jan Hamber, John Ogden, Vicky Meretsky, Jesse Grantham, Rob Ramey, John Schmitt, Fred Sibley, Bill Toone, Mike Wallace, and Art Risser, although this does not begin to do justice to the full array of collaborators involved. In addition, much of the current knowledge of vulture biology we have drawn upon has stemmed from the various research efforts of David Houston in Africa and the American tropics and of Peter Mundy in Africa.

For observations of various kite species, we are indebted to collaborators including Steve Beissinger, Rod Chandler, Gary Falxa, Rich Glinski, Dave Ellis, Paul Sykes, Herb Kale, and Tom Smith. Especially inspiring field companions in studies of Everglade Kites were Steve Beissinger, Gary Falxa, and the late Rod Chandler of Okeechobee, Florida, and much of the current knowledge of this species derives from their efforts. We were also especially grateful for the chance to join Tom Smith for a short while during his studies of Hook-billed Kites in Texas and Mexico.

For studies of the three accipiter species, we were privileged to work with Bill Mader, Dan Schmid, John Taapken, Jeff Lincer, Richard Reynolds, and Jim Wiley. Studies of the Puerto Rican Sharp-shinned Hawk were done in collaboration with Jim Wiley in the 1970s, and Jim and Carlos Delannoy have since followed the biology of that raptor in some detail.

For collaborations and an opportunity to visit projects concerning the buteonine hawks, we are indebted to Jim Wiley, Bill Mader, Jim Dawson, Rich Glinski, Arnold Moorhouse, and Jay Schnell; and for similar opportunities regarding the falcons, we thank Walter Spofford, Rich Glinski, Bill and Tom Mader, Jerry Swartz, Ernesto Enkerlin, and Dean Keddy-Hector. The late Walter Spofford was instrumental in introducing us to studies and observations of North American eagles and falcons, and his boundless enthusiasm for these birds serves as a continuing inspiration.

For opportunities and inspiration regarding the nocturnal species, we have drawn heavily on the contributions of Roger Payne, Sally Spofford, Bill Courser, Russell Duncan, Jeff Foote, Rod Drewein, Fred Gehlbach, Helen Carlson, Arnold Moorhouse, Dave Jasper, Bob Chapman, Jim Wiley, Steve Emslie, and Ted Swem. And as long-term field companions in many of these studies, we are especially grateful to Jim Shiflett and Dave Utterback. The drawings by the latter of many raptor species far surpass the photographs we offer here in conveying the aesthetic essence of these birds, and Dave has kindly allowed us to use one of these as a frontispiece for the owls section. Narca Craig has likewise contributed a most inspiring drawing of an Apache Goshawk to introduce the diurnal raptors section.

For numerous opportunities regarding diurnal and nocturnal raptors in Mexico, we owe a long-standing thanks to Ernesto Enkerlin and to his students and staff, including Diana Venegas-Holguín, Miguel Angel Cruz, and Javier Cruz, among others. Our work on raptors in Puerto Rico was aided immensely by the contributions of John Taapken, Carlos Delannoy, José Rivera, Jim Wiley, Clint Boal, Joseph Wunderle, and Howard Smith.

The written accounts presented in this book owe much to data assembled and made available in Arthur Cleveland Bent's *Life Histories of North American Birds*, Ralph Palmer's *Handbook of North American Birds*, Ian Newton's *Population Ecology of Raptors*, and Paul Johnsgard's thorough books on biology of these species. We have also relied heavily on information in James Duncan's *Owls of the World* and especially on the information provided on raptors by many expert authors in the recent Birds of North America series edited by Alan Poole and Frank Gill. The overall range maps we present for the various species are based primarily on the detailed range maps given by Johnsgard and in the recent Birds of North America series.

For identification of arthropods mentioned in text, we thank Jim Brock and Tom Eisner. For editorial expertise in preparing the manuscript, we are indebted to Elizabeth Knight for the 1991 version of this book and Gretchen Bratvold for the current one, and for help in preparing photographs for presentation, we thank Dave Utterback. Other than the cover, the authors took all photographs in the wild, although we acknowledge that minor digital wizardry resurrected some from the trash bin of inadvertent scratches and blemishes.

Introduction

SINCE ANCIENT TIMES, predatory birds have figured prominently in the art, ceremonies, and legends of most human societies. Fierce images of raptors abound in the cave paintings of bygone peoples around the world. Feathers of giant birds of prey once decorated the festive costumes of many tribes and clans. Ritual sacrifices of condors and eagles were formerly a widespread custom, and many of the earliest epic sagas featured raptors as sources of wisdom and power or agents of retribution. In manifestations ranging from mummies of falcons in the pyramids of Egypt to gold and turquoise owls fashioned by ancient artisans of Peru, raptors have permeated the traditions of virtually all civilizations over many thousands of years.

The cultural importance of raptors has not diminished in more modern times. Our national bird, the Bald Eagle, is a bird of prey, and many other countries have likewise chosen raptors as their national symbols. Similarly, innumerable other organizations, from baseball teams to rock bands, have adopted raptor names and logos. Condor Helicopters, Eagle Office Products, Falcon Realty, Hawkeye Heating and Cooling—the evidence of our bewitchment with these birds appears in strange and diverse places.

How and why did birds of prey become objects of this timeless veneration? Perhaps the bond we perceive with these bold avian aggressors traces to deep-rooted human traditions of hunting and warfare. Perhaps it reflects our intrinsic admiration and respect for creatures that can dominate the skies and kill without remorse. Perhaps it also stems from other, more primordial fears and emotions. Whatever the origins, our ties to birds of prey are indeed powerful.

This book is primarily a collection of the stories and memories of our encounters with birds of prey, both in professional and recreational settings, over a lifetime mainly devoted to field research on endangered birds. The fifty-three species of raptors considered in this book are all the birds of prey that have bred regularly in recent times within the confines of continental North America, north of Mexico. Included are species that are limited largely to cold climates, such as Snowy Owls, Gyrfalcons, and Rough-legged Hawks, as well as a substantial number of species, such as the Elf Owl, the Ferruginous Pygmy Owl, the Common Black Hawk, and the Aplomado Falcon, that are primarily tropical in distribution but that do reach the United States along its southern borders. As a group, the North American raptors occupy all major habitats on the continent, and in adapting to a great diversity of environmental conditions they have developed a great variety of lifestyles and personalities. Each species exhibits a unique range of behaviors and natural history characteristics that are useful for its particular role in nature; no two species are alike in the solutions they have found to the challenges of existence.

Raptors interact continually with many other wildlife species, often as their predators, but sometimes as their prey, sometimes as competitors for nest sites or food, and sometimes in other less obvious ways. Through these relationships, raptors encounter many of the same conservation problems faced by these other wildlife species. In fact, as was dramatically demonstrated during the era of organochlorine pesticides immediately after World War II, the sensitivity of raptors to various invisible yet pervasive forms of environmental contamination in their food supply can be especially great, and these birds can serve as valuable indicator species of the overall health of ecosystems. Because raptors often require relatively large expanses of habitat and feed on a great diversity of prey species, efforts to ensure their survival also aid the survival of many other creatures within their ranges. Thus, the measures taken to preserve from extinction species such as Everglade Kites and Spotted Owls have much wider significance than just the improved welfare of these particular species.

Of the North American raptor species, relatively few are currently listed as threatened or endangered on the continent, namely the California Condor (*Gymnogyps californianus*), the Everglade Kite (*Rostrhamus sociabilis*), the Aplomado Falcon (*Falco femoralis*), the Crested Caracara (*Caracara cheriway*), the Spotted Owl (*Strix occidentalis*), and the Ferruginous Pygmy Owl (*Glaucidium brasilianum*). A number of others, however, occur only in small populations in the United States and are vulnerable to sliding into the endangered category in the future. Perhaps the species most vulnerable to disappearing from the fauna of the United States, including both currently threatened and nonthreatened species, are a variety of tropical raptors that just barely reach the country's southern borders. However, all these species—the Everglade Kite (*Rostrhamus sociabilis*), the Hook-billed Kite (*Chondrohierax uncinatus*), the Swallow-tailed Kite (*Elanoides forficatus*), the Gray Hawk (*Asturina nitida*), the Short-tailed Hawk (*Buteo brachyurus*), the White-tailed Hawk (*Buteo albicaudatus*), the Zone-tailed Hawk (*Buteo albonotatus*), the Common Black Hawk (*Buteogallus anthracinus*), the Bay-winged Hawk (*Parabuteo unicinctus*), the Aplomado Falcon (*Falco femoralis*), the Crested Caracara (*Caracara cheriway*), the Whiskered Screech Owl (*Otus trichopsis*), and the Ferruginous Pygmy Owl (*Glaucidium brasilianum*) also occur in larger populations beyond the southern border of the United States, so they are not truly endangered as entire species at the present time. None of the North American raptors is known to have gone fully extinct in historical times, although some have come quite close to winking out, and it is clear from fossils that many raptor species disappeared from the continent at the end of the Pleistocene epoch about ten to twelve thousand years ago. The specific causes of the late Pleistocene extinctions have been a subject of heated debate and may well have been various. Many organisms other than raptors were also affected, and it was clearly a time of massive faunal and floral upheaval.

With about one-tenth of the North American raptors currently in some sort of official threatened or endangered status, the birds of prey deserve continued close attention from a conservation standpoint, although several other groups of birds have proportionately more endangered species. On a worldwide basis, the parrots, guans, and curassows, for example, have been declining much more alarmingly.

As a general view, we firmly support the conservation of raptors as wild creatures and can think of nothing more depressing than a world where raptors are found only in zoos. We also prefer to think of humans as a

---

Left: *A Northern Pygmy Owl peers from her nest entrance forty feet up a sycamore snag in southeastern Arizona. To acquire this nest hole, the pygmy owls successfully displaced a Flammulated Owl earlier occupying the site. The hole was originally excavated by woodpeckers.*

Between hunts for prey, a male Aplomado Falcon eyes the sky from a habitual perch near his nest in Tamaulipas, Mexico. Like many other falcons and many owls, aplomados characteristically occupy old stick nests made by various hawks or corvids.

part of nature, not as a species opposed to nature. This means neither a strict separation of our species from wild raptor populations nor a world in which humans must continually handle and manipulate wild raptors in order for them to survive. Overall, we personally support efforts to keep wild raptor populations as natural as possible and believe that efforts to sustain populations that involve continuing nursemaid attention from humans, such as those dependent on nest box programs or artificial feeding programs, are inherently more risky and less desirable in the long run than efforts that are focused on maintaining the health of natural ecosystems. We also believe that proponents have sometimes gone overboard with captive-breeding and release programs that are not always well justified for the conservation of species. Such efforts are often hugely expensive, and one often has to question whether the monies might not be much better spent in well-designed habitat conservation and restoration efforts. Some intensive conservation programs employing captive breeding and release are indeed necessary; many others are not and can actually detract from and compete with more fundamental ecological solutions to species endangerment.

In this book we have two major goals. First, by offering glimpses into the natural history of all of North America's raptors and by presenting a variety of photographs of these species carrying on their

accustomed affairs, we hope to awaken curiosity about the biology of birds of prey worldwide. Second, by detailing some of the problems faced by the North American species and by suggesting some solutions to specific threats, we hope to encourage a general interest in raptor conservation. In pursuit of these goals, we do not presume that the reader already knows a great deal about raptors or natural history, and we keep scientific jargon to a minimum. We do, however, consider many current topics of debate in raptor biology in the hopes the reader will be as interested in the unknowns about raptors as in the knowns.

Our presentation is based mainly on our personal experiences of more than a half century of observing these birds conducting their daily activities in natural environments. Our emphasis is strongly on field natural-history studies, and we recommend such studies as among the most exciting and rewarding pursuits a person can undertake, either as an amateur or professional ornithologist. Such studies are in fact the essential basis both for gaining a comprehensive biological understanding of these birds and for designing an effective framework for their conservation. These tasks are by no means complete even for the best-studied North American and European raptors. For many of the raptors in less populated parts of the world, essentially nothing is yet known, so the opportunities for new discoveries include virtually all aspects of their natural history. Such opportunities are especially great for many tropical birds of prey, some of which occur in very small numbers and are highly vulnerable to extinction. In the years ahead, a detailed understanding of the biology of these birds will be crucial for the development of successful measures to ensure their continued existence.

The values that birds of prey represent for those who have come to know them well are many but are difficult to communicate adequately on the printed page. Words, art, and photographs are at best only weak substitutes for actual experiences. Swirling masses of migrating Broad-winged Hawks can be described after a fashion, but the descriptions cannot bring to life the spectacle itself, just as there is no way to convey properly the unique sounds and smells of a troop of hungry Black Vultures and Crested Caracaras battling over a rotten raccoon carcass. Once experienced, such vivid impressions become engraved in an observer's consciousness, and their strength provides the primary motivation for further study of these birds. We hope this book stimulates readers to venture forth into the field to discover directly the value of such experiences. Learning how other species deal with the world is not only a fascinating activity in its own right, but also a highly instructive way to gain increased understanding of our own behavior. Like raptors, we too are both predators and prey, and much of our own biology finds close parallels in the biology of these birds.

Our planet's human population continues to swell, making it steadily more difficult to preserve the biological diversity on which our survival and quality of existence depend. Perhaps this is ultimately a hopeless battle, but to give up in the effort would be to guarantee defeat. We firmly believe it is unlikely that much can be achieved in solving the great challenges ahead without empathy and aesthetic appreciation for the intrinsic values of other species, and we hope this book contributes to that empathy in ways that may eventually lead to a more stable balance between our species and the natural world.

In Scheelite Canyon of Arizona's Huachuca Mountains, a fledgling Spotted Owl stretches one wing and leg in the late-afternoon sunlight. The Spotted Owls in this canyon are probably the best-known individuals of the species in all of North America. Spotted Owl conservation has been one of the most controversial issues involving wildlife species in recent decades because of conflicts with the timber industry.

Much has happened since the first edition of this book appeared in 1991, and we have revised the accounts of the diurnal raptors to incorporate new observations of our own and others made in more recent years. In addition, we have added accounts and photographs of all the owl species found regularly north of the Mexican border, so that the new edition considers both nocturnal and diurnal raptor species on an equal basis.

Our personal interest in owls actually preceded our interest in the diurnal raptors, and we have long wanted to return to observations and research on the nocturnal species. This became practical when we moved in the late 1980s to one of the regions of highest owl diversity in the United States—southern Arizona.

With Elf Owls and Western Screech Owls nesting in our backyard and with Burrowing Owls, Barn Owls, Great Horned Owls, Whiskered Owls, Long-eared Owls, Saw-whet Owls, Flammulated Owls, Spotted Owls, and Pygmy Owls all breeding within short distances, we presently live in a paradise of the nocturnal species and have become much more nocturnal ourselves as a result.

The present edition starts and ends with our most extended accounts for the North American raptors—the California Condor, the largest species, which we lived with on a daily basis in an intensive research and conservation effort of the 1980s, and the Elf Owl, the smallest species, which now monopolizes our lives each year from mid-March to early July. But as special as these two species are, we have found the process of becoming familiar with the lives of all the North American raptors to be a marvelous voyage of discovery and delight. The voyage continues and we hope it never ends.

Introduction

The Major Groups of North American Raptors

NORTH AMERICA'S BIRDS of prey fall into two basic groups: nocturnal raptors—the owls—and diurnal (daytime) raptors—hawks, harriers, kites, falcons, caracaras, eagles, ospreys, vultures, and condors. All these birds are meat eaters and all possess hooked bills adapted for tearing apart food. Further, they share much in their reproductive and foraging habits, and in their vulnerability to stresses such as environmental pollutants. Yet they have not all evolved from a single ancestral group of primordial raptors. Rather, today's birds of prey are believed to have evolved from a number of different kinds of early birds, and many of the behavioral and morphological traits shared by contemporary raptors were not characteristic of their early ancestors but developed convergently through time because the similar predatory lifestyles of various ancestral groups favored similar adaptations.

Thus, North America's raptors include the survivors of a variety of independent lines of evolution, although various subgroups of raptors do trace back to single ancestral groups. The owls, which themselves include two rather different lineages, stem from a source quite separate from the immediate ancestors of the diurnal raptors, while the diurnal raptors are quite clearly a hodgepodge. Most notably, the New World vultures have only a very distant common ancestry with other diurnal birds of prey, and instead are generally believed to find their closest relatives among the storks.

Like all other living creatures, the raptors of North America are classified in a hierarchical scheme of categories. The most basic and well-defined category is the SPECIES, which represents an assemblage of organisms (in this case, birds) that interbreed with one another. Species may sometimes be divided into geographic RACES (or SUBSPECIES) that differ from one another in subtle ways, but the various races of a species are all considered to be part of one interbreeding assemblage—one gene pool.

Species do not normally interbreed successfully with other species. If a species shares a great many characteristics with certain other species, however, and is believed to be very closely related to these other species, it may be classified in the same GENUS as these other species. A genus is thus a group of relatively similar species believed to be derived from a close common ancestral stock.

Each species is given a unique Latinized scientific name, which consists of a capitalized genus name followed by a lowercased species name, both always written in italics. For example, the scientific name of the Red-tailed Hawk, *Buteo jamaicensis*, consists of a genus name, *Buteo*, and a distinctive species name, *jamaicensis*, in this instance calling attention to the fact that the species was first described from the island of Jamaica in the West Indies. Other hawks in the genus *Buteo*, for example the Broad-winged Hawk (*Buteo platypterus*) and the Short-tailed Hawk (*Buteo brachyurus*), are all relatively similar to and presumably very closely related to the Red-tailed Hawk. When geographic races of a species are recognized, the race name follows the species name in the full scientific name, as in the Mexican race of the Northern Goshawk: *Accipiter gentilis apache*.

When species are classified in different genera (the plural of genus), they are considered less closely related to one another than when they are in the same genus. Nevertheless, genera that are believed to be relatively closely related to one another are placed in the same FAMILY. North America's diurnal raptors belong to one or another of four different families—the Vulturidae (or Cathartidae), the Accipitridae, the Pandionidae, and the Falconidae—and each family consists of one or more genera. For example, the family Vulturidae consists of seven living species in five genera—*Vultur* (one species), *Gymnogyps* (one species), *Cathartes* (three species), *Sarcoramphus* (one species), and *Coragyps* (one species)—and three of these species presently occur in North America. In contrast, the family Pandionidae consists of only one genus and species, *Pandion haliaetus*—the Osprey. That the Osprey is the only species in its family indicates that it does not have any truly close relatives among the other diurnal raptors.

Finally, three of the four families of North American diurnal raptors are classified together in one ORDER, the Falconiformes, which is a major division of the CLASS Aves, which includes all birds. The fourth family of diurnal raptors, the Vulturidae, is placed in a different order, the Ciconiiformes. The order including all owls is the Strigiformes.

Above: *As the smallest raptor in the world, the Elf Owl grows no bigger than a large sparrow and belongs to the family Strigidae. Adults approaching a nest with food almost always perch a few yards away before entering the nest. Crickets and grasshoppers are among the most commonly taken prey of this highly insectivorous species.*

Left: *A fledgling Merlin eyes his surroundings from a spruce in Alaska's White Mountains. One of a brood of five, he still depended completely on his parents for food and made only short journeys from treetop to treetop. Once they reach full independence, young Merlins, like many other falcons, have long pointed wings and are capable of impressively rapid flight and long migrations.*

The following example illustrates how raptors are classified, showing the full hierarchy of avian categories to which the southwestern desert subspecies of the Great Horned Owl belongs:

Class:	Aves—all birds
Order:	Strigiformes—all owls
Family:	Strigidae—typical owls
Genus:	*Bubo*—eagle owls
Species:	*Bubo virginianus*—Great Horned Owl
Subspecies:	*Bubo virginianus pallescens*—pale southwestern race of the Great Horned Owl

For many years it has been standard in ornithological publications to capitalize the common names of birds when they are given in full, but not when they are given only in part, and we follow this practice in this book. Thus Great Horned Owl is capitalized but horned owl is not. Capitalization of full common names is often not practiced in nonornithological works, where the Great Horned Owl is usually just the great horned owl.

Characteristics of Major Raptor Groups

The table at the end of this section summarizes the distribution of the fifty-three North American raptor species in various orders, families, and genera of birds. Perhaps the most useful category for understanding the relationships of species is the family. Each of the six families of North American raptors is believed to be a natural category of closely related species, although many of the relationships between families are much less well understood. The Tytonidae and Strigidae are families that are generally considered to be reasonably closely related and are consistently considered to be members of a single order, the Strigiformes. For the families in the Falconiformes, in contrast, ornithologists have long debated how close the Falconidae might be to the Accipitridae. These two families have long been grouped together in this order, but some experts believe the two families are quite unrelated. Similarly, the relationships of the Pandionidae have been a source of considerable debate, although this family has usually been included in the Falconiformes as well. Experts now largely agree that the Vulturidae are more closely linked to the storks (Ciconiiformes) than to other diurnal raptors. Indeed, the American Ornithologists' Union now places the Vulturidae in the Ciconiiformes, whereas they were formerly placed in the Falconiformes. Even so, the tradition of considering the vulturids alongside the other diurnal raptors has considerable merit and persists in most books on birds, including this one.

Before moving on to detailed accounts of individual raptor species, it is worthwhile to consider some of the major characteristics of the six raptor families found on the continent. Gaining familiarity with these general characteristics is an efficient way to learn many of the traits of individual species within the families and to appreciate the range of morphological, behavioral, and ecological features to be found in raptors in general.

Vulturidae

The New World vultures (Vulturidae or Cathartidae) are a tightly knit group of species sharing a large number of traits. All are primarily carrion feeders and possess naked heads, an adaptation that apparently reduces the risks of feather fouling for species that commonly insert their heads into the inner recesses of rotten carcasses, but also an adaptation potentially important in heat regulation. All also practice a curious mode of heat regulation known as urohidrosis (cooling off by drenching the legs with excrement), and all nest in caves or other cavities and sheltered places, laying their eggs directly on substrata of litter rather than in definable nests built of twigs. Further, all members of this group possess only weak talons more suited to walking than to grasping or killing prey, and all are essentially mute except for wheezes and snorts audible at close range.

The vulturids include the two largest living birds of prey: the California Condor (*Gymnogyps californianus*) and the Andean Condor (*Vultur gryphus*), both of which commonly exceed twenty pounds in weight and sometimes exceed ten feet in wingspread. Even larger vulturelike birds in a closely related family, Teratornithidae, roamed the New World only a few thousand years ago. The largest flying bird ever known to exist on the planet, *Argentavis magnificens*, was a member of this now-extinct group. Recently described from fossils found in Argentina, *Argentavis* had a wingspread estimated at an astounding twenty-three feet and a weight estimated at about 160 to 170 pounds.

At present, North America has only three living vulturid species—the California Condor, the Turkey Vulture (*Cathartes aura*), and the Black Vulture (*Coragyps atratus*)—although evidence suggests that a fourth species—the King Vulture (*Sarcoramphus papa*)—existed in Florida and Louisiana up until the time of the American Revolution. The King Vulture is still widespread in Central and South America and is commonly exhibited in North American zoos.

Accipitridae

The Accipitridae is a diverse assemblage of species, some with rather obscure relationships to fellow family members. This group includes the hawks of the genera *Buteo* and *Accipiter*, as well as eagles of the genus *Aquila* and harriers of the genus *Circus*. It also includes a number of raptors known as kites, which possess especially buoyant flight characteristics. The kites themselves are diverse. One subgroup, which includes the Black Kite (*Milvus migrans*) and the Mississippi Kite (*Ictinia mississippiensis*), exhibits a peculiar fusion of bones of the inner toe. Interestingly, this same anatomical trait is found in sea eagles of the genus *Haliaeetus*, very likely reflecting a close ancestral relationship. Thus, the Bald Eagle (*Haliaeetus leucocephalus*) apparently is much more closely allied to the Mississippi Kite than it is to the other North American eagle, the Golden Eagle (*Aquila chrysaetos*), which it more closely resembles in size and habits.

Within the Accipitridae, the largest group of species is the buteonine hawks, an assemblage made up primarily of species in the genus *Buteo*, but also including a number of other closely related species in genera such as *Buteogallus* and *Parabuteo*. Twelve of the fifty-three species of North American raptors are buteonine hawks, which can be characterized as medium-sized accipitrids with broad wings and relatively short tails, and which feed primarily on vertebrates. Confusingly, in the Old World, members of the genus *Buteo* are generally referred to as buzzards, while members of the genus *Accipiter* are referred to as hawks. In North America, members of both *Buteo* and *Accipiter* are commonly referred to as hawks, while "buzzard" is a term traditionally applied to certain vulturids. Nowadays, however, the term "buzzard" is rarely used for any North American raptor.

Left: *Near her nest in the hollow of a sycamore in Arizona's Chiricahua Mountains, a female Great Horned Owl of the race* pallescens *displays the awesome talons that allow her species to dominate the night skies throughout most of North America.*

At close range, the white banding of a Zone-tailed Hawk's tail is easy to detect, but this characteristic is much less obvious at the substantial distances from which potential prey generally observe this accipitrid species. Many researchers think the hawk's overall resemblance to the carrion-feeding Turkey Vulture is an example of aggressive mimicry, allowing the hawk to capture prey that mistake it for this unrelated and nonthreatening scavenger.

Most accipitrids are active predators. Their prey range from insects and snails to birds and large mammals, depending on the raptor in question. One group of accipitrids, the Old World vultures, has secondarily evolved to feed on carrion and exhibits many of the anatomical adaptations, especially of the head and feet, seen in the New World vultures. Nevertheless, the Old World vultures clearly reveal their accipitrid affinities by building nests of sticks and by lacking the trait of urohidrosis. Curiously, certain species of Old World vultures once occurred in North America, but disappeared by the end of the Pleistocene. Even more confusingly, the New World vultures first evolved in the Old World but now are limited to the New World.

Pandionidae

While the Pandionidae has generally been considered to be fairly closely related to the Accipitridae, most ornithologists continue to classify it as a separate family. This family consists of just one species, the Osprey (*Pandion haliaetus*), which possesses a number of very distinct anatomical features, especially in wing shape and in the structure of its talons. A fairly large species, the Osprey is a specialized predator of fish, and like the accipitrids, it builds substantial nests of twigs. Found worldwide in coastal, riverine, and lake habitats, it is one of the most successful and cosmopolitan of all raptors.

Falconidae

The Falconidae of North America include only two genera, *Caracara* and *Falco*. Like other genera in this family worldwide, these two genera differ from the accipitrids and the Osprey in a number of anatomical and behavioral respects. Both genera possess distinctive accessory bones attached to the base of the tailbone, for example, and both possess a tendency to attack prey with the talons and bill, rather than with just the talons. None of the species in the genus *Falco* is known to build nests, and members of this genus typically breed in old nests of other species or in caves and other natural cavities. In contrast, caracaras do build twig nests that are similar to accipitrid nests.

Like the vulturids and certain accipitrids, some falconids include carrion in their diets, though most are highly specialized as active predators. Species such as the Crested Caracara (*Caracara cheriway*), which does feed on some carrion, show the typical tendency for loss of feathers in the head region that is associated with this habit.

Tytonidae

Although closely related, the tytonid owls of the genera *Tyto* and *Phodilus* are quite different from the typical owls in the family Strigidae. Distinctive characteristics include heart-shaped facial disks, peculiar serrations on the middle claw, wishbones and breastbones that are fused together, and a lack of external "ear" tufts. Only one species of this family occurs in continental North America, the Barn Owl (*Tyto alba*), and the number of recognized species in the family worldwide has varied considerably in recent years, depending on which authority is consulted. This variability has been due to the existence of many isolated island populations in the genus Tyto that are sometimes considered distinctive species and sometimes merely races of other species. Recent genetic measurements suggest that *Tyto alba*, currently recognized as a single species having a nearly worldwide distribution, may ultimately be split into several species, each with a more limited distribution.

Like many of the typical strigid owls, the tytonid owls are highly nocturnal and rely heavily on hearing to find prey. Also like the strigid owls, falcons, and vulturids, the owls in this group do very little nest building, instead usually breeding in essentially unmodified caves, natural cavities in trees, and other sheltered locations. In certain regions, however, the Barn Owl is known to construct burrows in earthen banks.

Strigidae

The typical owls are a diverse group of birds, most of which are nocturnal, or at least crepuscular—that is, active in the dim light just after sunset or just before sunrise. Certain North American species, however, especially the Burrowing Owl (*Athene cunicularia* or *Speotyto cunicularia*), the Short-eared Owl (*Asio flammeus*), the Great Gray Owl (*Strix nebulosa*), the Northern Hawk Owl (*Surnia ulula*), the Northern Pygmy Owl (*Glaucidium gnoma*), and the Ferruginous Pygmy Owl (*Glaucidium brasilianum*), are active enough during the day that they don't fit the classifications of nocturnal or crepuscular very well.

Many of the strigid owls depend on hearing to find prey, and some are capable of hunting under extremely dark conditions. These owls have distinctive, rounded facial disks that serve to focus and amplify sounds for efficient detection and location of prey. Many of the species that depend on sound to find and capture prey also have very soft-feathered wings, which create very little noise in flight. These enable the owls both to better hear the sounds made by prey and to avoid alarming their prey in capture attempts. In contrast, the strigid owls that use their large eyes much more than their ears in hunting often lack distinctive facial disks, are noisier in flight, and rely on at least dim light to locate prey.

The strigid owls include both the smallest and the largest owls, as well as a great diversity of species of intermediate size. The very smallest species, the Elf Owl (*Micrathene whitneyi*) is about the size of a large sparrow and is considerably smaller than the smallest diurnal raptor. The heaviest is the Snowy Owl (*Nyctea scandiaca*), a species exceeding all diurnal raptors of North America in weight except the Bald and Golden Eagles and the California Condor.

Basic Classification of North American Raptors

ORDER	FAMILY	MAIN SUBGROUPS	GENERA	SPECIES
Ciconiiformes	Vulturidae (Cathartidae)	vultures	3	3
Falconiformes	Accipitridae	kites, harriers, accipiters, buteos and allies, eagles	13	23
	Pandionidae	ospreys	1	1
	Falconidae	falcons, caracaras	2	7
Strigiformes	Tytonidae	barn owls	1	1
	Strigidae	typical owls (various)	10	18

Observing and Studying Raptors

This book is about observing and enjoying raptors in the wild, and we wish to encourage the study of these birds as both a recreational and scientific activity. Nevertheless, because many raptor species are relatively uncommon and exhibit sensitivity to the approach of humans, it is valuable to consider some basic commonsense approaches to observing these birds to avoid significant negative consequences. Raptors can be observed and studied on a personal basis or as a social activity; each approach has merit. For someone just beginning to develop an interest in these species, joining the company of people experienced in raptor observations is a safe and efficient way to learn about many aspects of raptor behavior. Those who have already become facile in identifying and understanding these birds can point out what is normal raptor behavior and what is not—signaling when it is appropriate to back off in observations to avoid the risks of harmful effects. But once some familiarity with these concerns is gained, many bird-watchers may prefer to pursue raptor observations as an individual activity simply because of the enhanced flexibility one can enjoy when not involved in group activities.

Of the many ways people can experience and enjoy raptors, visits to migration concentration points provide an easy introduction to these birds. At strategic overlooks, such as Hawk Mountain in Pennsylvania, Cape May Point in New Jersey, Point Pelee in Ontario, Derby Hill in New York, and the Goshute Mountains in Nevada, it is sometimes possible to view thousands of raptors at very close range in a single day during appropriate times of the year. Experts are usually on hand to help with identifications, and the presence of numerous observers in no way threatens the security or behavior of the birds as they stream past. Massed flights of migratory raptors can be an extraordinarily impressive spectacle, and observations at migration lookouts represent a very rapid way to gain a first appreciation of at least the diurnal species.

Other positive ways to gain familiarity with these birds include joining local chapters of the Audubon Society and other conservation organizations, taking advantage of field trips guided by experts in these organizations, and participating in activities such as Christmas counts. These are the ways we began much of our early activities with raptors, and we learned a tremendous amount in the process and greatly appreciated the contact with some of the foremost experts on these birds at the time.

Much confusion exists regarding the behavioral sensitivity of raptors to close interactions with humans, and indeed there is tremendous variability in the reactions of various birds of prey to our own species. With some raptors, close approach, if prolonged, can be disturbing enough to cause harmful consequences such as nest desertions or nest failures. Other raptors readily habituate to humans and can be observed from very close distances without affecting their feeding rates, reproductive activities, and nesting success in any measurable way. Sometimes, however, familiarity with people can be a negative development, when the acclimated individuals become more susceptible to subsequent human predation as a result.

In evaluating potential impacts, observers should distinguish between effects on individual raptors and effects on raptor populations. Activities that threaten raptor populations are far more worrisome than activities that may negatively impact only single individuals, and while observers should be keenly sensitive to both sorts of impacts, effects on single individuals rarely constitute a threat to a whole species.

Further, when people attempt to shut down all contact of humans with raptor species in a belief this may be the only way to conserve species, they sometimes forget that such contact can potentially be highly beneficial to the conservation prospects of species, both by promoting aesthetic appreciation of the birds and by increasing understanding of their problems and needs. We well remember the passionate sentiments expressed by those who opposed all intensive conservation efforts for the endangered California Condor in the 1980s. Some even believed that passive observations of condor nests from enormous distances were unacceptably risky because of the "stress vibrations" transmitted to the birds by distant observers. Yet, as we came to witness directly during that decade, the condor is one of the more tolerant large bird species to the approach of humans, and wariness is by no means a reliable correlate of endangerment. Without the intensive measures of the 1980s, the California Condor would not exist today, and although viable wild condor populations have not yet been achieved, we remain optimistic that this goal will someday be realized.

In many regions, and particularly with various owl species, certain nesting pairs have become well known to the birding community. Yet these few pairs represent an insignificant fraction of the populations of the species, and although people may view them frequently, they usually habituate quite thoroughly to this activity. In our judgment, the opportunity for people to see these pairs is generally far more positive in the balance than any negative effects of the activity, as long as observations are brief and conducted without substantial disruption of the birds' activities. Nevertheless, debates over whether the public should be allowed to see these birds sometimes become extraordinarily emotional and polarized, with each side becoming steadily more convinced of the irrationality of the opposing side.

Owls are indeed a source of much contention. They can be very difficult to find and study because of their nocturnal habits, and it is common for bird-watchers and researchers to use tape-recorded calls (or vocal imitations) of the species in the field to stimulate individuals into vocalizing so they can be located, censused, observed, or photographed. This practice, however, can be disturbing to the birds—at the least, causing them to temporarily change activity patterns to confront apparent intruders into their territories. Yet the arguments over the use of tape recorders are strongly influenced by other considerations and are often based on very little data. Birders themselves can get very irritated (perhaps more so than the owls) at tracking down a calling owl only to find it is a *Sony walkmanensis*. Further, there is a pervasive belief

Left: *In March 1984, John Schmitt examines a radiotelemetered California Condor that had just perished from lead poisoning. The bird's digestive tract still contained a bullet fragment, likely ingested from the carcass of a hunter-shot mammal. This bird, together with numerous other condors poisoned in more recent years, gave evidence that ingested ammunition fragments were a major cause of the historic condor population's decline. Without intensive studies, including radio-telemetry research, this threat might never have been discovered.*

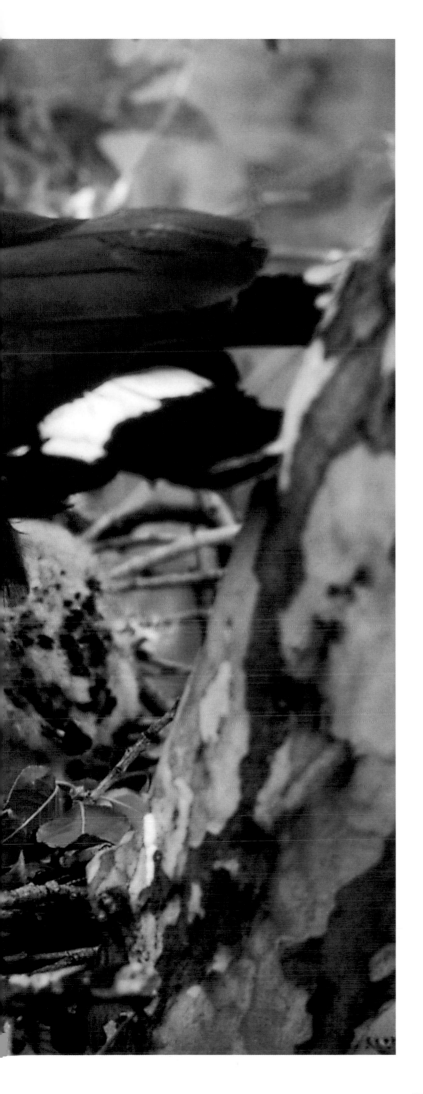

Above: *During 1976 and 1977, Helen collaborated with researcher Rich Glinski in a systematic survey of Common Black Hawk nesting habitats in the southwestern states. This effort, which entailed hikes up or down nearly all the region's permanent streams, yielded an estimate of about 220 to 250 pairs for North America, mostly concentrated in Arizona and New Mexico but with additional pairs in Texas and southern Utah.*

Left: *Accurate diet studies of raptors often demand long-term observations from blinds overlooking nests. We studied this Common Black Hawk nest from a treetop blind in an adjacent sycamore. In ripping apart a large fish for her nestling, the female adult swallowed some mouthfuls herself, but the prey was too big for the two birds to fully consume in a single meal.*

that while it might be acceptable for some birders under some circumstances to use recorders, if "everyone" were to do it, the practice would lead to great harm, causing nests to fail and other catastrophic consequences. In actuality, there is a paucity of rigorous data to suggest whether or not pairs subjected to frequent recorded vocalizations are less productive than pairs that are not. Nevertheless, agency managers in some regions have sought the banning of tape recorders from important owl habitats as a precautionary measure.

On the other side of the issue, the use of tape-recorded calls and vocal imitations has become a very important tool in the conservation of various owl species, as well as of some diurnal raptor species, allowing comprehensive censusing of populations. Determining how much use of tape-recorded calls might be beneficial versus detrimental to a species is often very difficult. Nevertheless, the issue will, no doubt, become increasingly important, with the progressive increase in use of field playback devices.

Efficiently observing some raptors demands a knowledge of peculiarities in their daily activity patterns. In Florida, Crested Caracaras commonly forage for road-killed armadillos, possums, and raccoons at first light. They are much more difficult to find later in the day.

Our own observations suggest that in heavily birded canyons of the southwestern United States (where many birders come to see the small owls and where nests are found early, are publicized, and are "staked out"), disturbance can be minimized if the owls are left alone for the first hour to hour and a half after their activities start in the evening. Like diurnal birds, the small owls do a great deal of feeding during the first hour of their workday, making this the period when risks of disturbance are highest. It is often possible, however, to watch a known nest hole shortly after sunset for the first appearance of the nesting female at the entrance, and then to retreat quickly before feedings get underway. This often affords a good ten minutes or more of study without the need for

flashlights or tape recordings, before feedings begin. Feedings can then proceed without any substantial risks of disturbing the birds' activities.

In our intensive observations of Elf and Flammulated Owls, we found that the adults habituated to us virtually completely even during the first hour of feedings if our presence was nightly and our behavior was consistent from the beginning of the breeding season. A good measure of disturbance for owls is measuring the "perch interval"— the length of time, usually several seconds, between when an incoming adult lands in sight of the nest and when it flies to the nest entrance. We found that when we began observations each night, the incoming adults would initially hesitate a few seconds longer than normal, but where they have been heavily persecuted. Unless an observer takes appropriate precautions, attempts to study these birds closely can quickly lead to regrettable consequences such as nest desertions.

In some diurnal raptors, an individual will exhibit different levels of wariness in different situations. Everglade Kites, for example, are usually quite approachable and safely observable on their foraging grounds, yet they tend to be extremely sensitive around their nests. In conducting reproductive studies of this species, we have found that it is rare to encounter pairs that tolerate blinds anywhere near nests, even in the late breeding stages. To avoid significant problems with this species, it is generally advisable to limit nesting observations to data taken through powerful telescopes at distances of several hundred yards.

Other raptors exhibit different peculiarities in their reactions to human disturbance, making it imperative that an observer has some knowledge of the usual patterns of a species' responsiveness to people before attempting close observations. Nevertheless, although there are typical patterns for species, particular individuals may differ greatly from others of the same species in their sensitivity to humans. On very rare occasions we have even found relatively approachable individuals in the Golden Eagles, perhaps the most generally wary species of all. By the same token, we have sometimes found unusually skittish individuals in species that are normally quite approachable. When the individual characteristics of raptors encountered in the field are unknown, it is always best to treat these birds as potentially very sensitive to disturbance, especially at their nests.

Observations at raptor nests should be made only with the utmost of caution, and only after an observer has had considerable field experience working with raptors in other contexts and has gained considerable sensitivity to their behavior. For the diurnal species, blinds are almost always a necessity for nest observations and should blend in well with surrounding vegetation. The disturbance involved in building blinds can itself represent a significant stress, and construction should generally be carried out in stages, always checking that the birds are accepting progressive developments. When problems arise, the efforts must be aborted quickly. As a general rule, it is unwise to install blinds in the nest-building and incubation stages. Raptors are most likely to tolerate the imposition of blinds during the later stages of breeding.

Observers pose special risks for species nesting in extremely hot or cold environments. In such environments, eggs or small chicks left uncovered can perish very quickly, and close parental attendance at the nest is essential for egg and chick survival. For such species, observers must take great care not to disrupt normal patterns of parental attendance.

Other risks to be avoided in working with nesting raptors involve inadvertent advertisement of the nests to other predators. It is essential to avoid making trails that lead to nests and to refrain from constructing blinds that are conspicuous and call attention to the location of nests.

Careless or poorly conceived efforts to study raptors have the potential for causing more harm than good. Thus, while we wish to encourage the study of raptorial birds, both as an intrinsically rewarding activity and as an essential and important part of ensuring their conservation, we also want to emphasize that birds of prey deserve special treatment in field observations because of their general scarcity and often unpredictable sensitivity to disturbance.

Egg collecting for scientific and recreational purposes was once a widespread activity in North America but has virtually disappeared in the past half century. Though generally regarded as harmful, the practice has had its benefits. A study of historically collected raptor eggs led to the discovery of why many raptor species were declining toward extinction during the organochlorine pesticide era after World War II — a crucial discovery for conservation. Crested Caracara nest trees drew egg collectors to the Kissimmee Prairie of central Florida in the 1920s and 1930s. In this photo from 1979, Rod Chandler of the National Audubon Society inspects a ladder of rusting nails on a cabbage palm trunk that had allowed a collector easy access to one of these early nests.

within five minutes were perching for the normal timing, strongly suggesting that any effects on feeding rates were near negligible.

Although some diurnal raptors are quite tolerant of nearby human activities, most tend to be fairly wary, no doubt because a long history of human harassment has favored the survival of individuals with considerable fear of our species. Certain raptors, especially the Golden Eagle and the Ferruginous Hawk, are extremely difficult to work with at close range, especially in regions

Observing and Studying Raptors

DIURNAL RAPTORS

Above: *A Florida Red-shouldered Hawk in flight reveals a finely-barred tawny breast and conspicuously banded tail. An inhabitant of wet woodlands, the red-shoulder preys on a variety of small aquatic and terrestrial species that are also taken by the hawk's nocturnal counterpart, the Barred Owl.*

Left: *Perched on a sycamore amid the needles of an Apache pine, an Apache Goshawk (Accipiter gentilis apache) lurks in partial concealment. These raptors are probably the most important predators of the Montezuma Quail, Steller's Jays, and Band-tailed Pigeons found in southeast Arizona, although they also take many squirrels and rabbits. Artist Narca Craig based this drawing on a scene near her home in the Chiricahua Mountains.*

California Condor
Gymnogyps californianus

THE IMMENSE, CARRION-FEEDING California Condor is the largest soaring bird of North America. Its huge wings approach ten feet in span and its weight often exceeds twenty pounds. Aloft it rarely flaps its wings, and on a glide through distant skies it sometimes looks more like a small airplane than a bird, often sailing for many miles without wavering from a straight-line path. No other bird on the continent exhibits such serene steadiness in flight or such grandeur in its aerial maneuvers.

The California Condor is also one of the few North American birds for which a reasonably comprehensive paleontological history can be traced back through the recent geological record. Fossils indicate that the species once ranged over nearly the entire continent, undoubtedly feasting on carcasses of the huge mammals of the ice ages. But with the disappearance of many of the great Pleistocene mammals of North America by about eleven thousand years ago, condors became restricted to the Pacific Coast region. Here, they still found good food supplies in whale carcasses and remains of other marine mammals and fish washed ashore, and in dead elk, pronghorn, mule deer, and bighorn sheep in the inland valleys. Condors were still common from British Columbia to Baja California when the first western explorers reached this region in the late eighteenth and early nineteenth centuries.

With the settlement of the West Coast by Europeans, however, the fortunes of the condor again began to worsen. Many birds were lost to indiscriminate shooting. Others were evidently killed by strychnine and cyanide poisoning campaigns that were aimed at eliminating wolves and grizzly bears as a threat to cattle and sheep. Many others were undoubtedly poisoned by ingestion of toxic lead ammunition fragments when they fed on the carcasses of animals killed by hunters. Condor populations disappeared first from Oregon and Washington, then from northern California and Baja California, and by 1940 the only remaining birds were limited to a region surrounding the southern San Joaquin Valley north of Los Angeles. Here, the historic population made its last stand in the wild.

Sadly, despite all efforts to reverse the decline, including the establishment of the magnificent Sespe Condor Sanctuary in the Los Padres National Forest in 1947, the species continued its steady slide toward extinction. By 1985, just nine individuals remained in the wild, including only a single breeding pair. Most observers were convinced that these last few birds would not survive much longer unless they were removed from the wild, and with the trapping of the last wild condor in early 1987, the species came to exist only in captivity. Fortunately, captive breeding quickly proved highly successful, and in 1992, just five years after the last wild condor was captured, first attempts to reestablish the species in the wild were begun.

Left: *California Condors bask in the early morning sun near their nest cave of 1983. Although successful in rearing a chick in 1981 and again in 1983, this pair perished over the winter of 1984 to 1985, a time of catastrophic mortality for the remnant wild population. The largest of the North American vultures, California Condors weigh nearly twenty pounds and sometimes have wings spanning nearly ten feet.*

The enormous size and unusual appearance of the condor, together with its well-known prehistoric association with the giant mammals of the Pleistocene, have given the species a curious reputation of being an obsolete "dinosaur" of a bird, long outlasting its proper place in the ages. At the same time, the great rarity of the condor, and its restriction in breeding to remote and spectacularly rugged montane habitats have made the species a popular symbol of a pristine world not yet defiled by civilization. Even the name "condor" evokes visions of a mystic creature from beyond ordinary reality—an image the species might not have if its earlier appellation of California Vulture had stuck. Perhaps more than any other North American bird, the California Condor has inspired a kind of reverence in our society, even among those who know and care very little about the natural world.

Unfortunately, the spiritual aura that surrounds the California Condor has often worked more to the species' detriment than to its favor. Over the decades, more than a few have considered it a sacrilege to subject such an exalted creature to the kinds of intensive high-tech conservation efforts that eventually became necessary to save the species from extinction. For some, the preservation of an image of the condor unsullied by the touch of man seemingly became more important than the preservation of the species itself. Besides being a victim of diverse ecological excesses of humanity, the condor has at times been a victim of its own wilderness mystique.

The declining fortunes of the condor were already well known to naturalists and ornithologists before the start of the twentieth century. Yet it was not until 1939 that the first concerted effort to determine and reverse the causes of decline was initiated. In that year, Carl Koford began an intensive study of the species for his doctorate degree at the University of California. Roughly one hundred and fifty condors still existed in the wild at that time, but they were exceedingly difficult to count and study because of their huge home ranges and the rugged character of their last nesting habitats. Although

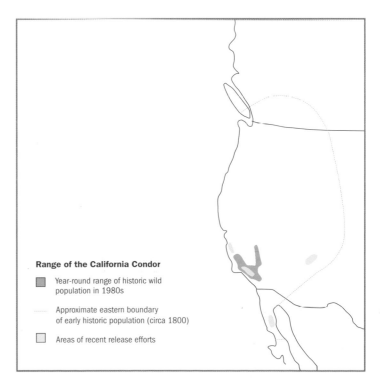

Range of the California Condor

Year-round range of historic wild population in 1980s

Approximate eastern boundary of early historic population (circa 1800)

Areas of recent release efforts

Remnants of a storm envelop the northern slopes of the Sespe Condor Sanctuary near Los Angeles. A major nesting region for condors both during historic times and in the recent release program, this sanctuary has also provided refuge for vigorous populations of black bears and mountain lions.

A pair of condors mutually preen on a talus slope near their nest cliff in 1981. After the disappearance of one of these birds in early 1982, the other nested with a new mate in 1984 in a giant sequoia a hundred miles distant.

Koford identified a number of stresses affecting the condor, it simply was not feasible at that time to determine which forces were contributing the most to the species' decline. Koford suggested, nevertheless, that with strict protection of the primary nesting region of the condor, the species might be able to endure. His recommendations led to the establishment of the Sespe Sanctuary, an eighty-three-square-mile region of canyons and cliffs in Ventura County that encompassed many of the known historic nest locations of the species.

Unfortunately, despite strict protection of the condor from disturbance in the Sespe region, the species' numbers continued to dwindle. A follow-up study in the early 1960s by Alden Miller of the University of California and rancher-biologists Ian and Eben MacMillan estimated a population decline of about 30 percent from the time of Koford's studies. Following this study and with passage of the first federal Endangered Species Act in 1966, the condor received full federal protection and expanded research attention. Fred Sibley of the U.S. Fish and Wildlife Service conducted studies through the late 1960s, and he was followed by Sanford Wilbur through the 1970s.

Because of widespread fears of harming the species, however, research during this period did not employ intensive techniques such as radiotelemetry and was still far too limited in scope to yield a definitive identification of the primary causes of decline. The decline of the species continued through the 1970s, and by the end of that decade the best estimates indicated that only about twenty-five birds might still exist. Primary causes of the decline remained controversial, with some parties believing that reproduction was failing in the population because of declining food supplies, and others believing that forces such as DDT contamination, illegal shooting, and poisoning with compound 1080 (a toxin used to kill ground squirrels) might be the most important stresses.

Clearly, what was needed to rescue the species was a greatly expanded research effort utilizing advanced techniques such as radiotelemetry to determine which causes of decline were truly important, coupled with the simultaneous formation of a captive population as a fail-safe approach in case these causes proved difficult to identify or impossible to remedy in the short period apparently left for the wild population. Congress authorized such a

Above: *California Condors have relatively short tails, distinctive white triangles on the undersides of the wings, and steady soaring flight. Normally flapping only to take off and land, they depend on air movements to stay aloft. Distinctive patterns of molt and feather damage visible during flight allowed reliable identification of individuals and censusing of the wild population in the 1980s.*

Left: *As the flakes of a late-spring snowstorm abate, a condor warming her single egg peers out the entrance of her nest cavity, a full hundred feet from the ground. One of only two condor nests ever found in giant sequoias, this site produced a young condor that was taken captive just before fledging in September 1984.*

program in late 1979 as a result of intensive lobbying efforts by the National Audubon Society, and in 1980 a new expanded conservation and research program for the species was inaugurated, with the U.S. Fish and Wildlife Service and the National Audubon Society sharing primary responsibilities for field activities. John Ogden became the first leader of operations for the National Audubon Society, and Noel was selected to fill a similar role for the U.S. Fish and Wildlife Service.

Still, certain influential opponents in the public continued to oppose all hands-on research with the species and sought all legal means available to prevent implementation of the new program, believing that the condor needed only to be given enough disturbance-free habitat to survive and recover. For several more years, the condor program remained a battleground for diverse interests, all of whom wanted to see the condor preserved, but who disagreed strongly with one another on how this might best be achieved. When Noel first accepted leadership of the U.S. Fish and Wildlife Service's

field condor program, we were intrigued by the challenge and were naively eager to have a chance to study this awesome bird. But if we had known what a quagmire of bitter controversy we were entering, we might well have avoided the opportunity.

Field efforts in the early 1980s were focused primarily on developing effective methods to census the wild population and on locating the last breeding pairs in the wild and studying their reproductive characteristics. By 1983, success in these efforts led to a much more intensive conservation program. Sadly, by that time the wild population had dropped below twenty individuals, and further operations became a desperate race against the clock.

An effective condor censusing method grew out of collaborative efforts with Eric Johnson and his students at a local university to photo-document individual differences of condors in their flight-feather patterns—differences resulting both from peculiarities in feather damage and from the great variability

California Condor

in molt patterns among individuals. These efforts soon established that each condor in the remnant population was unique in its flight-feather pattern, and when enough photographs were taken through time, it was possible to track each individual's survival and movements in great detail. Begun in late 1981, these efforts yielded a firm count of twenty-one condors for the late summer of 1982, down from a probable twenty-three condors earlier in the year. This was the first comprehensive count of the entire condor population ever achieved, and it was an important step in convincing skeptics that the species truly was in great jeopardy and needed fast and decisive aid if it was going to survive.

Photographic counts in the following years showed an alarming decline—to nineteen birds in 1983, fifteen in 1984, and only nine in 1985—yielding an overall mortality rate in the wild population exceeding 25 percent annually. This was far too high a mortality rate to allow population stability or increase under even the most optimistic reproductive conditions, but it was also still arguable that the population might be suffering significant reproductive problems as well. Determining whether the species was suffering major reproductive problems depended crucially on locating and observing all the remaining wild pairs of the species.

Finding the last nesting pairs of the species was a major challenge because the pairs were spread out over a very large region of rugged mountainous terrain mostly outside of the Sespe Sanctuary. Adding to the difficulties were the facts that nesting pairs often visited their nests only at infrequent intervals and that pairs frequently changed nest sites from year to year, sometimes moving many miles between successive nestings. Only with a staff of a dozen field workers patiently following birds to their nests each breeding season was it finally possible to locate all nesting pairs and track their reproductive success directly. The majority of adult condors turned out to be breeders and their success in fledging young from eggs averaged nearly 50 percent—statistics that did not suggest any major problems in reproduction. Thus, by 1984, it had become clear that the species' primary problem was not reproduction, but mortality, although the main causes of mortality still remained largely unknown.

The most significant result from the observations of nesting pairs came in 1982. In this year, a pair of condors under constant daylight surveillance chose a particularly poor nest cave for egg laying—one with a floor that sloped significantly to the outside. This also was a pair that had chronic problems in coordinating incubation duties. The adults bickered continuously over whose turn it was to warm the egg and often left the egg untended as the male repeatedly chased the female away from the nest cave. During one dispute, the egg rolled out of the nest cave, and shortly thereafter it fell over the edge of the cliff during a melee with Common Ravens, smashing on the rocks below. At the time, this incident seemed the greatest of tragedies. But as subsequent events unfolded, it became clear that it was the most fortunate thing that could possibly have happened for the species. The detailed documentation of this event and the events that followed totally revolutionized the course of the conservation program.

Forty days after the destruction of their egg, the pair laid a replacement egg. This was the first time replacement laying had ever been proven conclusively for the species, and the discovery had profound implications. Even though the second egg was also lost—again with raven involvement—a principle had been demonstrated that was to allow an enormous increase in reproduction of the population in the years that followed. With the solid documentation of

replacement clutching in hand, we obtained state and federal authorization to take and artificially incubate and rear first eggs from all condor pairs in 1983. The expectation was that each pair would respond by laying a replacement egg (a process known as multiple clutching) and that reproduction might be as much as doubled as a consequence.

The success of multiple clutching far exceeded expectations, for the total production of young condors in 1983 was six individuals from four pairs. This total should be compared with an average of two fledglings that the wild population had produced annually from 1980 through 1982. Results were even better in 1984, with seven young produced by five pairs. These young, together with a nestling taken captive in late 1982 when its male parent disappeared, a yearling trapped in poor health in late 1982, and Topatopa (a bird taken in 1967 as a starving fledgling), formed the original nucleus of a captive population at the Los Angeles and San Diego zoos, a population that was soon to offer the only hope for ultimate survival of the species.

The tremendous increase in reproduction produced by multiple clutching in 1983 and 1984, coupled with the good survival of breeding pairs in those years, encouraged the California Condor Recovery Team, an advisory group to the U.S. Fish and Wildlife Service, to develop a plan, later approved by state and federal authorities. Multiple clutching of wild pairs would continue at a near maximal rate, but once a minimum of five young were produced for the captive flock by each pair, further production of young from the pairs would be channeled back into the wild flock in an early release program. We all anticipated that these releases might serve to sustain the wild flock while efforts were continued to learn the causes of mortality and reverse these causes. At that time, the mortality rate, while considerable, appeared to be low enough that the increased productivity achievable by multiple clutching might be enough to largely counterbalance it.

Unfortunately, events of the winter of 1984–1985 revealed this strategy to be much too optimistic. Six adult condors were suddenly and unexpectedly lost from the wild population, mostly to unknown causes, and of the five wild pairs active in 1984, only one survived to breed in 1985—a near total collapse of the wild breeding population. No longer did a significant source of young birds exist to build up the captive flock, let alone to serve as a basis for an early release program, and by then concerns were increasing that the existing captive flock might not be diverse enough to be genetically viable. Mortality was clearly a much larger problem than had been appreciated earlier, and it had become highly questionable that the death rate could be sufficiently reduced to allow maintenance of the wild population.

Retrenchment was in order. Releases of captives to the wild in the near term could not be expected to greatly slow the decline and would at the same time jeopardize the chances for achieving a genetically viable captive population. Further, it had become clear that the entire future of the species was now totally dependent on achieving a viable captive population, and there was no point in compromising the chances for success in this endeavor. The remaining birds in the wild population had much more to contribute to conservation of the species as captives than by being left in the wild to die one by one.

Meanwhile, the discovery of a number of dead or dying condors revealed that the wild population was being stressed by mortality factors that were largely impractical to counteract in the near term. Three of four condors found dead or dying between 1983 and 1985, in part through radiotelemetry, were

Left: *A California Condor pauses before entering her nest cave in the Sespe Sanctuary during the summer of 1983. The most productive wild female of the 1980s, this bird also laid the smallest eggs ever documented for the species. Taken captive in 1986, she produced many additional young through the 1990s, then was returned to the wild in 2000. In late 2002, she was nearly lost to lead poisoning but was retrapped and successfully detoxified by emergency chelation therapy, and then was again released to the wild. Shortly afterward, in early 2003, she was shot and killed by a hunter, who was later apprehended and prosecuted.*

California Condor

suffering from independent instances of terminal lead poisoning, apparently resulting from ingestion of lead ammunition fragments in their carrion food. The fourth bird was an apparent victim of cyanide poisoning from a coyote trap.

While it was possible to counter the threat of cyanide poisoning by modifying cyanide trapping procedures (this activity was then under direct control by the U.S. Fish and Wildlife Service), it was not certain that this had been a major problem for the condor overall. Lead poisoning, on the other hand, had emerged as a critical problem, one that in all probability had been stressing the species severely since the first Europeans settled the region.

Unfortunately, lead poisoning was also a nearly insoluble problem at that time, in part because no good alternatives to lead bullets then existed for hunting species such as deer. Steel bullets or shot were not adequate substitutes for various reasons, and at the time there were no other nontoxic alternatives that might perform well in hunting such game. Furthermore, because hunting and predator-control activities, such as coyote shooting, were very widespread and popular activities in southern California (both legally and illegally), almost all observers agreed that a blanket prohibition of shooting in the condor range would be impossible to enforce and would almost certainly increase mortality risks to condors, via a backlash, instead of reducing them. Finally, an intensive effort in 1985 to get the remaining wild condors to feed mainly on "safe" clean carcasses provided by the research program proved to be only a partial success.

Instead, after a long and bitter debate over whether the last wild condors should be taken captive, including an unsuccessful lawsuit mounted by the National Audubon Society to prevent this action, a consensus at last emerged that the best hopes for the species did indeed reside in captive breeding of all the remaining individuals in the near term, followed by later reintroductions of their captive-born progeny into very specific regions in the wild where threats to the species could be minimized. In late 1986 and early 1987, the last of the wild condors were trapped for the captive-breeding program at the San Diego and Los Angeles zoos, yielding an original captive population of twenty-seven individuals: fourteen females and thirteen males.

Our personal involvement with the California Condor program ended in mid-1986, just as a decision to take the last wild birds captive was being finalized in the courts. The era of studies of the historic wild population was nearly over and an era of captive breeding and releases of captives to the wild was about to begin. For most participants it was a sobering time in the history of conservation of the species. The long battle to preserve the historic wild population had failed despite major efforts by dozens of people over the decades. Nevertheless, it was also a time of hope. A substantial captive population had been established, and research in Peru with releases to the wild of captive-reared Andean Condors strongly suggested that viable wild California Condor populations might someday be reestablished.

In more recent years, the condor conservation program has achieved tremendous success in certain respects, but it has had some continuing difficulties in others, and as before, it has remained a hotbed of controversy. Remarkable success has been achieved in captive breeding of the species and by 1998, just ten years after the first successful breeding of the species in captivity, more than one hundred and fifty condors were in existence, thanks to the dedicated efforts of the Zoological Society of San Diego, the Los Angeles Zoo, and the Peregrine Fund. Moreover, twenty-six of the twenty-seven original captives had parented

fertile eggs, and none of the original captives had died—a record rarely approached in captive-breeding programs for endangered species. The total of more than one hundred and fifty condors in 1998 matched the estimated number of condors alive in 1950, and the speed of increase was in significant measure a result of continued multiple-clutching efforts in captivity.

Releases back to the wild have not gone so smoothly, and the ultimate goal of self-sustaining wild populations has not yet been achieved. The most basic principle of animal reintroductions is that primary causes of extirpation need to be corrected before reestablishments are attempted. Otherwise, self-sustaining wild populations cannot be expected. In the case of the condor, it was clear that released birds needed to be protected from lead poisoning, and with ongoing use of lead ammunitions for hunting activities in the condor range, the only apparent way to eliminate lead from the diet of released condors was through a commitment to maintain released populations on subsidies of clean food. While earlier attempts to convert the historic wild population to a thorough dependency on subsidized food had not been successful, it appeared plausible that such a dependency might be achieved with releases of naive birds that had never learned the wide-ranging foraging habits of the historic wild population.

Indeed, for the first five years of releases, the condors did stay almost completely dependent on clean food subsidy. But beginning in 1997, cases of lead poisoning began to turn up in release populations both in California and in Arizona, as birds began to feed increasingly on carcasses not provided by the release program. By 2005, at least nine birds had been lost to lead poisoning and seventy-seven others had been saved from acute lead contamination only by trapping and emergency chelation therapy in captivity.

Clearly, clean food subsidy has provided only a partial solution to the lead poisoning threat. But even if food subsidy could be made a fully effective solution, most observers believe that it does not represent a satisfactory ultimate solution for conservation of the species, because subsidy-dependent populations are not truly self-sufficient and demand continued intensive investments into the indefinite future. In addition, subsidy-dependent populations are not truly naturally behaving populations and can be expected to evolve in directions quite divergent from original natural-foraging populations. For full success in species recovery, finding a way to remove all lead-contaminated carcasses from the range of the condor appears essential.

Fortunately, various nontoxic ammunitions with good hunting characteristics have been developed in recent years and are becoming available at reasonable cost. Replacement of lead ammunitions with these new ammunitions could solve the lead contamination problem without any appreciable penalties for hunters. All that is needed now is the political will and courage to implement such a substitution on a scale adequate to reduce the chances of lead exposure to very low levels. The replacement of lead ammunitions with nontoxic alternatives also offers benefits for other wildlife species and indeed for human health as well, since lead is also toxic for humans and is an inevitable contaminant in the flesh of game shot with lead ammunitions. With full replacement of lead ammunitions, released populations of condors could be converted into subsidy-free, naturally foraging populations with a potential for full self-sufficiency.

Lead contamination, however, is not the only problem faced by the release program. Especially in southern California, the released birds have proven to be highly attracted to humans and human structures and as a result have been

Left: *Some eleven thousand years ago, California Condors nested in cliffs in the Grand Canyon. Remains found by Steve Emslie in these old condor nest caves included bone fragments of extinct mammoths, camels, bison, horses, and mountain goats—evidently common foods for the condors of that time period. Efforts are underway to reestablish the condor in this region.*

California Condor

getting into a great variety of troubles, such as collisions with utility lines and chronic ingestion of trash. In part, these problems may be a result of food subsidy procedures, but they may also be a result of the fact that most birds released have not been reared by their own parents, but by puppets and various other artificial techniques. As yet, no thoroughly naturalistic releases, involving purely parent-reared birds raised far from human environments in naturalistic enclosures, have been attempted.

On the positive side, some released condors have been attempting to nest, and the breeders have generally chosen appropriate cliff-cave nest sites, many of them in historic breeding regions, such as the Sespe Sanctuary. The number of egg-laying pairs has remained relatively low, however, and divorce has been relatively frequent among pair members. Breeding success rates have also been low. So even though more than one hundred birds of all ages are now in the wild in release populations, the levels of breeding effort and success will have to rise substantially to match historical levels, and it is not yet clear that this will occur under current release techniques.

Thus, the last chapter on conservation of the California Condor is yet to be written, although much progress has been made. In the view of most conservationists, full success in conservation of the species will be achieved only when fully self-sustaining wild populations are created that are behaving in a species-typical manner—a level of success that has been achieved in other formerly endangered raptors, including Bald Eagles and Peregrine Falcons. A number of hurdles still remain for condors to join these species as fully recovered, but the problems identified so far appear to have solutions, and we remain optimistic that these problems will eventually be solved.

In the heat of endless debate over the best ways to conserve the condor, the real bird has sometimes been forgotten. Observing the historic wild condors as they pursued their daily activities gave us extraordinary experiences and provided insights into what sort of species the condor really is. These are the times we now recall most clearly, while memories of endless bureaucratic and political confrontations have faded into well-earned oblivion.

Observing the details of condor nesting activities was an especially rewarding part of the research efforts of the 1980s. As in earlier studies such as those of Carl Koford, condor pairs of the 1980s invariably produced single-egg clutches and nested mainly in caves on cliffs, although they occasionally adopted cavelike cavities in giant sequoia trees. Our observations of nests were conducted from long distances, usually at least a quarter mile away, so that the birds' behavior would not be significantly affected by the presence of observers and so that the full surroundings of nests would be in view. Once nests were found, they were monitored on a continuous basis during daylight hours to ensure that rare events, such as interactions with predators, would not be missed or misinterpreted, and so that the rates of crucial activities, such as feedings of young, could be accurately determined. Continuous monitoring demanded at least two observers per nest through the breeding season.

Few ornithologists ever have an opportunity to watch egg laying in a wild bird species, and in truth there is not always a great deal to see. Many birds lay their eggs inside nest structures that quite effectively conceal what is happening. Although condors do not lay eggs in well-defined nest structures, they usually lay them on the floors of caves that are difficult to see into from a distance. Nevertheless, in 1982 we were able to watch the entire egg-laying process of a condor whose shallow nest site was unusually favorable for observations. From a concealed location on a ridge about a third of a mile away, we could see the full extent of the cave's interior through a telescope, and the bird was always in full view when inside the cave. We had been expecting egg laying from this bird, because she had been spending increasing amounts of time in the site, patiently shaping the floor with her bill. But having never before witnessed the egg-laying process, we had no expectation of just how it might occur. When it finally did happen, the actual process was quick and surprising.

About two minutes before the event, the bird stood up and faced into the cave from just inside the entrance. A succession of tremors shook her body, and suddenly, the egg simply came shooting out to land in full view on the floor of the cave entrance. Amazingly, she laid it from a standing position, and the egg hit the ground with some apparent force, though it was evidently unharmed. Perhaps the loose litter she had gathered earlier at the laying position effectively cushioned the impact. She slowly pivoted to look at the faintly greenish white egg, then bent down with her bill almost touching it. Within a few minutes, she had settled down to commence incubation, tucking the egg in on top of her feet in the usual position adopted by vulturids.

Hatching was something we were fortunate to see at another nest of the same female, and this process held surprises as well. By May 11, 1980, we had been watching the incubation activities of the bird and her mate for some fifty-four days, again at a site whose interior was visible from a long distance. Unfortunately, our observation blind was so distant from this site that many details of events became lost in heat shimmer during the warmer parts of the day, when ambient temperatures sometimes exceeded 110 degrees Fahrenheit. The egg, in any event, was rarely in view, except during brief periods when the tending adult rose to roll and turn it before settling down again with ponderous care. Aside from this, we also glimpsed the egg every few days when the adults exchanged duties at the nest.

By midafternoon of May 11, the oppressive heat distorted the image in the telescope to such an extent that the incubating bird became a headless black blob. We strained to see whether the bird's eyes were open and alert. Normally, she would have been dozing quietly at this time of day, but today, despite soaring temperatures, she was fully awake. A little while earlier, when the bird had stood up to stretch, we had glimpsed what we thought might be a bad break in the shell, an irregular round hole about the size of a dime. This was alarming because still earlier in the day, the bird had shown difficulties in centering the egg on her toes before settling on it. In trying to slide one foot under the egg, she had accidentally kicked the egg nearly a foot across the floor. Could she have punched a toe in the shell hard enough to crack it?

The afternoon wore on, and the bird remained sitting. The heat built up and crested, then finally began to subside as shadows crept toward the nest cliff from across the canyon. One growing shadow at last began its ascent of the nest cliff, finally blanketing the nest itself by early evening. At last, the contrasty sunlight was gone, and the shimmer in the atmosphere began to disappear as the rocks surrounding the cave cooled. We wiped the eyepiece and centered the scope for the best viewing conditions of the day. Although we were a half mile from the nest, the telescope picked up details such as a bit of down stuck to the bristly face feathers of the adult, and even revealed the dark red color of her eye. She sat very still; then abruptly rose, and the egg was finally in clear view between her excrement-whitewashed legs.

There was indeed a break in the egg, and it was now closer to the size of a quarter. Wavering back and forth across the opening was a white spot. It was the chick's egg tooth, a tiny temporary spike on top of his bill that he was using to break free from his calcium prison. Remarkably, he had help. The adult reached down, and ever so gently for a bird this big, nibbled at the edges of the hole, slowly increasing its size in the patient process of hatching.

From first pipping of a condor egg to actual hatching takes close to three days, and we did not get to observe the final moment with this egg, because it happened two nights later. Nevertheless, it was clear that in these condors, unlike in many other birds, the process was a cooperative one between adult and chick, perhaps important in allowing the chick to conserve energy during his entry into the world.

Mated condor pairs commonly engage in a display called the pair flight, progressing close together in parallel fashion through their territories.

Once the chick had hatched, it wasn't long before he was leaving the nest to wander about on nearby slopes, but nearly six months passed before he at last took his first flight. Many additional months passed before he was finally independent of his parents. A full condor breeding cycle from egg laying to independence of a fledgling takes longer than a year, and while we occasionally saw a pair breed again in a year following a successful fledging, egg laying came very late in the breeding season of the second year in these cases.

Fledging is a process we witnessed at three different condor nests, one of them the same nest where we watched hatching in 1980. In none of the three cases were parent birds present at the time fledging occurred. First flights were not very long, nor were they highly controlled, especially in landing. The young birds, as they took off, appeared to have no idea where they were headed and only ended their flights when they collided with brushy slopes that loomed unexpectedly in front of them. Then followed a period of terrestrial wandering that eventually, sometimes days later, led the fledglings to sufficiently open locations that they could again take to the air. Repeated forays into the air led fairly soon to some minimal skills in avoiding inadvertent collisions with slopes and cliffs, though landings remained an approximate procedure for a much longer time. The entire process of becoming a skilled aerial performer takes a young condor many months of solo practice.

The chick whose hatching and fledging we watched in 1980 later became a central figure in the final history of the historic wild population.

During the early 1980s, we watched this bird slowly gain independence from his parents, then pick up associations with other condors, and gradually learn to travel the full range of the species. In 1986, now tagged and known as AC9, he initiated his first breeding attempt as a six-year-old, pairing with an old female who had lost her mate the previous year. This firmly established the capacity of the species to breed at this age. A year later he was the only known condor left in the wild. With his capture in early 1987, a new era of captive breeding began in efforts to prevent the extinction of the species.

Fortunately, the California Condor still exists. Its total numbers are far greater now than at any time in the past half century, and its prospects for survival and recovery in the long term are actually not all that bad, and not just in captivity. The species is truly a magnificent bird, and the intense excitement felt when one of these huge creatures sails by with the wind humming through its feathers lingers for a lifetime. A planet Earth bereft of California Condors would be a much-diminished place, and we believe that with the proper kinds of efforts, this remarkable bird can again be a viable member of wilderness communities. The condor will surely not survive without significant assistance from the very species that has been primarily responsible for its endangerment. But there is no reason to despair that either the bird or its aura will be destroyed by the steps that must be taken in the years ahead. *Gymnogyps californianus* shows no signs of losing its will to carry on, and it is much too powerful a creature to ever lose its capacity to capture our imagination and emotions.

California Condor

Turkey Vulture
Cathartes aura

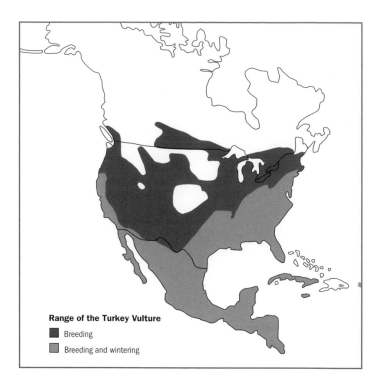

Range of the Turkey Vulture
- Breeding
- Breeding and wintering

ROOSTING GROUPS OF TURKEY VULTURES usually begin the day by spreading their wings and holding them either toward or away from the first rays of the rising sun. Their six-foot wingspans terminate in curved, fingerlike primary feathers that seem to clutch the air in a stylized embrace. Their purplish red naked heads, contrasting with their jet-black bodies, glisten with reflected morning light. Basking contentedly in the warm rays, the birds give no signs of haste to launch into more energetic endeavors and commonly keep their wings fully or partially extended for many minutes before finally folding them against their bodies once again. Until the morning breezes begin to stir, they remain indolently perched, occasionally preening their feathers, while most other birds have long since plunged into their daily routines of feeding, fighting, and reproduction.

Although the spread-wing display of the Turkey Vulture seems to be especially frequent after rainy or misty nights and may serve primarily to dry the flight feathers prior to the first foraging of the day, the exact purpose of the posture has long been debated. The same display is also highly developed in the other New World vultures, in the storks (which are generally acknowledged to be the closest living relatives of the New World vultures), and in the Old World vultures (which are only very distantly related to their New World counterparts). All these birds depend on soaring flight and cover long distances in their daily movements. Most are also at least moderately social in foraging and roosting behavior. In their massed spread-wing displays, they present tableaus of primeval natural splendor in a great variety of habitats around the world. A roost of many dozens of Turkey Vultures and Black Vultures in various stages of the spread-wing display is one of the most stirring spectacles to be found among the birds of North America.

Much more so than the other New World vultures, the species of the genus *Cathartes*—including the Turkey Vulture and the Yellow-headed and Greater Yellow-headed Vultures of Central and South America—are "honest" foragers. Using a refined sense of smell, they are usually the first species to discover a carcass, but often they lose control of the carcass to other scavengers if they do not feed quickly and discreetly enough. In contrast, other scavengers, such as California Condors, Black Vultures, and King Vultures, evidently lack olfactory skills, and these species appear to find food primarily by watching other scavengers, especially Turkey Vultures, but also each other and species such as Crested Caracaras, Common Ravens, and various eagles. This is not to imply that Turkey Vultures do not watch other scavengers, too, because they certainly do; nor to imply that condors, Black Vultures, and King Vultures never find food on their own, because they sometimes do. But as a rule in the New World, the first scavenger to locate a carcass, especially if it is not out in the open, is going to be a *Cathartes*, following its nose.

The ability of Turkey Vultures to find food by smell has not always been generally accepted. In early nineteenth-century experiments to test such a capacity, the noted ornithologist and artist John James Audubon failed to attract vultures to concealed carcasses, and he confidently concluded that these birds used only vision in locating carrion. Nevertheless, the olfactory lobes of a Turkey Vulture's brain are conspicuously large, and late twentieth-century studies by Kenneth Stager of the Los Angeles County Museum and David Houston of the University of Glasgow, as well as others, have established beyond any reasonable doubt that the species does indeed rely heavily on olfaction to find food. Audubon's failure to attract birds may have been a result of his using carcasses that were too far decayed to be acceptable or attractive as food.

By deliberately hiding freshly killed chicken carcasses in locations invisible from the skies in Panama, Houston was able to establish that while Turkey Vultures rarely find carcasses the day they are killed, they almost always find them on the second or third days when they are beginning to ripen, and they rarely visit them when they are four days along and in a stage of full-blown putrefaction. Since captive Turkey Vultures are happy to feed on fresh meat, it appears likely that the reason the wild individuals in Houston's study did not often find chicken carcasses on the first day was that the carcasses were still too fresh to give off enough odor to be detectable. By the second and third days, enough decay was taking place to make the carcasses noticeably pungent, and by the fourth day, there was no question of their giving off enough odor to be findable, but by then the quality of the meat was severely compromised by the buildup of microbial toxins and the carcasses were no longer attractive for the vultures.

Houston's thorough research has shown that were it not for *Cathartes* vultures, very few carcasses would ever be found by vertebrate scavengers in the heavily wooded regions of the American tropics. As it is, very few go undiscovered, so keen are the sensory abilities of the genus. In contrast, scavenging birds with comparable olfactory abilities are absent from the Old World tropics, and although open habitats of that part of the world are occupied by many vulture species, Old World forests are characteristically devoid of specialized avian scavengers.

In 1980, we had a chance to confirm firsthand the olfactory capacities of Peruvian Turkey Vultures while participating in a project to evaluate release methods for captive Andean Condors. The ability of the Turkey Vultures to sniff out food was often in evidence as we attempted to hide from their discovery a carcass we were saving for the condors. No matter how the carcasses were covered up from view with straw mats or whatever, they never were really concealed from the Turkey Vultures, who often walked right into camp in their efforts to track them down, invariably approaching the hidden bounty from downwind.

Throughout much of North, Central, and South America, the Turkey Vulture is the most familiar of the scavenging birds. Guided by a keen sense of smell, this species commonly forages close to the ground, sailing along with characteristic uptilted wings.

Distinctive wart patterns on the faces of Turkey Vultures are believed to result from bacterial infections caused by contact with decomposing carcasses.

In general, studies of both the nesting and the nonbreeding diet of Turkey Vultures have revealed a preponderance of relatively small prey species in their carrion food, especially when compared with the diets of California Condors and Black Vultures. In large part, this emphasis may reflect the ability of this species to find relatively small prey by smell. But it also probably reflects the difficulty this species has in competing with these other vulturids for space around larger carcasses. The Turkey Vulture seems to do best as a solitary forager, quickly finishing off small items before being challenged by its larger and more aggressive cousins.

On rare occasions, Turkey Vultures have been documented killing living prey, but the animals so taken have generally been near death. During the years we studied Everglade Kites in Florida, however, we once flushed a Turkey Vulture from a kite nest that had contained healthy living chicks only a few days earlier. All that was left in the nest was some freshly bloodied bones, and we wondered if this had been an instance of predation, rather than scavenging. Everglade Kites often harass Turkey Vultures that come close to their colonies, and we also sometimes saw Swallow-tailed Kites driving Turkey Vultures away from their nests. These observations suggest that this vulture may not always be an innocent scavenger.

Nevertheless, aside from occasional opportunities to get fresh meat in the form of defenseless prey and animals just dispatched by highway vehicles, Turkey Vultures normally have to deal with food that is at least somewhat decayed. To subsist on a diet of half-rotted meat, they necessarily have to contend with a variety of microbial toxins that permeate such food. Accordingly, their ability to tolerate botulism is known to greatly exceed that of many other birds. They also appear to be relatively insensitive to certain synthetic poisons, such as compound 1080, which has been used to kill mammals such as ground squirrels and coyotes. To other poisons, such as cyanide, the vulturids are apparently quite sensitive. In a pre-technological world, the major poisons found in carcasses were of microbial origin—poisons that vulturids were adapted to tolerate through their biochemical resistance mechanisms. The modern industrial world is now exposing these species to a cornucopia of new poisons that sometimes produce lethal effects in ways that vultures have never faced before. There is no reason to believe that the vulturids are inherently capable of surviving all these chemical stresses. Recent catastrophic declines of certain Asian vultures evidently produced by pharmaceutical contaminants in carcasses of livestock indicate a major

Turkey Vulture

In a photograph taken in 1956, roosting Turkey Vultures sun on a ledge above the immense Grand Canyon.

vulnerability of at least some scavengers to at least certain poisons that are not even toxic to other vertebrates.

Turkey Vultures occur virtually throughout South, Central, and North America to as far north as southern Canada. They are a familiar sight in most regions, often outranking the ubiquitous Red-tailed Hawk in conspicuousness, and perhaps also in abundance. Soaring buoyantly with their wings held tipped up above the horizontal plane, they circle endlessly in search of carrion and generally keep closer to the ground than do many other raptors.

North America's Turkey Vultures are largely migratory, withdrawing in winter to the southern United States, Mexico, Central America, and South America. Winter congregations of hundreds or even thousands of individuals sometimes develop. One enormous winter roost of several thousand birds has traditionally assembled in the tall Australian pines growing on the dikes at the south end of Lake Okeechobee in Florida, evidently attracted by a bountiful food supply of dead rats, rabbits, and snakes nearby. Much of this food supply is created fortuitously by the systematic burning of sugarcane fields during the winter harvest season.

Turkey Vultures are also highly gregarious during migration. In late October 1996 we visited the newly established raptor migration station in coastal Veracruz, Mexico, and on a single day we watched in complete amazement as more than a hundred thousand Turkey Vultures sailed silently southward overhead—a continuous river of birds stretching from horizon to horizon. The total Turkey Vulture count for the fall season in this location generally runs about a million and a half to two million individuals, clearly indicating that the Turkey Vulture is one of the most abundant raptors of more northerly regions. Other raptors using the same migratory flyway are Broad-winged and Swainson's Hawks, as well as lesser numbers of Swallow-tailed Kites.

Many of the Turkey Vultures and other raptors passing through Veracruz continue on south through Guatemala, Nicaragua, Costa Rica, and Panama, and on into South America, and it is possible to view this migration spectacle from many other locations along the way. At the very end of October 2004, we saw it as a daily occurrence in the La Selva preserve of Costa Rica. Here, the birds were especially impressive in midmorning, when they first left their overnight roosts to continue their steady southward procession close over the treetops. They became much less conspicuous later in the day when thermals allowed them to gain considerable altitude. The river of birds in this location consisted of about half Turkey Vultures and half Swainson's Hawks thoroughly intermixed with one another.

In California, where the Turkey Vulture is partially migratory and partially sedentary, we paid special attention to its ecological relationships with the California Condor during studies in the 1980s. At that time, these two species largely foraged in separate regions in the southern part of the condor range, though they came together in foraging in the northern part during summer. Except for overlap in a few localities, they also tended to nest in different regions, with the condors occupying the central parts of the mountains lying between the coast and the San Joaquin Valley while the Turkey Vultures nested close to the coast and close to the San Joaquin Valley. Very few Turkey Vultures used the central parts of the mountains except during migration.

We suspect that the main reason why condors nested historically in the central mountains had nothing to do with food supplies, since food was quite limited in this region and the condors rarely foraged there. But conspicuously absent from this region were appreciable numbers of Golden Eagles, which apparently constitute a strong threat to condor nestlings. The condor's powers of flight are sufficiently strong that commuting from nests in relatively enemy-free regions to distant foraging grounds does not pose a problem. In contrast, we suspect that Turkey Vultures, with their more modest flight capacity, were denied this same opportunity—it might simply have taken them too long to make round-trips. The Turkey Vultures nesting in the San Joaquin Valley foothills may never have had any option but to take their lumps from the abundant eagles there, and in fact, one of the two

Turkey Vulture

More than a million Turkey Vultures migrate south each fall through coastal Veracruz, Mexico. The birds in this photograph represent only a small sampling of a stream of more than a hundred thousand individuals that sailed past on a single October day in 1996. From horizon to horizon, the birds moved within a flexible narrow corridor, like a river in the sky.

nestling Turkey Vultures we radioed there in 1981 did wind up as an eagle victim after it fledged.

More difficult to explain was the absence of significant numbers of Turkey Vultures foraging in the foothills of the southern San Joaquin Valley, where the last historic wild condors did much of their foraging. Significant numbers of Turkey Vultures nested in these very same foothills, and food appeared to be abundant there. Yet the Turkey Vultures mostly dropped down to the floor of the San Joaquin Valley to forage in agricultural areas. Possibly they did so because the food supply on the valley floor was as good as or better than in the foothills, or because they faced less competition from ravens, condors, and eagles in the valley bottom. The last historic condors did not forage on the floor of the San Joaquin Valley, possibly in large part because this region lacks enough topographic relief to provide the consistent updrafts needed by this species to stay aloft. Turkey Vultures, with their much lighter wing-loading, appear to have no trouble maneuvering in the airspace of the valley bottom.

Admittedly, these hypotheses are tentative, and other factors may also have been involved in causing the historic nesting and foraging distributions of these species. Still, our preliminary hypotheses well illustrate the complexity of factors that may affect foraging patterns in these scavengers and that may affect the relationship between foraging and other important facets of the species' biology.

The resident Turkey Vultures of coastal Peru have conspicuously scarlet heads, and in 1980 we watched their behavior around a number of carcasses. As individuals switched around in controlling a food source, a very strange and rapid transformation in head color took place. Birds that took over a carcass often blanched their head color to a pale pinkish white as they defended the food, while individuals on the periphery maintained their full scarlet head coloration. In other Turkey Vultures seen at the same carcasses, the head remained bicolored, with the front half of the head scarlet and the rear of the head white—the typical coloration one sees in individuals of the race *ruficollis* in the high Andes. The color changes seen in the scarlet-headed individuals occurred in a matter of a few seconds and may have been important in signaling emotional states of individuals to each other.

By comparison, we have never noted such head-color changes in the North American form of the Turkey Vulture, which has a more purplish head color. Some of the Turkey Vultures we saw in Peru had such purplish heads and may have been wintering birds from North America. A careful study to sort out the significance of the various head colors seen in Peru would be of great interest. With such striking differences in head color, it seems possible that there might actually be several different species involved, rather than just subspecies of a single species. Regardless, visual stimuli, such as various head colors, appear to be important in the Turkey Vulture's world, just as are olfactory stimuli, but like other vulturids, various races of Turkey Vultures make little use of sounds in communicating with one another, limiting themselves to harsh grunts and hisses audible only at close range.

Turkey Vultures characteristically nest in caves in cliffs or in hollow logs or other sheltered locations on the ground. In Florida, they commonly use the ground-level labyrinths of palmetto thickets, as do Black Vultures, while in California all nests we located were in cliffs or boulder piles, similar to the sites used by wild condors. The spotted egg coloration of both Black and Turkey Vultures, however, contrasts with the plain white color of condor eggs, and suggests that for some reason these species may be more vulnerable to egg predators than are the condors. A comparable difference in egg coloration is found in the North American accipiters, where the smallest species—the Sharp-shinned Hawk—has camouflaged spotted eggs, while the larger species—the Cooper's Hawk and the Northern Goshawk—have plain white eggs.

Clutch size of the Turkey Vulture is most typically two eggs, but occasionally pairs lay just a single egg or three eggs. Both adults incubate eggs and care for the young, and nestlings are fed by regurgitation, as in other vulturids. Nestlings normally take about two months to reach fledging age, and they usually remain in the vicinity of their nests for another month beyond their first flights before joining communal roosts elsewhere. At fledging, individuals are black with dark downy heads, and the naked red-head coloration of full adults is usually achieved by a bird's second fall. This suggests that first breeding may sometimes occur in the following year, although the usual age of first breeding in the species has not yet been determined.

The present conservation status of the Turkey Vulture appears favorable for the most part, with a clear population expansion in the northeastern states in recent decades and generally stable populations elsewhere. The species has evidently not suffered nearly as strongly from lead poisoning as has the California Condor, although it is surely often exposed to lead ammunition fragments in carcasses. In part, the apparent absence of major problems with lead poisoning is probably due to a much greater reproductive potential in the Turkey Vulture than in the condor, but laboratory experiments also suggest that the species is simply much less sensitive to the toxic effects of lead than is its larger cousin.

Black Vulture
Coragyps atratus

Range of the Black Vulture

▓ Breeding and wintering

THE BLACK VULTURE of the New World is not to be confused with the immense Black Vulture of the Old World (*Aegypius monachus*), which ranges from Spain to Mongolia and rivals the California Condor in size. The American Black Vulture has a wingspread of less than five feet and is not much bigger than a barnyard rooster. Moreover, its bill is quite thin and weak in comparison to the bills of many other vultures.

Nevertheless, the Black Vulture is an aggressive and opportunistic bird. Single Black Vultures are not bulky enough to intimidate most other scavengers, but the species quickly gathers in large groups and often manages to overwhelm competitors by massed assaults, pitching into the feeding aggregations with reckless abandon. Where the Black Vulture occurs with the Andean Condor in South America, we have seen it repeatedly rushing in to grab scraps, even when this much larger species has had apparent full control of a carcass. Sometimes its boldness has even extended to snatching bites from right between the feet of a condor working intently on food.

The impetuousness of the Black Vulture contrasts with the more aloof personality of the similar-sized Turkey Vulture, and Turkey Vultures often appear to simply resign themselves to losing control of carcasses once Black Vultures move in. Much may depend on hunger and relative numbers of the two species, however, for sometimes Turkey Vultures defend food very aggressively.

Relatively flexible in behavior, the Black Vulture has adapted quite well to civilization in many regions, and in fact throughout much of Central and South America it is seen much more commonly in disturbed urban environments than in most natural environments. In many countries it has become a bird of the streets, docks, and garbage dumps, barely seeming to notice the confusion and noise inherent in such surroundings and feeding on all sorts of offal and food scraps resulting from human activities and the presence of domestic livestock.

In its urban tendencies and in many features of physical appearance, especially overall size and bill shape, the Black Vulture is very reminiscent of two Old World vultures, the Egyptian Vulture and the Hooded Vulture—species found throughout much of Africa and into southern Europe and southern Asia, in the case of the Egyptian Vulture. Nevertheless, these two Old World vultures are not at all closely related to the Black Vulture, and their behavioral and physical similarities to the Black Vulture have presumably evolved because of close similarities in the lifestyles of the three species and are an example of evolutionary convergence.

Black Vultures are more willing than other New World vultures to take living prey. Records exist of them capturing small turtles and consuming the eggs and young of colonial waterbirds on occasion. Groups of Black Vultures sometimes even successfully attack and dismember live skunks and possums. In Guyana, we watched groups clustering around cattle giving birth, apparently waiting for an opportunity to feed on afterbirths or on stillborn calves, or perhaps sometimes on live calves. Other foods taken include all forms of carrion and even dung from livestock.

The opportunistic feeding habits of Black Vultures bear a strong resemblance to those of Common Ravens, and perhaps as a result of competition, these two species for the most part inhabit separate ranges in North America. In California, for example, Black Vultures are absent, and Common Ravens, together with Turkey Vultures, have instead been the common small avian scavengers.

Yet judging from fossils in the La Brea Tar Pits and other California locations, the Common Raven and a very close relative of the contemporary Black Vulture did occur together in this region during the late Pleistocene, an epoch when the abundance and diversity of food was evidently much greater than in recent millennia, allowing the coexistence of substantially more species of scavengers. At that time, terrestrial environments were inhabited by mammoths, dire wolves, giant ground sloths, saber-toothed cats, and a great variety of other large mammals, while the skies hosted multiple species of condors, teratorns, eagles, and caracaras, in addition to ravens, close relatives of the Black Vulture and King Vulture, the Turkey Vulture, and two small species of Old World vultures, all potentially feeding to a greater or lesser extent on carcasses of the diverse mammals. The most astonishing of the avian carnivores was *Teratornis incredibilis*, a species with an estimated wingspread twice as great as that of the California Condor, but there were also other species larger than the California Condor, as well as a great variety of smaller scavenger species. Sadly, only a fraction of California's amazing Pleistocene mammals still survive today, and this much-reduced array, together with various introduced domestic mammals, now supports only a very limited number of avian scavenger species.

North American populations of the Black Vulture are centered in Florida and the other southeastern states, although the species has been edging northward in recent years and now can be found even in southern Pennsylvania. In Florida, where we have become most familiar with the species, it is abundant in the prairie regions of the south-central part of the state, where cattle grazing has been a dominant land use. Here it finds favorable nest sites mainly on the ground in the tangled patches of palmettos that dot the landscape.

Elsewhere in its range, the Black Vulture commonly nests in potholes and crevices in cliffs, hollow stumps, hollow trees, deserted buildings, and sometimes even on top of skyscrapers. Its main nest-site requirements, like those of the other vulturids, are relatively dark, sheltered places that have reasonably flat floors and are roomy enough to accommodate both nestlings and adults simultaneously. Like its close relatives, the Black Vulture does no nest building other than minor rearranging of twigs, pebbles, and other detritus already present in the sites.

Also generally important to nesting are nearby elevated snag or cliff perches from which the birds can monitor their surroundings effectively. Black Vultures are extremely watchful and secretive in approaching their nest sites, and such

A Black Vulture rips apart a possum carcass with its razor-sharp bill. Primarily dependent on carrion, this scavenger also takes some living—though relatively defenseless—prey.

perches allow them to carefully assess their surroundings before entering sites from which they can see very little. In the prairies of south-central Florida, for example, the start of the nesting season in late winter is signaled by pairs of the species perching for extended periods on conspicuous snags next to palmetto patches. Egg laying is signaled by the transformation of these pairs into single birds perched in the same locations. Finding nests then becomes a process of crawling on hands and knees through the nearby palmetto jungles and keeping one's nose attuned for the unmistakable putrid carrion stench of the species, all the while keeping one's ears and peripheral vision primed for warning signs of the lunker diamondback rattlesnakes that abound in this habitat.

All nests we have seen have been disgustingly odoriferous hollows in the dense vegetation, and all have been in ground locations apparently fully accessible for mammalian predators. Yet the nests have appeared to enjoy considerable safety from predation and have usually carried through successfully. Fresh tracks of raccoons and other terrestrial carnivores often go right past active nest clumps, so it is clear that the nests are often situated in places frequented by potential enemies, but are often left untouched. It seems unlikely that terrestrial carnivores would have difficulty finding the nests, considering the rank scent clouds in which they are imbedded, and it is tempting to hypothesize that the young vultures are simply not the most appetizing prey for these species, a repellency possibly reinforced by the nestlings' hair-trigger responses to regurgitate slimy carrion when approached closely. But exactly how most terrestrial predators may react to vulture nests, nestlings, and regurgitated carrion is a largely unstudied matter. Conceivably, regurgitated carrion may sometimes deter predators by its foul odor, but on the other hand, it might sometimes serve as a diversionary food offering that reduces threats by reducing a predator's hunger.

In any event, not all Black Vulture nests survive the threats of predators, and observers in some regions have found evidence for fairly frequent losses of nestlings to terrestrial mammals. Thus, it is quite uncertain how repellent or attractive the nests, young vultures, and their regurgitant may be in general, and the extent to which nests may be foul enough to discourage predators may vary from place to place. Much of the vulnerability of nests may depend on just how hungry potential predators are, what alternative foods they have available, and whether an adult vulture is present to defend a site at the time that a predator approaches.

One Black Vulture nest we located was in dense palmettos under a canopy of trees on the edge of a cypress swamp where we later studied nesting Short-tailed Hawks. Other nest sites we have seen have been in palmetto patches in much more open habitat where the nearest associated raptor species have been Burrowing Owls, Red-tailed Hawks, and Crested Caracaras. But regardless of where one is in the range of the species and the nature of surrounding habitat, clutch size of the species is almost invariably two eggs, and the eggs characteristically have an attractive greenish gray ground color overlaid with chocolate-colored blotches. Newly hatched chicks are covered with tan-colored down very similar to that of newly hatched Andean Condors, but distinctly different from the pure white down found in newly hatched Turkey Vultures and California Condors. Nestling Black Vultures grow relatively slowly for the size of the species, and most studies indicate that they usually do not fledge until they are two-and-a-half months

Left: *A Black Vulture (below) and Turkey Vulture (above) greet the dawn from a mangrove snag in Florida's Everglades National Park.*

Black Vulture

With its wings spread in a sunning posture, a Black Vulture basks on the edge of a Florida marsh.

old. Fledglings, however, are still dependent on their parents for food for many additional months and often do not achieve true independence until the spring or summer of the year following fledging.

Like other vulturids, Black Vultures make no sounds other than assorted wheezes, hisses, and snorts audible at close range. We have heard these noises emitted by birds defending their nests. Others have heard them given by birds engaged in mating activities. Vocalizations are better developed in the Old World vultures than in the vulturids, but even among the Old World species, vocalizations tend to be grunts and hisses that are much less frequently heard than the calls of most other raptors. In general, vocal communication is most valuable for birds living in densely vegetated regions, where vision is often obscured. The de-emphasis of vocalizations in vultures may result mainly from their preference for open-country habitat.

Black Vultures and Turkey Vultures commonly roost together at all seasons, but the numbers of individuals of either species using a particular roost fluctuate greatly from night to night because individuals change roosts frequently. Presumably because these vultures travel long distances in their daily activities, they cannot always efficiently return to the same roost each evening and need several roosts spaced through their ranges to avoid excessively long commutes.

Despite the flexibility in use of roosts, research with marked Black Vultures has shown that roosts often include mainly individuals that are quite closely related to one another. Furthermore, nonkin birds that attempt to join a roost are often attacked by birds already in the roost. Thus, because birds have been documented following one another to food sources from roosts, the

potential benefits of roosts with respect to foraging may be generally limited to birds within kinship groups and minimized for nonkin individuals.

Roosts are generally situated in tall live trees, though the birds often use nearby dead snags for sunning purposes. Except when they are returning to known food sources, Black Vultures generally leave the roosts later in the morning than do Turkey Vultures, and they likewise usually return to roosts later in the afternoon or evening than do Turkey Vultures. Not infrequently, both species circle and soar for several hours in the vicinity of their roosts before finally settling in, possibly inspecting the roost vicinity carefully for potential predators before deciding that it is safe to descend.

The generally late departures of Black Vultures from roosts are most likely a result of their relatively heavy-bodied physical proportions and heavy wing-loading. With a weight often exceeding four-and-a-half pounds and a wing area generally less than four square feet, the Black Vulture needs stronger air movements than does the Turkey Vulture to soar effectively, and such air movements normally develop fairly late in the morning. In accord with their differences in flight capacities, the foraging flights of the two species are also quite different. The Black Vulture cannot match the buoyant low-altitude coursing typical of the more light-bodied Turkey Vulture, and at low altitudes, Black Vultures are pretty much limited to labored fast-flapping to keep aloft. This sort of flight is energetically inefficient for foraging, and it is not generally used by the species except in takeoffs and during commutes to known locations of food visited in previous days. Instead, Black Vultures mainly prospect for food from considerable heights, where soaring conditions are better and where they are in a good position to observe the food-finding activities of other scavengers.

When a Black Vulture sailing high in the clouds first spots a feeding opportunity at a carcass, it begins a rapid descent and is immediately noticed by other Black Vultures at greater distances, who likewise begin descents converging on the food. Even more distant vultures follow as if drawn by an invisible force. The sky is soon swept clean of vultures, and a large group assembles around the carcass.

The presence of large feeding assemblages can facilitate the ripping apart of prey. With their relatively weak bills, Black Vultures often have difficulty getting through the tough hides of relatively large mammals and, in the absence of substantial wounds in this armor, the birds are often limited to feeding on easily accessible soft tissues such as eyes and tongues. Yet when numerous individuals pull in unison in a variety of directions at a point of weakness in an animal's hide, the birds can increase their leverage and sometimes penetrate to soft tissues that would otherwise be inaccessible for single birds.

Like other vulturids and like storks, their apparent close relatives, Black Vultures practice an unusual method of thermoregulation known as urohidrosis. In essence, they avoid overheating by deliberately voiding their own excretory wastes on their legs, cooling these appendages as the water portion of the waste material evaporates. The blood circulating under the evaporative surfaces of the legs is also cooled in the process, and when it is pumped through the rest of the body, it effectively cools the entire bird. During hot weather, the legs of all these species take on a conspicuous, chalky-white appearance, produced by a dried crust of uric acid crystals left plastered to the skin. An endless buildup of uric acid is in part prevented by the fact that all the species practicing urohidrosis are avid bathers. Urohidrosis presumably might have general advantages for large species with long legs living in hot environments, yet no birds other than vulturids, storks, and certain boobies are known to possess the trait.

The opportunistic behavior of the Black Vulture allows some optimism about this species' abilities to cope with future changes in the modern world. Nevertheless, the species has several vulnerabilities in its biology that have been of local importance in the United States. One weakness is nest-site availability. In regions where Black Vultures nest most commonly in hollow logs or hollow trees, timber management practices that reduce the average age of trees are significantly lowering the availability of such nest sites and forcing the birds to use more vulnerable thicket nest sites as alternatives, with consequent declines in nesting success. Such timbering practices may provide at least part of the explanation for reported local decreases in Black Vulture populations in the southeastern states in the mid-twentieth century. The deserted buildings sometimes used for nesting by the species have also been declining in abundance in some regions.

A second weakness is the strong dependency the species has come to have on humanity for its food supply. Changes in land use that reduce livestock rearing and that reduce the availability of livestock carcasses, garbage, or slaughterhouse wastes can have strong impacts on the Black Vulture's welfare. A thoroughly hygienic human environment does not leave much of a food supply for these scavengers.

Third, the willingness of the Black Vulture to attack newborn livestock has led to vigorous campaigns in some areas to trap and destroy the species. Such control efforts, commonly using giant self-baiting walk-in traps, were especially prevalent in Texas and Florida during the 1940s and 1950s, and the numbers of Black Vultures destroyed apparently reached the hundreds of thousands.

Finally, collisions with vehicles on high-speed roads have been taking a substantial toll of those Black Vultures that are attracted to road-killed mammals for food.

White patches at the bases of its fingerlike primary feathers allow ready identification of the Black Vulture in flight. Also characteristic are the relatively short tail and black naked head visible at close range.

In spite of these vulnerability factors, the North American range of the Black Vulture has been expanding northward in the past half century, and the species is still very common in many southern regions. It also remains a common species throughout much of Mexico and Central and South America, and in view of its strong association with urban environments in many regions, it may in fact be much more abundant now than it was before the dawn of civilization in the New World.

Black Vultures often nest in palmetto thickets in south-central Florida, laying their eggs on whatever litter is already present. The tan coloration of newly hatched Black Vultures resembles that of downy young Andean Condors, but differs from the white coloration of downy Turkey Vultures and California Condors.

Black Vulture

White-tailed Kite
Elanus leucurus

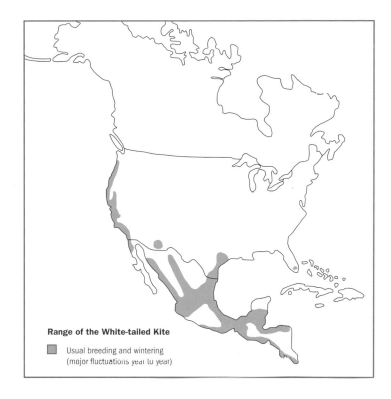

Range of the White-tailed Kite

□ Usual breeding and wintering
(major fluctuations year to year)

WITH A PURE WHITE HEAD, underparts, and tail, and with long black-and-white wings flashing conspicuously as it beats its way over open fields and meadows, the White-tailed Kite looks much like a wayward gull or tern, both in size and color pattern. This close resemblance has sometimes led to the species being overlooked, especially in areas where gulls habitually congregate on inland prairies. Yet the kite differs sufficiently from seabirds in flight characteristics that the species can be easily identified even from a considerable distance, if watched for any length of time.

The White-tailed Kite generally hunts from altitudes of about fifty to a hundred feet above the ground and feeds almost exclusively on small mammals. Advancing methodically across the terrain, it periodically stalls its forward progress to stare intently at a specific area from a stationary hover. In this maneuver the bird pivots to face directly into the wind, with its body tipped upward and its wings flexing deeply and rapidly, while its feet dangle loosely underneath. After scanning the ground for a few seconds, the kite resumes forward progress for perhaps another fifty yards, and again pulls up into a hover. The bird continues to advance and hover alternately until a prospective victim is finally sighted. Now the kite descends, either first to a lower hovering position, or quickly all the way to the ground. In the final descent, the bird's wings are generally held stiffly upward at about a forty-five-degree angle from horizontal, in a direct and powerful pounce.

A half century ago, the White-tailed Kite was a relatively rare species in the United States, limited largely to parts of central and western California and southern Texas. Concerned naturalists considered it a likely candidate for extinction in North America. Yet quite the opposite has happened. Since the mid-1960s, the species has undergone a massive population explosion, and its range has expanded to include large areas of Arizona and New Mexico, as well as most of California and Texas. There even have been sightings and breeding records for Mississippi, Louisiana, Oklahoma, Oregon, and Washington, and the bird has recently returned to Florida after a long absence.

The exact causes of the improved status of the White-tailed Kite are not certain, but whatever they are, they are not limited to North America. The kite has also been increasing in many other portions of its extensive range, which includes large parts of Central and South America. Some observers have attributed the widespread population growth to increases in open-field habitat, resulting from the clearing of forests and brushlands for pastures and croplands. Others have suggested that increased use of irrigation in agriculture and climatic changes, in particular increased temperatures and rainfall, have been the most important factors, possibly because of their beneficial effects on prey populations. Regardless of which factors have

been most important, the White-tailed Kite seems to have settled into a fairly comfortable relationship with modern agricultural practices, although some regions exhibit enormous population fluctuations from year to year and populations in some regions have shown overall declines in the most recent years.

Left: *Early in the breeding season, a female White-tailed Kite adjusts her wings on a habitual perch near her nest in Arizona's Sulfur Springs Valley. Relatively muscular toes and short talons adapt this species to a diet of small mammals.*

Above: *The male of the Sulfur Springs Valley pair arrives near his nest with a cotton rat. His mate will soon accept the prey at the perch before transporting it to the nest to feed their young.*

The female of the Sulfur Springs Valley pair prepares to brood her young in a nest lodged near the top of a cypress. During the early nesting stages, the male did all the hunting, while the female rarely, if ever, left the immediate nest vicinity.

One region the species has spread to is southern Arizona. Here, in the spring of 1987, we studied several pairs nesting in relatively short hackberries, gray thorns, and Arizona cypresses. We made especially close observations of one pair that nested in an Arizona cypress near an abandoned ranch in the Sulfur Springs Valley. The nest, only twenty-two feet from the ground, was well situated for study, and the birds proved to be vigorous and successful parents.

They were not alone. Groves of trees in open Arizona grassland-brushland habitats are magnets for nesting birds, and the cypress clump the kites had chosen attracted an astonishing density of avian neighbors. The kites' nesting tree also hosted a pair of Greater Roadrunners building their nest only six feet under the kite nest, as well as a pair of Western Kingbirds and a pair of House Sparrows lower down. An immediately adjacent cypress snag, a primary perch tree for the kites, held a pair of Loggerhead Shrikes, a pair of Northern Mockingbirds, and another pair of Western Kingbirds, despite the fact that the snag had only a few small living branches. Another immediately adjacent tree had a pair of Cassin's Kingbirds, a pair of Bullock's Orioles, and a pair of Mourning Doves, not to mention an occasional roosting Barn Owl. Still other nearby cypresses held nesting Great-tailed Grackles and additional pairs of kingbirds, while an old hollow fence post only a hundred feet from the kite nest contained a brood of four young Ash-throated Flycatchers.

The air in the vicinity was full of birds and their cries, as they fought with one another and carried on their breeding activities. The kingbirds were the most active and found the kites, especially the young kites after they had fledged, to be irresistible targets for their abundant aggression. Still clumsy and slow in flight, the fledgling kites could not fly anywhere in the vicinity without one or more of these pugnacious passerines soon landing on their backs, yanking out feathers with their bills as they rode. These were the same kingbirds that worked unceasingly to rip apart our burlap blind for nesting material and that occasionally startled us by grabbing a beakful of hair, unfortunately still attached, through spaces in the burlap.

But as annoying as the kingbirds were, our main concern was the close nesting of the roadrunners to the kites. Roadrunners are accomplished predators of vertebrates and were a significant threat to the kite eggs and young. Fortunately, nest attendance by the adult kites was very tight, and without any encouragement from us, the roadrunners abandoned their nest before egg laying. Moving to construct an alternative nest site in the rafters of an abandoned shed fifty yards away, they ultimately fledged a brood of two young while the kites raised their three youngsters unmolested.

As a number of biologists who have studied the White-tailed Kite have noted, the species appears to be limited to regions with good populations of

Above: *Adult White-tailed Kites often hover during hunting and usually forage from about fifty to one hundred feet above the ground.*

Right: *Fledgling White-tailed Kites possess necklaces of tan feathers, but the tan coloration is replaced by white a few months later.*

small mammals that are active during daylight hours. In some regions, such as much of California, the primary prey are meadow mice. Meadow mice do not occur widely in Arizona, however, and in our study area the diet of the kites proved to be virtually exclusively cotton rats. These were abundant in adjacent fields, and hunting forays of the kites usually ended successfully in no more than five to ten minutes. The kites, in fact, spent very little of the day foraging, even when food demands of their young were at a maximum in the middle of the late nestling stage. Further, the adults limited almost all hunting activity to the early morning and late afternoon, with a long siesta of perching and preening from about 9:30 a.m. to 3:30 p.m. each day, even when weather was cloudy.

The male kite did nearly all the foraging through the nestling period, and from our tower blind we could watch many of his hunting efforts through to successful prey captures. Towing his victims back to the nesting vicinity in his talons, the male announced his return with piercing chirps very reminiscent of the calls of Ospreys. Most often he landed on a nearby stub, where he was soon joined by his mate, who immediately took the prey from his talons in her bill. Sometimes, however, we saw talon-to-talon transfers that took place in midair over the blind. As the pair flew side by side into the wind, the female simply moved in close enough to reach over and grab the prey in her feet; then descended to perch near the nest.

While plucking the victim, the female uttered curious *ee-gritch* calls. Then, after a minute or two, she took the prey to the nest, often continuing to vocalize as she ripped off portions for the young. When she finished feeding the nestlings, the female flew off from the nest to cache

any uneaten portions of the prey on a nearby perch. In the early nestling period, she soon returned to brood or shade the young, occasionally flying off to collect sticks to fortify the nest. In the late nestling stage, she mainly occupied her time between feedings by guarding the nest from the top of a nearby cypress.

Between hunts, the male adult spent considerable time preening, and right through the nestling period he often mounted his mate in copulations. Mating activity late in the breeding cycle is rare in most raptors, and the overall frequency of copulations in this pair far exceeded what we have seen in observations of any other falconiform species.

White-tailed Kite

The adult male kite at the Sulfur Springs Valley nest often rested on the snaggy top of a cypress overlooking the nest vicinity.

all the way to the nest area itself. When an adult made a successful capture, off the fledglings would fly, each vying to be the first to reach the source of food. The first youngster to reach the parent, however, was not always the one to wind up with the prey. We sometimes saw triple plays in which the prey passed from parent to one young to a second young in quick succession.

Despite its extensive range, the White-tailed Kite is not known to engage in well-defined seasonal migrations anywhere. Instead, the species tends to be at least somewhat nomadic, appearing in some regions only during outbreaks of small mammals. Normally solitary or in pairs during the day, the species occasionally congregates in overnight roosts of up to several dozen individuals during the nonbreeding season. These roosts fluctuate in size and sometimes shift in location over a period of weeks or months. Most are situated in groves of trees in relatively open country, but occasionally the birds choose reed beds or sugarcane fields. This tendency to roost socially is also found in many other kite species and allows comprehensive censusing of regional populations if all roosts can be located and assessed.

The officially recognized relationship of the White-tailed Kite to other kites in the same genus has gone through an evolution symptomatic of classification changes that have been seen in many other bird species. In historical times, the species was known as the White-tailed Kite (*Elanus leucurus*), but during a period of widespread "lumping" of species that occurred in the late twentieth century, it was submerged in a larger species called the Black-shouldered Kite (*Elanus caeruleus*), which included close relatives in Africa, Eurasia, and Australia. More recently, recognition of significant differences among the various related forms of *Elanus* kites on the various continents has led to reconstituting the White-tailed Kite (*Elanus leucurus*) as a separate species limited to the New World. Thus, the bird we referred to as the Black-shouldered Kite in the first edition of this book is once again officially the White-tailed Kite, at least for now.

Other activities occasionally observed in the nesting adults included very conspicuous fluttering flights in the vicinity of the nest tree. We saw both adults participate in such flights, circling low and vibrating their wings rapidly above the horizontal plane as they simultaneously called excitedly with twittering vocalizations. The significance of these butterflylike flights was unclear. In observations of others, such flights have usually been performed only by males and have often involved a bird carrying a twig in the bill.

After fledging, the young kites still focused their activities around the nest tree for several weeks, and the adults continued to bring food to the nest. In time, however, food transfers began to take place on other nearby perches. A month after fledging, the young were consistently flying out to meet a parent returning with food, and transfers now took place midair. At this stage, the fledglings mostly spent their time on high perches near the nest, watching their parents hunt. Raising and lowering their conspicuous white tails in flashing displays and uttering intermittent begging screams, they appeared to be anxious to keep the adults informed of their locations and readiness to eat.

Off in the distance, the parent kites alternated hunting forays with spells of perching on mesquites and fence posts, and they now rarely returned

The usual criterion for determining whether different populations should be considered the same or different species is whether or not they can interbreed successfully. In situations where closely related species or subspecies occur on different continents, however, there is usually no way to determine if they might successfully interbreed, because the geographically separate populations never interact with one another. Thus, decisions about whether spatially separated forms should be considered separate species or only subspecies of a single species are necessarily arbitrary and are usually based on whether consistent differences in morphology or behavior exist between the populations. Still, such decisions tend to be quite subjective, and in recent decades "splitting" (creating multiple species from single species) has been much more prevalent than "lumping" (combining multiple species into single species). For better or worse, the number of officially recognized bird species has been growing steadily, in large part without discoveries of previously unknown populations.

Everglade (Snail) Kite
Rostrhamus sociabilis

A GIGANTIC AND BEWILDERING FRESHWATER marsh once dominated the central reaches of southern Florida from Lake Okeechobee to the southern tip of the peninsula. Its shallow waters flowed imperceptibly southward as a forty-to-sixty-mile-wide "river" that ultimately emptied into the mangrove-lined estuary of Florida Bay. Known variously as the Glades, the Never Glades, or the Everglades to early explorers, this entire region remained untraversed, unmapped, and unsettled until well into the nineteenth century. In the view of early Floridians, the region was so forbidding a wilderness it would likely remain inviolate forever.

Today, the Everglades are still a vast aquatic empire, although numerous dikes and canals, largely justified on the basis of flood control, have greatly distorted and tamed the flow of waters. Much of the original flow has been diverted via canals toward the coasts instead of passing down the peninsula, leaving southerly regions, including Everglades National Park at the tip of Florida, with much less water than before. In addition, large portions of the original marshes have been drained and converted into sugarcane fields and other croplands. These changes have both substantially reduced the extent of the Everglades and increasingly polluted the remaining wetlands with chemically contaminated runoff from the surrounding agricultural lands.

The effects of these changes on the wildlife of the region have been massive. Where once huge flocks of herons, storks, ibis, and spoonbills filled the skies, now only scattered individuals are seen. The deterioration

Range of the Everglade (Snail) Kite

☐ Breeding and wintering

has been especially obvious in Everglades National Park, but all portions of the Everglades, as well as the Kissimmee Prairie and St. John's marshland regions north of Lake Okeechobee have been affected. Belatedly, the poorly thought-out land and water management policies of the region have been recognized as an ecological disaster, and in the 1990s, an ambitious and hugely expensive effort was begun to return the region to something like

Soaring overhead, Everglade Kites display conspicuous white tail bases and wings that are narrow close to the body and wider farther out.

Everglade (Snail) Kite

A female Everglade Kite watches over her nest from a nearby perch in the eastern Everglades. Her long and relatively straight claws are not suited for killing snails but are adapted for plucking them from the water.

its original condition, especially by modifying the flow of water south through the existing system of canals and dikes. Nevertheless, it remains to be seen how successful this effort may be. With the rapidly increasing human population of the state, the many competing needs for water, and the inventive capacity of our species to create new environmentally damaging pesticides and fertilizers, full recovery of the Everglades ecosystem may prove very difficult to achieve.

Regardless of what the future may bring, the interior portions of the Everglades today are still an almost unrelievedly flat ecosystem in which dry land is virtually nonexistent, at least in years of normal rainfall. Yet the waters, except where canals have been dredged, are mostly no more than a few feet deep, allowing the development of endless shoals of saw grass, cattails, and half-submerged shrubs and trees. Only a few of these plants, mainly the clumps of willows and pond apples, rise even ten feet into the air. Distinctive landmarks are rare, the horizon stretches unbroken in all directions, and one slough looks pretty much like thousands of others. It's not a place for those who panic at the thought of getting lost.

In early times, extremely few people had an opportunity to face such anxieties, as the Everglades have always been virtually impenetrable by conventional boats. The tangled masses of submerged and floating plants quickly foul the most weed-proof outboard motors and in many regions are much too dense to allow ready passage even by canoes. And though most parts of the Everglades are shallow enough and hard-bottomed enough to be explored by wading, the fatigue involved in pushing through miles of vegetation-choked marsh and the ever-present risks of encountering cottonmouths and alligators have disheartened nearly all potential intruders on foot.

Shielded by the inaccessibility of its primary habitat, Florida's Everglade Kite, a race of the Snail Kite of Central and South America, was for many years the most mysterious of North America's birds of prey. Until the 1940s, only a few hardy souls had made concerted efforts to fight through the swamplands to locate the species. Most notable among these were Donald J. Nicholson, an early egg collector, and his notorious guide, Henry "Gator" Redding. For the great majority of naturalists, the kite continued to be known only as an extraordinarily elusive spirit they had never seen and probably never would, a medium-sized raptor with extremely long thin talons and a bizarrely curved bill that somehow were adapted for a strange specialized diet of aquatic snails. Beyond basic facts such as these, knowledge of the biology of the kite remained extremely fragmentary.

This situation changed dramatically following World War II with the advent of airboats. Admirably suited for traversing tangled aquatic habitats, these flat-bottomed craft with noisy airplane motors and propellers opened up the marshes for all who wanted to explore them. The alligators and other wildlife of the region suddenly lost a most precious asset—freedom from human disturbance and harassment. But at the same time, the Everglade Kite finally became easily accessible for study.

Unfortunately, by then the kite population had fallen to just a few dozen individuals. Many conservationists feared that the species might soon be lost from North America. In Florida, the kite feeds almost exclusively on a single species of freshwater mollusk: the Florida apple snail (*Pomacea paludosa*), a golf-ball-sized species with a dark brown shell. But by the 1950s, drainage activities to promote agriculture had wiped out major portions of the snail's Everglades habitat and had significantly weakened the vitality of the portions that were left. Snail populations and the kites feeding on them suffered greatly. Lake Okeechobee was the only place known to still support the kites with any reliability.

By the 1960s, however, the few surviving kites were inadvertently given a reprieve. Giant impoundments—the water conservation areas—were constructed that compartmentalized the remaining Everglades. Built mainly for water storage and flood control, the conservation areas created quite stable and high water levels in local areas, which led to the development of large and relatively healthy snail populations. The kites began to increase again as well. Thus, in the short term, the water conservation areas created very favorable local habitat for the kites, while at the same time the overall deterioration of the region continued. Damage was especially severe for localities downstream from the conservation areas in Everglades National Park.

With a new and still not fully tested water management regime now in place, what the future may hold for the Glades and the kites is not entirely predictable, and it is essential that the kite population be closely tracked in the years ahead. Fortunately, a practical method for monitoring the size of the kite population exists and has been pursued for nearly forty years, starting with the efforts of Paul Sykes of the U.S. Fish and Wildlife Service in the late 1960s. The species has a strong tendency to assemble in overnight roosts located in patches of emergent woody vegetation spaced irregularly through the range of the bird, and the kites can be reliably counted as they enter or leave these roosts in the evening or morning, respectively. If all active roosts can be found—and this takes continuous effort because roost locations change over time—it is then possible to come up with good counts of the entire population by combining simultaneous and near simultaneous counts from all roosts. Population counts in recent decades have shown substantial fluctuation from year to year, largely correlated with water levels, but the overall pattern has been a general increase from the early 1970s, when only about a hundred birds were found, through the late 1990s, when the totals peaked at roughly two thousand birds. A significant drought in 1999 and 2000 dropped the numbers back to roughly a thousand birds, and which way the population may trend in the future is highly uncertain.

Our first studies of the Everglade Kite grew out of behavioral research on its primary food animal—the apple snail—that we conducted during graduate student days at Cornell University in the mid-1960s. We were especially interested in the relationships of this snail with its various predators, and when we moved to Florida in 1967, we soon became aware that the apple snail occupies a central position in the food chains of the Everglades, serving as an important dietary focus for many of the region's aquatic animals, including various insects, crayfishes, fishes, turtles, and even young alligators. Three of Florida's birds feed especially heavily on apple snails—the Everglade Kite, the Limpkin, and the Boat-tailed Grackle—and we embarked on a study of the adaptations that these birds use to exploit their food supply.

The Everglade Kite's adaptations include an extremely long and thin, decurved upper bill, which the bird uses to cut the columellar muscle that holds an apple snail in its shell. To aid in cutting the same muscle, the Limpkin possesses a twisted asymmetrical lower bill. Historically, the exact functions of these specialized anatomical tools had long been misunderstood. The Boat-tailed Grackle is much less dependent on apple snails for food than are the other two birds and lacks specific anatomical specializations for snail feeding. Nevertheless, it too has developed efficient ways to extract apple snails from their shells. All three birds can commonly be found in the same regions, and we found it to be relatively uncommon for them to show signs of aggressive intolerance of one another.

Within the kite population itself, we also usually found harmonious relationships among individuals, regardless of whether they were slate-colored adult males or brown-streaked females and immatures. Consistent with its scientific name—*Rostrhamus sociabilis*—the Everglade Kite is a gregarious species, often feeding in loose assemblages and breeding in colonies of a dozen or more pairs. To be sure, solitary nesting and foraging are also quite common. But regardless of how closely or distantly birds are associated, it is rare to see any signs of individuals excluding one another

Everglade (Snail) Kite

Apple snails (Pomacea paludosa) *become vulnerable to capture when they come to the water surface to breathe. A foraging kite rarely gets more than its feet wet in procuring a victim.*

Everglade Kites almost always succeed in their attempts to grab snails, but this effort yielded only a cattail stalk.

from feeding territories. Very likely, snails are usually too thinly spread for defense of specific areas to offer an advantage that might exceed the cost of such behavior.

Nevertheless, we once observed vigorous defense of several adjacent sections of a canal in the eastern Everglades by several nonbreeding kites. These birds had discovered an incredibly abundant food supply in a limited area. Here, apple snails could be seen on nearly every submerged cattail stem, and the resident kites usually took only a few seconds to locate a victim on a given hunting foray. Intruding kites were driven away viciously and forced to forage in surrounding areas that had far inferior food supplies. Thus, under the proper circumstances, the Everglade Kite can be as aggressive as the most territorial of bird species, although ecological conditions do not usually warrant such behavior.

In the late 1970s, after an absence of several years, we returned to Florida to resume studies of the Everglade Kite, this time for the U.S. Fish and Wildlife Service. Also participating in these studies were Rod Chandler of the National Audubon Society and two collaborators supported by the National Wildlife Federation, Steve Beissinger and Gary Falxa. For our efforts we had the full-time use of an airboat, and we were able to cover the entire range of the kite in Florida, finding most nests, banding most young, and conducting intensive studies of the behavior of selected pairs.

Although Everglade Kites are often highly intolerant of blinds placed close to their nests (perhaps more so than any other North American raptor), many aspects of the breeding biology of this species are practical to study. In 1979 we watched the breeding cycles of two pairs on Lake Okeechobee from nearly the start of nest building through to independence of young sixteen weeks later. Our observations were made mainly from a lookout platform complete with a beach-umbrella canopy that we built atop a decapitated melaleuca tree about a quarter mile from the nests. From this vantage point, we were able to see essentially all nesting and foraging activities of the birds during two full-day observation periods each week. The kites generally hunted within a mile of the nests, flapping slowly over the sloughs, and we had an unobstructed view of nearly the entire foraging range from the observation platform.

The pairs had greatly varying success in capturing snails, mostly as a result of changes in weather conditions. On days of moderate temperatures, snails frequently came to the water's surface to breathe, and the kites rarely needed more than two or three minutes to locate a victim on a given foray. But on days following the passage of cold fronts, snails rarely came close enough to the surface to be vulnerable, and the kites had great difficulty in finding food, sometimes taking fifteen or twenty minutes or longer to make a capture. This difficulty may explain why the kites do not commonly breed as far north in Florida as their food supply extends. Despite Florida's reputation for balmy winter weather, cold fronts do roll down the peninsula all winter long. The severity of these fronts normally decreases markedly from north to south.

Once the young kites fledged from the nests we had under close observation, we found that they very quickly became as adept as adults in grabbing snails from the water's surface—perhaps not too surprising a result, since apple snails are not notably skilled in evading capture by kites. Nevertheless, the fledglings needed several weeks to develop the ability to extract snails from their shells. Successful snail extractions demand correct orientation of the shell for removal of the operculum (the "door" closing off the shell's entrance) and for insertion of the bird's long curved upper bill into the snail's soft parts. The young birds had special difficulty in learning how to hold a snail against a perch with the feet so that they could accomplish these tasks properly. Obviously unsure of how to proceed, they eyed their captured victims curiously; then often positioned them in orientations in which further progress was unlikely, if not impossible. Even worse, fledgling kites commonly fumbled snails in their clumsy efforts, and the snails fell to the water below and sank straight to the bottom. The young kites never attempted to retrieve such snails and soon took off on new hunting forays to begin the process anew. Only after many repeated attempts did the fledglings become expert in snail extractions, finally taking their places as fully competent members of the population.

In our general studies of the kite population, we discovered that survival of individuals can be extremely good when food supplies are favorable. In fact, all thirteen nestlings we provided with backpack radio transmitters on Lake Okeechobee in 1979 were still alive a year to a year and a half later (the lifetime of the transmitters). We know of only one other study—of Bald Eagles—that has documented such high survival of fledglings.

We also discovered what appeared to be a new threat to the species. A full 10 percent of the nestlings found in 1979 had small bloody holes chewed in their abdomens, evidently by nest-dwelling dermestid beetle larvae, which are normally only scavengers. In subsequent studies in the early 1980s, Steve Beissinger found the frequency of attack rising at times to as high as 25 percent. The great majority of nestlings survive these attacks, however, and overall, this threat does not appear to be severe enough to jeopardize the species.

But surely the most important biological discovery of all was the finding that in good years, with favorable water conditions and abundant snails, kite nests are almost always deserted by one parent or the other at about the time young reach fledging age. Females are as likely to desert as males, but regardless of which sex leaves, the remaining parent continues to provide for the brood until they reach independence—generally about another month. Meanwhile, the deserting bird is free to start a new breeding cycle with a new partner. Under poor conditions, neither parent deserts and both struggle to raise what young they have. Although desertion of mates in late nesting stages is known to occur in certain other raptor species, the Everglade Kite is evidently unique in that desertion can involve either sex.

Our early investigations into mate desertion raised many more questions than answers. What determines which parent deserts? What controls the precise timing of desertion? Why doesn't the species increase clutch size as an alternative to desertion? Solutions to these questions and many others were admirably explored in subsequent research by Steve Beissinger. In general, Beissinger has suggested that low clutch size (almost always two or three eggs in the 1970s) together with mate desertion may be a favored strategy when the probability of nesting successfully is low and nesting seasons are long, allowing frequent nesting attempts. Interestingly, clutch size of the kite appears to have been considerably higher in the early twentieth century before drainage projects caused massive deterioration of the Everglades. At that time, clutches of four, five, and sometimes even six eggs were often recorded by egg collectors. Whether mate desertion was less frequent in those early years was not documented, although one might expect this to have been the case.

In 1978, we confirmed that at least one color-banded male, who had a successful spring breeding on Lake Okeechobee, moved nearly a hundred miles south to breed again in one of the conservation areas during the early summer. The second nesting of this bird proved to be another successful one and constituted the first conclusive evidence of multiple brooding in the species. The fact that the kites frequently move long distances between successive broods may explain in part why the existence of multiple brooding was previously undetected, although we now know it is a frequent occurrence, closely linked with the mate-desertion phenomenon.

The discovery of multiple brooding, coupled with a finding that kites under good water conditions often breed before they are even a year old, revealed a tremendous reproductive potential for the species, an unusual trait for a bird on the endangered species list. Although nesting success of the kite is characteristically low—only about 13 percent of undisturbed nests produced fledglings during our years of study—the extended breeding season (sometimes continuing ten to eleven months of the year) and the numerous breeding attempts possible within a year allow the species to increase very rapidly when food supplies permit. Under good conditions, a breeding adult that consistently deserts its successive mates in the late stages can in theory produce as many as four successful broods of young in a single year, although whether this ever happens in fact has not been demonstrated.

One important cause of the high failure rate of nesting attempts has been a tendency for the species to nest in structurally unsound sites. Many nests we observed in flexible willow saplings, for example, collapsed during the breeding cycle, yet the kites commonly chose such sites, sometimes persistently rebuilding in exactly the same locations after previous nests had fallen. The best substrates tended to be substantial shrubs and trees such as pond apples, cocoa plums, cypresses, and melaleucas. Cattails proved the worst, and nests placed in this plant rarely succeeded in fledging young. They almost always slowly tipped over as nesting progressed and eventually dumped out their contents.

Everglade (Snail) Kite

Left: *At Wakulla Springs in northern Florida, a Florida apple snail lays eggs above the water surface on a cypress trunk. This aquatic snail normally lays eggs at night, but this female did not finish until just after sunrise. On completion of the task, she simply fell back into the water.*

Unfortunately, most kites on Lake Okeechobee have traditionally placed their nests in cattail beds and for many years produced very few young as a result. The problem, however, was largely solved in the early 1970s, when Rod Chandler began transferring cattail nests into specially built baskets mounted on poles in the original locations of the nests. These efforts greatly enhanced nesting success and contributed importantly to the increase of the species through the 1970s.

As a raptor almost totally dependent on a single variety of easy-to-catch prey, the Florida Everglade Kite enjoys an uncomplicated existence under good food conditions. But when food supplies fail, this species must be prepared to move long distances and to absorb heavy mortality. Although

Below: *A female kite brings in a snail for her brood in the eastern Everglades in 1968. This bird was raising her young no longer assisted by a mate; with most nests, one adult or the other deserts the site about the time the young reach fledging age.*

Downy nestling Everglade Kites are cryptic (camouflaged) in coloration, unlike the downy young of most other raptors.

food-stressed Everglade Kites have been seen taking unusual prey, such as small turtles and other snail species much smaller than *Pomacea paludosa*, their specialized anatomical adaptations for feeding on apple snails do not suit them well to such alternative fare. During the massive Florida drought of 1981–1982 *Pomacea* snails became very scarce in many regions, and the kite population suffered a major crash. Steve Beissinger observed a number of kites feeding on turtles at the time, but it took them hours to consume small individuals and they usually did not manage to extract more than a small fraction of the meat inside the shells. Likewise they were getting very little meat out of the *Vivipurus gruigiunus* snails they sometimes sampled. It is hard to imagine that the Florida kites could long survive anywhere in the absence of *Pomacea paludosa* snails. They appear to be trapped forever by their anatomical specializations, facing all the risks inherent in a single-food economy.

Other races of *Rostrhamus sociabilis* face somewhat more diverse food supplies. In Venezuela, for example, these kites take several other species of *Pomacea* snail, and they also feed quite heavily on freshwater crabs. In Colombia, we have seen them taking large snails of the genus *Marisa* as well as *Pomacea*. The full range of the kite extends as far south as Argentina, and it is a relatively common species in the marshlands of many South American countries, as well as in Cuba and various parts of Central America. Only in Florida is the species presently endangered.

The primary immediate threat to Florida's Everglade Kite remains the recurrent droughts that hit the state and reduce the open-water areas to a tiny fraction of their normal extent. When the rains fail, the kites leave the main Everglades almost completely and disperse widely, attempting to find apple snails wherever they can. Ultimate survival of the species in Florida may well depend on the continued existence and good health of deep-water refugia such as Lake Okeechobee, which have traditionally served to tide the species over hard times until the rains have returned. Unfortunately, pollution

has begun to affect the health of Lake Okeechobee, and with the ceaseless growth of the human population along the coasts of southern Florida, other deep-water refugia may suffer increasing pollution stress as well, making the species increasingly vulnerable to the effects of droughts.

In addition to problems with water supplies, the kite has faced significant difficulties with the invasion of the Everglades by an exotic species of tree—the melaleuca (*Melaleuca quinquenervia*)—which has rapidly converted parts of the conservation areas and Lake Okeechobee into aquatic woodland. The melaleuca, a native of Australia, is exceedingly well adapted to conditions of long term submersion alternating with periods of dry downs and fires, and it has spread throughout much of the Everglades unchecked by natural enemies. When present in low densities, it provides excellent nest trees for the kites, but in the long term it changes open Everglades habitat into forest conditions unsuitable for the species. Efforts are now finally being made to remove the melaleucas from some regions, such as Lake Okeechobee, but it remains to be seen how successful these efforts will prove to be overall.

Even much more threatening to the stability of the Everglades is the long-term prospect of rising sea levels and changed climatic patterns caused by global warming trends. Some projections suggest that vast areas of the Everglades, which lie only a few feet above sea level, could well be inundated with salt water within the next century or two, and it is questionable whether even massive dike construction can prevent this development. While the Everglade Kite population might conceivably survive such a massive disruption of its primary habitat by moving north (if warming trends also allow apple snail populations to expand northward), it is highly uncertain that such adjustments would occur smoothly enough and rapidly enough to keep pace with the projected rapidity of sea level changes. Long-term survival of the Everglade Kite in Florida is at best precarious, despite the relatively vigorous population the species has maintained in recent years.

Everglade (Snail) Kite

Hook-billed Kite
Chondrohierax uncinatus

LIKE THE EVERGLADE KITE, the Hook-billed Kite feeds almost exclusively on mollusks—a highly unusual trait among raptors. But whereas the Everglade Kite preys almost exclusively on aquatic snails, the Hook-billed Kite specializes on terrestrial species, and whereas the Everglade Kite is generally a bird of open marshes, the Hook-billed Kite is a bird of densely forested areas. Both species are medium-sized—a bit larger than the Broad-winged Hawk—but they are not closely related, and they diverge markedly in behavior and anatomy.

In fact, the hook-bill is by far the oddest raptor we have ever had a chance to observe. Its repetitive calls are quite musical and are reminiscent of the mellow vocalizations of the Field Sparrow. Its frail nest consists of only a handful of twigs and looks very much like that of a dove. Stranger still, its fleshy feet are sometimes employed like those of a parrot in manipulating prey. Although snails are usually braced with one foot against a perch during extractions, the birds sometimes hold them free of the perch, working on

Range of the Hook-billed Kite
■ Breeding and wintering

The presumed male of one pair of Hook-billed Kites studied near Tampico, Mexico, feeds an extracted snail to a recent fledgling. Feeding rates were at times as high as one snail every six minutes.

The presumed female hook-bill at one nest brought many whole snails to her young. These she extracted in full view of her nestlings. Characteristically, she clutched a snail in her left foot, then dropped the shell once she removed the soft parts.

them much as a small child might attack an ice-cream cone held not quite upright in one hand.

The snail-extraction method used by the hook-bill has little of the elegance of the method used by the Everglade Kite. Rather than subtly severing the columellar muscle of the snail without damaging the shell, the hook-bill uses brute force and fractures the base of the shell with its bill, then pulls out the exposed soft parts. Correspondingly, the bill of the species is much stouter than that of the Everglade Kite and is structured to withstand the continuous wear and tear inherent in crushing dozens of shells on a daily basis. In profile, the hook-bill's bill projects proportionately much farther forward from the head than the bill of most fellow members of the Accipitridae and is most reminiscent of the huge prow of a Bald Eagle.

The hook-bill also exhibits other physical characteristics that set it apart from other North American raptors. Adults have glassy white eyes that give them an oddly crazed expression. And between the eye and bill is a peculiar greenish patch of skin topped by a yellowish patch, both of unknown significance. Lastly, the legs of the kite are so short as to look like stumps and

give the species an unnatural "sawed-off" appearance in profile. Altogether, the Hook-billed Kite is a most unusual bird of prey, both in appearance and behavior, and it is perhaps the least familiar raptor of all the North American species to most ornithologists as well as to general nature enthusiasts.

The Hook-billed Kite is basically a Central and South American species that occurs as far north as Texas in the thorn-scrub vegetation along the Rio Grande. Nesting records exist for the Santa Ana Refuge and a few other locations in southern Texas, but the species is erratic in distribution and is not found in these locations in all years, likely because of major fluctuations in snail populations. For those seeking to find and study the species, this fluid and inconsistent distribution is a source of great frustration. Very few nests have ever been found for the species and many facets of its biology still remain unexplored.

The most thorough studies yet accomplished have been those of Tom Smith, who doggedly pursued the species for his graduate research with Stan Temple at the University of Wisconsin in the late 1970s and early 1980s. Smith, who had earlier helped us with research on the Everglade

Hook-billed Kite

All kites observed in the Tampico population, including this probable male, were the small-billed variety. The species' legs are characteristically short, giving the birds a "sawed-off" appearance when perched.

Kite, was mainly interested in the significance of a curious variability in bill size that was apparent in collections of museum skins of the species. Museum specimens indicated that some populations of hook-bills had bills of relatively uniform size. In other regions, two markedly different forms of the species occurred—one with a very large bill and the other with a smaller, but still substantial bill. The two bill types did not seem to have any consistent relationships with variable characteristics of plumage coloration, body size, sex, or age of the birds, but in some regions the difference between the two bill sizes was great enough that some observers had even proposed that more than one species of hook-bill might exist. Most evidence, however, suggested that the two bill sizes belonged to a single highly variable species. In his research efforts Tom Smith focused specifically on how the bill size variability related to variability in snail sizes in various prey populations.

Tom Smith's first searches for the species were in southern Texas locations where the hook-bills had been documented nesting in earlier years. But although he located old nests of hook-bills and found promising piles of hook-bill-damaged snail shells, no active pairs were in evidence, so he headed across the Mexican border to continue the search. Several weeks later he phoned to invite us to join him in observations of a loose nesting colony of the small-billed form of the species he had located in thorn scrub two hundred miles south of the Texas border. The opportunity to assist in observations of how the hook-bill's method of extracting snails might differ from the method used by Everglade Kites was too intriguing to pass up, and within several days Noel flew to Tampico, Mexico, to participate in these studies.

The Mexican hook-bills were feeding exclusively on small white-shelled terrestrial snails that were extremely abundant in the region surrounding the colony. These were not active snails crawling about on the ground and vegetation, but dormant aestivating snails clinging in a state of motionless torpor to tree trunks and twigs. As such, the snails were highly conspicuous and obviously were not much of a challenge to capture. The birds were taking them at a rapid rate. At one of the two nests he observed, a nest with two young just at fledging age, Noel recorded long stretches when visits of adults to the nest were as frequent as one trip every six to seven minutes. Though we have seen Elf and Eastern Screen Owls provisioning their nestlings with insects at even greater frequencies than this, we know of no other raptor comparable in size to the hook-bill that can match this rate of prey deliveries. The similar-sized Everglade Kite takes snails that are much more massive than the snails the hook-bills were eating, and not surprisingly, we have never observed Everglade Kites bringing prey to their nests at anything like the rate seen with the hook-bills.

The Mexican hook-bills flew from tree to tree with accipiterlike alternations of flapping and gliding, and they were not seen circling in the sky, although soaring individuals have been seen elsewhere by other observers. The birds brought snails to the nest vicinity quite surreptitiously and extracted them either at the nest itself or on a perch nearby. Piles of many dozens of shells with characteristic hook-bill damage had accumulated under some perches. The vocalizations of the adults did not carry far, and often the crunch of a snail being processed nearby was the first signal that an adult had returned to the nest vicinity.

Hook-billed Kite nests are often small and frail, unlike those of most diurnal raptors. Youngsters close to fledging have attractive cream underparts marked with black barring.

The hook-bills usually transported snails still in their shells. Sometimes they carried the shell crosswise in the bill, sometimes with the upper bill inserted in the snail's aperture. Both sexes of adults fed the young independently, and the youngsters, although right at fledging age, were not yet attempting extractions on their own. The youngsters had attractive cream-colored underparts and were very different in appearance from the adults. Basic coloration of the adults presumed to be males was gray, while their mates were much browner. Plumage variation is great in the species, however, and both sexes are sometimes almost completely black. The hook-bill is one of the few exceptions to the usual rule that polychromatic raptors tend to be birds of open country.

In accordance with what one might suspect about the function of bill dimorphism in the Hook-billed Kite, there was only one kind of tree snail—a small species (*Rhabdotus alternatus*)—for the small-billed Tampico population to exploit. Later, Tom Smith was able to document that in regions farther south, where the hook-bills were strongly dimorphic in bill size, snails of differing size classes were available as food. In some places, the different prey sizes were produced by multiple snail species, but in other places, the different sizes represented different age classes within single species.

Thus, the hypothesis that the dimorphism might be related to availability of different sized prey snails appeared to be well supported by field data. Evidently, small-billed kites simply do not have the bill strength needed to fracture large snails, while the large-billed kites find their bills too large and clumsy to be well suited for tackling small snails. The presence of both large- and small-billed kites in a region with a diversity of snail sizes allows much more thorough exploitation of available food resources than would be the case with only a single bill size. Nevertheless, such dimorphism in bill size unrelated to sex is highly unusual in birds, and very likely reflects the discontinuous distributions of snail sizes to be found in many regions.

Little is known about long-term population trends of the Hook-billed Kite throughout much of its range. But at least in northeastern Mexico, habitat destruction represents an apparently serious threat to the long-term welfare of the species. One by one, the thorn-scrub woodlands of this region are being bulldozed into cropland, and in fact the habitat of the colony of hook-bills found near Tampico in 1979 was completely obliterated later in the same year. With such massive changes occurring, it is worth pondering how long hook-bills can continue to exist in this region and how long they can continue to turn up farther north in Texas, even in protected areas.

Hook-billed Kite

Elsewhere, other populations are even more vulnerable to loss. Two distinctive subspecies of the hook-bill, on Cuba and Grenada, are now exceedingly rare and considered highly endangered, possibly mainly because of habitat destruction, but also because of persecution from farmers who mistakenly imagine them as threats to poultry. The population on Cuba, only recently rediscovered, is distinctive enough that it is often considered a separate species. In both of these island habitats, the kites are consistently small-billed and feed on small snails that are quite uniformly sized.

Despite the precarious status of many hook-bill populations, it's hard to find a following for the Hook-billed Kite among conservationists and ornithologists, in thought-provoking contrast to the fraternities of devotees who revere more well-known species such as the California Condor and the Peregrine Falcon. In fact, the Hook-billed Kite commands so little attention that it is one of the very few species of birds breeding in North America that is not covered in the recent comprehensive *Birds of North America*, a series of monographs edited by Alan Poole and Frank Gill. But is this bizarre raptor, with its many extraordinary adaptations, any less worthy of our concern than any other bird species?

Left: *Estivating (dormant) snails of the species* Rhabdotus alternatus *evidently made up the entire diet of the hook-bills near Tampico.*

Below: *Huge piles of damaged shells accumulated under perches that the hook-bills used for snail extractions.*

Opposite: *A glassy white iris and exposed green and yellow skin patches between the eyes and bill give the hook-bill an unusual appearance.*

Hook-billed Kite

Mississippi Kite

Ictinia mississippiensis

Range of the Mississippi Kite
■ Breeding

LONG POINTED WINGS and a long tail give the Mississippi Kite a deceptively falconlike silhouette as it soars overhead. Nevertheless, the gregarious habits and buoyant flight of this species, coupled with its apparent reluctance to beat its wings, soon dispel any doubts about its true identity. In size, the Mississippi Kite, like the White-tailed Kite, is only somewhat larger than a common city pigeon. In coloration it is almost uniformly a battleship gray. Adults, however, have a whitish patch along the trailing edge of the topsides of their wings, formed by the pale upper surfaces of their inner flight feathers. This patch is most apparent when flying individuals tilt their shoulders toward the observer below.

Aloft, the Mississippi Kite is pure pleasure for the eyes. Totally at home on the winds, this species exhibits an exquisite acrobatic grace in its movements and an ease of progression that is rivaled by few other raptors. Gliding, circling, and swooping with its companions, it sails tirelessly across the skies, sometimes ascending so high above the ground that it ultimately disappears from view, lost in the clouds or glare from the sun.

The underlying reason for the Mississippi Kite's penchant for the stratosphere is a search for prey, mainly high-flying insects such as dragonflies. These it grabs in its talons after quick flapping dashes and swoops, or sometimes with nothing more than almost imperceptible slight shifts in flight direction and altitude. Occasionally, the species also takes flying birds, bats, and other vertebrates, and rarely, it even takes carrion, but its overall dependence on large airborne insects is very strong.

With such a diet and such hunting behavior, it is not surprising to find that the Mississippi Kite is a late riser. Only with the thermal stimulation of midmorning sunlight do many of its prey species take to the air, and only with the air movements created by the sun can the kites themselves stay airborne with maximal efficiency. Until conditions are right, the kites commonly gather on conspicuous snags, preening their soft gray feathers and intermittently scanning their surroundings.

Sometimes, especially when flying conditions do not permit soaring, Mississippi Kites also hunt from perches, waiting for prey to fly by, flapping over to grab them, and gliding quickly back to their stations. Such hunting behavior is sufficiently frequent that it may explain the strong tendency of the species to nest near towering trees with dead branches that can provide strategic vantage points for sighting prey.

A dependence on insects also appears to explain the relatively late breeding cycle characteristic of the species, for in most regions the greatest availability of large flying insects occurs in summer, not springtime. Unlike the many raptor species that begin breeding in March and April, Mississippi Kites do not commonly commence egg laying till late May and early June, and young are often not on the wing until August.

In addition, the Mississippi Kite's tendency to take large flying insects high in the air appears to explain its tolerance for a great variety of habitat types in its nesting distribution across the southern United States. Such prey can be found in abundance over diverse ecological zones. In some regions, for example in northern Florida, Mississippi Kites are characteristic birds of heavily forested river swamps. In other regions, such as in parts of Texas and Oklahoma, they can be found coursing over endless swales of mesquite or oak scrublands. In still other regions, such as in other parts of Texas, Oklahoma, and Kansas, they gather in shelterbelts in the midst of open-field habitats. In recent years, they have also become familiar nesting birds along the tree-lined fairways of suburban golf courses in some southwestern states, posing a nuisance, if not a hazard, to golfers by their tendency to defend their nests with aggressive swooping dives.

Still another habitat type occupied by Mississippi Kites is one where we have become most familiar with the species—the cottonwood riparian zones of the southwestern states, for example along the San Pedro, Gila, and Verde rivers in Arizona. Here the kites have settled primarily in regions dominated by both cottonwoods and salt cedars. Both tree species are primary food plants for the Apache cicadas on which the kites feed extensively.

During June 1987, we observed the activities of one of Arizona's Mississippi Kite colonies along the San Pedro River. Here, several dozen kites had settled along a five-mile stretch of the river that also hosted at least four pairs of Gray Hawks, several pairs of Cooper's Hawks, and a pair of Common Black Hawks, as well as many Gila Woodpeckers, Bewick's Wrens, Western Kingbirds, Vermilion Flycatchers, Blue Grosbeaks, Summer Tanagers, and uncountable numbers of Yellow-breasted Chats, Yellow Warblers, and Bell's Vireos. A low elevation riparian region snaking through hillsides of saguaro cacti and other Sonoran Desert vegetation, the lower San Pedro Valley hosts some of the highest densities of birds found in the entire Southwest.

Many of the kites roosted in a small grove of huge cottonwoods on the west side of the river, while nests were scattered several hundred yards apart, mainly on the river's east side near the tops of tall, slender cottonwoods that defied safe ascent. Salt cedar was common in the area, though the abundance of mesquite and other woody vegetation—especially mature cottonwoods—was truly impressive.

Right: *In flight, the Mississippi Kite ranks among the most graceful of all birds, soaring most of the time rather than flapping. Its buoyancy facilitates a long migration to South America each fall. Migrating kites commonly travel in flocks, alternately circling upward in thermals and gliding long distances with little energy expenditure.*

Early in the breeding season, a male Mississippi Kite of southern Arizona passes his mate a cicada.

The kites commonly foraged right over the crowns of the cottonwoods on the east side of the river, catching the lift of the winds deflected upward by the treetops. But sometimes they ascended to prodigious heights, capturing and eating endless numbers of cicadas on the wing. Often it was impossible to detect any kites in the area without scanning the skies carefully with binoculars. But a few minutes later, a dozen or more birds would appear at close range, joining one another, dispersing again, then coming together in a constantly evolving aerial ballet of graceful movements and associations.

Prior to egg laying, the female kites often spent much of their time perched quietly on dead branches high in the cottonwoods. Their mates meanwhile worked hard to satisfy not only their own food needs, but much of the females' needs as well. Coursing the skies in the vicinity, the males brought in many of their insect victims in plummeting swoops, transferring the prey from foot to bill in the last few moments before landing beside their mates, then relinquishing the food in quick bill-to-bill passes. Some of the swooping approaches, however, ended not in food transfers, but in copulations, with the males balancing on the backs of the females for about ten seconds.

Some of the kites did not appear to be breeders, and of these, many wore the plumage of one-year-olds: banded tails and mottled underwing coverts. Others that were associated with nests drifted in and out of the foraging groups, returning periodically to their nest locations to feed small young or to assist in incubation or in the shading or brooding of young. When we approached their nests or roosts too closely we were greeted with the characteristic *wheet-phew* vocalizations that signify alarm.

Late June temperatures along the lower San Pedro can reach wilting levels well above 100 degrees Fahrenheit, and our primary desire at midday was to take refuge in the shade and to swill volumes of liquids. The kites, however, remained quite active through this period, perhaps finding cooler conditions aloft. Gray Hawks also commonly made an appearance at this time, leaving the shelter of the dense cottonwood groves to land on the gravel bars at the river's edge and drink. We occasionally saw the kites do likewise. The San Pedro floodplain at this time of year is an oven, and only when the summer monsoons arrive in July, with daily thunderstorms and cloud shelter from the sun, do conditions become more bearable.

A Mississippi Kite incubates her eggs high in a cottonwood in Texas. Mississippi Kites, like Hook-billed Kites, raise small broods, commonly one or two young. Nesting comes later in the year than for any other diurnal raptor of North America, probably a reflection of the kite's reliance on large insects as food.

In a thorough study of Arizona's Mississippi Kites in the late 1970s, researchers Rich Glinski and Robert Ohmart determined that the species appeared to be thriving only in riparian zones that had a mix of cottonwoods (*Populus fremontii*) and salt cedar (*Tamarix chinensis*), like those found along stretches of the San Pedro River. But salt cedar is an aggressive exotic species that appears to be completely replacing cottonwoods over wide areas, and it is not clear whether the kites could have existed in the state before the arrival of this tree or whether they have a stable future here. The kites were only first recorded in the state in the early 1970s, when the salt cedar invasion was well underway. Should the invasion ever go to completion, the kites might well disappear once again.

In most of its breeding range, however, the Mississippi Kite is not in any way dependent on or threatened by salt cedar, and its overall status appears to be robust. Thus, it would be perverse to argue for the preservation of exotic salt cedar in Arizona's riparian zones for the sake of the kite, especially in view of the apparently severe threat that this plant poses for native cottonwood forests and a host of bird species closely dependent on these forests. Unfortunately, salt cedar is extremely difficult to remove once established, because it spreads readily from seed, is highly resistant to fire, and is capable of sprouting from even small root sections. Successful eradication efforts entail high levels of persistence and major financial investments. The

resources needed for full removal of this species are simply unavailable in most regions. Like the exotic melaleuca tree and the Brazilian pepper tree usurping native environments in Florida, salt cedar has proved far more of a curse than a blessing in its new home in North America.

Like the Swallow-tailed Kite, the Mississippi Kite is highly migratory, retiring to South America via Central America for a large fraction of the year. The migratory flights of Mississippi Kites, while not as familiar to North Americans as the migratory flights of Broad-winged Hawks and Swainson's Hawks, are sometimes impressive. In late April 1988, we observed a dense flock of more than two hundred individuals of this species heading methodically northward across the flat coastal plain of southern Texas near the Laguna Atascosa Refuge. Like many other migrating raptors, the kites moved across the landscape by alternating periods of circling upward in columns of rising air with periods of coasting in long glides in their chosen direction of travel. The migrating flock remained well integrated and closely packed till it finally faded from view in the distance.

In early December 2002, we had a chance to observe Mississippi Kites on their wintering grounds in western Brazil near the city of Cuiabá. Here, the birds exhibited the same highly gregarious foraging and roosting

Above: *During November 2002, we found wintering Mississippi Kites associating with Plumbeous Kites near the city of Cuiabá in southwestern Brazil. The two species are closely related and sometimes considered to be only subspecies of a single species. In the field, the most prominent difference between the two is a rufous patch visible at the base of the primaries in the Plumbeous Kite but absent in adult Mississippi Kites.*

behavior we had seen on their breeding grounds. Adding to the sociality, the very similar Plumbeous Kite sometimes joined them in combined aggregations. Distinguishing these two species is not always easy, although the rusty patches visible in the wings of flying Plumbeous Kites allow their identification under good viewing conditions. In perched birds, the wing tips tend to extend farther beyond the tail tips in Plumbeous Kites than in Mississippi Kites, but some individual Mississippi Kites also have wing tips that extend significantly beyond their tail tips, making this characteristic a relatively unreliable one for separating the species. Some ornithologists even maintain that the two species are not really separate species and might best be considered subspecies of a single species.

The Mississippi Kite, like the White-tailed Kite, experienced a significant increase in overall numbers and range in the late twentieth century, reoccupying many previously abandoned regions and forming new populations in some areas that it was never known to occupy historically. It now can be found nearly coast to coast across the southern states during the summer months. The broad tolerances of this species for urban and other disturbed habitats and the relative security of its food supply from destruction by human activities allow considerable optimism for its conservation in the years ahead. Nevertheless, the biology of the Mississippi Kite is still known only imperfectly, especially on the wintering grounds in South America, so the full array of threats this raptor may face in the future cannot be specified with certainty. Its ability to survive the many new ecological stresses challenging our planet, from global warming to ozone depletion, is unknown, just as it is for all other raptors.

Left: *Mississippi Kites commonly forage from high soaring flight, but when winds are deficient, they hunt from snaggy perches that give them good vantage points for detecting potential prey.*

Swallow-tailed Kite
Elanoides forficatus

SAILING AND CIRCLING AMONG the treetops, with its long, forked tail twisting in the air currents, its wings flapping but rarely, the Swallow-tailed Kite is surely the most elegant of all the world's raptors. Weighing about a pound and formally attired in striking, black-and-white plumage, it is a species that occurs as far south as Argentina and can be found in a variety of moist habitats, ranging from lowland rain forests to steep mountainous slopes. In North America it is often associated with extensive swamps of the southeastern states, at home among the towering cypresses, the tupelo gums, the Spanish moss, and the bromeliads, but it also occurs in drier, pine habitats and sometimes in mangroves and other cover types. North of the Mexican border the species is most common in Florida, especially in southwestern regions of the state, but it was once found in river bottoms as far north as Wisconsin and Minnesota. It suffered a major decline in the late nineteenth and early twentieth centuries, disappearing almost completely from the many tributaries of the mighty Mississippi River, although the causes of this decline are uncertain.

In North America the swallow-tails are present for only about half of the year, usually arriving in early March and withdrawing again to Central and South America by the end of September. During this period they have ample time to breed, most commonly fledging one or two young per nest. Throughout its breeding range, the species nests at the very tops of the tallest trees available, and consequently it is a challenge to study. Many nests are more than a hundred feet from the ground, lodged in branches too slender to support a person's weight. In addition, most nests are impossible to view clearly from blinds in other trees because no nearby trees rise high enough to overlook the nests.

Aware of these problems, we were very pleased to discover a population of swallow-tails in low mangroves along the southwestern coast of Florida, not far from the boundary of Everglades National Park. Here, tree heights rarely exceeded forty-five feet, well within the reach of a good extension ladder, and nests were fully visible from our tower blind, allowing us to carry out an intensive study of breeding biology of the species. The two biggest difficulties in observing this population proved to be moving around through the mud and tangles of mangrove roots, and surviving the assaults of hordes of biting insects. Nowhere else in North America have we ever encountered such diabolical swarms of mosquitoes, no-see-ums, and deerflies as occur in this region.

We took little comfort in observing that the swallow-tails had their share of misery from the insects as well. Their problems, however, seemed limited to the mosquitoes. We saw no signs that either deerflies or no-see-ums were ever attracted to the swallow-tails. Furthermore, the kites had help in combating the mosquitoes from the resident dragonflies. These miniature fighter planes darted endlessly through the mosquito clouds that formed around the kite nests, destroying victim after victim.

It was tempting to speculate that the tendency of the swallow-tails to place their nests at the very tops of the highest black mangroves constituted an adaptation to escape the mosquitoes. But it could just as well have reflected the difficulty these long-winged raptors would have had in maneuvering through heavier vegetation farther down the trunks. Their nest placement, however, carried penalties of several sorts, for nests situated at the tops of trees are vulnerable to the winds and to attacks from other aerial predators. At one nest we studied closely in 1972, both young were tossed out to their destruction in the swamp below as high winds of thunderstorms buffeted the area. At another nest, we found the remains of one adult kite right under

Range of the Swallow-tailed Kite

■ Current breeding

▤ Historic U.S. breeding (no longer occupied)

Swallow-tailed Kites generally carry nesting material in their feet but usually transfer it to the bill just before landing. Sexes are alike in coloration and contribute about equally to nest construction and other reproductive activities.

Usnea lichen (Ramalina usnea) *makes a common nest material in Florida. Kites bring it in especially frequently in the late nestling period, when it effectively covers debris in the nest.*

Amid a swarm of mosquitoes, an adult swallow-tail passes a green anole to a youngster. Mosquitoes were a staple food of dragonflies and tree frogs in the mangroves but provoked almost constant head-shaking in the nestling kites when wind velocities were low.

Swallow-tailed Kite

the nest, apparently a victim of another raptor—most likely a Bald Eagle or a Great Horned Owl, both common in the region.

Altogether, we had an opportunity to closely follow the natural history of three pairs of swallow-tails through their breeding cycles in the mangroves, two in 1969 and one in 1972. The contrasts we found between the behavior of the birds in these two years were enormous and well illustrated the dangers of attempting to generalize about the biology of a species from a single year's data.

In 1969, the diet of the breeding pairs was heavily slanted toward tree frogs, which were widespread in the mangroves and which the kites captured on the wing by swoops into the canopy. Food was abundant in this year, and the kites had no apparent difficulties raising their young. In the early stages of the breeding cycle, we often observed males feeding their mates at the nests, and incubation switches between adults were frequent.

The extreme drought of 1971, however, effectively wiped out the tree frog population of the mangroves, and a major scarcity of food characterized the kites' 1972 breeding season. The adults spent long periods away from the nest we had under close study, apparently hunting steadily to satisfy their own food needs, and incubation switches at the nest were infrequent. We only very rarely saw the male feed his mate at the nest, and we observed no tree frogs whatsoever in the diet of the pair. Instead, the kites were attempting to carry on by concentrating on green anoles (a small lizard) and nestling birds for food. Feeding rates at the 1972 nest averaged less than half the rates seen at the 1969 nests, and although the 1972 nest failed because storms tossed the young out of the nest, we seriously question whether the adults could have fledged young in any case, in view of the poor food supply.

A comparison of the two years suggested a strong local dependence of the kites on tree frogs for food. While they also took a variety of other food types, including anoles, snakes, and large flying insects, of these only the anoles were brought to nests with any frequency. Observers of successfully nesting swallow-tails in other regions have reported much higher use of insects than we observed, and why the birds were bringing in so few insects is not entirely clear. One possibility is that the availability of large flying insects may actually be comparatively low in mangrove habitat, despite our battles with biting varieties and the seeming abundance of dragonflies around nests.

The tree frogs in the mangroves were all green tree frogs and the similar-looking squirrel tree frogs. The occurrence of tree frogs in this habitat may depend on a freshening of the brackish waters during the summer rainy season. Although they spend much of their lives in arboreal locations, these amphibians are tied to fresh water for egg laying and may be able to breed only in years of normal or high rainfall.

One of the most interesting aspects of the behavior of the young kites was the development of their ability to recognize their own species and whether or not their parents were carrying food. Newly hatched nestlings gave cheeping cries more or less continuously during the daylight hours, and especially during feedings. At about one week of age, the cheeping cries of the young reliably followed the *eeep* calls of the female adult at the nest as the male approached with food. At this time, the young also responded with cheeping cries when Great Crested Flycatchers gave *weep* calls in the vicinity of the nest. The similarity of these calls to the *eeep* calls of the kites is apparent to the human ear as well. By two weeks of age, the young no longer responded to calls of the flycatchers. They did, however, call whenever adults came to the nest, with or without food, and whenever other large birds such

Left: *A male swallow-tail leaves his nest, vocalizing with* klee klee klee *calls, after passing a nestling bird prey to the female.*

Shortly after passing his mate food, a male swallow-tail prepares to land on her back for copulation.

Mating is a noisy and conspicuous affair for swallow-tails and is generally performed on high, exposed branches.

as Common Grackles and Pileated Woodpeckers flew past the nest. By three weeks of age, the young no longer responded to large birds of other species flying past, but they still called when kites flew nearby with or without food. At five weeks of age, the young often did not respond vocally when adults flew past without food.

Another intriguing feature of the behavior of nestling swallow-tails in the study area, especially when compared with the behavior of nestlings of other hawks and kites, was their apparent disinclination to loft excrement over the nest edge. We repeatedly observed young backing up to the nest rim in typical accipitrid fashion. Then, instead of ejecting a stream off into space, they just dribbled excrement directly down onto the nest rim. The extensive nest building by adults late in the nesting cycle, primarily using Spanish moss or usnea lichens, served to cover the accumulation quite effectively, but it left us wondering why these birds were not exhibiting the normal accipitrid pattern of lobbing waste material beyond the limits of the nest. Possibly, since telltale excrement did not tend to accumulate on the ground under the swallow-tail nests, it was an adaptation to reduce the conspicuousness of the nests to terrestrial predators capable of climbing to the nests, especially raccoons, which abound in the mangrove habitat. The availability of absorbent materials such as Spanish moss and usnea in the habitats occupied by the kites may have facilitated the development of such a trait. Swallow-tailed kites in certain other regions have been reported to have more typical defecation behavior.

Swallow-tailed Kites will defend quite small areas around nests from other members of their species, but they are not known to defend exclusive foraging ranges. Radiotelemetry studies in South Carolina and Florida have revealed that foraging ranges of nesting Swallow-tailed Kites can be many square miles in extent and are probably much too large to be feasible to defend. In fact, these birds often forage together in groups throughout the year, especially when pursuing flying insects, and they often nest fairly close together in loose colonies. Further, nesting colonies commonly include some extra, nonbreeding birds. One important advantage of this sociality may lie in enhanced abilities to detect and deter potential predators. We have seen numerous examples of cooperative assault of the species on Bald Eagles and various owls. Incubating kites are able to see eagles from an amazing distance, and they rapidly sound the alarm, soon to be joined by their mates and other kites in a mass effort to drive off the enemy.

One of the most unusual aspects of Swallow-tailed Kite biology is the fact that the species sometimes consumes plant foods. Fruit eating has been recorded for Costa Rica, Colombia, and Guatemala, and in late February 2001 we had a chance to observe such behavior directly in Ecuador. Individuals in a flock of nine foraging swallow-tails we observed in the foothills of the western Andes repeatedly peeled off into swoops into a small grove of palm trees, grabbing palm fruits in their talons, and then circling up in the sky to feed on these fruits in flight. Fruit feeding is a very uncommon occurrence in raptors, but when it does occur, for example with the Palm-nut Vulture of Africa, it often involves the oily and energy-rich fruits of various palms.

During the years we studied Everglade Kites on Lake Okeechobee, we became aware of a spectacular concentration of Swallow-tailed Kites that forms annually in this region between July and mid-September. Studied more recently by researchers Brian Millsap and Ken Meyer, the birds appear to gather after breeding to put on energy stores prior to their autumnal migration to Central and South America. Soaring in the updrafts created by the Australian pines and melaleucas planted on the dikes surrounding the lake, these birds may be taking advantage of the large numbers of insects associated with the lake region. In August 1987 in a remote cypress swamp west of the lake, Millsap located a roost of these swallow-tails that consisted of more than thirteen

A green tree frog (Hyla cinerea) *rests on a mangrove trunk. This species was a common food for the resident swallow-tails in 1969 but disappeared from their diet in 1972, evidently eliminated from the region by the drought of 1971.*

hundred individuals packed into an area of only about two to three acres. He suggested that this might represent as many as 50 percent of the swallow-tails breeding in the United States. Although the total North American population of the Swallow-tailed Kite can be estimated only crudely, future monitoring of this roost and others may give a practical means for assessing overall population trends of the species in the United States.

More recent estimates have suggested only about a thousand breeding pairs and perhaps a maximum of about five thousand individuals of Swallow-tailed Kites in North America in the postbreeding season. Judging from the massive shrinkage in the species' range prior to the mid-twentieth century, the swallow-tails must have declined tremendously in numbers up until that time, and the population still left in North America today must be considered relatively precarious. Although the species has recently increased in a few local regions, for example eastern Texas, populations in other southeastern regions have recently disappeared, and present overall population trends are uncertain.

Causes of the historic decline are speculative and may be various, including shooting and general habitat losses. Habitat changes presumably detrimental for the species are continuing, especially in Florida, and this raises major concerns about the viability of the North American population. In the stronghold of the species in southwestern Florida, analyses suggest that 88 percent of the pine forests were lost between 1900 and 1989, as were nearly 60 percent of the freshwater marshes. Although the swallow-tail has been documented breeding in suburban Miami and even using exotic trees such as Australian pines for nesting, habitat alteration in southern Florida has been massive, and the human population continues to increase in many regions occupied by the species. Little of the species' habitat is in protected status, and it is highly uncertain that it can adapt fully to the changes taking place. Loss of this splendid species from the fauna of North America would be a tragedy, and it appears crucial that expanded research and conservation efforts on its behalf be developed.

Swallow-tailed Kite

Northern Harrier
Circus cyaneus

An agile raptor of open swamps and fields, the Northern Harrier hunts steadily from flight, coursing low over the ground and catching small birds and rodents at short range with lightning-fast strikes. Very light bodied and buoyant, this species normally flaps only intermittently, and instead remains airborne primarily by banking and sailing in a seemingly haphazard manner, exploiting the subtle uplifts provided by the winds blowing across irregular terrain, sometimes perching momentarily on the ground, then continuing on in a steady hunt for prey. With a relatively long tail and a wingspread of about three-and-a-half to four feet, the species is large enough to soar effectively, but usually does so only sparingly, preferring to stay close to the ground except during migration.

In color pattern, Northern Harriers fall into two major categories. Adult females and immatures of both sexes possess a basically brown plumage that blends in well with their surroundings. Adult males are almost pure white underneath and pale gray above, with striking black outer primary feathers. All ages and sexes exhibit a conspicuous white patch at the base of the tail formed by the upper tail coverts, and this field mark is one of the most diagnostic characteristics of the species, usually easily visible even from long distances.

The prey taken by the species vary substantially from region to region, with a strong emphasis on small rodents in more northerly regions across Canada and into Alaska, and with a more diversified diet including small birds, reptiles, amphibians, and large insects in more southerly regions. In coastal marshes of the southeastern states, wintering birds take almost exclusively passerine birds and small waterbirds. The entire range of the species includes nearly all of Canada south of arctic regions, nearly all of the United States and Mexico, the west coast of Central America, and the larger islands of the West Indies; but the species is strongly migratory and rarely breeds south of the northern tier of states in New England and the Midwest, or south of the Great Basin and Great Plains states in the west.

Unique among North America's diurnal raptors, Northern Harriers have a prominent sound-focusing facial disk. This anatomical feature is shared with most owls and helps give the latter their distinctive "owlish" appearance. Facial disks enable the birds that possess them to capture unseen prey concealed in densely cluttered layers of vegetation, provided the prey make at least some audible sounds. Studies of the acoustic abilities of Northern Harriers have shown that this raptor is indeed capable of locating prey by sound alone and with an accuracy comparable to that of the most accomplished owls hunting in total darkness.

At one blind we set up on a Northern Harrier nest, we were amazed and frustrated by the abilities of the birds to detect the slightest noises we might make, even though the blind was positioned at a fair distance from

Range of the Northern Harrier
- Breeding
- Breeding and wintering
- Wintering

the nest. Only when rain showers provided a cover of white noise were we able to scratch, stretch, and move about relatively normally without causing alarm in the birds.

The harrier nest we had under observation held only a single chick and two inviable eggs, although harriers commonly raise much larger broods. The nest itself was a simple platform of grasses on the ground, as is typical for the species, and it was tucked in a thick carpet of waist-high brush on the floodplain of a high valley in central Alaska. Here, the birds' close neighbors were a pair of Merlins nesting in a patch of spruce on the side of the valley. Also conspicuous in the area were numerous caribou, Dall's sheep, Long-tailed Jaegers, ptarmigan, and red foxes. The harriers eventually fledged their single youngster successfully, although we watched grizzly bears foraging within a few yards of the nest on a number of occasions and often wondered how long it might be before one of these predators discovered the nest.

We also found Northern Harriers in close wintering association with Merlins at the opposite corner of the continent in southern Florida. Here, during the late winter of 1979, we set up a treetop platform for observing Everglade Kites in one area of Lake Okeechobee that by chance also hosted a nightly congregation of hundreds of thousands of roosting Tree Swallows. Not surprisingly, this extraordinary concentration of potential prey proved highly attractive to the bird-feeding raptors that hunted the marshes.

Each evening, as sunset approached, the swallows gathered high overhead in a cloudlike assemblage that steadily grew larger and denser while continuously changing shape, much like a vast swarm of honeybees. Meanwhile, Northern Harriers and Merlins gathered ominously below.

Left: *A female Northern Harrier returns to her nest in central Alaska carrying nesting material. An inhabitant of open fields and marshes, this species characteristically nests on the ground and feeds on small rodents and birds.*

Above: *When discovered, the nest in central Alaska contained only a single chick and two addled eggs, a low reproductive output for a normally prolific species.*

Occasionally, portions of the swarm made abortive dives toward the marsh, but these overanxious groups soon returned to the main swarm high overhead, and it was not until the last moments of daylight that the birds began a serious descent to roost in the saw grass. Now, in a tight, swirling, tornadolike vortex, and with a great roar of wings, the swallows poured from the sky into the marsh.

As they took up roosting locations, the swallows were vulnerable to their avian predators for a period of just a few minutes until full darkness enveloped the region. In the dim light and at a distance, it was often difficult to discern exactly how many raptors were drawn in, but on one evening when the roost was fairly close, we were sure of two Northern Harriers and three Merlins simultaneously active in the aggregation, and there could have been more. Although the swallows moved their specific roost location each night to a different part of the marsh, both raptor species kept track of their movements, unerringly converging on the tornado of descending birds to reap their nightly harvest.

The day we had first constructed our treetop lookout in the marsh, we had discovered the feathers and detached wings of swallows caught in branches of the lookout tree and had wondered what their origin might have been. But after discovering the roost during the first evening of observations, we realized we had usurped a favorite plucking tree from the raptors. Apparently, this caused the Merlins and Northern Harriers little grief, and they simply switched to other perches in the vicinity.

The steady toll of a few swallows each evening represented only a tiny percentage of the total mass of perhaps half a million individuals in the roost. Yet such predation acting over many generations of swallows most likely explains the evolution of their highly specialized roost-formation behavior. As long as the swallows remained in an amorphous cloud high above the marsh, they were easily able to avoid the raptors, but once they came in to roost they had little in the way of defenses. Apparently the best they could do was to minimize the amount of daylight time they spent in

Right: *The female Northern Harrier gets soaked while sheltering her chick from a rain shower. Prominent owl-like facial disks function as sound collectors and give the species keen powers of hearing.*

Northern Harrier

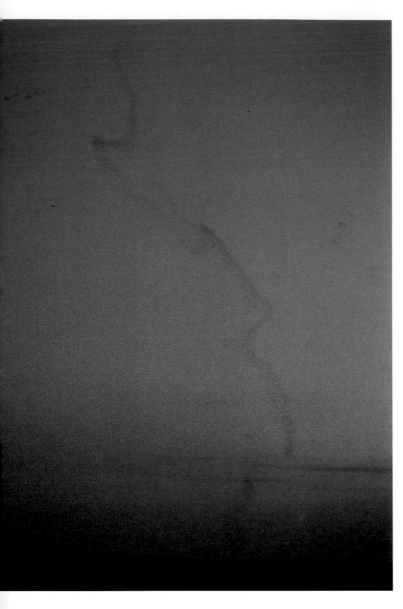

During early 1979, a vortex of several hundred thousand wintering Tree Swallows descended each evening after sunset to the saw grass of Florida's Lake Okeechobee. The precise roost location was never the same in two consecutive nights, but Northern Harriers and Merlins always converged to capture swallows during the few minutes between roost formation and complete darkness.

the roost. In the mornings, the swallows left their roost at first light and we saw no comparable raids by the raptors.

The powerful nightly spectacle of swallows pouring into the marshes pursued by their raptorial enemies continued until March 23, when the swallows finally departed on their annual spring migration to more temperate regions. The Northern Harriers and Merlins did not follow them immediately, though they too disappeared from the lake soon thereafter.

Northern Harriers themselves are well known to have a strong tendency to roost communally on the ground during the winter, although the functions of these roosts, like the communal roosts of many other birds, have been controversial. Some biologists have favored the idea that communal roosts might function mainly to transfer information about foraging conditions, and indeed, evidence with Black Vulture roosts seems to indicate clearly that individuals often do follow one another from roosts to discover food sources. Foraging arguments alone, however, do not explain why well-fed individuals might want to join communal roosts, unless they might be associated with close kin in the roosts. Kinship groups appear to be frequent in roosts of

Black Vultures, but this has not been demonstrated for Northern Harriers. Furthermore, in at least some circumstances, as we have seen with wintering birds in Arizona and New Mexico, individual harriers vigorously defend exclusive hunting grounds, so it is not entirely clear that poorly fed birds might gain foraging benefits by following well-fed individuals.

The possible functions of communal harrier roosts are not limited to foraging considerations. For example, individuals clustered in groups can potentially increase their ability to detect and escape predators. Northern Harriers disturbed at roosts by terrestrial mammals quickly communicate their alarm to other members of their roosting assemblages, and all are soon aware of the threat. Thus, the chances of a roosting harrier being taken completely by surprise by a predator may plausibly be very low for grouped individuals. On the other hand, the presence of numbers of harriers roosting close together might lure in predators, much as Tree Swallow roosts obviously attract harriers.

In general, however, we think it more likely that harrier roosts may reduce predation threats than increase them. We also remain doubtful that the roosts might offer significant advantages in communicating foraging information. Nevertheless, comprehensive experiments to elucidate the function of harrier roosts have not yet been designed and carried out, and such experiments should take into account the possibility that the roosts might actually serve multiple functions, potentially including some functions that are as yet entirely unsuspected.

Northern Harriers are also known to nest in loose colonies, especially when prey mammals are very abundant. Sometimes in these colonial situations they practice polygamy, with certain males simultaneously raising several broods with several mates. To what extent polygamy in this species is attributable to unbalanced sex ratios on the nesting ground, or to the superior attractiveness and capabilities of particular males, is an intriguing question. Many studies have indeed shown an apparent preponderance of females in wild harrier populations, and most have shown that on average females produce fewer young when paired polygamously than when paired monogamously. Males, on the other hand, have quite consistently produced more young when paired polygamously than when paired monogamously. Do females that join males that are already nesting with other females really have any alternatives other than not breeding at all? Many of these latecomer females are faced with raising their broods almost unaided in the later stages of nesting because of lapsing male attentiveness, and many fail to do so successfully. The much increased occurrence of polygamy in years of high prey populations suggests that for unattached females, joining a harem is sometimes worthwhile and sometimes not.

Among the most spectacular aerial displays given by any raptor species are the sky-dancing swoops of male harriers in the early breeding season. With deep, slow wing beats, a displaying bird rises and falls in a series of nearly vertical dives and climbs, often turning over upside down at the apex of his ascents, only to regain his orientation as he plunges earthward in the next phase of display. Sky-dancing displays are normally given in full view of a prospective mate, and the nearby female, often perched on the ground, but sometimes coursing below, has ample opportunity to judge the physical prowess of the male. The displays may also function in alerting other males to the territorial claims of the displaying bird. The conspicuous deep wing beats and obvious swoops make the displaying bird readily observable from great distances and may significantly reduce his overall energy expenditures in laying claim to a full territory. Occasionally, females also engage in the swooping displays, but most commonly they remain passive observers. Displays tend to be most intense when pairs or polygamous groups are nesting within sight of each other, but they are also

This wintering female in Arizona's San Simon Valley vigorously defended her feeding territory from other Northern Harriers. Easy to recognize because of a missing primary feather, she roosted many miles from her feeding territory.

performed with great fervor by young, unmated males and by males whose mates have died during the breeding season.

Northern Harriers also have a variety of vocal displays, including a long, rapid series of *keks* given by both sexes in courtship and distress, a piercing descending scream given by females soliciting food from their mates, and a chuckling call given by females arriving at the nest with food for their nestlings. As in most diurnal raptors, females perform all incubation and ripping apart of food for their young, while their mates concentrate on capturing food for their families. In prey transfers, flying females characteristically catch prey dropped by their mates in midair, then take the prey to the nest. Nestlings begin to move around on foot in the nest vicinity at about two weeks of age, about the same time that adult females begin hunting. First flights of nestlings occur at four to five weeks of age, with males characteristically flying at a somewhat earlier age than females. Activities continue to center near the nest location for about a month after first flights, with adults continuing to provision their still-dependent young.

The overall conservation of the Northern Harrier is perhaps most critically dependent on habitat considerations. While harriers can, to a considerable extent, forage in disturbed habitats such as those found in many agricultural regions, they have difficulty nesting successfully in these regions unless the soil is not tilled and the hay fields are left uncut through the entire breeding season. Unfortunately, the intensification of agriculture has led to a progressive loss of fallow fields and marshes, with major impacts on harrier populations in many areas. For example, it is now difficult to find nesting harriers anywhere in southern California, although the species was a regular breeder in this region a half century ago.

Harriers are far from the only creatures that have been adversely affected by massive losses of wetlands. Another associated species facing similar difficulties is the Short-eared Owl. The basic productivity of marshland habitats makes them extremely valuable for a great diversity of wildlife species. Yet preservation of wetland habitats is one of the most difficult of conservation tasks, in large part because the drainage of marshes has been one of the most economically attractive ways to create new lands for agricultural and urban development.

Northern Harrier

Accipiters

Northern Goshawk
Accipiter gentilis

A HANDSOME, DARK-CROWNED RAPTOR with a white eye stripe and a finely barred gray breast, the Northern Goshawk is a living nightmare for squirrels, jays, grouse, rabbits, and other similar-sized mammals and birds. Weaving through the mature forests at speeds almost too fast to follow, this raptor rarely gives its intended victims much time to react. For those who allow their vigilance to lapse, the first awareness of danger often comes as goshawk talons are already piercing deeply into internal organs. About the only true refuge from this formidable predator is a hole in the ground or brush too dense for it to enter.

Like the other North American accipiters, the Cooper's Hawk and the Sharp-shinned Hawk, the Northern Goshawk is adapted for maneuvering in woodland habitat by its relatively short wings and long tail. All three species are capable of rapid bursts of speed and quick changes in direction. They rely heavily on agility and stealth in making kills and in avoiding injury to themselves in an airspace cluttered with trunks and branches. Rarely observed for more than a few moments as they streak down a trail or ravine in headlong pursuit of prey, the accipiters are superbly crafted killing machines—the supreme experts in close combat among the raptors of North America.

The Northern Goshawk is the largest of the accipiters, with females sometimes exceeding three pounds in weight. It also has the fiercest disposition and takes the largest and most challenging prey. The ferocity of the species extends as well to a renowned willingness to defend its nests aggressively from people. Cackling angrily and diving repeatedly in blazing swoops, almost always from behind, the goshawks usually succeed in forcing intruders into a hasty retreat. As we learned directly in a 1969–1972 study of all three accipiters in Arizona and New Mexico, those foolhardy enough to attempt unprotected climbs to nests often find their hats removed and clothing and skin shredded by the talons of these birds. In breeding studies of goshawks, we generally carried leafy branches as we approached and checked nests. Armed with these improvised shields we were usually, but not always, able to fend off attacks without being struck.

Goshawk nests tend to be situated in more open woodlands than those inhabited by Cooper's Hawks and Sharp-shinned Hawks. In our study area, we often found goshawks breeding in mature Chihuahua pines and Douglas firs, although they also used ponderosa pines and Apache pines. Nests were substantial platforms of sticks lined with chunks of the outer bark of various conifers, and most often the hawks placed them in the lower branches of the canopy zone. Several nests were well suited for observations from nearby blinds, and from these positions of concealment, we made intensive studies of the diet and behavior of a number of pairs.

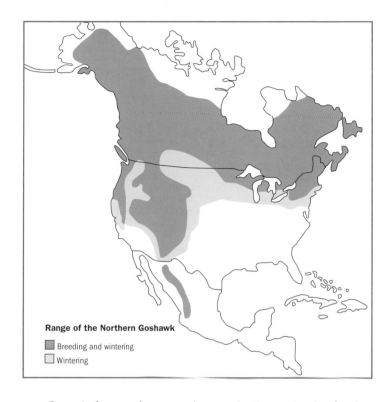

Range of the Northern Goshawk

▪ Breeding and wintering
▪ Wintering

One pair that nested two years in succession in towering Apache pines became our primary study pair. The male was an especially beautiful black-backed individual, whereas his mate had more brownish gray upperparts. Surprisingly, this pair ate birds exclusively, mainly Band-tailed Pigeons, Steller's Jays, and Mexican Jays, while other pairs took squirrels and rabbits in addition to avian prey. These differences in diet did not appear to be a strict reflection of availability of prey types for the various pairs, because it was clear that many squirrels and rabbits lived in the hunting range of our primary study pair, yet these goshawks apparently never captured them. Furthermore, when we again studied goshawks in the very same territory seventeen years later (almost surely different birds by this time), they were frequently taking squirrels and rabbits as prey. Perhaps the first pair we observed in the territory avoided mammalian prey because of bad experiences, possibly injury, encountered in previous attempts to capture such prey. Whatever the cause, the diets of some pairs sometimes deviate significantly from the norm for reasons other than overall availability of prey.

In most regions of North America, the most usual clutch size for the Northern Goshawk is three eggs. In our Arizona–New Mexico study area, however, we often found single-egg clutches, and the average was close to two eggs, suggesting that the region is not optimal habitat for the species. The main habitat deficiency may be the absence of any populations of grouse in the region. Instead of grouse, we found the local goshawks taking Montezuma Quail with frequency, but these quail are themselves not notably abundant, though they draw visiting birders to the region in search of Mexican "specialty" birds.

Left: *A female Northern Goshawk makes an early morning landing at her nest eighty feet up an Apache pine. Goshawks typically place their nests close to main trunks in the lower canopy zone, and the birds commonly approach them on the level or by shooting upward from below. Like other North American accipiters, Northern Goshawks are woodland raptors that feed mainly on vertebrates.*

Above: *On a transfer perch a hundred feet from his nest, a male goshawk stands on a completely plucked Montezuma Quail and waits for his mate to respond to his repeated* guck *food calls.*

In the early stages of breeding, the male of each observed goshawk pair caught almost all the prey consumed by himself, his mate, and his brood. He characteristically brought prey destined for his mate or brood to a horizontal limb fifty to one hundred yards from the nest—usually referred to as a transfer perch. Here he summoned the female with *guck* calls, and she soon flew over to take the prey and feed, or to prepare the food for the young. Meanwhile, the male flew to the nest and took a short turn incubating eggs or brooding small young. The male often had thoroughly bloodstained belly feathers during the intensive period of hunting in the breeding season, a testimony to his predominant role in provisioning the family.

The female only started hunting in the mid-nestling stage, when the food needs of the brood rose to a maximum and when the young were old enough to maintain body temperatures without being brooded continuously. Prior to this stage, a hungry female awaiting prey from her mate uttered plaintive *weer* calls audible from hundreds of yards away. The same vocalizations were also used later as begging calls by goshawk fledglings, and they were expertly imitated by Steller's Jays in the vicinity.

The young were downy white when they first hatched, but they gradually took on a streaked brown coloration as they developed juvenile feathers.

Wing and tail feathers were among the first to appear through the down, and the last wisps of down did not disappear from the youngsters' heads until they had reached fledging age. By this time the youngsters had also become quite active, especially the males, and often engaged in mock "captures" of pieces of bark or pinecones in the nest. Just before fledging, they began to move out onto limbs immediately adjacent to the nest structure itself, intermittently exercising their wings with rapid bursts of flapping.

In 1969, we watched the lone youngster of our primary study pair take his first flight from a nest high in a tall pine rising from the bottom of a steep ravine. The youngster was actually blown off the nest in a strong gust of wind at a time when both adults were off hunting, and he came spiraling down to the ground almost directly under the nest. His fledging appeared to be premature and clumsy, and we were greatly concerned about this youngster's survival. We were especially concerned about the adults' abilities to find and feed him and his own ability to avoid the many terrestrial predators in the region if he stayed on the ground.

Our fears were unfounded. The young goshawk appeared to be unruffled by his surprise fledging and immediately walked over to the small

Left: *Female Northern Goshawks, larger than their mates, are formidable in nest defense. They also are more likely than their mates to encounter nest predators because of their primary duties in incubation and feeding of chicks. The species' strong legs and feet suit the birds well both for repelling enemies and for capturing medium-sized birds and mammals.*

Northern Goshawk

Greenery collection is especially frequent during the latter stages of the breeding cycle and may have multiple functions.

A droplet of salty fluid clings to the tip of an adult female's bill during a feeding. Like many other raptors, goshawks rid their bodies of excess salt via fluid secretions from their nostrils.

stream under the nest and began to bathe and drink. Through the rest of the afternoon, he gradually worked his way on foot up one slope of the steep-sided ravine until he was almost directly under our blind and at a considerably higher elevation than the nest. Then, in a totally confident flight he took off straight for the nest tree, losing altitude all the way, to be sure, but landing expertly on the nest itself—which he did not leave again for several days. Although this sequence of maneuvers may have been entirely accidental and not a premeditated solution to a difficult problem, we will always suspect that there was something remarkably intelligent going on in this young goshawk's consciousness.

Our primary study pair laid only a single egg during our second year of observations, and unfortunately this egg proved to be infertile. When it did not hatch by the expected date, we decided to foster a young Cooper's Hawk into the nest so that we could continue to get diet information on the pair. The goshawks immediately accepted the nestling, and this youngster went on to become perhaps the best-fed nestling Cooper's Hawk in history. The adults kept it in a state of bulging repletion throughout the nesting cycle, and it ultimately fledged successfully, despite its portly condition.

The goshawk uses more greenery in nest construction than does any other North American raptor. Pine sprigs are favored building material in many

Right: *The Northern Goshawks of southern Arizona and northwestern Mexico belong to the race apache, a name honoring the Native Americans who once resided in the region. Apache Goshawks are heavier and have longer wings than other races of the species and tend to be darker in coloration.*

Following a feeding of her young, a female Northern Goshawk in Arizona provides shelter and shade for her nestlings.

areas, but in regions lacking pine, the species uses leafy branches of other trees. The top surfaces of goshawk nests often wind up looking much like shaggy green carpets toward the end of the breeding cycle.

Greenery collection is also common in many other species of the family Accipitridae, though its general functions have been long debated. Does the greenery help camouflage the nests from enemies? Does it serve as a signal of current occupancy of nests to intruders? Does it help sanitize nests by covering over waste materials? Does it deter nest arthropods by releasing aromatic chemicals? Does it strengthen nests—especially for species that reuse nests year after year? Does it reduce the incidence of fungal infections (Aspergillosus) of the lungs of nestlings? The trait could serve multiple functions, and the functions could vary from species to species. In the Swallow-tailed Kite, which often brings in Spanish moss late in the breeding season, plausibly to cover fecal material building up on the nest rim, greenery could well serve a very different purpose than the pine sprigs used by

goshawks, since young goshawks are much more adept in lofting excrement beyond the limits of their nests. Assuming a single overall function for the trait is unwarranted.

Cooper's Hawks use lesser amounts of greenery in their nests than do Northern Goshawks, and we have never found greenery in a Sharp-shinned Hawk nest. We long puzzled over the differences among the three North American accipiter species in this habit and sought reasonable adaptive explanations for the differences. But we now wonder if the differences may reflect nothing more profound than differing abilities of these species to break off green living branches. In close observations of Sharp-shinned Hawks in Puerto Rico during the early 1970s, we watched birds struggling repeatedly to snap off leafy branches for nesting material. They were unsuccessful in doing so, apparently not out of desire, but simply because they lacked the requisite strength. The failure of a raptor to collect greenery should not be assumed to reflect that the species would not benefit from the use of greenery.

In the late 1980s, we found our sympathies toward Northern Goshawks undergoing a subtle change when we began a program of experimental reintroductions of Thick-billed Parrots into the pine forests of Arizona for the Arizona Game and Fish Department. Thick-billed Parrots, at about fifteen inches in length and three-quarters of a pound in weight, are ideal-sized prey for goshawks, and it was only a day or two after the first releases when we became aware of just how fully the local goshawks appreciated our efforts. The parrots, thrust into their new wilderness home from captivity, had not yet developed full flight strength, and we saw numerous tail chases of the parrots by these raptors and by Red-tailed Hawks, as well. We also began finding piles of parrot feathers that bore clear witness to raptor success. In one case, we got to what was left of a radioed parrot just in time to flush a goshawk from the remains.

Nevertheless, the parrots that made it through their first few weeks in the wild were soon in much better physical condition and were a much better match for the hawks. Their losses declined markedly. Extremely fast when in good condition, Thick-billed Parrots can easily outdistance a goshawk in level flight, and as long as they stay together in flocks they are very difficult for a goshawk to approach undetected. In addition to speed and flocking, their defenses include unceasing vigilance and a tendency to feed high up in trees, where they are difficult to surprise. The first flock member to spot an approaching raptor gives an alarm call to which all immediately respond by taking to the open air as a group and circling up out of reach. The goshawk's main hope for success lies in finding birds feeding in vegetation dense enough that it can get relatively close before being detected. With luck, it can then grab a parrot that has not yet attained full flight speed. Such opportunities are quite uncommon, and their rarity has allowed wild parrot populations to coexist with goshawks in the mountains of Mexico over the long term. Our close observations of Thick-billed Parrots under attack by goshawks gave us a keen appreciation of just how finely tuned the ageless battles between predator and prey can become.

Goshawks have made a dramatic comeback in the northeastern states in recent decades, probably largely because of the increasing area and maturity of the forests there. A century ago, the landscape of New England was very different from what it is now, with most lands devoted to various forms of agriculture. But farming in this hilly, rocky country did not compete well with farming in the midwestern states and California, and large areas of New England have been allowed to return to woodlands. The goshawks have benefited greatly from this reforestation.

In the Rocky Mountain states and California, as well as in much of Canada and Alaska, the Northern Goshawk is still a regular, if not abundant species. The goshawk also occurs regularly in the forests of northern Europe and Asia, and it has recently been reestablished in the wild in Great Britain, where it sometimes breeds in young forest plantations that bear little resemblance to the mature old-growth forests that the species commonly occupies when available. Evidently, the most crucial requirement for goshawk breeding is a good food supply, not mature forests.

In the montane coniferous forests of extreme southeastern Arizona, southwestern New Mexico, and the adjacent Sierra Madre of Mexico, goshawks are larger and darker than in more northerly populations, and some experts consider these birds a separate race, the Apache Goshawk (*Accipiter gentilis apache*). Our work on these birds has confirmed their significantly larger size, both in weight and wing length, and supports recognition of the birds as a distinctive race. Nesting territories of the Apache Goshawk have been very stable over time; one we know of has been regularly occupied for the past seventy years. Yet the birds are not abundant and face a number of significant threats to their survival.

Perhaps the most worrisome problem for the Apache Goshawk in recent years has been the loss of nesting territories to intense wildfires, a threat also stressing Spotted Owls in the Southwest. Each year since 1994,

After fledging, Northern Goshawk youngsters are strongly attracted to streams and often drink and bathe on a daily basis.

wildfires have incinerated the habitat of one or more historic Apache Goshawk pairs in the Sky Island mountain ranges, and as discussed in the chapter on the Spotted Owl, recent wildfires have been far more destructive than the wildfires known for the region in historic times.

Another worrisome stress is fatal collisions with house windows. During winter, Apache Goshawks commonly descend to relatively low elevations of the mountains, where they are attracted to prey birds gathering around the feeding stations maintained by local residents. In attempting to capture such birds, both the goshawks and local Cooper's Hawks sometimes perish by crashing into windows next to feeders. With increasing settlement of the region and increasing interest in feeding small birds, the losses to such collisions have likely been a steadily increasing threat. And while the enhanced prey supply produced by feeding stations might appear to represent a benefit to these accipiters, in the balance the hawks might be better off if the feeding stations did not exist.

The overall distribution of the Northern Goshawk is large and varied and provides the species as a whole with considerable security from extinction. The species has never been officially considered threatened or endangered in North America, although it deserves continued close monitoring because of its overall sparse population densities. A status survey of the Northern Goshawk made in 1998 in response to a petition to list it as threatened or endangered yielded more than three thousand identified territories known to be recently active in just the contiguous western United States. Undoubtedly, additional territories in this region were undocumented, and had the number of territories in Canada, Alaska, Mexico, and the eastern United States been included, the total would surely have been much larger.

Northern Goshawk

Cooper's Hawk
Accipiter cooperii

I N THE LATE 1960s, the ornithological world awoke to the realization that a number of raptors in North America and western Europe were heading rapidly toward extinction. In eastern North America, Bald Eagles and Ospreys were in severe decline, while the Peregrine Falcon was already almost entirely wiped out. Counts of Cooper's Hawks and Sharp-shinned Hawks at migration lookouts such as Hawk Mountain, Pennsylvania, had also dropped alarmingly. The widespread declines were unprecedented, and what all the affected species seemed to share was the fact that they fed primarily on birds or large fish. Raptors feeding mainly on mammals and insects were maintaining stable populations.

The main cause of decline of the affected species turned out to be contamination with chlorinated-hydrocarbon pesticides, which came into widespread use after World War II. Much attention was initially focused on DDT (or more specifically its major metabolic breakdown product, DDE),

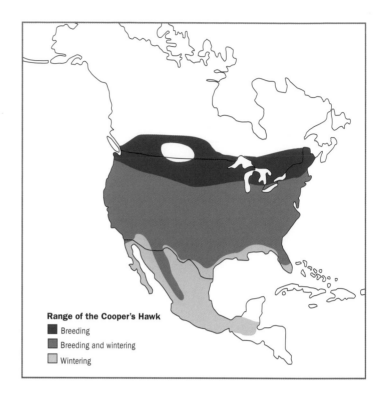

Range of the Cooper's Hawk
- Breeding
- Breeding and wintering
- Wintering

Above: *Direct feeding of nestlings by male Cooper's Hawks is exceedingly rare. This male assumed such duties when a predator killed his mate midway through nesting.*

Right: *A female Cooper's Hawk dismembers a Band-tailed Pigeon for her nestlings. In our observations, band-tails were captured more frequently by females than by males and also served as a staple prey for Northern Goshawks.*

Cooper's Hawk

Male Cooper's Hawks are characteristically darker in coloration than their mates and normally incubate eggs only while their mates consume prey on transfer perches.

Cooper's Hawks commonly mate on transfer perches after the male has passed food to the female. Mountings generally last about eight seconds and are accompanied by wild vocalizations.

which was causing drastic thinning of eggshells, high rates of egg breakage, and extremely low reproductive success. But it later became clear that in many regions, Dieldrin and some related toxins, which cause direct mortality of raptors at relatively low concentrations, were also having severe effects. While a variety of organochlorine contaminants additional to DDT were clearly involved, DDT received a disproportionate amount of attention from researchers and the popular press. Many in the public today still mistakenly blame DDT alone for the widespread raptor declines of the organochlorine era.

Like many other chlorinated hydrocarbons, Dieldrin and DDE are extremely stable. When they are ingested as diet contaminants, they lodge preferentially in fatty tissues and are excreted only with difficulty. Because they are so readily stored,

their concentrations in body tissues soon come to exceed their concentrations in ingested food. For this reason, levels of contamination tend to increase at each step of a food chain. Concentrations are relatively low in plants; are higher in herbivorous insects and mammals; still higher in carnivorous insects, birds, mammals, and fish; and highest of all in species that feed on other carnivorous species. During the period these pesticides were used freely in agriculture, the raptor species residing at the ends of the longest food chains—those feeding on birds and large fish—were ingesting especially contaminated food, and not surprisingly these were the species suffering the most.

The three species of North American accipiters—the Northern Goshawk, the Cooper's Hawk, and the Sharp-shinned Hawk—well illustrated the differing levels of stress suffered by species positioned at different levels of food chains. The diet of both Cooper's Hawks and Sharp-shinned Hawks is generally focused quite heavily on prey that tend to be relatively contaminated with organochlorines, primarily small birds, many of them insectivorous. In contrast, Northern Goshawks feed much more heavily on herbivorous mammals and herbivorous birds, which generally exhibit much lower levels of contamination. Thus, while both Cooper's Hawk and Sharp-shinned Hawk populations suffered severe declines during the organochlorine pesticide era, it is understandable why Northern Goshawk populations were largely spared the systematic declines.

The most severe declines of Cooper's Hawks and Sharp-shinned Hawks took place in the eastern states, where use of organochlorine pesticides was most widespread and intensive. The situation was somewhat different in the southwestern states of Arizona and New Mexico. Here, use of chlorinated-hydrocarbon pesticides was not as great as in the eastern states because grazing is a much more predominant land use than farming. In addition, Cooper's Hawks, in particular, are much less thoroughly focused on small birds in their diet here than in the eastern states, taking many small mammals and reptiles. In detailed studies of all three accipiters in Arizona and New Mexico in the late 1960s and early 1970s, we found that populations were still holding up reasonably well despite moderate levels of contamination with organochlorines.

In the eastern United States, however, a considerable amount of evidence had accumulated on the insidiously harmful effects of DDT (DDE) on a great variety of species. In 1972 the federal government finally instituted a ban on the use of this chemical, based largely on its carcinogenic potential for humans. Dieldrin use was also greatly restricted shortly thereafter. In Canada, curtailment of DDT use occurred even sooner than in the United States.

Eastern accipiter populations quickly began to recover. Counts of Sharp-shinned Hawks at Hawk Mountain, Pennsylvania, rose fairly rapidly. Cooper's Hawk counts increased more slowly, but just as convincingly, and both species now appear to have regained much of the abundance in the East that they enjoyed before the organochlorine pesticide era.

In contrast, the Cooper's Hawk populations we had studied in the late 1960s and early 1970s in Arizona and New Mexico, which had been remarkably stable in spite of some DDE stress, have declined substantially in more recent years. In 1987 we re-censused much of our old study area in Arizona and New Mexico and found only about 50 percent of the historic territories still active with breeding pairs. A more thorough census in 1988 confirmed the overall decline. Reproductive success of the active territories was normal in both years, and we saw no case of egg breakage to suggest DDE stress. We do not yet know the full cause of this local decline and the extent to which the decline represents a long-term trend, but populations have continued to be quite sparse in more recent decades and we suspect this may be mainly a reflection of long-term declines in populations of prey birds, possibly due in part to long-term drought conditions and loss of wintering habitat.

The overall breeding range of the Cooper's Hawk closely matches the borders of the lower United States, although some Cooper's Hawks do

A last view of the world for many a small bird. Cooper's Hawks typically rely on surprise to capture prey. Their short wings and long tails allow them to make rapid changes in direction in cluttered forest habitats.

breed in extreme southern Canada and extreme northern Mexico, and many individuals winter as far south as central Mexico. In Cuba, a very similar accipiter, Gundlach's Hawk, replaces the species, but neither species occurs elsewhere in the West Indies.

With a weight generally running in the vicinity of a pound, the Cooper's Hawk is a medium sized raptor well adapted for maneuvering in woodland habitats with its relatively short wings, long legs, and long, banded tail. In general coloration, both sexes tend toward inconspicuous browns and salmons, though adult males are distinctly bluer in their upperparts than are females. Juveniles of both sexes are heavily streaked with brown and are especially well camouflaged in their normal surroundings.

Juveniles normally take two years to become fully adult in plumage, but they sometimes breed at one year of age, especially under conditions where unoccupied spaces are available in the territorial arrays of the species. Clutch size usually ranges between three and five eggs laid at intervals of about two days between eggs. Incubation takes about thirty-five days, and young fledge at about five weeks of age. As in other accipiters, males do virtually all the hunting for their families through the incubation and early nestling periods, but both male and female adults hunt intensively during the late nestling and fledgling dependency periods. Males bringing prey to their mates characteristically announce their arrival with sharp *kik* calls, while females soliciting food or working on prey utter distinctive *caw* calls.

Strictly solitary in behavior, except during breeding, Cooper's Hawks are experts in ambush and surprise attack, appearing from nowhere and stopping at nothing in the pursuit of prey. They do not hesitate to enter quite brushy vegetation and sometimes even run on the ground in impetuous efforts to claim a victim. High-strung and restless on the hunt, they fully deserve their reputation as eager and capable avian executioners. We have even run across individual pairs that have specialized in taking prey as difficult to capture as swifts, bringing them to their nests on a nearly daily basis, though we have never been fortunate enough to see just how they have captured such prey.

As predators predominantly of small birds, Cooper's Hawks appear to be constrained in their breeding by major seasonal trends in prey availability. During our studies, egg laying of the hawks generally coincided with the arrival of a pulse of spring migrant songbirds, while the rearing of hawk nestlings coincided with the availability of large numbers of easy-to-capture fledgling songbirds in June and early July. After mid-July, however, most fledgling songbirds had reached independence and lost much of their vulnerability to the hawks, resulting in a period of apparent declining food availability for the hawks. The hawks, however, still had fully dependent nestlings and fledglings through to the end of summer in many cases, and perhaps not surprisingly some late nestling and fledgling hawks did not make it through to their own independence.

Under conditions of extremely low food, Cooper's Hawk nestlings practice cannibalism of their nest mates, and we directly observed this happening at several Arizona nests during the drought year of 1971. The process began with larger members of broods pecking repeatedly at the back of the head of one of their smaller siblings. When blood was finally drawn, the attackers, apparently greatly stimulated by the newly red color of their sibling's head, began to peck with greatly increased vigor, and this soon led to death of the chick and its consumption by its siblings.

From a human perspective, cannibalism seems a brutal way for nestlings to stave off starvation, but in the absence of such behavior, even more chicks might starve in food-stressed nests than actually occurs. By the inexorable logic of natural selection, bringing the number of young into balance with available food supplies maximizes the number of surviving young. The genes producing cannibalism evidently have value or the behavior would not occur.

In some raptors, for example certain Old World eagle species, pairs almost invariably lay two eggs, yet rear only a single young, because the older

Cooper's Hawk

A first-year female's tail feathers show heavy molt during late stages of her first nesting season. Males normally do not molt until nesting is over, probably because they need full flight capacities to fulfill their primary role of capturing prey for their families.

chick routinely kills its later-hatching sibling during development. Under such conditions one might well ask why the pairs bother to lay two eggs, but it appears that the laying of two eggs may occur mainly as a hedge against infertility in these species. If pairs laid but single eggs, they would risk fledging no young at all in some years simply because of failure of some single eggs to hatch. Laying two eggs greatly increases the chances that at least one may be fertile, and if two hatch, one chick can be efficiently sacrificed by siblicide to ensure brood size will not exceed provisioning capacities of the adults.

The tamest wild hawk we have ever dealt with was a nesting female Cooper's Hawk in 1969. This bird and her mate had placed their nest about twenty feet up in a box elder just ten feet from a heavily traveled road. We constructed a blind on a platform in a tree about twelve feet from the nest, but soon discovered that the blind was totally unnecessary. Because of the stifling heat inside the blind, we took it down and made further observations just sitting on the platform. The female was so extremely nonchalant that she often fed her young with her back to the platform, which meant that her body obscured our view of the prey and sometimes prevented us from making prey identifications. Since we were attempting to gain as much information as possible on feeding habits of the species, we needed an efficient solution to this problem. The solution was equipping the platform with a long stick with which we could reach over and gently move the female's tail to one side so we could view the prey. Her response to this adjustment of her person was never more than a momentary glance in our direction.

Her tolerance ceased, however, whenever one of us climbed the nest tree itself for periodic measurements of the young. Now she stood glowering on the nest edge until the climber reached nest level. Then she would leap

A female Cooper's Hawk assists the hatching of a chick by pulling away the eggshell with her bill.

onto the top of the climber's head and foot his or her scalp aggressively with her talons, often drawing blood in the ensuing fracas.

While most other Cooper's Hawks in our study area defended their nests very aggressively, even to the extent of flailing at climbers who scaled their nest trees weeks after young had fledged, we did find occasional pairs that were quite wary of people. In general, however, the Cooper's Hawks of this region were easy to work with, in great contrast to the Cooper's Hawks of the eastern states, which are renowned for their skittish behavior. The relatively bold behavior of southwestern Cooper's Hawks may reflect less human persecution in their history than eastern birds have suffered.

Nevertheless, as our studies of Cooper's Hawks progressed, we became increasingly worried that as certain individuals became accustomed to our presence, their chances for survival might decrease. Birds that people can easily approach may be highly susceptible to molestation. We normally banded all young Cooper's Hawks we located in the study area, but only a small fraction were exposed to us on more than the day of banding. The returns we received from recoveries of our banded individuals, however, were limited almost exclusively to birds that had had an opportunity to become very familiar with us, either through repeated days of observation from nearby blinds and platforms or through repeated handling for weighing and measuring through the nestling period. Further, essentially all these recovered birds were victims of various forms of human predation. The recovery rate of tamed or partially tamed nestlings was much greater than that of untamed nestlings, a fact suggesting that we were not doing the birds a favor by allowing them to see us at close range on a repeated basis.

Many conservationists assume that the negative consequences to be most worried about in human disturbance of nesting wild birds are problems such as lowered feeding rates, desertion of nests, and lowered net reproduction. With at least some species, however, such problems may be of less importance than becoming so unafraid of humans that it reduces their survival rate. Wildness is often an overwhelmingly important characteristic for species subject to direct human predation. Cooper's Hawks have long been the target of retribution by farmers because of their attraction to free-ranging poultry, so they are one of the species where taming effects could be most significant.

Sharp-shinned Hawk

Accipiter striatus

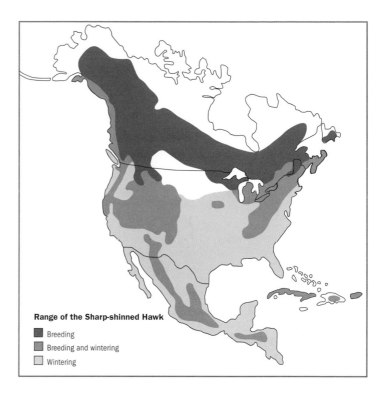

Range of the Sharp-shinned Hawk
- Breeding
- Breeding and wintering
- Wintering

DENSE STANDS OF IMMATURE Douglas firs in the West and hemlocks in the East provide favored nesting habitat for the most secretive of North America's diurnal raptors, the Sharp-shinned Hawk. A single-minded predator of small birds, this is not a species that survives by intimidation, but one that relies on stealth and camouflage, both in gaining close approach to its victims and in avoiding capture by larger raptors. No larger than a jay and feathered mainly in browns and grays, the sharp-shin is named for a sharp keel of unknown function on the leading edge of its legs.

In its habitual surroundings of forests and forest edges, the sharp-shin is an animated spook, a high-strung flying machine dashing pell-mell through extremely tight squeezes in the vegetation. It rarely perches in conspicuous locations and rarely flies above the canopy, except during migration. So even though it is a commoner species than is often recognized, it is a difficult species to find and study closely.

The Sharp-shinned Hawks of Puerto Rico are more intensely colored and extroverted than their mainland relatives and tend to inhabit high mountainous regions. In the early breeding season of 1974, this male divided his attentions between two mates in adjacent territories, then finally nested with only one. Although common at that time, the Puerto Rican sharp-shin has since disappeared almost completely from the island's easterly regions and is now considered endangered.

Sharp-shinned Hawk

Chocolate-colored blotches mark the eggs of Arizona's Sharp-shinned Hawks, making them much less conspicuous than the pure white eggs of Cooper's Hawks and Northern Goshawks. Also reducing their conspicuousness, Arizona's sharp-shins, unlike nesting Cooper's Hawks and Northern Goshawks, avoid displaying their white undertail coverts in activities around nests.

The sharp-shin is very similar in appearance to the somewhat larger Cooper's Hawk and is often confused with that species. The two species do not normally overlap in size, but in both, females are much larger than males, and a large female sharp-shin is sufficiently close to a small male Cooper's Hawk in measurements that even experienced raptor biologists often mistake one for the other. The two species are colored very similarly, occupy similar habitats, and fly with similar alternations of flapping and sailing. Moreover, their small differences in shape are often very difficult to discern under field conditions. Sharp-shinned Hawks tend to have tails that are more squared off at the end than the rounded tails of Cooper's Hawks, and the head of a flying individual tends to project farther in front of the wings in a Cooper's Hawk than in a Sharp-shinned Hawk. But at best, these and other differences are quite subtle and variable, making it easy to misidentify the species. In addition, while any small- to medium-sized accipiter seen in northern Canada and Alaska will likely be a sharp-shin, the ranges of sharp-shins and Cooper's coincide almost completely in the lower United States, making range an unreliable way to distinguish the species in most of North America.

Perhaps the most reliable way to differentiate sharp-shins from Cooper's Hawks is through vocalizations. Alas, they do not commonly vocalize except near nests. The repetitive *kew kew kew kew kew...* alarm calls of the sharp-shin are much more mellow than the strident *kek kek kek kek kek kek kek kek...* alarm calls of the Cooper's Hawk, and once these calls are heard they are easy to remember.

The Sharp-shinned Hawk exhibits the strongest difference in size between sexes of any raptor in North America. Male sharp-shins average about three-and-one-half ounces in weight, while females average almost twice as much at about six-and-one-third ounces. Females also exceed males in size in nearly all other raptors, while the reverse is true for most nonraptorial birds. Explaining the size superiority of females among raptors has been one of the most contentious topics in raptor biology, and the number of different hypotheses advanced to rationalize the phenomenon continues to increase without apparent end. No consensus has yet developed about what factors are most important in producing the pattern.

Nevertheless, the extent of size difference between sexes appears to be strongly related to the extent that a raptor species takes birds as prey. Thus, the greatest sexual size differences are found in species like the Sharp-shinned Hawk that have diets composed almost exclusively of other birds, while sexual size differences are quite modest in species that take mainly mammals, insects, other invertebrates, or carrion. The best-known explanations for the sexual size differences center on potential advantages in reducing food competition between sexes and on potential advantages in promoting clear-cut dominance relationships within pairs and harmonious pair bonds. Certainly the size differences between sexes often do result in differences in diet of the sexes, but biologists continue to debate whether

The Sharp-shinned Hawk feeds almost exclusively on small birds, but the female at this Arizona nest occasionally ripped apart lizards for her young.

these differences are the primary cause of the dimorphism or only a secondary effect.

Our data for both sharp-shins and Cooper's Hawks in Arizona and New Mexico confirm that males and females of these species do take significantly different prey during the breeding season. In our observations, sharp-shin females often captured prey the size of grosbeaks and robins, while males mainly took birds the size of juncos and smaller. In Cooper's Hawks, females quite frequently captured jays and pigeons, while males more commonly took chipmunks and robin-sized birds. It is hard to believe that these sexual differences in diet were unimportant to the overall foraging success of pairs, and we find it difficult to believe that strong sexual size differences would be retained if they led to appreciable disadvantages in foraging. More plausible is the view that the sexual size differences may be an adaptation to increase food supplies available to pairs during the breeding season, especially for species where prey vulnerability and availability may tend to decline in the late breeding season when both adults are hunting.

The Sharp-shinned Hawk is the last of the accipiters to initiate breeding activity in the spring, generally beginning nest building in late April or early May in the southwestern states. New nests are built each year, and they are only occasionally placed on top of old nests. Building on top

of old nests is much more common in Cooper's Hawks and Northern Goshawks. Both sexes of sharp-shins participate in nest construction, much like Cooper's Hawks and Northern Goshawks, and the birds use their feet and bills to break off dead twigs from standing trees in the vicinity of the nest, then carry them to the nest in direct flights under the canopy. Nest-building activities are concentrated in the early to midmorning hours and are interspersed with bouts of mating activity, preening, and foraging. Nests are usually placed on horizontal branches against the main trunks of conifers and characteristically are lined with chips of the outer bark of trees. The surrounding vegetation is often so dense that the nests are quite difficult to find. The best clue to a nest area often is finding prey bird feathers scattered on the ground.

During the early stages of breeding, the male does essentially all of the hunting while his mate remains in the nest vicinity. On his return with prey, the male announces his arrival at a perch near the nest with a repetitive high-pitched *kew kew kew kew kew*, which sounds similar to the species' typical alarm call. The female soon flies in to take the prey with repeated *eee* calls, which also continue while she is feeding. As egg laying approaches, the female becomes more and more lethargic, often just perching for long periods, fluffed up and quiescent, apparently saving her reserves for egg formation.

Female sharp-shins usually lay eggs on alternate days, a pattern found

Sharp-shinned Hawk

Male sharp-shin nestlings (top two birds) typically mature more rapidly and leave the nest several days earlier than their female siblings (bottom two birds). This developmental difference reflects the huge size difference between sexes.

in many raptor species. Clutch size in the Southwest is most commonly four or five eggs. Unlike the plain bluish white eggs of Northern Goshawks and Cooper's Hawks, sharp-shin eggs are usually highly camouflaged with brown blotches and speckling, giving them a very attractive appearance. Incubation lasts about thirty-four or thirty-five days and generally begins with the laying of the next-to-last egg.

Females do all the incubation of eggs and cover them almost constantly except when working on prey brought in by males. As a female feeds, a male sometimes flies to the nest and occasionally even spreads out his breast feathers as if to settle on the eggs, but we have never seen a male actually follow through and cover the eggs. At best, the males might do so only ineffectively because of their relatively small size. In this respect, male Sharp-shinned Hawks differ markedly from male Northern Goshawks and Cooper's Hawks, which generally do cover eggs while their mates feed on prey. During the nest-building and incubation periods, males usually feed their mates three or four times per day.

For about the first half of the nestling period, females continue to attend their nests, brooding the nestlings when they are not feeding them. But thereafter, females also begin to hunt and supply food for the brood. Throughout the nestling period, the female rips apart prey for the young, and if the male returns with prey at a time when the female is off hunting, he drops the prey in the nest cup, leaving it for the female to handle when she returns. By the late nestling stage, pairs commonly bring as many as ten to twelve prey to the nest daily. Begging calls of the young are very similar to the *eee* calls of female adults soliciting food from their mates.

The nestling period lasts about four weeks, but males develop more quickly than females and generally fledge several days earlier. Fledging generally occurs in mid to late July and is a gradual process, with youngsters first moving out to branches near the nest and quickly returning when adults arrive at the nest with food. At this stage, youngsters begin ripping apart prey for themselves, although most feedings still take place at the nest supervised by the adult female. In time, the fledglings begin to fly out to meet returning parents and take prey from them at locations away from the nest vicinity. Young usually remain dependent on adults until mid to late August and are slow to develop their own ability to hunt.

Most mainland populations of the Sharp-shinned Hawk are apparently seasonal migrants, but Sharp-shinned Hawks are year-round residents on Puerto Rico in the West Indies, where a very intensely colored race of the species has evolved and where there are no other accipiters. In studies of the Puerto Rican sharp-shins in the Luquillo Mountains in the early 1970s, we found that these birds were dissimilar from mainland sharp-shins in a variety of ways that seemed likely a result of their historic isolation from other accipiters and their relative freedom from predation. In general, their behavior was much more conspicuous than the behavior of mainland sharp-shins. Thus, they commonly displayed their white

After fledging, young sharp-shins remain in the nest area for several weeks, dependent on their parents for food but steadily improving in flight capacities.

undertail coverts around nests, something we have never seen in mainland sharp-shins, although this same display is commonly seen in Cooper's Hawks and Northern Goshawks around nests. Further, they frequently gave the conspicuous aerial diving displays high over their nesting areas that are also seen commonly in Cooper's Hawks and Northern Goshawks, but which we have never seen in sharp-shins of Arizona and New Mexico. Finally, their eggs, which are characteristically heavily spotted in coloration on the mainland, are almost pure white on this island. Thus, we found the sharp-shins of Puerto Rico to be much easier to find than sharp-shins on the mainland, and this presumably was as true for potential predators of the species as for biologists and consequently left the species vulnerable should new predators become established on the island.

Ominously, we did find evidence of predation on some sharp-shin eggs and chicks in the Luquillo Mountains, and all evidence suggested that the culprit was the Pearly-eyed Thrasher, a highly predacious species that had only recently become common in the mountains. The pearly-eye was also a major threat to eggs and chicks of the endangered Puerto Rican Parrot, the species on which our research efforts were mainly concentrated at the time, and it appeared that both parrots and sharp-shins lacked effective

natural defenses against this relatively new enemy. In more recent years, the sharp-shin has all but disappeared from the Luquillo Mountains, and we strongly suspect that the primary cause has been the population explosion of thrashers in this region.

In recognition of this species' declining fortunes, the federal government has recently classified the Puerto Rican Sharp-shinned Hawk as endangered. But while effective means (involving modification of cavity nests) have been developed for protecting Puerto Rican Parrot nests from thrashers, no practical means are known for protecting Puerto Rican sharp-shin nests from these birds, and the sharp-shin currently persists mainly in regions where the thrasher is still relatively uncommon.

On the mainland, the Sharp-shinned Hawk is presently a relatively common species, although it was one of the species to suffer a major decline during the organochlorine pesticide era. Its major dietary emphasis on insectivorous birds places the species in a relatively vulnerable position with respect to toxic materials that increase in concentrations up food chains, and it is accordingly a species that deserves continued close study in the future.

Sharp-shinned Hawk

Broad-winged Hawk
Buteo platypterus

THE BROAD-WINGED HAWK is probably the most abundant diurnal raptor of the eastern woodlands of North America, where it feeds mainly on a great variety of small vertebrates, ranging from toads and frogs to chipmunks and nestling birds. Its thin, plaintive calls drifting through the mature oaks and beeches sound much like those of another resident of the same habitats, the Wood Pewee, and together these two species seem to embody the peaceful spirit of upland deciduous and mixed deciduous-coniferous forests.

The broad-wing is a relatively small buteo, usually slightly less than a pound in weight and not quite three feet in wingspread. Above, it is largely brown, and its largely white underparts are marked mainly with brown streaks and bars appropriate for concealment in wooded surroundings. Rarely found far from cover, this raptor is much more often heard than seen, but it sometimes can be observed rising above the canopy with a snake or mouse in its talons. During fall migration, the broad-wing becomes one of the most commonly observed raptor species of the eastern states, as it consistently flies above the treetops following ridgelines and other topographic features on its annual trek south toward Central and South America.

Less tied to swampy regions in its nesting habits than the Red-shouldered Hawk, the broad-wing nevertheless often settles near bogs and wet depressions and usually places its twiggy nest well below the treetops in the first main crotch of a moderately large tree. The first broad-wing nest we ever watched in detail from a blind was not far from a bog and was situated in a tall oak in a heavily wooded region of upstate New York in the early 1960s. The dense surrounding deciduous woodlands were shared with species such as Red-eyed Vireos, Ovenbirds, Black-throated Blue Warblers, Scarlet Tanagers, chipmunks, and red-spotted newts, offering the hawks a diverse and abundant food supply.

Yet we came to know the Broad-winged Hawk most intimately some ten years later in a completely different setting—the virgin wilderness of the Luquillo Mountains in eastern Puerto Rico, where we also studied the Red-tailed Hawk, the Sharp-shinned Hawk, and the Puerto Rican Parrot in collaboration with Jim Wiley of the U.S. Fish and Wildlife Service and his wife, Beth. Here, a tiny resident population of a distinctive subspecies of the broad-wing lives in company with tropical hummingbirds, bananaquits, parrots, and todies. Nesting in bromeliad-laden hardwoods and coping with nearly two hundred inches of rain per year, this population faces a very different world from that of its migratory relatives in the eastern United States. Still, the Puerto Rican birds are clearly Broad-winged Hawks, with vocalizations and behavior similar to mainland populations of the species.

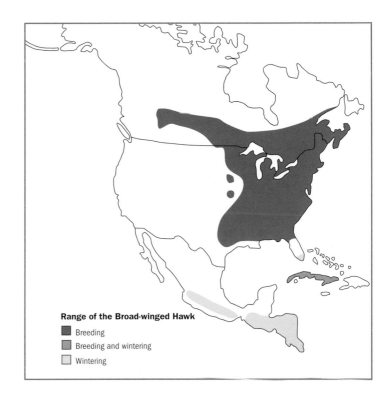

Range of the Broad-winged Hawk
- Breeding
- Breeding and wintering
- Wintering

In early 1976, we located three Broad-winged Hawk nests in Puerto Rico's Luquillo Mountains—the first nests ever recorded of the Puerto Rican subspecies—and one of the three was very suitable for detailed observations. We made an intensive study of the diet of the birds at this nest, because we were anxious to determine if the species represented any significant threats of predation to the endangered Puerto Rican Parrot.

Like the Broad-winged Hawk on the mainland, we found that the Puerto Rican subspecies was feeding mainly on small vertebrates, especially frogs and lizards, though we also saw occasional rats and frequent centipedes, and sometimes birds, some even as large as nestling pigeons. Overall, this diet was very similar to what we were documenting for the Red-tailed Hawk in the Luquillo Mountains. The broad-wing, however, is a much smaller bird (less than half as heavy as a red-tail), and it did not match the capacities of its larger cousin in taking some of the larger prey available. Our data indicated fewer rats in broad-wing diet than in red-tail diet, and while we found evidence of red-tails even occasionally taking mongooses, we found no evidence of broad-wings doing so. Puerto Rican Parrots are considerably larger than the prey normally taken by the broad-wings.

Nevertheless, with both red-tails and broad-wings taking pretty much the same sorts of foods in the Luquillo Mountains, it is of considerable interest that they have apparently been able to coexist in harmony, especially in view of the high density of red-tails in the region and the exceedingly aggressive territoriality red-tails show to one another. The red-tails passively tolerated the broad-wings and did not exclude them from their territories, suggesting strongly that the two species had reached some sort of ecological accommodation.

Left: *Broad-winged Hawks are the most abundant diurnal raptor in heavily forested regions of the eastern states. In 1963, this pair nested in the sturdy crotch of an oak atop a hill of upstate New York. The birds' plaintive calls sounded much like the vocalizations of Eastern Wood Pewees inhabiting the same woodland.*

Broad-winged Hawk

In the fall, most North American Broad-winged Hawks migrate southwest to northern Mexico, then on to points farther south. Broad-wings that winter in the Florida Keys are mostly immatures that likely missed their proper bearings in their first fall migration. The wintering individuals in the Keys are sometimes mistaken for light-phased Short-tailed Hawks, as they are about the same size and sometimes have nearly clear white underparts.

The truce between the red-tails and broad-wings seemed mainly to result from differences in their hunting behavior. The red-tails, at least on the windward slopes of the mountains, hunted mainly from the air and mostly exploited the animal life of the upper branches of the forest canopy. In contrast, we never saw the broad-wings hunting from flight, and virtually all their foraging activities were concentrated well beneath the forest crown, where they characteristically watched for prey from low perches. Thus, in the region where the broad-wings coexisted with the red-tails, the two species were using quite different habitats and were not actually hunting and eating the same specific prey populations. Despite their similarities in diet, our observations indicated they were not in major competition with each other for food.

Consistent with this explanation is the fact that broad-wings in the Luquillo Mountains normally occur only on the windward slopes, whereas red-tails occur on all sides of the mountains. On the leeward slopes, the red-tails have few updrafts to utilize for aerial hunting, and accordingly they hunt mainly from perches at all levels within the forest—hunting behavior like that shown by Broad-winged Hawks on the windward slopes. Consequently, if the broad-wings were present in the same leeward areas, the two species would almost surely be hunting the same food supplies. Very likely the broad-wings do not occupy leeward slopes because of this potential competition and their inability to dominate red-tails.

Although we never saw them hunt from the air, the Puerto Rican broad-wings frequently soared into the skies and sometimes engaged in dramatic aerial displays. In these displays one bird locked talons with another, and the two descended rapidly toward the forest canopy, whirling around like a windmill running wild, and separating only moments before they collided with the treetops. Whether we were watching courtship or fights in these encounters was not clear. But in other species where such whirling displays have been seen, particularly certain eagles and kites, they have commonly involved male-female pairs, suggesting courtship activity. Regardless of function, these whirling displays are among the most striking avian spectacles known, and they were especially impressive in the misty setting provided by the steep-sloped rain forests of the Luquillo Mountains.

In the eastern United States, broad-wings provide another of the most impressive avian spectacles to be seen in North America—massed fall migration to the tropical regions of Central and South America. Viewed from strategic lookouts along the Appalachian Mountains, the fall flights of broad-wings bring ever-increasing numbers of hawk watchers together from all over the world.

Easily the most famous of the migration observation points is Hawk Mountain, located along the Kittatinny Ridge of eastern Pennsylvania. In good flight years, broad-wings drift and soar by the thousands past the slopes of Hawk Mountain from late August to early October. From this location, it is also possible to see at close range essentially all other species of diurnal raptors that occur in the eastern states and Canada. Flights tend to be especially dramatic during the periods of fresh northwest winds that follow cold fronts. And although some other raptor observation points in North America surpass Hawk Mountain in their tallies of migrating raptors, none exceeds this site in scenic beauty or in general biological and historical interest. The numbers of raptor observers migrating to Hawk Mountain each fall have grown to exceed the numbers of migrating hawks by a considerable margin.

The broad-wings and other raptors of Hawk Mountain have unique significance in the history of raptor conservation, for it was here in the mid-1930s that Rosalie Edge and Maurice and Irma Broun, the founder and first guardians of Hawk Mountain Sanctuary, began a lonely but ultimately successful battle to stop the senseless slaughter of migrating hawks that was at that time a socially acceptable pastime. Until these efforts, droves of gunners gathered each fall to fire endlessly at the raptors passing by the mountain lookouts. The carcasses of dead and dying hawks accumulated by the hundreds in the forests below.

The halting of the raptor massacres at Hawk Mountain was at first viewed as a strange misunderstanding of local customs perpetrated by outsiders unfamiliar with the serious threats raptors posed to human society. But in time, similar efforts have spread throughout the country, creating a whole new climate of interest in and respect for birds of prey, with incalculably positive implications for wildlife conservation in general. What was once a minority viewpoint toward raptors has become a growing consensus that seems destined to endure. The lonely defenders of Hawk Mountain have left a unique and priceless legacy.

The overall breeding range of the Broad-winged Hawk includes pretty much the entire eastern half of the United States, with the exception of most of Florida and the eastern fringe of the Great Plains. In Canada, the birds breed in a southerly band extending from Nova Scotia to as far west as central Alberta. Most of the spring migration in the species is concentrated in March and April, with the great bulk of egg laying occurring in May in the northeastern states, and with young usually fledged from nests before the end of July. As in other similar-sized raptors, first breeding sometimes occurs at one year of age, when the birds still retain some juvenile feathers, but the average age of first breeding is undocumented.

Nest building generally takes about three weeks; clutch size is almost always two or three eggs; and incubation, performed mainly by females, takes very close to a month, with the chicks hatching asynchronously. Young fledge at five to six weeks of age and remain at least partially dependent on their parents up to about two months after fledging. Fall migration generally begins in late August or early September, and very few birds are still present in the northern states and Canada by the end of October.

Fall Broad-winged Hawk counts at Hawk Mountain have shown an apparent slow decline over the last few decades, although it is not clear whether this represents a shift in migratory patterns or an overall decline in eastern populations. Counts at some other hawk migration sites in the eastern and midwestern states have shown relative stability or systematic increases over the same years, so the evidence for an overall decline in the species is unclear. Recent counts along the migration route in eastern Mexico suggest a total population for the species that may include as many as two million individuals.

The Broad-winged Hawk feeds low enough in food chains that it was spared the population declines many raptors experienced immediately after World War II, when chlorinated hydrocarbon pesticides came into widespread use. The species has long suffered to some extent from shooting and other forms of human harassment, but it has been much safer from

One of the first Puerto Rican Broad-winged Hawk nests ever found was this structure in 1976 concealed in air plants high in a ridge-top tree of the Luquillo Mountains. The nest's two youngsters matured on a diet of frogs, centipedes, and nestling birds from nearby forested habitats.

Broad-winged Hawk

From the North Lookout of Pennsylvania's Hawk Mountain, observers sometimes see thousands of migrating Broad-winged Hawks during a single fall day. Most other diurnal raptors of the northeastern states also stream past the ridgeline, but in lesser numbers. Once an assembly point for gunners participating in a senseless slaughter of raptors, Hawk Mountain became a sanctuary protecting all birds of prey in the mid-1930s and has served as North America's most renowned gathering place for raptor enthusiasts ever since.

such stresses than many other raptors because of its preference for forested habitats and avoidance of open areas. The broad-wing has never been a significant threat to poultry, and whereas many individuals of the species were shot historically along migration pathways, this activity has now disappeared almost completely.

Most conservation concern for the species now centers on the small nonmigratory island populations of the Caribbean. In 1994 the Puerto Rican population of the species that we studied in the 1970s was officially classified as endangered, with a total population estimate of just 124 birds. Traditionally, about half these birds have been located in the Luquillo Mountains and half in another population toward the west end of the island centered in a region of rugged limestone hills. Judging from reports of early ornithologists, these populations have not changed greatly in size for at least the last century and have been the only appreciable populations on the island through this entire period. If so, these hawks may now be highly inbred and deficient in genetic variability, yet they seem vigorous and productive. It would be of great interest to directly determine the amount of genetic variability in the two Puerto Rican populations to test current theories regarding genetic threats to populations that remain quite small for long periods and to determine how much interchange there may be between the two populations.

Setting genetic concerns aside, the prospects for the Puerto Rican subspecies of the broad-wing may not be all that grim, in view of the progressive reforestation occurring on Puerto Rico in recent decades. Perhaps of much more concern is the status of the Puerto Rican Sharp-shinned Hawk, a raptor that has also been recently classified as endangered and has experienced a dramatic decline, if not extirpation, in the Luquillo Mountains in the decades since the 1970s.

Broad-winged Hawks are among the earliest of the raptors migrating past Hawk Mountain in the fall. The broad-wing migration starts here in late August, peaks in September, and dwindles to nothing in October. Farther south in Panama, the broad-wing fall migration peaks in October.

Red-tailed Hawk

Buteo jamaicensis

ONE OF THE MOST FAMILIAR raptors of North America, the Red-tailed Hawk is a fairly large species, weighing about two-and-a-half to three pounds and exhibiting a wingspread of about four feet. Distributed coast to coast from Alaska and northern Canada south to Florida, Mexico, and Costa Rica, as well as throughout much of the West Indies, this species has an extremely wide range, and it occupies more ecological zones than any other raptor of North America, with the possible exceptions of the Great Horned Owl and the American Kestrel. Moreover, in physical appearance the red-tail exhibits such a variety of patterns from place to place that it was originally described as several different species. Only more recently have detailed studies revealed the prevalence of numerous intergrades linking together the various geographic forms within the species.

In its many guises, the red-tail varies from pure white to completely black underneath, though the most frequent ventral color pattern is a distinct cummerbund of dark spots contrasting with a light throat and upper breast. Upperparts vary from light brown to black. Even the tail color is highly inconsistent, ranging from solid red to banded brown and gray, with an almost infinite diversity of spotting and streaking patterns.

The great variability of the red-tail extends also to behavior and ecology. Powerfully proportioned, with a relatively short tail and sturdy broad wings, this raptor is well adapted for hunting from soaring flight, but it is also a skilled perch hunter and at times is capable of rapid pursuits of quite elusive prey. With such versatility, it is difficult to characterize the feeding preferences or habitat tolerances of the species. Although it is generally considered a predator of small- and medium-sized mammals, it also feeds quite heavily on birds, in some places preys heavily on terrestrial crabs, in others takes mainly snakes, and even sometimes takes carrion. And while it is generally characterized as a raptor of relatively open or mixed habitats, it occupies regions ranging from treeless open deserts to extensive rain forests. Its bulky stick nests are correspondingly placed in a great variety of sites, ranging from the arms of saguaro cacti to potholes in towering cliffs to the tops of vine-tangled trees.

In southerly portions of its range, the red-tail is a year-round resident in its nesting territories, but Canadian populations are mostly migratory, withdrawing

The most common diurnal raptor of eastern Puerto Rico's dense rain forests, Red-tailed Hawks feed on a variety of vertebrates and invertebrates such as lizards and giant centipedes. Hanging in the winds over the treetops, the hawks make most kills in the upper canopy and constitute the principal mortality threat to the endangered Puerto Rican Parrot.

Red-tailed Hawk

Dark-phased red-tails are less abundant than light-phased red-tails and occur most commonly in the western states.

to more southerly regions in the United States during winter. The start of the breeding season is advertised by spectacular courtship flights in which both adults soar high over their territory, often dangling their legs conspicuously, vocalizing excitedly, and swooping dramatically on one another. Both sexes contribute to nest building and other nesting activities, such as incubation, but males are the primary providers of food in early stages of the breeding cycle, and they typically incubate eggs for only short periods during the day.

Pairs tend to be very loyal to their territories from year to year and often reuse old nests when Great Horned Owls haven't usurped them. The Great Horned Owl, in fact, is more than just a nest-site competitor; in some regions this species appears to be a major cause of nesting failure for the red-tails through predation on nestlings. These two species have an uneasy relationship, evidently due to their very similar body sizes, geographic ranges, overall diets, and their ability to kill each other. The similarities of the two also extend to a usual clutch size of about two eggs and productivity generally running somewhere between one and two young per active pair.

Yet in overall appearance, diurnal versus nocturnal habits, and behavioral characteristics such as vocalizations, red-tails are strikingly different from horned owls. Great Horned Owls usually vocalize with a mellow series of syncopated, low-pitched hoots, while the red-tail's most characteristic vocalization is an extremely harsh descending scream that is given when a bird is disturbed near its nest or engaged in territorial disputes with other red-tails. Often lasting more than two seconds, this vocalization is commonly called the *keearr* cry and leaves no doubt of the bird's displeasure. Red-tails also have other vocalizations, for example short piping chirps given during their courtship flights, but except for the *peep* calls of young nestlings, their calls tend to be quite rough and unmusical.

Our most intensive studies of red-tails, like our most intensive observations of the Broad-winged Hawk, were made in one of the species' most unusual habitats—the dense rain forests of the Luquillo Mountains of eastern Puerto Rico, a region where the Great Horned Owl does not occur. Here, our primary research responsibilities in the early 1970s were studies of the endangered Puerto Rican Parrot, but we soon recognized that the red-tail was probably the most important mortality threat faced by the adult parrots, and thus it was crucial to study the habits of the red-tails as well.

Red-tailed Hawks are more densely concentrated in the Luquillo Mountains than has ever been documented anywhere else, averaging more than two pairs per square mile on east-facing slopes, but rising to more than four pairs per square mile on slopes near the tops of the highest peaks. The high densities are apparently a result of good food supplies combined with superb foraging conditions. The extremely steady updrafts caused by the northeasterly trades interacting with the mountain topography allow the red-tails to hang effortlessly over the canopy as they hunt, inspecting all crannies of the treetops below with hardly a wing beat and efficiently capturing any prey foolish enough to be visible from the sky.

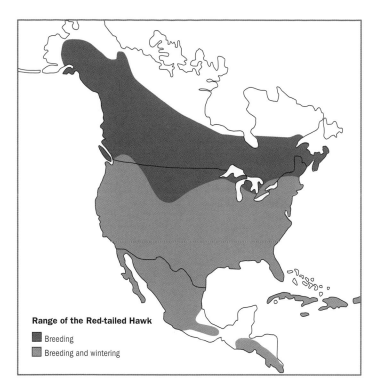

Range of the Red-tailed Hawk

■ Breeding
■ Breeding and wintering

A "Harlan's Hawk" lands at its nest in the Yukon Territory in 1968. Once considered a distinct species characterized by dark longitudinal streaks and spotting on the tail, this highly variable raptor is now merged taxonomically with the red-tail.

The high red-tail density in the upper Luquillo Mountains is especially remarkable because closed-canopy forest does not initially appear at all similar to the open and mixed habitats that red-tails generally occupy on the continent. Nevertheless, our observations revealed that Luquillo's red-tails are well adapted to local conditions, treating the surface of the forest canopy very much as if it were an open field and making most of their kills at canopy level.

From above-canopy lookouts, we found it relatively easy to map out red-tail territories by watching the pairs interact with neighboring pairs at territorial boundaries. These boundaries proved exceedingly stable over the several-year period of our investigations in the early 1970s, and they were still virtually unchanged in a follow-up study in 1998, more than two decades and a major hurricane later. Such extreme constancy suggests that the red-tail population of the region has been close to saturation in density for many years. Yet although all pairs under study built nests, well under half were successful in fledging young in any year, and it was rare for a nest to fledge more than a single young. This relatively low productivity may have been a direct result of the close packing of territories and the large amounts of time and energy that pairs were obliged to spend in territorial defense while also committed to foraging for their broods.

Within our principal study area on the northeastern side of the mountains, red-tail pairs claimed essentially all lands. Although we sometimes saw a nonresident individual pass through a territory, such birds were characteristically chased vigorously by the territory owners and driven successively by adjacent pairs to distant regions beyond the territories in view. Only by flying at great altitudes above the territories were intruders able to escape harassment.

Red-tail nests were difficult to study in the Luquillo Mountains. Even though we could spot the nests high up in tall trees from our above-canopy lookouts, finding them again from the ground was troublesome because of the density of rain-forest vegetation and the distances involved. Often the nests were completely invisible from the ground below, and it sometimes took several days of climbing to the canopy in nearby trees to pin down a nest location. Even then, nests were often in such dense tangles of vines and epiphytes that they could not be observed from nearby blinds.

Nevertheless, we finally located a nest in a vine-shrouded Cecropia tree that was well suited for close observations. When first found, the nest contained a single chick, who was still largely downy but past the stage where he needed steady brooding by the adult female—just the age when growth rates and food needs were at a maximum. Feedings at the nest were quite frequent—several prey per day—except for one day when a weather system moving into the area becalmed the usually dependable trade winds. On this day, the adults did not bring a single item of food to the nest. No doubt the main problem was the fact that aerial foraging is not feasible in windless cloudy weather, but for whatever reasons, the adults' success in perch hunting must also have been unusually low.

On days of more favorable weather, the prey brought to the nest ranged from native lizards, centipedes, crabs, and pigeons to the introduced rats and mongooses. The most interesting prey were the giant centipedes, many inches long, which were delivered still alive, though obviously in stunned condition. The chick had great difficulty dismembering and swallowing these tough-skinned arthropods and frequently failed to do so. As they revived, some of the centipedes just crawled off the nest and down the trunk of the nest tree.

The great diversity of prey species the red-tails brought to the nest indicated considerable foraging flexibility, and suggested that they were feeding on nearly all animal species of appropriate size in their environment. Puerto Rican Parrots were well within the size range of prey taken, and

Red-tailed Hawk

A light-phased red-tail rests on a rock during its first fall migration in eastern Oregon. Light-phased birds commonly, but not invariably, sport dark cummerbunds.

although we saw no parrots delivered as prey at the intensively studied nest, other observations indicated that the red-tails were indeed a major threat to this species. Several times we saw red-tails try but fail to capture adult parrots, and at one parrot nest in 1975, a red-tail once crawled down inside the hollow nest stub (four feet deep and eleven inches in internal diameter) in an attempt to grab nestling parrots. Further, we obtained strong circumstantial evidence—plucked remains—of a successful attack on a breeding female parrot near her nest in 1976. It was both ironic and highly unfortunate that the last remaining habitat of this highly endangered parrot species turned out to largely coincide with the exact region of highest density known anywhere for this most versatile natural predator. Although the red-tails were by no means the only threat faced by the parrot population, conservation of the parrot was surely not helped by this circumstance. At one point in 1975 the entire wild population of the parrot dropped to a low of thirteen individuals, and while the species still persists today, its last natural habitat

appears to be far from ideal (in part because of the abundant red-tails), even though the forests are still in largely pristine condition.

About the only sort of potential prey we did not see the Luquillo red-tails capture was snakes, although this omission was most likely due to nothing more than the scarcity of arboreal snakes in the region. In other parts of its range, the red-tail is renowned as a snake predator. For example, at one old red-tail nest in a cliff pothole in California, a site later used for nesting by a pair of California Condors, we found the tail rattles of four different western rattlesnakes in the litter. The red-tail's fondness for snakes may exceed that of any other North American raptor.

In northwestern Canada and Alaska, at the opposite corner of the species' range from Puerto Rico, the red-tail occurs as a form that for many years was given full species status as "Harlan's Hawk." As originally described, Harlan's Hawk (*Buteo harlani*) was supposedly separable from the red-tail by a tail

High over Florida's Everglades National Park, a Red-tailed Hawk endures aggressive diving attacks from a small flock of crows. Although renowned as a predator of mammals, red-tails also pose a substantial threat to small- and medium-sized birds.

coloration that is normally gray in adults and shows spotting and longitudinal dark streaks instead of the transverse dark bars that are usual for western red-tails. The problem in conceiving of Harlan's Hawk as a true species, however, has always been the difficulty in finding two Harlan's Hawk individuals that look alike in tail coloration. Just about every conceivable intermediate condition between red and gray tails with varying amounts of longitudinal and transverse barring and spots can be found in large samples of museum skins collected in the western states, Canada, and Alaska. Some individuals have red tails or partially red tails combined with longitudinal streaks, while others have transverse bars on tails that are mostly gray, and many individuals have both transverse bars and longitudinal streaks on the very same feathers. With this kind of mishmash in tail color characteristics, the general consensus in recent years has been that Harlan's Hawk is not a separable, reproductively isolated species. Until strong evidence for its distinctiveness is found, the form, if even that is a proper term, should best be considered a color variant of the red-tail that breeds in the northwestern corner of the continent.

In 1968 we had an opportunity to watch several pairs of relatively pure Harlan's Hawks at their nests in the Yukon Territory of Canada and near Fairbanks, Alaska. We saw and heard nothing in the behavior of these birds to suggest that they were anything but red-tails. The long, harsh *keearr* alarm vocalizations, the kinds of nest construction, diet, hunting behavior, in fact everything we could determine fell within the variability we had seen for the species elsewhere.

Among other well-marked color variants of the red-tail are melanistic, or black, individuals, which are most common in the western states. Red-tails also seem, more than other North American species of raptors, to have a tendency toward albinism, producing white and partially white individuals. One of the most striking raptors we have ever seen was such a bird—completely white except for a brilliant red tail—perched on a snag in an open field east of Lake Okeechobee, Florida, in 1979.

Because of its great flexibility in food habits and variability in other characteristics, the Red-tailed Hawk is especially well positioned to survive ecological disasters. By virtue of its relatively low position in food chains, the red-tail was spared the devastating population declines many other diurnal raptors suffered in the organochlorine pesticide era, and for the same reason it may well survive future chemical catastrophes. Further, its adaptability to human-modified habitats, and its general lack of interference with human interests, together with its tolerance of climatic extremes ranging from harsh deserts to humid rain forests, probably equip it, as much as any raptor could be equipped, to withstand the challenges of a changing planet. The species has been doing very well in recent years, expanding its range and numbers in the face of the multitudes of changes humans have brought to the landscape.

Red-tailed Hawk

Red-shouldered Hawk

Buteo lineatus

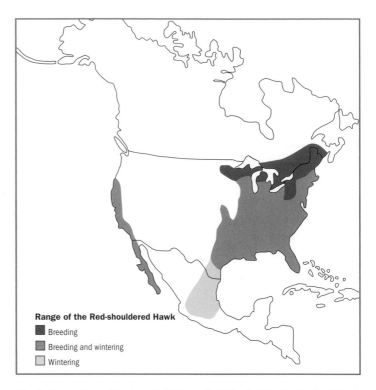

Range of the Red-shouldered Hawk
- Breeding
- Breeding and wintering
- Wintering

BOTH THE RED-SHOULDERED HAWK and the Broad-winged Hawk are characteristic woodland buteos of the eastern states. But whereas the broad-wings are mainly birds of upland deciduous and mixed deciduous-coniferous forests, red-shoulders are found primarily in moist river bottoms and wooded swamps. Diets of the two species are quite similar—mostly small forest vertebrates—although the red-shoulders feed especially heavily on aquatic animals such as frogs and crayfishes. In many respects, the red-shoulders most closely resemble the Common Black Hawks of the Southwest in their habitat preferences and diet. They are not commonly found in the same range as the black hawks, however, most likely because the two species would be in strong competition if they shared the same turf. Nevertheless, a geographically disjunct population of red-shoulders does occur farther west than the black hawk range—in coastal California—again associated primarily with riparian woodland.

Red-shoulders, broad-wings, and black hawks are all almost exclusively perch hunters, watching intently for prey from low positions within the forest canopy, then descending to capture it in short pounces. In this respect, they are similar to yet another raptor of the riparian zone of the southwestern states, the Gray Hawk. But the Gray Hawk takes few aquatic creatures as prey and specializes mainly on lizards, thus avoiding severe direct competition with the black hawks occurring in the same region. Together, the above four species are the woodland buteonine raptors of North America and form an ecological group distinct from the open-country buteonines of the continent, which include species such as the Swainson's Hawk, Rough-legged Hawk, Ferruginous Hawk, and White-tailed Hawk. The Red-tailed Hawk and Short-tailed Hawk are mostly allied with the open-country species in their foraging ecology, and although they also sometimes nest in heavily wooded regions, they usually do not capture prey under the forest canopy.

Somewhat larger than the Broad-winged Hawk, the Red-shouldered Hawk has a wingspread up to three-and-a-half feet and a weight averaging roughly one-and-a-third pounds. Adults possess a rich orange-chestnut barred breast

Florida's Red-shouldered Hawks have lighter-colored heads than more northerly red-shoulders. They also tend to be less wary than their northern relatives and frequently hunt in open habitats.

A female red-shoulder in upstate New York arrives with a short-tailed shrew for her brood. Red-shoulders were still common in this region in the 1960s when this photo was taken, but have since disappeared almost completely. The causes of disappearance here and elsewhere in the northeastern states have remained enigmatic. In California, the species has adapted well to highly disturbed habitats.

and a similarly hued shoulder patch. The tail is black with white bands, while the upper sides of the wings are basically black with numerous white spots. From below, the bases of the primary feathers of a soaring bird appear light in color, creating a white "window" patch toward the ends of the wings. The head color is generally brown, but in birds from Florida the brown is so pale it appears almost white from a distance.

The vocalizations of the Red-shouldered Hawk, as well as other morphological and behavioral similarities, serve to link this species closely with Ridgway's Hawk on the island of Hispaniola in the Caribbean, and it seems likely that these two species share a close common ancestry. Ridgway's Hawk in effect appears to be a population of Red-shouldered Hawks that has evolved to fill the normal niche of the Broad-winged Hawk on Hispaniola—that of a mainly upland forest buteo—and it is of special interest that Hispaniola is the only major island of the West Indies, except for Jamaica, that lacks a resident population of Broad-winged Hawks. Very likely, ecological space is too limited on Hispaniola to allow coexistence

of two woodland buteo species. Perhaps the Red-shouldered Hawk got to the island first, became well adapted to local conditions there as Ridgway's Hawk, and has been able to exclude colonization by Broad-winged Hawks ever since. Meanwhile, Broad-winged Hawks may have been the first to reach other islands in the region, serving as a barrier to the further spread of Ridgway's Hawk.

The Red-shouldered Hawk reaches peak abundance in the Spanish-moss-draped cypress swamps and river bottoms of the southeastern states, especially in Florida. Its *kleeah* proclamations resounding through the swamps in early spring are among the most pleasant sounds in nature—sounds that seem to announce the end of winter and the beginning of the breeding season for many species. The wet woodlands of this part of the country are seemingly filled with pairs of red-shoulders. In bottomlands like those that border Fisheating Creek in central Florida, pairs occur with almost metronomic regularity as one proceeds along the watercourses.

Red-shouldered Hawk

The Patuxent River bottoms in Maryland once hosted a dense population of Red-shouldered Hawks, but nearly four-fifths of the birds have disappeared since the mid-1970s. Though not virgin, these forests still include some of the state's most impressive stands of old-growth timber.

more suitable for Red-tailed Hawks and Great Horned Owls than for the red-shoulders. Still, the species has also declined in many of the best-preserved river-bottom habitats in the region, and it has remained uncommon in many areas where regrowth of secondary woodlands has returned the lands to a more forested condition. A number of northeastern states have listed the red-shoulder as a species worthy of special conservation concern because of its greatly diminished populations.

One of the eastern regions where red-shoulders once occurred in dense and apparently healthy populations is the Patuxent River bottoms of Maryland, especially the stretch of this river running through the Patuxent Wildlife Research Center. For many decades, researchers at the center have tracked the health of the local red-shoulder population, and it has suffered a massive progressive decline over the years, despite the lack of any cutting or development of the forests in the region. While there have been some habitat changes in the region—including an increase in the age and maturity of the forests in general and the creation of beaver ponds along the watercourses—the overall extent of habitat change has been limited and the sorts of changes occurring have not all been clearly detrimental for red-shoulders. Red-tailed Hawks have moved into some areas formerly occupied by the red-shoulders, but this may well have been a result, rather than a cause, of the red-shoulder's decline.

Another formerly dense red-shoulder population once resided in the Pocomoke River bottoms of the eastern shore of Maryland. Yet recent preliminary surveys of this region by Jim Wiley now indicate a near absence of the species, again despite generally increasing maturity of the swamp forests. Recent habitat changes have been minimal and generally beneficial, so it seems very likely that the decline has been caused by other, unknown factors. In the absence of strong evidence for particular factors, the possibilities deserving consideration are many and include potential stresses ranging from exotic diseases to toxic chemicals to widespread declines in key prey species. The recent massive declines of griffon vultures in Asia, first interpreted as a disease problem but later shown to be a toxic chemical problem, stand as a clear example that mysterious declines sometimes need very careful and creative research to be well understood.

Often exceedingly tame, Florida's red-shoulders are a common sight perched along hammock edges and drainage ditches, patiently scanning the ground for potential prey. Anglers of the region learn to guard their catches and bait buckets well when this species appears in the vicinity. Nesting everywhere from dense cypress swamps to hammocks in relatively open marshes and even in saltwater areas dominated by mangroves, the red-shoulder has adapted to virtually all aquatic regions of the state. The major factor that appears to limit its distribution in these regions is the presence of adequate numbers of hunting perches. Red-shoulders are rarely seen in truly open Everglades habitat, where snags are few and far between.

In years past, Red-shouldered Hawks were also abundant in the moist woodlands of the northeastern states, though they have been showing a major overall decline in this region, especially during the past half century. In part, the decline may have occurred because fragmentation of the original forests during the nineteenth century created huge areas of open habitat

In contrast to the declining red-shoulder populations of the northeastern states, the populations of species along the West Coast have remained vigorous despite even much more massive habitat changes caused by encroaching civilization. The red-shoulders of southern California, for example, have become familiar birds of suburbia and the freeways, often nesting in groves of eucalyptus and other exotic trees. It is hard to imagine a much more thoroughly disturbed region in the United States than the riparian zones of southern California, and it is notable that the species has been able to accommodate itself as well as it has to the habitat changes taking place there.

The ability of a number of raptors to adapt to urban conditions is now a subject of great interest among biologists and may well be of great importance to the future conservation of these species. Examples of species making such adaptations include the European Sparrowhawks invading urban areas of Scotland, and the Merlins occupying urban areas of Saskatchewan. Many of the Peregrine Falcons released in reestablishment efforts in the eastern United States have also adopted urban environments, as have Cooper's Hawks and Bay-winged Hawks in Tucson, Arizona.

At a nest along the Patuxent River in 1977, nothing hinted at the massive population decline to follow. The three youngsters were well fed and cared for, and the species was abundant up and down the river. The forests then, as now, were fully protected as part of the Patuxent Wildlife Research Center and adjacent federal areas.

In many ways, the Red-shouldered Hawk is an ideal species for biological research. In most regions it is relatively tolerant of close observations, and it often occupies territories that are sufficiently small that much of what happens in the activities of a pair can be seen from a single, well-chosen vantage point if the topography is right. Despite these advantages, wildlife biologists have undertaken relatively few intensive studies of this species.

Some of the most significant studies have been those of Jim Wiley, who has concentrated on observations from blinds and lookouts in both Florida and California. Wiley's research efforts have revealed many interesting facets to the behavior and ecology of this species, including the fact that the size of prey brought to nests bears a strong relationship to where it is caught. In his observations, the adults almost never brought small prey such as insects to nests unless they were caught in the near vicinity, while larger prey were brought in both from relatively close and relatively great distances. This feature of nest provisioning seems to make excellent intuitive sense, because the costs of transporting small items from great distances could well exceed the benefits gained. It seems likely that other raptors may make similar decisions in provisioning their young, but determining whether this is so poses formidable practical difficulties with many species. The Red-shouldered Hawk is one of the few for

which such data can be collected with accuracy and rigor in at least some habitats.

Our own studies of this species have been limited, although we have frequently observed red-shoulders incidental to other field studies in Florida and other eastern states. Our most focused observations of this species were in 1976 and 1977, when we lived in a forest cabin just off the east end of the Patuxent Research Center in Maryland. Here, we frequently hiked the towering old-growth woodlands of the Patuxent River and observed the local red-shoulders on a daily basis. One pair nested near the edge of the clearing where we lived, and we set up a blind to watch nesting activities of another pair along the main part of the river farther to the north. Far more wary than the red-shoulders of Florida, the Maryland birds were nonetheless very similar in diet and general behavior, and their abundance at that time still rivaled that of the species in the very best Florida habitats. The pairs we observed were highly productive of young, and the species had already survived the period of organochlorine pesticides after World War II with at most only minimal detrimental effects. We had no premonition at the time that the species was in the early stages of a massive regional decline. Surely, the red-shoulder is a species deserving of much expanded conservation research in the years ahead.

Red-shouldered Hawk

Gray Hawk

Asturina nitida

A LONG THE SOUTHERN BORDERS of Arizona, New Mexico, and Texas, birds typical of Mexico and Central American countries intermingle with more temperate species in a region of especially high avian diversity. Nowhere else in North America is the variety of raptors so great. Among the tropical species that attain their northern limits here is an intriguing woodland buteonine that was once known by the colorful name of Mexican Goshawk but in recent years has usually been referred to as the Gray Hawk. A very handsome raptor with a three-foot wingspread, a solid gray head and back, and a finely barred gray breast, this species is one of several raptors that are found almost exclusively in the linear bands of cottonwoods and mesquites that parallel the major streams of the region.

Studies in the 1970s indicated that only about fifty-five pairs of Gray Hawks were to be found north of the Mexican border, almost all of them in Arizona's San Pedro and Santa Cruz drainage basins, including Sonoita Creek. More recently, the population has grown to an

Range of the Gray Hawk
■ Breeding
■ Breeding and wintering

An adult Gray Hawk circles near her nest along the San Pedro River of southeastern Arizona. In this region, the species rarely strays far from well-developed riparian forests.

estimated eighty pairs for Arizona, and about ten pairs are now known to be breeding along the Rio Grande in southern Texas. Although this increase is encouraging, the North American populations are still quite small, and the species remains in a highly vulnerable status north of Mexico.

Of major concern is the health of the riparian cottonwood groves in which not only Gray Hawks but also Common Black Hawks, and to a lesser extent Zone-tailed Hawks, usually nest. Cottonwood seedlings are unable to survive in areas that are heavily grazed, and few cottonwood areas free of cattle remain in the Southwest. In many riparian zones, the only cottonwoods left are old giants that are slowly dying out, with no younger trees coming along to replace them. The few areas where cattle have been excluded, however, exhibit healthy regeneration of cottonwoods.

A prime example of how dependent Gray Hawks are on healthy riparian communities can be seen in the recent history of Guadelupe Canyon along the Arizona–New Mexico border, a location we have been surveying for raptors since the late 1960s. Prior to the 1980s, heavy cattle grazing had removed much of the low vegetation from the canyon floor, regeneration of cottonwoods was virtually nil, mature cottonwoods were progressively dying out, and Gray Hawks were nowhere to be found. But

immediately following the curtailment of cattle grazing in this canyon in the 1980s, young cottonwoods quickly colonized the stream sides, followed by colonization of the regenerating areas by Gray Hawks about twenty years later. Without the removal of grazing pressures, at least periodically, riparian zones offer poor long-term survival prospects either for cottonwoods or Gray Hawks, not to mention many other bird species. When not abused, the riparian cottonwood forests of the Southwest are among the richest habitats in overall avian diversity known anywhere on the continent.

The cottonwood communities of the Southwest are jeopardized by more than excessive cattle grazing. Another severe threat is the widespread invasion of the bottomlands of many river systems by an exotic tree known as salt cedar, or tamarisk. A native of the Old World, this species has been widely introduced into the Southwest to control erosion along streams. Once established, it often completely overwhelms the native riparian vegetation and creates a dense monoculture of very brushy, dark woodland that most birds use very little. Difficult to eradicate, salt cedar is having major effects on native wildlife resources. Approximately half the avian species found in the southwestern states, including both Gray Hawks and Common Black Hawks, are crucially dependent on natural or relatively natural riparian vegetation, so the stakes in stalling or reversing the encroachment of salt cedar are enormous.

Left: *A female Gray Hawk guards her nest high in a cottonwood along the Santa Cruz River near Nogales, Arizona. The Gray Hawk population has increased north of the Mexican border in recent years but still numbers less than one hundred pairs. Principal threats to the species include loss of mesquite-hackberry foraging areas to cutting and loss of cottonwood nesting areas to overgrazing. Overuse of groundwater supplies, however, may be the biggest threat of all, as Gray Hawks are very closely associated with permanent streams in Arizona.*

Gray Hawk

Intensive studies of the Gray Hawk by Rich Glinski and Brent Bibles, the preeminent researchers of this species, have revealed another habitat requirement for the species—access of the birds to substantial hunting areas that are relatively heavily wooded but open at ground level. Such hunting areas are provided by the mature mesquite-hackberry forests that characteristically grow in bands parallel to the cottonwood strips along rivers, but farther away from the water. The Gray Hawk depends critically on lizards for food, and these it generally hunts from low perches within such forested areas. Unfortunately, the large mesquites adjoining the cottonwood riparian zone in many regions have been heavily cut for firewood, because this is one of the best woods known for heating and cooking. In other areas, ceaseless pumping of groundwater supplies has lowered the water table to a point where neither mature mesquite nor cottonwood forests can survive. As a result, mature mesquite woodlands have disappeared from many regions, for example along the Santa Cruz River near Tucson. Although low brushy mesquite has been spreading rapidly in the Southwest at the expense of good grassland, few areas have mature enough mesquites to offer good hunting grounds for Gray Hawks.

That both cottonwood nesting areas and mesquite-hackberry hunting grounds are critical for Gray Hawks is illustrated by this raptor's absence from most of Aravaipa Canyon, a well-watered tributary of the San Pedro River in Arizona. This canyon possesses an excellent riparian zone of cottonwoods and sycamores suitable for Gray Hawk nesting, but it is too deeply incised in the surrounding terrain and too scoured by floods to permit the existence of extensive mesquite-hackberry forests suitable for the species' foraging needs. Gray Hawks do thrive farther downstream where the Aravaipa widens out to join the San Pedro, but they are normally absent from central regions of the canyon.

Despite the overwhelmingly positive value that cottonwoods represent for southwestern avian communities, this tree does pose a number of hazards for those interested in studying member species of these communities. Cottonwoods have very brittle branches, so it is essential when climbing these trees to stick to main trunks to avoid a sudden catastrophic return to ground level. But main trunks also pose problems, including very thick bark to which it is sometimes difficult to attach blind supports securely. Possibly the most unsafe blind we have ever constructed and trusted was in a cottonwood overlooking a Gray Hawk nest in southern Arizona. Nevertheless, this blind gave an excellent viewpoint from which to observe the nesting activities of the hawks on another trunk of the same cottonwood.

The adult Gray Hawks, obviously uninterested in our substandard blind, confidently fed their two young a diet of lizards and small mammals. Though we did not see any avian prey, extensive observations of other Arizona pairs by Rich Glinski have revealed that these hawks also take birds with some frequency. Glinski's overall data indicate that the species' diet consists of about 80 percent lizards and snakes, 10 percent mammals, and 10 percent birds. A major dependence on spiny and whiptail lizards is clear.

Also unmistakable in Glinski's data is the absence of aquatic prey in the species' diet. Yet, for some reason, the Gray Hawks of Arizona appear to be tightly tied to habitats with permanently flowing streams. We have never found them resident in completely dry canyons, whether vegetated with cottonwoods or not, and others have found them in such areas only rarely. Conceivably, since we have watched Gray Hawks coming to streams to drink, their usual prey of lizards may not provide enough moisture to

In Arizona, the Gray Hawk's diet includes about 80 percent reptiles, especially lizards. Mammals, such as this cotton rat brought to a nest along the Santa Cruz River, compose only about 10 percent of prey, and birds, another 10 percent.

satisfy their water needs, and they may require such additional accessible water sources to avoid dehydration. Other raptors of this region, such as Zone-tailed Hawks and Red-tailed Hawks, often nest in completely dry canyons, but the tissues of their typical prey may have enough moisture content to free them from such a dependency. These speculations are untested, however, and are surely not the only possible explanation for the different habitat tolerances of these species. The apparent tie to permanent streams in the Gray Hawks of the region may alternatively be more ecological than physiological, resulting from the favorable vegetation structure and relatively vigorous prey populations in ecosystems with water tables close to the surface.

As a migratory species, the Gray Hawk arrives in Arizona in middle to late March and begins nesting activities immediately. Nest building involves both sexes and is concentrated in April. Females normally lay eggs in early May and incubate for about thirty-three days. Males provide food during incubation but do not assist in warming eggs. The usual clutch is either two or three eggs, and the usual brood of two or three young in successful pairs stays in the nest for five to six weeks before fledging. Following fledging, young Gray Hawks remain dependent on their parents for another month or two. Productivity in Arizona has averaged about 1.2 young fledged per

Almost all Gray Hawk nests in Arizona have been found along streams with reliable above-surface flows, such as this short stretch still persisting along the Santa Cruz River. An important watercourse in the nineteenth century, the Santa Cruz is now usually dry along most of its length and has lost almost all of its Gray Hawks.

active pair, and predation on nests by Great Horned Owls and Red-tailed Hawks is suspected as one of the most significant factors reducing nesting success. The birds normally head south again to northern Mexico by early October, although occasionally, birds have been seen remaining in Arizona during the winter.

Like Common Black Hawks, Gray Hawks are not often seen soaring overhead except during the courtship and nest-building stages of the breeding season, when soaring at low elevations above the canopy is fairly common during the early afternoon, possibly mainly to advertise territory occupancy. Most activities are conducted within cover. Indeed, it is a challenge to observe Gray Hawks hunting because of the heavily wooded nature of their preferred foraging habitat. Most commonly, they hunt by perching on low branches and examining their surroundings carefully for prey. If no potential prey are spotted within about twenty minutes on a perch, the bird moves to a new perch and repeats the process. When a potential victim is spotted, either on the ground or on vegetation, it is taken in a quick pounce or pursuit. Most hunting activity is concentrated in midmorning and early evening. Small lizards are generally swallowed whole, but larger ones are dismembered prior to ingestion.

One almost always hears Gray Hawks before seeing them, and their loud descending alarm calls are an excellent indication that an active nest may be nearby. Other vocalizations include a very musical note of rising and falling inflection that sounds more like the call of a peacock than that

of a typical raptor. This call carries very clearly through the galleries of cottonwoods, and it is one of the first sounds heard in the dim light before dawn as resident Gray Hawk pairs announce their territorial holdings to one another.

In flight, Gray Hawks are relatively swift and accipiterlike, with rapid series of wing beats followed by glides. Their body proportions, with relatively short wings and long tails, also resemble those of accipiters. Further, Gray Hawks, like accipiters, often hunt by interspersing short flights with episodes of perching and scanning their surroundings. Thus, the old name applied to the species, Mexican Goshawk, is actually fairly appropriate, though the species is not closely allied with the true goshawks in ancestry.

Instead, the Gray Hawk has generally been classified in the genus *Buteo* and has often been considered a close relative of some other woodland buteos, particularly the Red-shouldered Hawk. Many features of coloration and body proportions—for example, shape of the legs and feet—suggest a close relationship of these two species. The black-and-white banding of the tail is closely similar in both, and both exhibit similar wing shape and a parallel pattern of wing banding that is visible when the birds are soaring overhead. The similarities of these two species set them apart from typical buteos in a number of ways, and some ornithologists have urged their separation, along with the Roadside Hawk and Ridgway's Hawk, into a distinct genus, *Asturina*, the genus in which the Gray Hawk resided before it was placed in *Buteo*. But although the American Ornithologists' Union has recently returned the Gray Hawk to *Asturina*, it has left the Red-shouldered Hawk, the Roadside Hawk, and Ridgway's Hawk in *Buteo*, apparently based on a belief that many of the similarities among these species could be due to evolutionary convergence rather than close common ancestry. The ultimate generic placement of all these species will probably be resolved only with comprehensive genetic studies.

The major task for conservation of the Gray Hawk is to prevent habitat loss and degradation. Fortunately, some significant progress has been made toward long-term protection of crucial portions of the species' range in Arizona. In 1966, the Nature Conservancy established the Patagonia–Sonoita Creek Reserve along two miles of permanently flowing water hosting several pairs of Gray Hawks. A much bigger step came in 1988, when the Bureau of Land Management created the San Pedro National Conservation Area. This second preserve presently includes forty miles of cottonwood bottomlands along the San Pedro River, one of the last low-elevation permanent streams in Arizona. The San Pedro drainage hosts approximately half of the Gray Hawk pairs that nest in Arizona, and about half of these pairs are found within the boundaries of the preserve. Moreover, since the preserve's establishment and the cessation of grazing activities within its boundaries, the number of Gray Hawk territories within the preserve has increased from eleven to twenty-four, an increase paralleled by a dramatic increase in populations of all bird species in general within the preserve. Clearly, this preserve, together with the Patagonia–Sonoita Creek Reserve, represents a major advance toward guaranteeing a North American future not only for the Gray Hawk, but also for many other southern bird species dependent on riparian cottonwood forests.

The San Pedro reserve, however, is not an island invulnerable to outside influences. Perhaps most worrisome in the long run is the continuing rapid growth of the nearby city of Sierra Vista, whose water demands, supplied largely by pumping of groundwater, could ultimately lower water tables in the region enough to compromise the viability of the San Pedro River itself, much as Tucson has destroyed the viability of Rillito Creek and the nearby Santa Cruz River by pumping of groundwater. Another more unpredictable threat comes from the extensive copper-mining activity practiced upstream from the reserve and across the border in northern Sonora, Mexico. A catastrophic spill of mining wastes could result in major long-term toxic contamination of the reserve and produce massive effects on its component species.

Gray Hawk

Short-tailed Hawk
Buteo brachyurus

HISTORICALLY, THE SHORT-TAILED HAWK was found only in Florida within the United States. In recent years, however, an apparent northward expansion of populations in Mexico has led to sightings in southern Texas, and the species has also turned up as a breeding bird in the Huachuca and Chiricahua Mountains of southeastern Arizona. In Florida, where the population is believed to include several hundred birds, the short-tail is a bird of the flatlands, mainly associated with groves of tall pines, hardwood hammocks, and cypress or mangrove swamps in the southern and central parts of the state. Sightings in Texas and nearby Tamaulipas, Mexico, have also been in flatlands, often associated with cypress-lined rivers. In Arizona, the topography of the species' habitat is completely different, and the bird is found in very high-elevation mountainous terrain cloaked in coniferous forests. We have also seen the species in similar montane habitat in the northern Sierra Madre of Mexico, just south of the border, in Chihuahua. The species' range extends south along the mountains and coastal strips of Mexico to tropical lowland regions throughout much of Central and South America. In a 1988 expedition we made to tributary streams of the Amazon River in southeastern Peru, the Short-tailed Hawk was by far the most common raptor observed.

With a wingspread of just under three feet, the short-tail is just slightly larger than a Broad-winged Hawk and is one of the smallest buteos of North America. In both sexes it occurs in two distinct color phases—white underneath with brownish gray upperparts and completely brownish black above and below. Unfortunately, neither pattern is very conspicuous at the

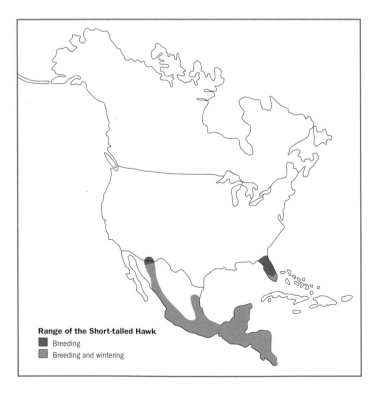

Range of the Short-tailed Hawk
- Breeding
- Breeding and wintering

Right: *A female dark-phased Short-tailed Hawk rests on her nest edge in a south-central Florida cypress swamp in 1979. The nest, placed atop bromeliads and orchids in one of the region's tallest cypresses, was nearly a hundred feet from the ground. The male provisioned the nest with a steady supply of small prey birds, but the single chick did not survive to fledging.*

Short-tailed Hawk

Access to the cypress nest tree of the dark-phased pair was through hip-deep sloughs clogged with muck and aquatic vegetation. Though a tranquil location in the dazzling morning sunlight, the swamp was buffeted by violent thunderstorms on most summer afternoons.

distances one usually sees the bird, and until one becomes familiar with the species' style of hunting and with its squealing vocalizations, it is a raptor that is very easy to overlook.

In Florida, short-tails most commonly hunt by making use of the updrafts that form along the boundaries between tall isolated groves of cypresses or pines and the surrounding low prairies and marshes. These cliffs of vegetation deflect any moving air upward into standing waves that can support almost effortless soaring by large birds. As the morning breezes begin to stir, the short-tails rise from the trees to take positions over such vegetational features and commonly reach altitudes of several hundred feet from the ground. Other large birds move into the air columns about the same time, and the short-tails soon become hard to pick out among the many soaring vultures, anhingas, storks, kites, and other raptors. At such heights it is difficult to see field marks, and usually the best way to find the species is to look for tiny aerial specks that do not move. The short-tail rarely circles when hunting. Instead, it just hangs in the air, facing into the wind for long periods. Hang-hunting in updrafts high above topographic features is also the foraging style of short-tails in Arizona, but the usual foraging elevations observed for the species in this state have exceeded 8,000 feet above sea level. Very little of Arizona is this high in elevation, and consequently the species may never achieve more than a tiny population in the state.

Short-tails primarily feed on small birds—an unusual diet for a buteo—and like other raptors feeding heavily on birds, the species exhibits a considerable size difference (greater than 10 percent) between the sexes.

Florida's short-tails capture prey in long stoops, sometimes in the canopy of hammocks, but perhaps as often in the open fields surrounding wooded areas. One of the most accessible and reliable places to watch this species hunting, especially in winter, is over the prairies of Everglades National Park near Flamingo. Short-tails are also often seen foraging over Anhinga Trail in the same park. Another place where there is a good chance of seeing the species at any time of year is in Corkscrew Swamp Sanctuary in Collier County, Florida. In Arizona, the species has been seen regularly hunting at high elevations in Miller Canyon of the Huachuca Mountains and near Barfoot Park in the Chiricahua Mountains.

Despite its relatively inconspicuous nature, the short-tail is one of the most attractive raptors found within the borders of the United States, and we long hoped for a chance to observe it closely. We were especially interested in studying a nesting cycle of this species, because its diet is heavily focused on small birds, and we wanted to determine if the species faced the same seasonal stresses in food supplies we had found in the bird-feeding accipiters.

An opportunity to hunt for nests of the Short-tailed Hawk finally materialized in 1978 and 1979, when we were studying Everglade Kites on Lake Okeechobee in Florida. In both years, we made intensive searches of the swamps and hammocks northwest of this lake, especially along Fisheating Creek, where many previous sightings of short-tails had been reported. Eventually, we found an active pair, but this was only after dozens of fruitless searches that led us to wonder if the species could have suffered a significant decline in the region.

Our searches in 1978 yielded only a lone territorial bird, a light-phased individual that built several nests along Fisheating Creek but never acquired a mate. Pure white underneath and dark above, with attractive chestnut patches on the sides of the neck, this bird was noticeably smaller than the Red-tailed Hawks and Red-shouldered Hawks occupying the same region, and it spent long periods circling over its nest grove and giving squealing calls in an apparent effort to attract a partner.

Expanded efforts in the following year finally turned up a pair of dark-phased short-tails in a remote cypress swamp farther north. These birds had solid black bodies and were active in flight over the very heart of the swamp. Viewing the swamp from the prairies outside, we strongly suspected a nesting was in progress when we saw the presumed male bird streak into the swamp carrying prey. But it was already late spring and the cypresses were rapidly leafing out, making it difficult to spot a nest from the ground, especially considering the abundance of nestlike bromeliads on the cypress branches. We had to get closer, and this meant slogging through opaque, waist-deep waters, stubbing our shins on innumerable cypress knees and submerged logs, until we finally saw the male adult overhead carrying a twig. He flew straight to one of the air plants in a nearby cypress, making a twisting, flapping landing. At last we had an active nest. Better still, the nest was not yet completed, so it appeared we had a chance to follow a full breeding cycle of the species.

The nest was placed atop a mass of bromeliads and flowering orchids nearly a hundred feet from the ground in one of the tallest cypresses in the region. This may have been a renesting effort after a failure earlier in the year because it was the latest nest ever recorded for the species in Florida (incubation began on about May 26, whereas it usually begins between mid-March and late April). An unoccupied nest in a nearby cypress, apparently also of short-tails, suggested that the swamp had been occupied by the species before the current nesting, although there was no way to determine conclusively if this second nest dated from the same year.

The height of the active nest and the density of nearby vegetation made good observations from the ground impossible. To view the nest adequately

A solitary light-phased Short-tailed Hawk did considerable nest building along Fisheating Creek in 1978 before abandoning efforts to attract a mate.

unknown, although it became reluctant to take food toward the end, possibly because of disease or parasite problems, and may well have perished as a result.

Our efforts to find and study Short-tailed Hawks took us into some of the most pristine wildlife areas of Florida. They also gave us one of the most extraordinary wildlife experiences to be hoped for in this age—a moment in which we believed we had seen a true avian will-o-the-wisp, an Ivory-billed Woodpecker. The last well-documented population of the ivory-bill in the states had disappeared from the bottomland swamps of Louisiana in the 1940s, and by the late 1970s, many considered the ivory-bill to be extinct. New sightings were generally viewed with considerable skepticism. None of the recent sightings had been clear enough or long enough or substantiated well enough with photographs to have gained full acceptance. Our sighting was not troubled by these problems but nevertheless reinforced the caution with which contemporary ivory-bill sightings should be regarded.

The bird in question was in a hammock northeast of Archbold Biological Station, and we sighted it during a hike to find short-tails in the spring of 1979. The bird had been feeding on a log on the ground,

we constructed a blind near the top of a neighboring cypress on a side limb that slanted up into the sky at an alarming 45-degree angle. Although we had some misgivings about the safety of this effort, the limb proved to be strong, and we wound up with a blind perched at the highest point in the swamp, with a spectacular view not only of the Short-tailed Hawk nest some thirty feet away, but also of the entire region. Swallow-tailed Kites, nesting several hundred yards away, cruised past the blind with regularity, and far below were Wild Turkeys, Wood Storks, Barred Owls, deer, bobcats, and raccoons. Overhead, we could watch the aerial activities of the short-tails, as well as the ominous buildup of thunderheads that drenched the swamp with rain each afternoon.

Shortly after we began observations of the pair from the treetop blind, we saw the adult female successfully defend her nest from a formidable enemy. As she sat incubating, a large yellow rat snake appeared, threading its way upward through the plants supporting the nest. Once she became aware of the snake, the female spread her wings fully and held them extended in an impressive display that greatly increased her apparent size and ferocity. The snake circled the nest's perimeter as the female swayed over her clutch, and by footing aggressively at the snake, she managed to drive it into a quick retreat back down the trunk of the cypress.

The short-tails hatched their single chick on June 29, and the male adult began bringing prey to the nest to pass to the female for feeding to the youngster. The pair fed exclusively on other birds, mainly from the surrounding prairie region, and we had our first good look at a Bachman's Sparrow as a prey item brought to this nest. But sadly, the single chick in the nest lost vigor about a week after hatching and soon disappeared, so we were unable to study a full nesting cycle. Causes of the chick's difficulties were

and when we startled it, the bird flew up to land on the vertical trunk of a pine about fifty feet away. Immediately apparent was the fact that it was a very large woodpecker and had large and conspicuous white triangles on its back formed by the white secondary feathers of the folded wings—the most diagnostic field mark of the ivory-bill that distinguishes this species from the otherwise quite similar Pileated Woodpecker. Had the bird flown on at this point, we would have had no doubt whatsoever that we had seen a living ivory-bill.

But the bird did not fly immediately, and instead it shifted from one side of the trunk to the other for perhaps another thirty seconds, allowing ample opportunity for a careful inspection of its plumage with binoculars. Unfortunately, a detailed look revealed that in fact the white triangles on the bird's wings were not pure white but were somewhat cream-colored, and in fact the white area on the left wing was slightly marred by two black secondary feathers intermixed with the white ones. Furthermore, the bird did not have the pure white bill of an ivory-bill, but the typical black bill of a Pileated Woodpecker, and the details of the bird's head color pattern matched a Pileated Woodpecker in all respects. Clearly, this was not really an Ivory-billed Woodpecker, but was most likely a freak Pileated Woodpecker (or less likely a hybrid of the two species), bearing most of the wing coloration of an ivory-bill.

With the sighting of this bird, thoughts of Short-tailed Hawks had vanished for a time, and in truth even if a screaming short-tail had circled low overhead, we might not have noticed it. We hiked back toward home wondering just how many of the ivory-bill sightings of previous decades might trace to similar sources.

Short-tailed Hawk

A dark-phased short-tail hunts over the prairies near Flamingo in Everglades National Park. Hanging high in the wind, short-tails circle infrequently and generally capture prey in long stoops out of the sky.

The potential for mistaken identifications of odd Pileated Woodpeckers as ivory-bills did not end with our sighting of 1979. Reports from early 2005, more than twenty-five years later, have claimed the continued existence of ivory-bills in Arkansas based largely on multiple recent sightings and a controversial low-resolution video recording of at least one large woodpecker with the same field mark we observed—white secondary patches. The bird seen may indeed be an ivory-bill, and its especially large apparent size in sightings to date supports this judgment, but such size judgments are difficult to make, and our sighting of 1979 at least raises the alternative possibility of another aberrant Pileated Woodpecker masquerading as its more famous cousin. One can only hope that such is not the case, and that future sightings will be of sufficient quality and detail to fully confirm the bird's true identity.

The Short-tailed Hawk itself is a species that is frequently misidentified because of its resemblance to other species. In particular, wintering Broad-winged Hawks in southern Florida are often nearly pure white underneath and are very similar in size and shape to short-tails. Often such broad-wings are found in the Florida Keys, and many records of short-tails from

this area have undoubtedly been misidentified broad-wings. In general, the hawks of the genus *Buteo* are especially hard to differentiate, because many are so variable in plumage. A knowledge of behavior and ecology of the various species is as important as good eyesight in resolving the many ambiguities.

Outside of occasional cases of Short-tailed Hawks being shot or suffering from collisions with vehicles or windows, the species is apparently largely free from major direct impacts of humanity—one of the benefits of its largely inconspicuous habits. With a diet primarily of small birds, however, it resides high in food chains and is presumably a species vulnerable to environmental pollutants. No detailed studies were made of the species during the organochlorine era following World War II, so it is unknown to what extent it may have suffered from DDT and related toxins. Monitoring efforts in recent years suggest a reasonably stable population in Florida and expanding populations in the Southwest, but no more than a few hundred individuals presently exist in North America, and the species clearly deserves more intensive study to identify population stresses and to design effective long-term conservation strategies.

Swainson's Hawk
Buteo swainsoni

Range of the Swainson's Hawk
■ Breeding
□ Wintering
Most winter in South America

ONLY ONE WOODLAND BUTEO, the Broad-winged Hawk, and one open-country buteo, the Swainson's Hawk, regularly migrate all the way from North America to South America in the fall. All other North American buteos, with the possible exception of the Zone-tailed Hawk, go no farther south than Central America, and some barely reach the Mexican border. On their journeys, Swainson's and broad-wings characteristically take a land-based path through eastern Mexico and Central America and across the Panamanian isthmus, where they pass by in huge assemblages of tens of thousands of birds. Swainson's Hawks characteristically finish their fall migrations in the pampas of Argentina, settling in habitats similar to the open grasslands and brushlands they occupy in western North America during the summer. The winter destination of most migrating broad-wings is the forests of northern South America, though some get no farther than southern Central America.

The entire southward migration for Swainson's Hawks takes about a month and a half to two months, and biologists have long speculated about whether these birds take any food at all during most of this long journey. We have commonly seen premigratory or early migratory flocks foraging for grasshoppers in Arizona and northern Mexico in late summer, but no one has witnessed prey capture attempts in the fall migratory swarms in Costa Rica and Panama. Further, at sites in this latter region where flocks of Swainson's Hawks have roosted overnight, no one has found traces of pellets or fecal material. In northern South America, where the migration route passes over some open-country locations, foraging would seem to be feasible, although it has not been documented. Farther south, satellite radiotelemetry studies have indicated that the species travels directly over the Amazonian jungle in its migration path, hardly the sort of habitat the species normally hunts.

Calculations on the energy requirements of migration suggest that Swainson's Hawks could put on enough fat to enable them to survive the entire trip without eating, providing the birds do not use any significant amounts of flapping flight en route. This restriction accords well with field observations that indicate soaring and gliding as the overwhelmingly predominant modes of travel. Nevertheless, some of the birds reaching Argentina have arrived in severely weakened condition, a result suggesting that the long migratory journey may have approached the limits of their energy reserves.

Regardless of the extent to which they may feed during migration, the fact that nearly all Swainson's Hawks and Broad-winged Hawks migrate in a narrow stream through Panama has offered an opportunity to make minimum counts of the entire populations of these species. The main practical difficulty in making such counts is that the birds often pass by so quickly and in such dense swarms that it is frequently impossible to keep up in direct visual-based tabulations. To some extent this problem can be solved by photographing large swarms and later analyzing the numbers of birds in the photographs. Using such methods in the 1980s, Neal Smith of the Smithsonian Institution was able to document for both Swainson's Hawks and Broad-winged Hawks that several hundred thousand individuals passed through Panama each year. The general magnitude of these counts has been confirmed more recently by tabulations of these species passing through coastal Veracruz, Mexico.

Of the North American raptors in other genera, only a few make comparable seasonal migrations, most notably Swallow-tailed Kites, Mississippi Kites, and some populations of Turkey Vultures, Peregrine Falcons, and Ospreys. One important factor that may prevent most other raptors from making a full migration to South America is the difficulty they have flying across long stretches of water. Eastern raptors, in particular, face a formidable barrier to southward progress in the Gulf of Mexico, unless they swing far to the west in their routes of travel. Soaring conditions are generally poor over water, and most raptors have to rely on powered flapping flight to cross such barriers, an energetically expensive way to progress for large birds. Thus, it may be difficult for many raptor species to develop or maintain efficient migration routes taking them into South America. Only five species—the Osprey, the Swallow-tailed Kite, the Northern Harrier, the Peregrine Falcon, and the Merlin—are known to move regularly into the West Indies or across the Gulf of Mexico in migration, and these are all species that relative to their body size have especially long, powerful wings suiting them for such arduous journeys.

Though its wings are not long enough to place it among the species comfortable with long overwater migrations, the Swainson's Hawk has relatively long pointed wings for a buteo, which may be a reflection of its strongly migratory habits. At least a rough correlation between wing length and length of migration exists in many avian groups. For example, the nonmigratory Sharp-shinned Hawks of Puerto Rico have much shorter wings than migratory populations of sharp-shins on the mainland, although they are very similar in weight to mainland sharp-shins. In both body weight and wing length, the Swainson's Hawk is extremely similar to the Rough-legged Hawk, another strongly migratory species, and both these raptors have longer wings than the less-migratory Red-tailed Hawk, which significantly exceeds them in body weight.

A few of North America's Swainson's Hawks and Broad-winged Hawks fail to follow the usual fall migration path through Mexico and Central America. Mostly, these stragglers end up wintering in southern Florida. Evidence suggests that these birds may primarily be individuals that missed their bearings in their first fall migration and got "trapped" in southern portions of the peninsula by the oceans to the east, south, and west. Most individuals of these species wintering in Florida have been juveniles not yet experienced in migration. Further, there have been actual sightings of migrating flocks of broad-wings circling over Key West, heading tentatively out to sea, then returning once again to the safety of land. Some flocks have been seen to fight onward to the south, but the finding of weak and starving individuals on the

A pair of Swainson's Hawks nesting in southwestern New Mexico's Chihuahuan Desert in 1972 consisted of a light-phased male and an intermediate-phased female. Fully dark-phased individuals are rare in most regions.

Dry Tortugas not much farther along suggests that individuals that continue south over the Gulf of Mexico may generally be doomed.

During the late 1960s, we sometimes watched Florida's wintering Swainson's Hawks foraging in agricultural lands near Everglades National Park. Here the birds had learned to follow tractors while farmers plowed their fields for planting. This process exposed many small rodents to view—some of which were crippled as the blades of the plows cut through the soil. Processions of Swainson's Hawks commonly drifted along behind, diving intermittently to the ground to grab these unfortunate creatures, and the birds involved seemed to be swallowing as many prey as they could possibly hold. Occasionally, the hawks collided in midair when more than one bird attempted to capture the same rodent simultaneously, but for the most part the hawks appeared to be having an extraordinarily nonstressful time foraging. The main challenge they faced appeared to be locating operating tractors.

The Swainson's Hawk, like many other buteos, exhibits a great variety of color patterns, from completely black to primarily white underneath. In

its most common adult coloration, the species has a white throat and belly separated by a dark brownish band across the upper breast. Intermediate-colored adults have a reduced white throat and a white belly heavily marked with rufous-brown barring. Completely dark adults are generally rare, although they evidently comprise a majority of breeding females in northeastern California.

On its breeding grounds in the western states and western Canada, the Swainson's Hawk is known mainly as a predator of small mammals and insects, but like many other large raptors taking both invertebrate and vertebrate prey, this species normally brings only vertebrates to nests as food for developing nestlings. In part, this reliance on vertebrate prey during breeding may stem from the fact that vertebrate skeletons offer a rich source of calcium for bone development of nestlings. But more important, it may stem from the high transport costs of satisfying the energy and protein needs of developing nestlings with relatively small prey such as insects.

In any event, the diet we have seen at several nests of Swainson's Hawks in the southwestern states has been exclusively small mammals, lizards, and

The New Mexico Swainson's pair nested in a well-developed soaptree yucca, a species possessing roots that were once used as a source of shampoo.

129

In flight around his nest, a male Swainson's Hawk exhibits the typical two-toned wing coloration and long pointed wing shape that allow observers to identify this species from long distances.

birds. These are the sorts of prey the species evidently needs for successful breeding, despite the fact that stomach analyses of Swainson's Hawks over the years, many of them of birds outside the breeding season, have shown a very high proportion of insects in the diet. The reliance on vertebrates vanishes once breeding is over. In fact, our experience in attempting to trap the species for telemetry studies in September suggests that Swainson's Hawks ignore vertebrate baits at this season and seem to prefer grasshoppers to all other foods.

Swainson's Hawks most usually return to their North American breeding grounds in March, and most eggs are laid in late April or early May after a nest-building phase that involves both adults and generally lasts one to two weeks. Most clutches consist of two to three eggs that are usually plain white in color, although a minority have reddish brown or purplish blotches around the larger end. Incubation begins with the first egg laid and generally averages thirty-four or thirty-five days, with eggs hatching asynchronously. Nestlings remain in the nest for about six weeks, but brood reduction is common, with

the youngest and smallest nestling often consumed, if not killed, by its older siblings. After fledging, the youngsters remain within the nesting territory dependent on adults for about a month, although young have abandoned their natal territories as early as two to three weeks after fledging in some cases. The availability in late summer of large, easy-to-capture grasshoppers may facilitate relatively early achievement of independence.

One nest we watched in western New Mexico in 1971 was in the top of a sturdy soaptree yucca that reached about twenty feet into the sky. The pair attending the nest included a light-colored male and an intermediate-colored female, and the nest contained two downy white nestlings. Swainson's Hawks were very common in this region, nesting in everything from mesquites to cottonwoods. Despite the heavily overgrazed, brushy conditions of the land, the hawks found an abundance of ground squirrels and small birds to capture, and we even once saw the male adult bring in a banner-tailed kangaroo rat to the nest in the middle of the day. Kangaroo rats are quite strictly nocturnal, and the capture may have been accomplished by the bird thrusting its talons

In the nonbreeding season, Swainson's Hawks prey heavily on insects such as grasshoppers, but nesting pairs typically focus on vertebrate prey. Here, a Swainson's Hawk lands with a lizard victim near its nest in central Texas in 1967.

into the loose earth at the entrance of an active burrow—a method both Swainson's and Ferruginous Hawks are known to use to capture gophers in other regions. We have never directly witnessed such a prey capture, but we have found kangaroo-rat remains in other Swainson's Hawk nests, suggesting that such captures may be a regular occurrence.

Like most buteos, Swainson's Hawks are highly territorial and are dispersed in distribution during the breeding season. But once breeding is finished, the species becomes one of the most social of raptors in most aspects of behavior, including foraging, overnight roosting, and migrating. One intriguing social foraging method we have seen practiced by the species in late summer is fire following. When the grasslands are aflame, whether a result of deliberate burning practices or of lightning strikes or other accidental events, Swainson's Hawks stream in from miles around to take advantage of the prey species suddenly deprived of cover and safety. Such behavior is also well known for other raptor species of open country, such as White-tailed Hawks and Aplomado Falcons.

Swainson's Hawks present a number of difficult conservation challenges. To some extent, the species has adjusted well to agricultural practices. For example, a number of researchers have noted that where trees have been planted as hedgerows and around farm structures, Swainson's Hawk populations have increased due to greater nest-site availability. The suitability of agricultural lands for Swainson's Hawks, however, depends on the specific characteristics of agricultural practices. As a general rule, pasturelands and

hay fields provide good foraging habitat. Wheat fields and alfalfa fields do not, apparently because they provide too much cover for prey.

Thus, it is not surprising that Swainson's Hawks have had difficulty surviving in some agricultural regions, and it is clear that over the long term the species has suffered major declines in many regions, including southern Canada, parts of the northwestern United States, and California. At least in part, these declines have likely been related to changes in land-use practices that have affected prey populations and prey availability on the nesting grounds, although it is not clear that all regional declines have had the same causes.

Further, as investigated by Boise State University researcher Mark Bechard and his collaborators, wintering Swainson's Hawks have been suffering major losses in Argentina in recent years resulting from poisoning by organophosphate pesticides used to kill grasshoppers. Studies of banded and telemetered birds indicate that individuals in specific regions on the wintering grounds are mixtures of birds from diverse North American sources, so such poisoning threats are likely affecting breeding populations in general, rather than just certain breeding populations.

Thus, even though the Swainson's Hawk is still an abundant and welcome sight in many western regions, it has declined massively in others and it remains vulnerable to a variety of forces whose future impacts are very difficult to predict. Because this species winters almost completely in regions south of the borders of North America, its long-term conservation can be only partially controlled by policies on the breeding grounds, and for full success in ensuring the bird's persistence, international cooperation is essential.

Swainson's Hawk

Rough-legged Hawk
Buteo lagopus

Ｆ ROM THE PEAKS OF the Brooks Range a number of snow-fed rivers gradually descend Alaska's North Slope. The Sagavanirktok, the Kuparuk, the Itkillik, and the Colville are among the largest, and as they leave the steeper mountains, they meander first through rolling foothills, then push across a broad plain of tundra and lakes, finally reaching the Arctic Ocean after journeys of up to several hundred miles.

The lands these rivers traverse are all underlain by permafrost and support only a low carpet of plants. Nevertheless, the surface of the vegetation is so uneven that it is a challenge to walk across without stumbling or twisting an ankle. Often drenched by low-lying mists, the terrain is covered with a mosaic of grass and sedge clumps, sphagnum moss, dwarf willows, tiny birches, and miniature rhododendrons interspersed with numerous soggy depressions and pools that nurture dense midsummer swarms of mosquitoes and other insects. The Arctic Circle lies hundreds of miles to the south, and the sun never rises very high, but it never sets in the summer months and sweeps endlessly around all 360 degrees of the horizon. In winter the sun vanishes completely in one extended period of alternating twilight and darkness enhanced at times by periods of moonlight and the aurora borealis.

Although the overall relief of the region is modest, the rivers of the North Slope have cut low bluffs here and there along their courses. Mostly too small to be called cliffs, these patches of rock and talus are adequate, nevertheless, to support thriving populations of nesting raptors during the summer, primarily Peregrine Falcons, Gyrfalcons, and Rough-legged Hawks. Common Ravens also live here, though in lesser abundance, and like the rough-

Range of the Rough-legged Hawk
- ■ Breeding
- ☐ Wintering

Right: *The Rough-legged Hawks of Alaska's North Slope typically build their nests on low cliffs overlooking the rivers that drain the Brooks Range. A rough-leg pair in 1987 selected a site on an easily accessible rib of gravel and rock descending to the Sagavanirktok River. Small mammal prey were evidently in short supply, and the pair reared its single scrawny chick mainly on small birds. The male adult attending this nest was nearly all black, except for white tail banding.*

Rough-legged Hawk

In flight over her nest, a female rough-leg screams in defiance at the approach of potential predators. Although some individuals of this highly variable species are difficult to identify, this bird displays the white tail base characteristic of the species and the dark belly band and dark wing patches found in many individuals.

legs, they provide an important service to the Peregrine Falcons and Gyrfalcons by constructing stick nests that these species can subsequently occupy. Golden Eagles, common on the cliffs of the Brooks Range, occur only on some of the higher escarpments along the southern fringe of the region.

On the tundra landscape between the rivers, the North Slope raptors find a variety of prey. Small mammals, primarily lemmings and various species of voles, form the main food of the Rough-legged Hawks, while the resident ptarmigan and ground squirrels sustain the Gyrfalcons. The Peregrine Falcons take mainly small birds, while the ravens, as is their custom elsewhere, feed opportunistically on a variety of plant and animal species, many of them as carrion. Certain of these food species, particularly the small mammals, exhibit dramatic cycles of abundance and scarcity, and the Rough-legged Hawks especially, because they are heavily dependent on such prey, have to contend with severe fluctuations in food availability. Under good prey conditions pairs can easily fledge three and sometimes four young

in a year, but when prey numbers collapse, the average fledgling production sometimes drops to less than a single youngster per pair.

The focus of rough-legs on small mammals is to some extent surprising and reminiscent of the similar focus of Great Gray Owls on small rodents—both are relatively large raptors that one would believe could take larger prey than they normally do. At a weight often exceeding two pounds, the rough-leg approaches the Red-tailed Hawk in mass, and we have sometimes seen it with prey as large as Willow Ptarmigan. Nevertheless, most studies have shown that the diet of the species is heavily skewed toward small mammals throughout the year, and only a few have shown substantial use of ptarmigan and other relatively large birds or mammals.

Breeding almost exclusively in treeless regions of tundra, Rough-legged Hawks and Gyrfalcons compete for honors as the most thoroughly arctic nesters of North America's diurnal raptors. The breeding distributions of the two species overlap broadly, and although the Gyrfalcons of some

Another Alaskan rough-leg nest in 1987 was on a gentle slope of the tundra far from any river. The parent birds enjoyed a relatively favorable prey supply of small mammals in their home range and kept their three young in vigorous good health.

Rough-legged Hawk

regions extend closer to the pole than the rough-legs, Gyrfalcons also regularly breed farther south in the mountains of interior Alaska and Canada. The rough-legs mostly avoid high mountain regions. Building nests of dwarf willow and birch branches on exposed ledges and slopes, they make the best of what few woody materials are available in their surroundings, and their nests tend to be substantial, perhaps in part for the thermal advantages such structures offer.

In winter, the rough-legs leave their arctic breeding grounds, and in the New World they migrate as far south as northern Mexico. Those we have had an opportunity to observe in winter in southern Arizona have chosen open grassland habitats year after year, and we have never seen them in terrain with more than small amounts of brush. At least superficially, grassland is the closest habitat match to tundra that Arizona has to offer.

Normally, rough-legs are the most common of all the arctic raptors, but in July 1987, when we had an opportunity to visit Alaska's North Slope for several weeks, small mammals were at a low point in their cycle of abundance in most areas, and we found more pairs of Gyrfalcons than of rough-legs. Numerous old rough-leg territories along the river bluffs were host only to empty nests, and the few pairs that were attempting to breed were having only modest success.

One nest we watched from a blind held but a single youngster, and a very scrawny one at that. His parents, apparently unable to find adequate numbers of small mammals, were bringing in mostly small birds, and the youngster appeared to be in a state of acute hunger. In view of the apparent food stress at this nest, we were curious whether the parent birds might be attempting to increase prey captures by extending their hunting activities through the late evening and early morning hours. Certainly there was enough light around the clock to make this possible. But although we watched for signs of such an adjustment in a twenty-four-hour vigil, activities ceased at about nine at night, and the pair did not resume hunting until an hour of the morning that would be appropriate for raptors in the lower states. A twenty-four-hour watch of an active Golden Eagle nest nearby revealed a very similar schedule of activities. These raptors of the midnight sun likely needed their rest as much as did their observers.

Rough-legged Hawks are extremely diverse in coloration, with hardly two birds alike, and they vary from completely dark to mostly white underneath and from basically brown to black above. The adults of the pair with a single chick included a light-phased female and a most strikingly beautiful black-phased male. Both exhibited the broad black subterminal band to the tail typical of the species, but beyond this they were quite different in appearance. The female, heavily streaked with dark brown and with a black belly and black patches near the bases of her primary feathers, remained in close attendance at the nest. The all-dark male, arriving only at irregular intervals, was reminiscent of a Zone-tailed Hawk, differing mainly in the amount of white banding at the base of the tail.

A similarity to zone-tails was also apparent in alarm vocalizations of the two species—in both, a high, thin descending scream that breaks up into a sort of yodeling when the birds beat their wings in flight. Nevertheless, aside from these visual and vocal similarities, rough-legs and zone-tails are very different birds in behavior and ecology and probably encounter each other only rarely in nature. By the time the southernmost wintering rough-legs from the arctic reach the summer range of the zone-tail in Arizona, New Mexico, Texas, and northern Mexico, the zone-tails have normally long departed for a wintering

After landing with prey, the female at the tundra nest tarries for only a few moments before returning to the skies.

Rough-legged Hawk

small cliff a quarter mile away. Old rough-leg nests on the cliff suggested that it might have been the rough-legs' usual home.

This second pair of rough-legs was occupying a region with much better small mammal populations than those available to the first pair and was doing much better in provisioning its brood. We saw only small mammals brought in to this nest and found only fur as prey remains at the site. In directly observing the adults' activities, we found that they had little trouble locating prey. Hunting much in the manner of White-tailed Hawks, they alternated periods of circling with bouts of hanging, facing into the breeze high over the tundra and intently scanning the landscape below. On sighting prey, they either descended in long direct stoops or sometimes interrupted their descents with periods of hovering, possibly assessing continuing movements of their potential victims.

While the first pair of rough-legs was somehow succeeding in the very midst of a wolf pack, the second pair was situated only a short distance from an active den of five red foxes. That they too were unmolested in spite of this tangible threat and in spite of the total vulnerability of their nest site to such predators was again noteworthy, as was the fact that both rough-leg nests were surviving what appeared to be a substantial threat of aerial predation by nearby nesting Gyrfalcons. Perhaps the persistence of both nests was due to the close attendance they received from the adult females and the ability of the females to spot approaching predators and intercept and harass them at long distances from their nests.

Like most other raptors found in the far north, the Rough-legged Hawk has a circumpolar distribution. Peregrines, Gyrfalcons, Merlins, Golden Eagles, Ospreys, Northern Goshawks, and Northern Harriers, among the diurnal raptors; and Snowy Owls, Boreal Owls, Hawk Owls, Great Gray Owls, and Short-eared Owls among the nocturnal species, all occur both in the New World and the Old World. Very few raptor species limited to more southerly latitudes can make this claim. Very likely, this effect is largely traceable to the fact that only minor oceanic barriers to dispersal have existed between northwestern Alaska and Siberia over the ages. Indeed, during periods of low sea levels in the late Pleistocene, these two regions were connected by land.

The name Rough-legged Hawk is derived from the feathering of the legs found in this species, an unusual characteristic for a buteo, but a characteristic found also in the Ferruginous Hawk and Golden Eagle among the diurnal raptors, and in most owl, ptarmigan, and grouse species, some of which even have feathered toes. Presumably the feathering of legs and toes helps conserve heat for these extremities, and this is why the characteristic seems to be associated primarily with birds of cold climates or nocturnal habits. The correlation of feathering of legs and toes with cold climates is not perfect, however, as none of the falcons, including the Gyrfalcon, have such feathering, and some species with leg-feathering, for example a number of eagle species in the genus *Aquila*, live only at quite low latitudes.

For the most part, the Rough-legged Hawk, like the Gyrfalcon, has suffered very little from the advances of civilization, primarily because it nests so far north of developed regions. On its wintering grounds, however, the rough-leg is vulnerable to human pressures such as shooting, habitat destruction, and collisions with power lines and automobiles. Such pressures have certainly been taking their toll, though there have been no indications of long-term declines of the species at migration overlooks such as Hawk Mountain in Pennsylvania or in studies of arctic breeding populations. Presumably, over the long term, productivity on the nesting grounds has been enough to compensate for the chronic wintering losses.

Following a meal, one of the young at the tundra nest lofts excrement far beyond the nest's limits, the typical sanitation behavior of nestling accipitrids.

range farther south. Spatial overlap of the two species is most likely in the early spring, since rough-legs sometimes linger in the southwestern states until late April and zone-tails usually return to this region in March.

The nest with the single rough-leg chick rested on an inconsequential rib of gravel and rock projecting from a low bluff overlooking the Sagavanirktok River. Between visits of adults to the nest, we watched the activities of a family of seven arctic wolves not more than a couple hundred yards away on the floodplain directly below. We wondered how the rough-legs could possibly survive predation by these canines, as it was an easy stroll to reach the nest from the top of the bluff, and just as easy a stroll from the bottom of the bluff to the top. Five of the wolves were just pups, tumbling and wrestling with each other on the green tundra carpet, and like the rough-legs, they ranged from light-colored to black. In the late evening and early morning hours, the pack held extended mournful choruses in response to the calling of other wolves perhaps another mile or two upriver—possibly members of a different pack. The nearby remains of a wolf-slain caribou gave testimony to a recent feast, and we could only wish the rough-leg family the best of luck in the weeks that lay ahead.

Perhaps the rough-legs' choice of such a vulnerable nest site was dictated by the fact that a pair of Gyrfalcons was occupying what may have been their customary nest on a more substantial and protected small cliff a quarter mile away. For the most part, the rough-leg and Gyrfalcon pairs appeared to be avoiding one another, although we did see occasional aggressive aerial encounters. Other observers, however, have sometimes reported much closer nestings of these two species, and they generally appear to tolerate one another to a greater degree than do adjacent pairs of rough-legs.

Avoidance of nesting Gyrfalcons may also have been the reason why another rough-leg pair of 1987, about seventy miles away, nested completely apart from any cliff whatsoever. This nest, with three young close to fledging in mid-July, was placed on nothing more than a gentle slope of the tundra, and here again Gyrfalcons were nesting in the nearest and only locally available

Ferruginous Hawk
Buteo regalis

THE FERRUGINOUS HAWK is a very solidly built, "chesty" raptor inhabiting the Great Plains and intermontane grasslands of the western states and southern Canada. But although it is the largest North American *Buteo*, with females often weighing more than four pounds, it is one of the least familiar members of this genus for most naturalists. Formerly known as the Ferruginous Rough-legged Hawk because of its feathered legs, it is a much more heavy-bodied bird than the true Rough-legged Hawk, and much more powerful. The rusty color of the bird's leg, back, and shoulder feathers is the source of the term "ferruginous."

The Ferruginous Hawk feeds nearly exclusively on medium-sized mammals such as gophers, ground squirrels, and rabbits. It is so thoroughly adapted to open country that it commonly rests right on the ground and hunts from the ground, even in areas that offer apparently suitable perches in the form of posts, snags, and telephone poles. Because of its terrestrial tendencies, the species is often overlooked and its abundance is sometimes underestimated.

Ferruginous Hawks, like many other buteos, occur in various light and dark color phases (distinct color types). In typical light phase, the species is nearly pure white when viewed in flight from below, with a conspicuous rufous V formed by the legs against the lower abdomen and tail. The topsides of the wings are basically gray with rufous patches. In the much rarer dark phase, the body is solidly black with a rufous wash, and the wings are two toned black and white when viewed from below. The tail in both dark and light phases is basically a dirty white underneath, and this is often a very useful field mark for distinguishing this species from most other large raptors at a distance.

In addition to Ferruginous Hawks, other North American buteos exhibiting a tendency toward multiple color phases are Red-tailed Hawks, Short-tailed Hawks, Swainson's Hawks, Rough-legged Hawks, and White-tailed Hawks. At least on this continent, the trait seems somehow related to habitat, because the preceding species are all most commonly found in open habitats, while the woodland raptors, with only very rare exceptions, do not exhibit such polychromatism. Giving added support to this conclusion is the fact that dark color phases of the Red-tailed Hawk are virtually absent from the forested regions of the eastern states and West Indies, and only in the open country of the western states does this species exhibit a full array of color phases. Among the woodland buteos, only the Broad-winged Hawk shows any tendency toward color phases, but here again the tendency toward dark individuals is limited to the most western population, which nests in Alberta, and dark individuals in this species are quite rare.

Just why there is such a strong tendency toward multiple color phases in the open-country buteos is one of the more interesting unresolved questions in the biology of raptors. Perhaps variability in coloration aids the birds in recognizing other individuals at a distance—for example, mates versus territorial intruders—and perhaps this is why the trait is mainly limited to species in open habitats that can frequently see one another at great distances, distances often too great for vocal cues to be equally useful. Alternatively, the trait could in some way relate to interactions with prey species, perhaps increasing the difficulties prey might have in recognizing their predators. Studies of the Red-tailed Hawk conducted in Arkansas have suggested that different color-phased birds actually tend to position themselves differently in perching, perhaps to make themselves maximally inconspicuous to prey. In most species exhibiting color phases, light-phased individuals greatly outnumber dark-phased individuals, and this fact may

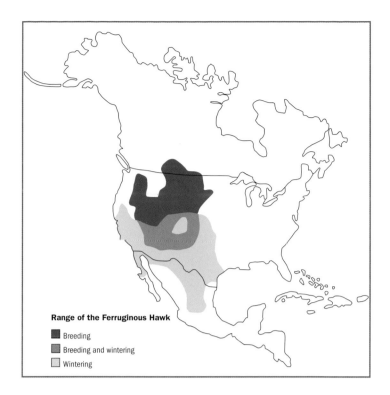

Range of the Ferruginous Hawk

■ Breeding
■ Breeding and wintering
□ Wintering

ultimately prove important in elucidating the significance of the variability. Among the variable North American raptors, a preponderance of dark-phased individuals is known only for the Florida population of Short-tailed Hawks and for females of the northeastern California population of Swainson's Hawks.

In keeping with its strong open-country habitat preferences, the Ferruginous Hawk is one of the few raptors that commonly nests on the ground, although where cliffs, bushes, or trees are available within its range, the species readily uses them, presumably because they give superior protection from terrestrial predators. An active nest we examined in southern Idaho in 1981 was placed in the top of a low juniper adjacent to a region of sagebrush and grassland stretching unbroken to the horizon. The nest itself was a bulky structure,

A dark-phased Ferruginous Hawk strokes through the late-spring skies of northern New Mexico in 1968. A powerful predator of small- and medium-sized mammals, this species almost always inhabits open country, where it commonly perches on the ground.

A pair of light-phased Ferruginous Hawks occupied a bulky nest in the top of a juniper on the edge of a vast region of southeastern Idaho prairie in 1981. The same nest was again active when checked in 1991 and 2004 and may also have been active in all other years between 1981 and 2004.

consisting mainly of massive dead branches of juniper. These were far larger than the branches generally used in nest construction by other similar-sized buteos and accipiters, suggesting an uncommon degree of strength in the species. Other observers have similarly reported unusually large materials incorporated into Ferruginous Hawk nests. In the latter part of the nineteenth century, during the period of rampant slaughter of bison on the Great Plains, Ferruginous Hawks were sometimes found attending nests constructed largely of ribs taken from skeletons of these giant mammals. Observations of Ferruginous Hawks carrying relatively large prey, such as adult rabbits, further suggest a substantial physical prowess in this species. Yet in spite of these clear manifestations of power, the talons of the Ferruginous Hawk are actually quite small for a raptor of this size.

The Idaho Ferruginous Hawk nest we first found active in 1981 was again active in both 1991 and 2004. On our last visit it held four young close to fledging in mid-June, and the size of the nest had increased to massive, eaglelike proportions—considerably more than a meter in both diameter and depth. We don't know whether the nest had been used continuously over the decades, but the substantial size increase of the structure was consistent with such a possibility. One Ferruginous Hawk nest on record is known to have been active for thirty-two consecutive years, so a precedent for such long-term use exists.

We saw only light-phased adults in all our visits over the twenty-four-year period. Thus, we cannot rule out the possibility that the same two adults could have been involved throughout. Such longevity would be surprising, however, as the maximum life span in the Ferruginous Hawk has been estimated at only about twenty years. More likely, replacements, perhaps many replacements, had occurred in the identities of the birds in attendance.

Most Ferruginous Hawks are seasonal migrants, and pair formation occurs most commonly in late February to early March, at least in southern portions of the breeding range. Nest building occurs generally in March in southern latitudes and in April in northern portions of the range. Both members of pairs share in nest construction activities, with males doing the bulk of collecting materials and females predominating in arranging of materials. Eggs appear most commonly in late April or early May, and clutch size is relatively large for such a large buteo, often averaging more than three or four eggs in years of high populations of prey mammals. Both sexes incubate, but females predominate, and eggs usually hatch after about thirty-two days. Nestlings normally fledge at about six to seven weeks of age, leaving the nest most commonly in July and remaining dependent on their parents for about a month after fledging.

Ferruginous Hawks often hunt right from the ground, perching on hillsides where they have a view of their surroundings and from which they can take off in short shallow glides to surprise victims leaving cover. At other times they hunt from low perches. In still other circumstances, such as we have observed in wintering birds in Arizona, they perch in loose groups on the ground among burrows of mammals such as gophers, waiting for unwary prey to become vulnerable at close range. Under such conditions the hawks sometimes make successful captures by thrusting their talons into the piles of loose earth the mammals are pushing up from below. In addition, Ferruginous Hawks sometimes hover over open fields, much like American Kestrels, Rough-legged Hawks, and White-tailed Kites, and they sometimes hunt from soaring flight.

The active nest contained two newly hatched young in June 1981 and was composed largely of massive juniper branches—branches far larger than those used by other buteos in nest construction. A century ago, following the period of unrestrained bison slaughter on the Great Plains, Ferruginous Hawks sometimes built their nests largely with ribs scavenged from bison skeletons.

In studying Ferruginous Hawks using various hunting methods in Idaho, James Wakely of Pennsylvania State University found that males of this species were successful in 16.6 percent of their capture attempts overall. Success was consistently greater than 20 percent, however, for birds hunting on the ground among mammal burrows and for birds hunting from high soaring or hovering flight. Birds hunting from low flight were less successful, and those hunting from low perches did worst of all, with only about 10 percent of their attempts resulting in kills. Yet in spite of the relatively low success rate in hunting from low perches, this was the most commonly used hunting method, possibly because it requires only low energy expenditure, yields a relatively high rate of return on investment, and at the same time allows the birds to be vigilant for their own predators.

Of special interest, the Ferruginous Hawks in Wakely's studies did not concentrate their foraging efforts on areas where prey density was greatest but in areas where prey vulnerability was highest because of a dearth of cover. In earlier times, many ecologists assumed that habitat quality for raptors could be specified simply by counting prey numbers or measuring prey biomass per unit area. More recent studies, however, have clearly demonstrated that for many species, prey abundance is not equivalent to prey availability. And while the data obtained from prey censusing efforts are a start toward understanding why birds of prey concentrate their foraging efforts in certain areas, the best way to measure habitat quality for these species is to study

By late June 2004, the Idaho nest had increased in size—to well over a yard in diameter—and held four healthy youngsters close to fledging.

Ferruginous Hawk

In all three visits to the Idaho nest, both nesting adults were of the light phase, although there could well have been multiple replacements of the adults during the twenty-four years between first and last visits.

their rates of prey captures relative to their foraging expenditures in various habitats. Prey numbers are often only a small component in the equation, and such factors as availability of hunting perches for the raptors, density of concealing vegetation, and age and activity levels of the prey are commonly far more important. As a general rule, most individuals of most prey species are simply not highly vulnerable to capture most of the time.

In the winter of 1987, Noel encountered a most unusual Ferruginous Hawk with our friend Arnold Moorhouse on one of his raptor census routes in the Sulfur Springs Valley of Arizona. This bird was perched on the ground, and attracted attention because it was only able to flutter and stagger ineffectively. Because of its obvious difficulties, the bird was captured to examine it for signs of injury.

In the hand, the bird seemed in good weight, and indeed it had a crop bulging with food. There were no broken bones or signs of recent injury. Close examination, however, revealed that one of the bird's eyes was highly unusual—it had what appeared to be two pupils, which lent the bird a decidedly unnerving appearance. Had the bird been shot? Was one of the pupils actually an entry point for a lead pellet? If so, the eye had healed over remarkably well. There was no disfiguration to its shape, and the cornea appeared unblemished. Further, there were no ragged edges to either of the irises surrounding the pupils. It all looked relatively natural, yet at the

same time horribly supernatural. Until one sees such a bird, it is easy to forget how confidently we all rely on the cosmic rule of one pupil per eye in vertebrates.

Whether the bird's inability to fly was in some way related to its unusual eye was unclear, but regardless, it was surprising that the bird seemed to be in reasonably good physical condition. Somehow it was surviving in spite of its handicaps, though how it was managing to feed itself remains a mystery.

Around their nests, Ferruginous Hawks have a reputation for being acutely sensitive to human activities, and they are one of the falconiform species most likely to desert nests, at least early-stage nests, after disturbance. Perhaps not surprisingly, studies indicate that nesting success in these hawks depends heavily on the degree of remoteness of nest sites from developed areas. Such sensitivity argues for great caution in conducting reproductive studies with this species, and overall conservation of the species apparently must include effective safeguards to minimize human activities on the breeding grounds. The Ferruginous Hawk has the smallest total range of any of the buteos found in North America, and recent rough estimates suggest that its total population might include only about ten thousand to twenty thousand individuals. In the event of future environmental stresses, the species could quickly drop to a truly threatened status. For this reason, the Ferruginous Hawk merits special concern and continued close monitoring.

White-tailed Hawk
Buteo albicaudatus

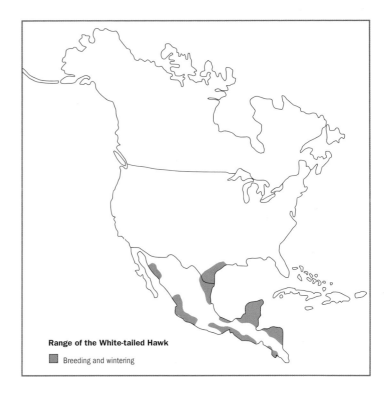

Range of the White-tailed Hawk

- Breeding and wintering

THE SOUTHEASTERLY SEA winds blow humid, warm, strong, and steady, bringing mostly cloudy skies to the southern coast of Texas. These forces create a unique combination of direct and indirect environmental conditions that are important to the ecology of one of the most attractive of North America's raptors, the White-tailed Hawk. The white-tail is one of the larger buteos of the continent, with a wingspread usually exceeding four feet and a weight usually exceeding two pounds, and its wide distribution extends as far south as southern South America. North of the Mexican border, however, it rarely occurs anywhere else but along the southeastern coast of the Lone Star State. In parts of South America it is geographically replaced by two other very similar buteos, the Red-backed Buzzard and Gurney's Buzzard. All are presently considered separate species, but it is possible they might better be considered geographic races of a single species.

In Texas, the white-tail is frequently seen in the flat transitional habitats between the coastal beaches and the dense thorn-scrub vegetation farther inland. In this zone of open grasslands and marshes with scattered low shrubs, prickly pear, and Spanish daggers, the hawk finds very favorable hunting conditions for its primary prey of rabbits, small mammals, and diverse birds, reptiles, and arthropods. Here the species occurs in dense populations, with pairs defending regularly spaced territories against other white-tails and intruders such as Crested Caracaras.

A prime example of good white-tail habitat is the coastal pastureland region lying just inland from Port Mansfield south through the Laguna Atascosa National Wildlife Refuge. Here, in the spring of 1987 and 1988, we had an opportunity to watch the activities of half a dozen pairs and become familiar with many aspects of their behavior. The birds had spaced their nests at distances of approximately a mile, and the low relief and open nature of the habitat allowed us to observe the entire foraging ranges of specific pairs from single vantage points.

Though they often hunt from perches, especially during the early morning and evening hours, White-tailed Hawks are accomplished aerial hunters who prosper in the coastal gales. Hanging high in the sky, they face directly into the wind. Their long wings beat only rarely but nevertheless are kept in constant motion, extending in and out from the body while simultaneously their tails flex up and down. With these minor postural adjustments, the birds maintain a nearly stationary position in the face of continual vagaries of the winds. Normally, the birds spend about a third of each day in such aerial hunting during the time they have young in the nest.

Poised perhaps two hundred feet from the ground, a foraging white-tail is not conspicuous to human observers, but it has a commanding view of the terrain and any potential prey leaving cover. Characteristically, the hawk remains in one position during an extended, leisurely inspection of the ground below, then drifts to another position, moving from one end of its territory to the other and back again in stages. When prey is sighted, the hawk begins an approach, which is often a long, uninterrupted stoop to the ground. Sometimes, however, the bird descends in phases, pulling up short at intermediate heights, sometimes hovering for a second or two as if pondering the possibilities of success. Then finally, it either continues on down in a capture attempt, or thinking the better of the situation, shifts over to soar back up to greater altitudes to resume general scanning.

In many respects this hunting behavior strongly resembles the usual hunting method of the Short-tailed Hawk. Both species forage from such high altitudes

A landscape featuring prickly pear, Spanish daggers, and scattered mesquites and huisache, southern Texas's windswept coastal plain forms the White-tailed Hawk's principal North American habitat. This raptor also occurs in scattered open habitats south to Argentina. Throughout its range, it preys mainly on small terrestrial mammals, reptiles, and birds.

In flight, the White-tailed Hawk resembles the light-phased Short-tailed Hawk in coloration and behavior but not in size. Both species have light-colored tails with a dark subterminal or terminal band, light underparts, and dark cheeks. Moreover, both commonly hunt by hanging high in the wind, patiently inspecting the terrain below.

that they are likely to be overlooked, and both hang in the wind as they patiently inspect the terrain for potential victims. Furthermore, the shape and coloration for the light-phased forms of both species have some close similarities. Both species have a short tail relative to their wingspread, and in both the tail is basically white with a dark band near the tip. Further, both have dark gray or brown upperparts and largely white underparts, with dark cheeks and a chestnut patch in the shoulder or neck region. Major differences between the species lie in overall size and in the fact that they concentrate on quite different prey—birds in the case of the short-tail, and predominantly mammals in the case of the larger white-tail, although the white-tails also take birds and other prey types with fair frequency. While the underlying causes of the visual similarity of these two raptors are not obvious, they represent an intriguing subject for future research.

Alarm cries of the White-tailed Hawk are a curious *raa kadick kadick kadick* when disturbed at the nest, but the birds are not at all bold in defending nests and mainly circle so high overhead and at such a distance that you hardly notice their scolding. Possibly because of the battering winds in the region, the white-tails generally place their bulky, coarse nests in compact shrubs relatively close to the ground, eschewing sites in taller and less stable vegetation. Nests are often in bushes or Spanish daggers on small rises or dunes, where the birds have an unobstructed view of their surroundings and can detect the approach of potential predators from a great distance.

A female White-tailed Hawk gently descends to her nest in the brisk southeasterly winds of coastal Texas in 1988. Blowing almost constantly, these winds provide steady uplift for nearly effortless hang-hunting.

White-tails commonly line their nests with grasses—often whole grass plants including roots. Though an unusual lining for a raptor nest, grass provides a relatively soft substrate for eggs and chicks, similar to the moss lining of Swallow-tailed Kite nests. The single-egg clutch in this nest was atypical, as most white-tail nests in the region held two young.

One nest we watched from a distance for a number of days was placed about eight feet from the ground in a mesquite tangled with vines. This nest was deeply concave and lined with grass. It held but a single egg, which we suspected may have been inviable, because most pairs in the region already had chicks at fledging age. This pair attended their egg only fitfully, and it appeared that they might well have been in the process of desertion, after having incubated long past the expected hatching date. Nevertheless, detailed studies of nesting pairs by Craig Farquhar of Texas A&M University have revealed that normal incubation of this species is surprisingly inconsistent. Pairs frequently leave their eggs unattended for several hours at a time, yet with no apparent detrimental effects on hatching success. This style of incubation represents a strong departure from the usual falconiform pattern. It is possible that what we first interpreted as desertion behavior was in fact only typical incubation behavior.

At another nest only about four feet from the ground, we watched adults alternately feeding one fledged chick on the ground near the nest and another chick still in the nest. Two other nests slightly higher above the ground also held two chicks apiece. Thus, two chicks per nest appeared to be the norm, and they were very dark in color, quite unlike their parents in general appearance. Dark-phased adult white-tails also occur, but they are unknown for North America. We have encountered them in grassland habitats of western Brazil.

Studies indicate that nestling white-tails normally fledge at about fifty days of age, but they remain at least partially dependent on their parents for an extremely long period after fledging—about seven months—after which the adults begin a new nesting effort and literally chase their fledglings out of the nesting territory.

Aside from resident Bay-winged Hawks, Crested Caracaras, White-tailed Kites, Black Vultures, and Turkey Vultures, we found few other raptors in the region occupied by the Texas white-tails. Migrating flocks of Broad-winged Hawks, Swainson's Hawks, and Mississippi Kites passed through in the early breeding season, but they were largely gone by the time the white-tails had young in their nests. The white-tails themselves are not normally migratory, and breeding pairs usually remain on territory throughout the year, although there is some dispersal of nonbreeders in the nonbreeding season.

Near Aldama in coastal Tamaulipas, Mexico, a White-tailed Hawk preens her tail feathers during a break from nest duties.

Although some Red-tailed Hawks winter in the range of the white-tails, the virtual absence of Red-tailed Hawks during the breeding seasons we observed was especially interesting in view of the widespread distribution and abundance of this species in North America. Whether the rarity of red-tails here might be a result of this species being an inferior competitor to the white-tails, or the result of other more subtle factors, is not immediately obvious. Red-tailed Hawks are certainly capable of thriving in some habitats with strong winds, such as the dense population we have studied in the very windy upper elevations of the Luquillo Mountains of eastern Puerto Rico. Likewise, it is questionable that the absence of tall trees for nesting in coastal Texas might be a serious impediment for red-tails, as this species readily nests in quite low yuccas in the grassland regions of New Mexico. A detailed comparative study of the red-tails and white-tails of southern Texas, examining what factors limit distributions and reproductive success and how the two species interact, could be of considerable interest in understanding why these species occupy the habitats they do.

Intensive studies of the White-tailed Hawk by researchers Mark Kopeny and Craig Farquhar have revealed that the species has been relatively stable and perhaps increasing in Texas in recent years, although its overall numbers have apparently been considerably lower than they were a century ago. Historically, the species was also occasionally recorded in Arizona and New Mexico, and it was sometimes known to breed in southern Arizona in the nineteenth century. In Texas, the overall ecology of the species appears to be quite compatible with the cattle grazing practiced on most of the coastal prairies and scrublands. As long as these lands are not plowed under for crops, are not allowed to grow up to dense brush, or are not detrimentally overgrazed, the White-tailed Hawk should be able to endure as a local resident, provided future climatic trends do not disrupt the region's basic ecology.

White-tailed Hawk

Zone-tailed Hawk
Buteo albonotatus

I T WAS A COOL SPRING MORNING in the San Simon Valley of eastern Arizona in 1970. Alongside the road, the usual Turkey Vultures were circling leisurely overhead in a tireless quest for carrion, while Cactus Wrens, Mourning Doves, and Gambel's Quail called from the mesquite thickets. A peaceful scene; nothing out of the ordinary; nothing to suggest violence or stress. Then suddenly, one Turkey Vulture from a group of three partially folded its wings and powered into a stoop toward the ground in a remarkably unvulturelike maneuver. The stoop, as it turned out, was directed at a Mourning Dove, which just barely avoided capture by dodging to one side as the vulture came barreling in at a shallow angle out of the sun.

Was this really a Turkey Vulture? It certainly looked like one as it circled back up into the sky and hastened to rejoin its flock mates, who had moved a half mile down the valley. The long wings tipped up at an angle from horizontal and the two-toned pattern of the wings all seemed normal for the species. A closer look through binoculars, however, revealed that what seemed like a vulture's naked head was really just a bright yellow cere merging with a conspicuous naked patch of skin in front of the bird's eyes. The bird's head was otherwise fully feathered. And what we had taken to be a vulture's excrement-covered white feet lying flush against its tail was actually a white band of the hawk's tail itself. What had appeared to be a Turkey Vulture acting very strangely was really a Zone-tailed Hawk doing what it apparently knows best—using its Turkey Vulture–like appearance to get close to unsuspecting prey.

That the Zone-tailed Hawk might be a true mimic of the Turkey Vulture was first pointed out by Edwin Willis of the University of California in 1963 and has been vigorously debated ever since. Willis noted the close similarity in size, coloration, and flight characteristics of the two species, and the fact that zone-tails do not occur outside the range of the Turkey Vulture. He also called attention to the curious black coloration of juvenile zone-tails, representing an abrupt departure from the usual brown-streaked appearance of other young buteos, but which might be expected in a species dependent at all ages on its visual resemblance to the dark Turkey Vulture. Only at close range can white speckles be seen on the body feathers of juvenile zone-tails. From any distance they appear solid black. Willis's hypothesis was an excellent one, and one we have come to believe is very possibly correct after watching this species on numerous occasions in southern Arizona and New Mexico.

The close association of zone-tails with Turkey Vultures extends much further than Willis noted, for we have found that zone-tails in southern Arizona and New Mexico frequently nest very close to Turkey Vulture roosts, and the species has a strong tendency to fly with groups of Turkey Vultures as it hunts. While it is not difficult to tell the two species apart when they are at very close range, at the usual distances above the terrain that they forage, their similarity is very deceptive. On more than one occasion we thought we were photographing a zone-tail in a group of Turkey Vultures, only to find that once the photos were processed, many were of a Turkey Vulture alone. It is reasonable to suppose that other visually oriented species may also have difficulty in distinguishing these two species. Further, it seems plausible that for those kinds of prey that can learn over time the needlessness of responding in panic to soaring Turkey Vultures, the close resemblance of the two species may allow zone-tails an important advantage in making close approaches without causing alarm.

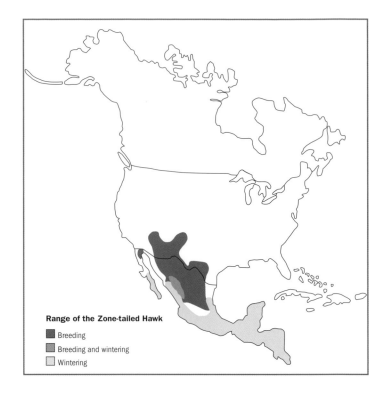

Range of the Zone-tailed Hawk
■ Breeding
■ Breeding and wintering
□ Wintering

Small birds are one sort of prey that might be capable of learning that Turkey Vultures are not a threat, and as we learned in observations of foraging zone-tails and in close study of pairs of zone-tails at their nests, small birds, such as meadowlarks and doves, form an important part of the zone-tail's diet. It would be remarkable if a slow-cruising raptor like the zone-tail were able to catch such prey without some special adaptations.

The relatively long toes and claws of the zone-tail also strongly suggest that birds might be frequent in its diet. These characteristics are not usually found in buteo hawks, but they are conspicuous in bird-specialists such as Peregrine Falcons and certain accipiters, presumably aiding these species in grasping prey covered by loose feathers. Another feature consistent with a substantial focus on birds in the diet of zone-tails is a quite strong difference in sizes of the sexes, with female zone-tails normally weighing about 40 percent more than males. Zone-tails also take considerable numbers of lizards and mammals (in some areas they seem to concentrate on lizards), and these are also prey that might be capable of learning Turkey Vultures are normally no danger.

Zone-tails do not always hunt together with Turkey Vultures, and when they are flying alone they appear to have greater difficulty deceiving potential prey. Over a period of several days, we once watched the reactions of Mourning Doves feeding in an open field in southern Arizona as Turkey Vultures and zone-tails came in over the region. As long as the vultures and zone-tails came in as a group, we saw relatively little response in the doves, but if a zone-tail came in alone they took off in a startled panic. Remarkably, they also often took off in alarm if Turkey Vultures came in singly. The doves seemed to have difficulty telling the two species apart, and they appeared to decide whether to flee at least in part on the basis of how many Turkey Vulture–like birds were foraging together.

We saw the same responses repeatedly, so it seemed likely that we were observing a real difference in the responses of the doves to single and grouped birds. These observations suggested a strong advantage for zone-tails that ally themselves with Turkey Vultures in foraging. The apparent extent of this advantage was reflected in the success rates in capture attempts we recorded over the years in the southwestern states. Of a total of forty-five attempts at prey when zone-tails were foraging alone, only 6.7 percent were successful. In contrast, of ten attempts made in the presence of Turkey Vultures, 30 percent succeeded, a statistically significant difference that suggests zone-tails do indeed have better foraging success when they are near groups of Turkey Vultures. Nevertheless, the sample size of observations is quite small. To adequately test the validity of these proposed relationships, the differences noted need to be confirmed in additional regions and populations.

In our observations of actual prey capture attempts, a zone-tail almost always delayed its stoop until after it had spotted prey and flown on some distance in typical leisurely Turkey Vulture fashion, although its eyes remained obviously fixed on the prey. Once it had soared on out of view of the prey, it half closed its wings and doubled back in a shallow stoop, taking full advantage of cover to get as close as possible to the prospective victim without being seen. As it neared the prey, the zone-tail finally darted around a rock or bush at the last instant, catching its victim by surprise.

Thus, the Zone-tailed Hawk apparently uses its resemblance to the Turkey Vulture mainly to locate prey without unduly alarming it, and not actually to approach prey in capture attempts. The Jekyll-Hyde transformation of a slow-cruising zone-tail into a rapidly approaching feathered demon normally takes place instantaneously and out of the prey's view, leaving the prey with almost no warning and very little time to escape once the hawk's stoop becomes visible to the prey. The same flight agility seen in zone-tails making capture attempts also becomes quickly apparent to researchers climbing to zone-tail nests. This hawk typically defends its nests very aggressively, with highly maneuverable dives and swoops.

Zone-tail hunts are fascinating to witness. The main impediment to making observations lies in finding zone-tails in the first place. We have found it worthwhile to scan every group of Turkey Vultures

At her nest high in a cottonwood in southern Arizona, a female Zone-tailed Hawk and her single chick await the return of the male with food. Most prey at this nest consisted of open-country birds such as meadowlarks.

encountered in the zone-tail's range. More than occasionally one individual in the group turns out to be one of these "invisible" black buteos.

The kind of mimicry potentially shown by the zone-tail is known as aggressive mimicry, and for this type of mimicry, as well as for some other types, the whole system can break down if the mimic becomes too numerous relative to the model species. Zone-tailed hawks, while not exceedingly rare, are very thinly spread in the southwestern states, and it is uncommon to find two pairs nesting closer than about five or six miles from one another, a sparse distribution consistent with the mimicry hypothesis. Overall, in a Texas-to-Arizona survey of this species Helen conducted with fellow raptor researcher Rich Glinski in 1976, a total of only about a hundred known nesting locations were documented north of the Mexican border. Although

many additional pairs undoubtedly exist in the states (Glinski has recently made a revised estimate of 125 pairs for Arizona alone) and although zone-tails also occur south through Central America and into South America, they are not known to occur in dense concentrations anywhere.

The most unexpected setting in which we have encountered Zone-tailed Hawks was the floodplain rain forests along the Manu River in southeastern Peru. Here in the spring of 1989, we found a zone-tail regularly hunting over a swale of dead palms that was home for a small nesting colony of Blue and Gold Macaws. Also cruising regularly over the area were Greater Yellow-headed Vultures, which are very similar at a distance to the Turkey Vulture and may serve as an alternative model species for the zone-tails of this region. Twice in one morning we watched the zone-tail dive into

Zone-tailed Hawk

Arizona's zone-tails often nest in tall streamside sycamores, and at high elevations they commonly breed in pines. In Texas, zone-tails sometimes build nests on cliffs.

Female Zone-tailed Hawks average more than 40 percent heavier than their mates, a strong size difference between sexes consistent with a diet that includes many small birds. Also consistent with such a diet are the zone-tail's relatively long toes.

a vine-covered tree close by the macaw nests. Once it came up with a struggling lizard in its talons. We were not able to determine if the second attempt was also successful. Nevertheless, it is noteworthy that the bird returned to make a second capture attempt in the very same tree it had earlier hunted successfully. It was clearly the same bird, judging from several flight feather peculiarities.

In the desert near Yuma, Arizona, zone-tails sometimes nest in modest-sized ironwoods, but in most of Arizona, they characteristically nest high in tall trees, often in cottonwoods or sycamores along desert streams, but sometimes in pines in more mountainous regions. In contrast, some Texas zone-tails nest on cliff ledges. Two eggs comprise a normal clutch, and the eggs are usually white but sometimes are marked with dark blotches, as is typical for most buteos. While not unusually large for a medium-sized buteo, the eggs are of considerable size, a fact that was first learned under singular circumstances by a renowned ornithologist of the 1870s, Major Charles Bendire. It is worth repeating his account of this discovery, which appears in his *Life Histories of North American Birds*, as a cautionary tale:

> *On May 3, I paid a second visit to this locality [Rillito Creek near Tucson] and found one of the birds [zone-tails] on the nest, where it*

remained until I rode up to the tree and rapped on it with the butt of my shotgun. This caused it to fly off about 50 yards farther up, on the opposite site of the dry creek bed, where it alighted in a smaller tree. As the bird appeared so very tame I concluded to examine the nest before attempting to secure the parent, and it was well I did so. Climbing to the nest I found another egg, and at the same instant saw from my elevated position something else which could not have been observed from the ground, namely, several Apache Indians crouched down on the side of a little canon which opened into the creek bed about 80 yards farther up. They were evidently watching me, their heads being raised just to a level with the top of the canon.

> *In those days Apache Indians were not the most desirable neighbors, especially when one was up a tree and unarmed; I therefore descended as leisurely as possible knowing that if I showed any especial haste in getting down they would suspect me of having seen them; the egg I had placed in my mouth as the quickest and safest way that I could think of to dispose of it—and rather an uncomfortable large mouthful it was, too—nevertheless I reached the ground safely, and with my horse and shotgun, lost no time in getting to high and open ground. . . . I found it no easy matter to remove the egg from my mouth without injury, but I finally succeeded, though my jaws ached for some time afterward.*

In flight, the Zone-tailed Hawk resembles the Turkey Vulture in its uptilted two-toned wings, overall black coloration, and slow progress in flight. Research ers have debated for decades whether the zone-tail uses this resemblance to aid in the capture of prey that consider the Turkey Vulture innocuous.

Those who ignore the lessons of history are sometimes condemned to relive them. Having forgotten all about Major Bendire's travails, Noel indeed had the misfortune to replicate them with a different species—coincidentally not all that far from where Bendire made his famous getaway. The setting was a particularly high Cooper's Hawk nest of 1970 that we were checking periodically to follow its progress. On the occasion in question, Noel could see from the ground that the nest contained well-developed nestlings, but on making the climb he found, unexpectedly, that the nest also contained an especially large, but inviable, egg. Since we were then routinely analyzing accipiter eggs for pesticide residues, it was important to collect this egg.

Unfortunately, there was no obvious way to get the egg safely to the ground. Noel had made the climb without any sort of pack and needed both hands free for the descent. Needless to say, the possibility of climbing all the way down and then all the way back up with a proper container was too much trouble. Consequently, without any premonitions of disaster, he casually slid the egg into his mouth.

The descent of the tree was uneventful, except for our unsuspecting victim's growing appreciation that a whole addled Cooper's Hawk egg can have a very peculiar and unpleasant flavor. When it came time to remove the egg at the base of the tree, however, he found, like Major Bendire, that this was a most difficult task. Jaws open only just so far, and the egg proved

to be almost impossible to grasp and advance past the front teeth. The realization of this fact, coupled with a realization that the essence of stale Cooper's Hawk was rapidly soaking off the shell and heading straight for nausea centers of the brain, led to dark thoughts about oxygen deprivation, catastrophic convulsions, and cardiac arrest.

Did Major Bendire experience the same desperate worries? His published account is silent about such matters. Since the egg he collected was fresh, rather than addled, he presumably missed out on the nausea factor with his egg. But any advantage here might well have been overwhelmed by the urgency of his predicament with respect to the Apaches. In any event, the jammed Cooper's Hawk egg, like Major Bendire's zone-tail egg, only came free after a seemingly interminable period of painful jaw contortions.

In the long run, conservation of the Zone-tailed Hawk may depend significantly on the good health of its apparent model species, the Turkey Vulture. In overall status, the Turkey Vulture appears to be holding up well in recent years and even expanding in range in northeastern regions. But should Turkey Vulture populations of the Southwest ever drop below some hypothetical threshold, the zone-tails could face significant declines in hunting efficiency. Assuming the zone-tail is a true mimic, its effective conservation may only be possible if considered in tandem with conservation of the model species upon which it depends.

Zone-tailed Hawk

Common Black Hawk

Buteogallus anthracinus

Range of the Common Black Hawk
■ Breeding
■ Breeding and wintering

A T REST, THE COMMON BLACK HAWK is a virtual twin of the Zone-tailed Hawk, just as the zone-tail is a twin of the Turkey Vulture in flight. Black hawks and zone-tails are very close to the same size, with wingspreads slightly greater than four feet, and both are completely dark in color, except for white bands on the tail. Moreover, both species can often be found nesting in the very same river bottoms in the southwestern states. The great similarity in appearance and range of these two hawks led to considerable confusion in early records of their occurrence, even among experienced naturalists. Confusions between the two continue to bedevil bird-watchers.

Yet the two species can be distinguished readily by vocalizations, by their shape in flight, and by the prey they feed on. It does not seem likely that they are true mimics of each other. Soaring overhead, the black hawk displays much broader wings than the zone-tail, and its tail is quite short, projecting only a short distance beyond the trailing edge of the wings, quite unlike the long tail of the zone-tail. Another characteristic helping to distinguish these two species in flight is the presence of a small white patch at the base of the outer primary feathers in the black hawk and the absence of this patch in the zone-tail. Once these differences are learned, it is relatively simple to separate the two species under most conditions.

Only during migration are Common Black Hawks likely to occur at any distance from a permanent stream, so during much of the year any large black raptor with a white band on the tail flying over dry desert regions will almost surely turn out to be a zone-tail. The black hawk is closely tied to aquatic ecosystems, both for feeding and nesting, and while zone-tails sometimes nest near black hawks, they feed in a great variety of ecological zones, many of them far from water. Were it not for the fact that tall trees are concentrated near streams in the desert regions, the zone-tails probably would not show any significant tendency to nest in the same areas as black hawks.

Unlike the zone-tails, black hawks are perch hunters, carefully scanning the riparian forest floor and streambeds from positions relatively low in trees or from prominent rocks in the watercourses. From such vantage points they are able to locate the fish, frogs, snakes, lizards, and aquatic insects that form their usual diet, and they normally capture prey in short descending pounces. Although black hawks eat a mix of terrestrial and aquatic prey, aquatic creatures make up the bulk of the species' diet throughout its North American range.

Farther south, in Central and South America, the Common Black Hawk also concentrates on aquatic fare. There it often occurs in mangrove swamps, where it is an enthusiastic predator of crabs and is known regionally as the Crab Hawk. In November 2004 we watched Common Black Hawks habitually foraging for crabs in the ocean surf zone of Corcovado National Park in Costa Rica. Perching on floating piles of flotsam heaving in the waves, these birds scanned their surroundings intently and with great success made rapid flapping sorties at nearby crabs that were crawling out of the water onto loose debris.

North of the Mexican border, the Common Black Hawk breeds nearly exclusively along well-wooded permanent watercourses of the southwestern states. Such habitat is quite limited in the region, making it feasible to estimate the size of the population in the United States. In 1976 and 1977, Helen collaborated with Arizona researcher Rich Glinski in hiking many of the remaining permanent streams of Arizona and New Mexico to find nesting pairs and evaluate detailed habitat preferences of the species. The project traversed some of the wildest country of the Southwest and yielded an overall estimate of about two hundred and twenty to two hundred and fifty pairs. These were concentrated largely in Arizona and, to a lesser extent, in New Mexico, although a few pairs also occurred in Texas and occasionally in southern Utah.

The center of black hawk distribution north of the border is along the streams draining the Mogollon Rim country into the Salt, Gila, and Verde rivers of central Arizona. This is a wild, roadless region of forested mountain streams that still remain largely inaccessible to all but the most dedicated hikers. Here, in the best riparian habitats, black hawk pairs are spaced at intervals as close as a mile to a mile and a half from one another.

The streams of this region are notable for placid stretches lined with cottonwoods, sycamores, walnuts, and alders alternating with vertical red-rock gorges too narrow to allow the growth of any riparian vegetation. In many stretches, the only way to follow the canyon bottoms is to wade and swim down the watercourses themselves, hoping that forward progress will not be blocked by impassable waterfalls or chutes. The polished rock surfaces slickened by a surface layer of algae often urge the hiker along faster than seems safe, and sometimes it is impossible to see far enough ahead to anticipate difficult stretches before being thrust into them. Too narrow and too broken up with boulders and debris to allow boating or rafting, many of these streams present an unending succession of unpredictable challenges and should not be attempted alone or without waterproof containers for food and other gear. A flash flood from a summer thunderstorm can close off escape routes along the canyon bottoms within minutes and leave a hiker stranded for many hours.

Despite these difficulties, the black hawk's domain is an entrancingly beautiful one of stream-chiseled rock formations and grotesque, flood-battered tree trunks piled high with debris on their upstream sides. The deep

Right: *At a nest in a sycamore along a Gila River tributary in Arizona, Common Black Hawks supplied their single chick with a variety of aquatic foods. Included were garter snakes, frogs, and some fish so large the birds could hardly carry them.*

The Common Black Hawk and the Zone-tailed Hawk have similar color patterns, but in flight, the black hawk distinguishes itself by its broader wings and shorter tail.

clear pools provide welcome refreshment from the midday heat, as well as a source of aquatic insects to sustain many of the resident birds of the region. American Dippers concentrate on the larvae and nymphs of these insects, submerging themselves completely beneath the water's surface to hunt their victims. Emerging adult insects are vulnerable to Black Phoebes sallying from boulder to boulder along the water's edge. Those insects reaching higher elevations above the water must take their chances with swifts and swallows coursing ceaselessly overhead. Canyon Wrens also take their toll and proclaim their ownership of the precipitous rocky walls with loud cascading calls that ring and echo down the chasms.

The black hawks are most commonly found along the more peaceful stretches, but they generally keep just ahead and out of sight around the bend. Only at nests do they make a stand and challenge an intruder with angry cries, flying from tree to tree, landing on rocky outcrops of the canyon walls, or circling overhead. The alarm calls of the hawks are very reminiscent of the alarm cries of Bald Eagles—a series of sputtering staccato notes very different from the long drawn-out tremulous screams of nesting Zone-tailed Hawks.

In 1976 and 1977, we watched several pairs of black hawks from treetop blinds. Our primary study pair was nesting sixty feet up in a tall sycamore along a tributary of the Gila River. The nest was a substantial platform of twigs in a sturdy crotch, and the adults kept it well decorated with greenery. It held a single chick who was fed a diet of frogs, fish, and snakes, some of which were so large that the adults were barely able to carry them to the nest. Such nests are often strong enough to be reused for many years by the hawks. Probably more than half the nests we have found over the years have been built on limb junctions where large dead branches had fallen into live crotches, providing especially well-braced support for the structures.

Common Black Hawks nesting in North America generally arrive in March and depart again in October. Egg laying normally starts in April, and the clutch usually consists of only one or two eggs. Young most commonly hatch in late May and fledge in July, but they remain dependent on their parents for food through August and into September. As they develop, juvenile black hawks, unlike juvenile zone-tails, acquire a streaked brown plumage similar to the juvenile plumage of almost all buteonine raptors. After fledging, they tend to remain within the territory of their parents until their first fall migration. Black hawks normally migrate solitarily, though we have sometimes seen a number pass by during a single October day along mountain ridgelines of southern Arizona.

For many years, Jay Schnell, a biologist living along Aravaipa Creek in eastern Arizona, made a thorough study of the Common Black Hawks in his home canyon. This population is especially dependent on aquatic prey because the

Right: *The Common Black Hawk's vocalizations differ markedly from those of the Zone-tailed Hawk and allow certain identification of the birds around nests. Whereas zone-tails sound alarm with thin descending whistles, black hawks give a long series of sputtering short notes similar to the calls of Bald Eagles.*

In Costa Rica's Corcovado National Park, Common Black Hawks often hunt for marine crabs on floating masses of detritus in the surf zone. From perched positions on the detritus, the hawks make quick flying dashes to capture their prey.

creek bottom is narrowly incised in a region of towering cliffs and the area of bottomland floodplain adjoining the stream is quite minimal. In close observations of nests, Schnell has found that more than 70 percent of the birds' diet is fish and frogs, mostly caught within quite short distances of the nests.

The black hawk pairs of Aravaipa have formed an exceedingly stable array over the years, and this canyon constitutes one of the most reliable, and certainly one of the most spectacular, locations for finding the species in North America. Here, black hawk pairs are interspersed with pairs of Zone-tailed Hawks and Cooper's Hawks along the riparian zone. Higher slopes and cliffs of the canyon host Peregrine Falcons, Prairie Falcons, and Golden Eagles. Fortunately, a large portion of the canyon is protected in a preserve of the Nature Conservancy and a wilderness area of the Bureau of Land Management, and the security of this thriving community of diurnal raptors appears to be well ensured.

Although the North American population of Common Black Hawks appears to be self-sustaining at present, the species exhibits a relatively low reproductive rate and it is not a raptor that could absorb much in the way of increased threats of mortality. These birds are vulnerable to losses of riparian habitats due to both overgrazing and invasion by salt cedar, and they may also be vulnerable to spread of the exotic watercress into permanent streams. Dense mats of this surface plant may significantly obscure the visibility of prey, just as dense mats of floating water hyacinth are a problem for Everglade Kites in some areas of Florida, although this potential effect has not received comprehensive study. Furthermore, the riparian zones of Arizona and New Mexico are in high demand as recreation areas and for housing developments. In accessible riparian areas, Common Black Hawks have not been faring well in the face of human disturbance and harassment. One nesting female of a pair we had been monitoring along a heavily used creek in east-central Arizona in 1977 was shot right on her nest, a fate that others have likely met as well.

The conservation of the Common Black Hawk depends on maintaining important regions of riparian habitat, like that found in Aravaipa Canyon, free from excessive development and disturbance. Less than half of the known black hawk nesting territories are on public lands, and the long-term future of many of the private lands on which the bird lives is uncertain. Unfortunately, black hawks do not occur commonly in the recently created San Pedro National Conservation Area of the Bureau of Land Management, a riparian preserve of crucial importance to the conservation of Gray Hawks. The primary protection for the species at present comes from the remoteness of many regions where it does occur.

Bay-winged (Harris's) Hawk

Parabuteo unicinctus

Range of the Bay-winged Hawk

Breeding and wintering

ONE OF THE MOST CHARACTERISTIC birds of the Sonoran Desert of southern Arizona is the Bay-winged Hawk, also known as Harris's Hawk. These hawks often place their nests in the arms of giant saguaro cacti and perch on their prickly tops as they hunt for the diverse mammals and birds that constitute their prey. This same desert is also home to a variety of other raptors, ranging from Elf and Great Horned Owls to Red-tailed Hawks, and its complex vegetation supports surprisingly high densities of prey in spite of the overall scarcity of water.

Yet Bay-winged Hawks are not limited to saguaro-dominated deserts. They also do well in various thorn-scrub brushlands that lack this enormous cactus. Moreover, they have been expanding their range in some of these latter habitats in recent years. The Bay-winged Hawk, as a whole, has a

A fledgling Bay-winged Hawk ends his first tentative flight atop the fruit-laden arm of a saguaro. Fledglings, especially males, often retain an association with their parents for several years and assist in caring for later broods.

North American distribution that extends from the Colorado River basin in the west to central Texas in the east, and it also occurs as a common raptor in brushy country south through Central America and into South America.

The bay-wing is a medium-sized raptor—about one-and-a-half to two-and-a-quarter pounds in weight—with an overall dark brown coloration set off by handsome chestnut patches on the legs and shoulders. The underwing coverts are also a rich chestnut color and give the bird a very attractive pattern in flight. From a distance, another of the most obvious features of coloration is a conspicuously white base to the tail, visible both from above and below. Immatures are fairly similar to adults in appearance but have a streaked brown-and-white breast instead of a solid dark-brown breast.

The biology of the bay-wing is highly unusual for a raptor. Unlike any other North American hawks, bay-wings commonly breed in groups, with more than two adult birds attending many nests. They also hunt in groups and commonly breed several times a year. Moreover, they occupy some of the most challenging thermal environments of any North American raptor, with ambient temperatures often rising significantly above optimal incubation and brooding temperatures.

Intensive research on these peculiarities was started by Tucson researcher Bill Mader in the early 1970s and has been continued in more recent years by a succession of other researchers. Mader's pioneering studies in Arizona revealed that many nests of Bay-winged Hawks were attended by trios of adults, consisting in every case studied of a female with two males. And in at least several cases, both males copulated frequently, and apparently successfully, with the female, so it seems very possible that true polyandry was involved, with both males contributing genetically to the broods. Whether or not both males actually fertilized eggs, all members of the trios studied helped feed the broods and defend the nests. Overall, the trios were much more successful producing young than were pairs, a result since confirmed in other studies.

More recent research on a large color-banded Arizona population conducted by Jim Dawson, Bob Sheehy, and Bill Mannan of the University of Arizona has revealed an astonishing diversity of additional reproductive patterns in the species. In this 1990s study, Bay-winged Hawks also commonly bred in groups, but the groups usually consisted of more than three birds, often including peripheral individuals who rarely came close to nests, but who nevertheless passed food to the "core" bay-wings attending the nests. The existence of these peripheral individuals was only determined by careful, long-term observations from blinds. The composition of groups attending nests was highly variable, ranging from pairs, to polygynous assemblages of one male with several females, to a more common association of one female with several males. One nest Dawson showed us in 1989 was tended by two males and two females. Each male copulated with both females, and both females closely attended the brood.

The breeding groups in this Arizona study appeared to be primarily family groups in which fledglings, especially males, remained associated with their parents for several years. Some group members, however, were immigrants from other families, and helpers were by no means restricted to young males. While more than one male typically attempted copulations with the single egg-laying female found in most groups, usually only one male copulated successfully with this female. So while polyandry and polygyny definitely occurred in some groups, as demonstrated conclusively by DNA analyses of offspring, the usual pattern appeared to be monogamous pairs assisted by one or more nonbreeding helpers, mostly previous offspring.

Monogamous pairs assisted by helpers have also been the usual pattern reported for Bay-winged Hawks in New Mexico. But farther east, in Texas,

Known as "gang hawks" for their tendency to hunt in groups, Bay-winged Hawks in flight reveal conspicuous white tail bars often hard to see in perched birds.

several studies of bay-wings have indicated that group breeding is rare. Thus, the reproductive strategies employed by the species vary considerably both within areas and on a geographic basis. The causes of this variability still await full resolution.

Within groups, Bay-winged Hawks are surprisingly docile raptors, rarely showing strong aggression to one another, although studies have shown that groups do maintain well-defined territories, defended from other groups by aggressive interactions when intrusions occur. For the most part, territorial violations are rare, with the various groups avoiding trespass of each other's territorial boundaries. When violations occur, however, the intruders are quickly driven from the territories by harassing flights of the territory owners. Early reports that the species was nonterritorial, based on nesting birds tolerating apparent intruders, seem to trace mainly to instances in which observers were unaware that the "intruders" were actually group members.

The extent of tolerance between individuals within groups is often extraordinary. In fact, the birds commonly land and perch peacefully on top of one another on saguaros under circumstances that apparently have nothing to do with mating behavior or aggression. Such behavior, known as "backstanding," sometimes involves as many as two birds stacked up in series on top of a third for periods up to several minutes.

At least in part, this great mutual tolerance is very likely related to frequent cooperative hunting within groups. As first studied by Bill Mader and later investigated by others, group hunting is highly developed in the species, and groups enjoy much greater success in foraging than do individuals. In part, the increase in success with group size occurs because team hunting makes it feasible for the hawks to kill prey that are normally safe from capture, especially prey that have taken cover in dense vegetation. With some individuals working actively to flush a prospective prey from cover while others stand by ready to capture it in the open, the prey has few chances for escape. In one such capture we witnessed with Jim Dawson in 1989, a group of five bay-wings piled in successively on a cottontail rabbit, diving right into the brush and quickly dispatching the unlucky animal.

The prey taken are frequently large enough to provide food for several individuals, so all can share in the rewards of group hunts. The birds find

Left: *Arizona's Bay-winged Hawks often use giant saguaro limbs as hunting perches. From such viewpoints, they can efficiently detect the rabbits and quail that form a large portion of their diet.*

Bay-winged (Harris's) Hawk

The female adult at a nest in Arizona's Sonoran Desert in 1974 was highly solicitous of her young, often shading them from the broiling midday sun and patiently feeding them the prey supplied by the two male adults in her breeding group.

themselves highly interdependent in foraging as a result. The advantages of cooperative foraging may also underlie the strong tendency for the species to breed in groups. When only a single male and female cooperate in breeding, group hunting is difficult during much of the breeding cycle—the incubation and early nestling periods.

Bay-winged Hawks are primarily dependent on mammals such as rabbits for food, but studies from blinds indicate that they also take birds regularly. Bill Mader compared his direct blind observations of the kinds and amounts of prey adults brought to nests with the feather, fur, and bone remains found in the nests during the same periods of time. By direct observations, more than 35 percent of the diet was birds, but by examination of prey remains, the proportion of birds was only 17.5 percent, a twofold difference presumably resulting from a relative impermanence of bird remains in nests. Jim Dawson has confirmed a similar bias against detecting prey remains of birds in Bay-winged Hawk nests. Thus, prey remains in nests can give highly unrealistic evidence of diet in this species.

The same problem occurs with other species. Jim Wiley of the U.S. Fish and Wildlife Service, for example, has found major biases in using prey remains to establish the nesting diet of Red-shouldered Hawks, and we have found unacceptably large biases in using such data to determine the nesting diet of Cooper's Hawks. Comprehensive observations of raptors from blinds are often the only way to gain reliable information on many aspects of their biology.

The Bay-winged Hawk's relatively strong use of birds for food is reflected in its possession of two morphological features that seem to cut across

essentially all groups of raptors. Like other raptors that take substantial numbers of birds, bay-wings have relatively long toes and claws and exhibit a strong size difference between the sexes. The long toes and claws apparently aid in gripping elusive prey covered by hard-to-grasp feathers. Just how the size difference between sexes relates to bird feeding has been much more controversial, as is discussed in the chapter on the Sharp-shinned Hawk. The Bay-winged Hawk, despite its extremely unusual breeding and foraging habits, exhibits the expected amount of size dimorphism for its diet, a fact that may prove crucial in the ultimate evaluation of various hypotheses concerning the function of size dimorphism.

The tendency of Bay-winged Hawks to breed more than once a year places this species among a very limited group of raptors. The only other North American falconiforms known to regularly produce more than one brood a year are Everglade Kites, White-tailed Kites, some populations of American Kestrels, and some Crested Caracaras. Among the owls, the only species regularly producing multiple broods is the Barn Owl. All these species occur mainly in the southern reaches of North America and are largely year-round residents in their breeding ranges. The nesting cycles of most raptors are sufficiently long that seasonal constraints largely rule out multiple brooding, especially if the species are migratory.

In the Everglade Kite, extremely long breeding seasons coupled with highly unpredictable food supplies have apparently been important factors leading to the development of regular mate desertion as a component of multiple brooding. Bay-winged Hawks have a breeding season roughly as long as that of the Everglade Kite (ten months of the year in some areas), yet mate desertion is at most a very rare occurrence in this species, and the composition of breeding groups tends to be quite stable in successive breeding attempts. Under good conditions, groups have begun new breeding attempts long before fledglings from previous breeding attempts have become independent—thus overlapping their investments in nesting attempts through time. Such overlap may be one of the important advantages of group breeding, because with additional individuals to care for fledglings, the adults are indeed able to carry on more than one breeding attempt simultaneously.

Why have Everglade Kites developed a mate-desertion strategy coupled with ephemeral use of nesting territories while Bay-winged Hawks, at least in some areas, have adopted a strategy of overlapping broods, with stable pair bonds, helpers at nests, and stable territories? The differences may be a result of the regularity with which the two species approach the limits of their respective food supplies. Everglade Kites, with their boom-or-bust population trends, may be chronically "underpopulated" under good food conditions, and individuals may generally have little difficulty finding good new feeding areas and forming new pair relationships. Bay-winged Hawks, with their much more stable populations, may commonly approach saturation of their favored habitats. With few openings available for new pairs to exploit, mate desertion and ephemeral pair bonds would likely be unprofitable strategies, especially if they might lead to reductions in the sizes and hunting success of foraging groups.

In August 1974, we joined Bill Mader for several days of observing Bay-winged Hawk nests in his study area. One nest was twenty feet up in a saguaro cactus, and here we saw the single youngster take his first flight and make his first uncertain landing on the thorny top of a fruit-laden saguaro limb. Stepping gingerly on the thorns, he had his first taste of a chronic problem that all bay-wings have to cope with in this region—impalement. By the time they reach independence, bay-wings must learn how to pull cactus thorns out of the bottoms of their feet or suffer severe consequences. Most become adept in this process, using their bills to pluck out the offending needles from one foot while standing on the other, never seeming to conclude that perching on cactus might not be worth the pain and trouble involved.

Another nest we observed with Bill Mader was about ten feet up in a palo verde and held only downy chicks. The adults tending this nest were remarkable in that they were also still caring for a hopelessly crippled fledgling from a previous nesting attempt. Injured by some accident, possibly a fall from the nest, this fledgling could not fly or forage effectively on its own, and there was no apparent hope that it would ever improve. While the efforts of the adults to rear this fledgling were doomed to failure and were a wasted investment in a genetic sense, the adults very likely had no way to determine whether the fledgling was beyond recovery. What emotions these hawks may have felt in continuing their solicitous care can only be conjectured, but for us it brought to mind parallels with human treatment of the infirm and terminally ill.

By standing in the nest cup and providing shade in which the youngsters could huddle, the adults at the palo verde nest sheltered their brood as best they could from the hot midday sun. Midsummer temperatures in the deserts near Tucson often reach 110 to 115 degrees Fahrenheit, a severe stress for all wildlife in the area. That the Bay-winged Hawk can breed successfully in such a rigorous environment may depend on the availability of water sources within reasonable commutes of nests. Much of the water available to wildlife in the Tucson region presently comes in the form of artificially constructed cattle ponds, and Jim Dawson has frequently observed the hawks gathering at such ponds to drink and sometimes to stand for long periods in the water. Where such ponds have not been created, the hawks seem to be much more sparse.

Sadly, the original saguaro habitats of Arizona are being rapidly converted into housing developments as suburbia engulfs the southern reaches of

Nestling Bay-winged Hawks in the Sonoran Desert face some of the most rigorous temperature extremes endured by any diurnal raptor species. Daytime temperatures during the breeding season can reach 110 to 115 degrees Fahrenheit, and pairs tend to nest only where they have access to reliable water supplies.

the state. The entire region between Tucson and Phoenix is on its way to becoming a giant sprawling city, and this is having major impacts, both positive and negative, on the bay-wings living there. As mentioned above, one aspect of bay-wing biology that has greatly benefited from human practices, at least in the short term, is access to water supplies, not only at cattle ponds, but also at swimming pools and suburban birdbaths. It is also encouraging to see that this species can still breed in suburban areas, often nesting in backyard ornamental trees and feeding on the birds attracted to bird feeders. But on the negative side, the bay-wing also suffers substantially from electrocutions on power poles and from a disease (trichomoniasis) it contracts by feeding on urban pigeons and doves. In the face of these and other challenges, it is not clear how viable urban populations of the species may prove in the long run, although they appear to be coping remarkably well so far.

The overall future of the Bay-winged Hawk in North America is questionable from several standpoints. In general, the bay-wing is highly dependent on a brushy habitat structure with numerous scattered hunting perches for foraging, and the species has apparently been suffering substantial declines in Texas and some regions of Arizona and New Mexico as more and more mesquite habitats are cleared for cattle grazing. In Arizona, the population nesting in saguaro-dominated habitats may face almost total urbanization of its range in the decades just ahead, with as yet difficult to predict consequences. A crucial question is to what extent water availability may limit both human and bay-wing populations in the region, as groundwater supplies are continuing to be depleted rapidly. External water supplies from the Colorado River, already in use in the Phoenix and Tucson regions, are finite in amount and offer only a temporary reprieve. The overriding consideration for all species in the region—both human and wildlife—may prove to be the extent to which continued human population growth affects the future availability of water supplies.

Bay-winged (Harris's) Hawk

Osprey
Pandion haliaetus

NO RAPTOR EXHIBITS GREATER skills in capturing fish than the Osprey. Certain other species, such as the Bald Eagle and the Common Black Hawk, also take fish with fair frequency. But none pursues this prey with anything like the Osprey's single-minded focus, and none captures fish with the same heroic crashing dives from high in the sky.

Aiding the Osprey in its foraging are a number of anatomical peculiarities. Dense, oily feathers minimize waterlogging of the plumage. Curiously crooked wings may adapt the species for jolting collisions with the water's surface and subsequent liftoffs into the air. Unusually long legs with very short stiff feathers facilitate penetration of the bird's talons through the water to the depths occupied by prey. Highly curved talons and feet soled with spiny spicules help it grip slippery prey. The species is clearly a specialist locked anatomically to its food supply, much as the Everglade Kite is structurally matched to a diet of snails with its long, nearly straight talons and bizarrely shaped bill. To be sure, Ospreys have occasionally been documented taking nonpiscine prey such as birds and mammals, but such events are highly exceptional.

The Osprey is also unusual in being the only diurnal raptor besides the Peregrine Falcon to have a nearly worldwide distribution. Never found far from water, except during migration, this species is entirely dependent on healthy aquatic ecosystems, and where fish are especially abundant, it is sometimes found nesting in substantial colonies. Gardiner's Island and Plum Island in Long Island Sound were once famous for their huge Osprey colonies, and large colonies also once existed in various Florida locations. For example, Donald J. Nicholson, an early Florida egg collector, found seventy-five occupied Osprey nests on relatively modest-sized Lake Istokpoga in 1910, and we counted as many as a couple dozen Osprey nests simultaneously active on a single small island in the northern keys of Florida Bay during the late 1960s.

In general, Ospreys are well known for their choices of highly conspicuous nesting sites at the tops of towering trees and dead snags, or on power poles, duck blinds, channel markers, communications towers, chimneys of houses, and even billboards. One renowned pair in southern Florida built their nest atop the boom of a temporarily idle construction crane. The owner, to his everlasting credit, permanently retired the crane from active duty, allowing the Ospreys to follow through with numerous annual nesting efforts.

Sometimes, however, elevated nest substrates are simply unavailable in regions of favorable food supplies. Under such conditions, Ospreys occasionally build nests right on the ground, if sites exist that are safe from terrestrial predators. We saw ground nests on uninhabited Florida Keys in the 1960s and 1970s, and ground nesting was a common trait for the

Range of the Osprey
- Breeding
- Breeding and wintering
- Wintering

Osprey colony of some three hundred pairs on Gardiner's Island in the early twentieth century.

Although Ospreys do not hesitate to make deep dives that carry them completely under the water in their attempts to capture fish, they most typically take moderate-sized fish such as mullet and menhaden, which often occur close to the surface. Nevertheless, Ospreys may occasionally tackle fish too large to lift from the water and may not always be able to extricate their talons from such prey in time to avoid drowning. Reports of large dead fish being recovered with Osprey skeletons still attached apparently trace to such blunders.

Ospreys may also make fatal mistakes in attempting to take fish capable of counterattack. On one occasion, as we were boating in northern Florida Bay, we happened upon an Osprey floating at the surface that may have made just such an error. This bird appeared totally exhausted and was so waterlogged that it made no effort to flee our approach. When we hauled it into our skiff, we found that it had a deep abdominal gash, which had allowed seawater to enter its body cavity, apparently weighing the bird down to such an extent that it was impossible for it to become airborne. After allowing the seawater to drain from its body cavity, we wrapped the bird in spare clothing to prevent it from struggling and to allow it to regain its normal body temperature. Later we gave the bird to John Ogden of the National Park Service, who was then studying the Ospreys of the region. The bird recovered quite quickly, and Ogden was able to release it successfully near where we had found it. Although we can only speculate about what had happened to this Osprey, one plausible scenario is that it may have grabbed a

Left: *Darkness descends on an Osprey nest in a black mangrove snag in Everglades National Park. The species favors such snags, where available, but sometimes nests right on the ground, especially on predator-free islands.*

When landing at the nest, an Osprey descends into the wind, feet outstretched to cushion the impact.

Through most of the breeding cycle, male Ospreys capture all prey for their families while their mates care for eggs and nestlings. This nest in the Florida Keys, built largely of turtle grass, was only five feet off the ground.

large sea catfish by the tail, only to have the dangerous pectoral spines of its struggling victim slash into its abdomen.

Although they sometimes hunt from perches, Ospreys, like Everglade Kites, are usually very active in foraging, generally using flapping flight and hovering as they search for food from heights of about fifty to one hundred feet above the water's surface. For a relatively large bird such as the Osprey, such flight is energetically demanding, but often few opportunities exist for the species to hunt from perches, and the thermals, or topographic updrafts, necessary for continuous soaring are characteristically missing over bodies of water.

Colin Pennycuick, a specialist in avian flight physiology, has calculated that sustained flapping flight is energetically impossible for birds that exceed about twenty pounds in weight, and indeed the larger vultures, such as the California Condor, do not employ flapping flight for more than brief bursts. The Osprey falls well below this aerodynamic limit, at a body weight of three to four pounds and a wingspread of five to six feet, although it is far larger than many raptors that hunt primarily from soaring flight. Only when migrating over terrestrial regions is the Osprey able to consistently conserve energy by soaring in thermals and topographic updrafts. But even in migration, Ospreys commonly carry fish, as if they might be greatly concerned about keeping their energy reserves in good shape.

In their breeding activities, Ospreys are highly conspicuous both visually and vocally. Male Ospreys sometimes carry prey for extended periods during display flights over their nesting areas, flapping and hovering vigorously, their bodies inclined at a steep, almost vertical angle, and at the same time calling repeatedly with loud *chereeeeks*. These flights are highly conspicuous and may serve primarily to convince females of the physical stamina of their mates. Females generally remain perched at their nests during these displays, just as they remain very attentive at their nests during most of the nesting cycle. The males do almost all hunting through to the end of the nestling period.

In migratory populations, males usually arrive back on the breeding grounds earlier than females. Pairs are formed at nest sites, and males guard their mates from the attentions of other males very closely, almost always escorting their mates in flight and chasing off any intruders from the vicinity. Clutch size averages about three eggs, and nesting cycles for the species are relatively long, with incubation averaging about thirty-nine days and a nestling period lasting about two months. After fledging, young remain dependent on their parents for food for periods up to two months and more, while they simultaneously develop hunting skills. Their first successful captures of fish are generally seen within two to three weeks of fledging, but success rates are very low at first. One study documented only one success per four to five tries at one month after fledging, increasing to three successes per five tries by four months of age.

Adult Ospreys are basically black above and white underneath. They have white heads, except for a black crown and a broad horizontal black line from the bill through the eye to the back of the neck. Nestling Ospreys, in

Osprey

On occasion, Ospreys tackle fish that are risky to handle. This may have been the history of this waterlogged bird we found floating in Florida Bay in 1971 with a deep gash in its abdomen.

contrast to nestlings of most other raptors, are highly cryptic, or camouflaged, in their first down. Their mottled pattern makes them almost impossible to see in their nests from above. Such coloration suggests significant threats of predation from other avian species, as does the cryptic spotted coloration of Osprey eggs and the very close attendance of female Ospreys at their nests. In North America, the threats may come primarily from Bald Eagles and various crows and ravens, and the conspicuous nature of Osprey nests makes them obvious targets for such species.

Osprey nests have also been favored targets for predation by people, especially by egg collectors, although this has been much more of a problem in Europe than in North America. Egg collecting as a hobby has now fortunately died out almost completely in the New World. Harassment by egg collectors, however, was an important factor in the loss of the Osprey population of Britain around the beginning of the twentieth century, and it has been a major obstacle to the natural reestablishment of the species in Scotland, despite massive efforts to guard vulnerable nests. Nevertheless, the Ospreys, which returned on their own to Scotland in the 1950s, apparently repopulating the country from Scandinavia, are still continuing to increase and may yet come close to approaching their original abundance.

Both European and North American populations of Ospreys exhibit a curious migration pattern unknown for other raptors. Yearlings from north temperate regions migrate south in typical falconiform fashion, wintering in African and tropical American locations, respectively. But then instead of

returning to their summer homes the following spring, the young Ospreys almost always remain on the wintering ground through another whole year. They finally move northward in their third calendar year to enter the breeding populations near the nest sites where they hatched. Assuming adequate year-round food supplies in the wintering areas, and assuming that birds might still be too inexperienced in foraging to breed successfully in their second year, such a strategy, avoiding unnecessary migration, seems very sensible. Similar migratory strategies may eventually be documented in other long-lived species with delayed maturity and extensive migrations.

The Osprey was one of the species most severely stressed by organochlorine pesticides during the period after World War II. Especially affected were the coastal populations of the northeastern states, such as those bordering on Long Island Sound, which were once among the densest populations of Ospreys known anywhere in the world. By the 1960s, the northeastern population of Ospreys had crashed to near extinction, although a few pairs hung on in the region, attempting, mostly unsuccessfully, to hatch eggs. At least some of the decline was due to direct mortality from Dieldrin poisoning, but the surviving pairs were clearly also under heavy stress from DDE. With the banning of Dieldrin and DDE in the early 1970s, the Osprey population began a slow but steady recovery throughout most of its North American range.

In addition to controlling environmental pollutants, overall conservation of the Osprey depends even more on ensuring the basic productivity of its foraging habitat, and in many areas, on ensuring that suitable nest sites are available. In past decades, coastal farmers of the eastern states often encouraged Ospreys to breed near their homes by constructing artificial nests atop wagon wheels mounted on poles. Their rationale was that territorial Ospreys would protect domestic animals, such as chickens, from attack by other raptors but would pose no threat to domestic animals themselves. In areas where good fish supplies have existed and nest sites have been in short supply, such efforts have often enhanced Osprey numbers significantly. In fact, the Osprey populations in many regions of North America are now almost completely dependent on artificial nest structures of various sorts. In many studies, nesting success has been much higher at artificial sites than at natural sites, in large part because the greater stability of artificial sites decreases the number of failures due to nest collapse. Nevertheless, attempts in some regions to increase Osprey populations with such structures have shown that these efforts will not accomplish very much in areas where fish populations are relatively low.

Population estimates made in 2001 for the lower United States by compilers Alan Poole and colleagues indicate about sixteen thousand to nineteen thousand pairs—more than a doubling of the estimate of about eight thousand pairs for the early 1980s. These birds are concentrated in five main regions—the Atlantic Coast, Florida and the Gulf Coast, the Great Lakes, the northern Rocky Mountains, and the Pacific Northwest. Canada's Osprey population is also substantial, with a rough estimate of ten thousand to twelve thousand pairs. Numbers in Alaska are relatively modest at about two hundred pairs, possibly because of strong competition from dense Bald Eagle populations. Overall the species appears to have increased greatly from the depths of the organochlorine era, with recent declines seen in only a few areas, such as Florida Bay.

Above: *Although capable of elegant soaring flight, Ospreys hunt from flapping flight for the most part, as the thermals and updrafts that permit soaring flight are generally absent over large bodies of water.*

Below: *Ospreys defend their nests aggressively, harassing intruders with awesome dives and angry vocalizations.*

Osprey

Golden Eagle
Aquila chrysaetos

GOLDEN EAGLES ARE the most formidable of all raptor species in North America. Records exist for them even killing grown deer and pronghorn antelope, and they are known to kill foxes and coyotes with some frequency. The list of documented prey for this species includes most of the medium-large mammals on the continent, though, to be sure, many of the largest prey taken have been animals incapacitated by injury or hobbled by deep snow. Many of the largest prey have also been attacked under conditions of dire food stress for the eagles, when no other prey were available. Under normal conditions, the eagles usually concentrate on prey the size of rabbits or ground squirrels, and they are frequently attracted to carrion.

Regardless, Golden Eagles certainly take larger prey on average than do any other North American raptors, and they normally dominate all others in disputes over food. The amount of violence they exhibit as they take control of contested food supplies is awesome. We have seen a number of eagles missing eyes and bearing other wounds—very likely resulting from battles with other eagles over prey.

Even California Condors, the largest birds of prey on the continent, normally refrain from challenging Golden Eagles at carcasses, and there are records of these eagles killing young condors. We once observed such an attempt directly, and it was surely the most intense scene of avian aggression we have ever witnessed. Circling high above the line of cliffs from which he had fledged a few months earlier, the young condor was awaiting the return of his parents with food. It was late March 1980, and the youngster was not yet capable of foraging independently, though he was daily gaining experience in flight maneuvers. Suddenly, the leisurely circling of the condor was interrupted by the arrival of another large bird. In a searing stoop from distant crags to the south, an adult Golden Eagle came storming in to lock its talons to the condor in midair. Despite being considerably smaller than the condor, the eagle had apparently lethal intentions, and the two birds began a tumultuous free-fall toward the ground, breaking apart only moments before they crashed into the top of the cliff. The condor just barely fought off the attack and fled quickly down the canyon out of reach of his assailant.

Undoubtedly, the condor's appreciation of his place in the universe had changed forever. He might still be the largest bird to sail the skies, but he knew now that he was not the fiercest. In watching this incident, we too gained a new appreciation of the natural world and who its avian rulers really are.

Golden Eagles generally weigh about ten pounds and have a wingspread of six to seven feet. Individuals vary considerably in size, however, and some females reach thirteen pounds and have wingspreads close to eight feet. The most striking physical characteristics of the species are its massive talons and legs that are feathered down to the toes. In coloration, both juveniles and adults are basically dark brown with a shaggy golden glaze to the back of

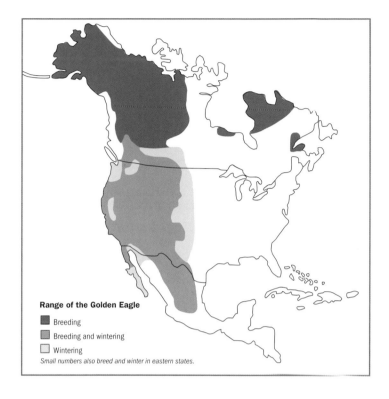

Range of the Golden Eagle

■ Breeding
■ Breeding and wintering
□ Wintering
Small numbers also breed and winter in eastern states.

the head and neck, although immatures are marked also with a conspicuous white tail base and white patches on the undersides of their wings at the bases of the outer secondary and inner primary feathers. These white patches are gradually lost with progressive molts until the birds finally achieve an overall brown coloration at about five years of age.

During the early 1980s, we spent many days in blinds overlooking calf carcasses set out to attract condors in the foothills of California's southern San Joaquin Valley. For the most part, however, we watched Common Raven and Golden Eagle behavior rather than condor behavior. The ravens fed in massed groups, while the eagles were loners, intolerant of any other birds on the carcasses while they fed, especially other eagles. When an eagle was feeding, all others usually waited, perched on the ground at some distance from the carcass. Normally it took each eagle about a half hour to forty-five minutes to fill its crop. Then it either took off on its own volition or was displaced by the next in line, sometimes in a flurry of flashing talons as each bird went for the other.

So many eagles inhabited the region that a carcass was sometimes attended almost continuously through an entire day. At times, we saw more than a dozen birds waiting their turn. It was often very difficult for condors to break into the loop to get food, and after landing in the vicinity and waiting for a while, the condors attracted to the food commonly took off again, probably hoping to find a less thoroughly guarded carcass elsewhere.

Golden Eagles are indeed very fond of carrion, but in most regions they are primarily predators of medium-sized mammals. They also take considerable numbers of fairly large birds. One population of the species studied by raptor

Left: *Still weeks away from fledging, a young Golden Eagle exercises its wings at a nest amid flowering fire-weed in central Alaska.*

In this central Alaska canyon, a Golden Eagle pair raised a single youngster in the summer of 1968. The nest was placed in a cleft on the side of a huge boulder projecting from the canyon side, immediately below a recently active wolf den.

researcher Yossi Leshem in his native Israel is heavily dependent on large lizards for prey and characteristically raises more young (often three per nest) than any other known Golden Eagle population in the world.

In addition, some Golden Eagles in Israel feed heavily on tortoises, which they kill by carrying them high in the air and dropping them to smash on rocks below. At one nest studied by Leshem near Jerusalem, about a third of the diet was comprised of these creatures. In researching historical precedents for these observations, he discovered that tortoise predation by Golden Eagles is apparently a very ancient trait. It was even described by the Roman natural historian Pliny, who attributed the death of the Greek poet Aeschylus to an eagle that apparently mistook his bald head for a rock and successfully aimed a tortoise at it. This tale just may have been borrowed from the supermarket tabloids of ancient Athens, but the studies in Israel at least bring it into the realm of possibility. Clearly, the Golden Eagle is a very adaptable species in its feeding habits, and it is not to be underestimated in its capacity for unusual exploits.

Unfortunately, in some regions the appetite of the Golden Eagle for carrion has given the species a largely unfair reputation of being a major threat to sheep.

Direct observations of eagles killing lambs are very rare, but nevertheless, ranchers have sometimes interpreted sightings of eagles feeding on stillborn lambs as predation. In the 1950s and 1960s, ranchers sponsored a massive slaughter of wintering eagles from airplanes in Texas, based on the assumption that the eagles were a major menace. In studying this slaughter, Walter Spofford, one of the foremost experts on the species, estimated that more than twenty thousand eagles had been shot in the twenty years between 1941 and 1961. Yet the many careful studies that have been conducted subsequently of eagle predation on livestock have generally shown that eagles take very few domestic animals, except as carrion, and are rarely a significant source of their mortality. At the same time, eagles clearly offer benefits to ranchers in many areas by feeding heavily on the rabbits and ground squirrels that compete with their stock for forage.

Even granting that Golden Eagles may kill lambs on occasion, and forgetting for the moment that their rabbit killing is generally an economic assist for ranchers, it is difficult to believe that the expense of airplane campaigns to slaughter eagles might ever be cost-effective. The fact that no one has attempted to justify such campaigns with hard economic data suggests that more than economic motives may have been involved.

Left: *Golden Eagles feed on carrion as well as living prey, and fights over carcasses sometimes become sufficiently violent to lead to injury of participants. Here, two immature eagles battle for possession of a calf carcass put out for condors in southern California.*

Golden Eagle

In our observations, the Golden Eagles nesting on Alaska's North Slope in 1987 preyed exclusively on arctic ground squirrels. No sheep remains were found at this nest, despite an abundance of Dall's sheep on nearby slopes.

Perhaps the main motive for such slaughter has been a primordial human drive to do battle with wild creatures perceived as powerful and evil. Historically, the targets of such persecution were mostly large and dangerous predators such as grizzly bears, but now that grizzlies and wolves have been eliminated from most regions, it's up to the eagles, coyotes, and foxes to fill that need. Unfortunately, the emotionalism surrounding the eagle-livestock issue has often precluded rational discussion and research, and although the hunting of eagles from airplanes has been illegal since 1962, human harassment of eagles may not cease completely until the frontier ethic itself has passed completely into history.

Despite the fact that some Golden Eagles are still shot or poisoned in the belief that they threaten livestock, many populations of the species still appear to be vigorous, and in many areas more eagles have probably been lost to electrocution on power poles than to deliberate slaughter by humans. The wingspread of the Golden Eagle is sufficiently large that these birds are able to complete circuits between wires if, as they land on one, they brush another simultaneously. Intensive studies of this problem by raptor conservationists Morley Nelson, Erv Boeker, and others have led to recommended changes in the design of power poles to make them safe for perching by large raptors. In some of the western states, rapid progress has been made in reducing such deaths by installing these better-designed poles.

Another more recently developed threat to the species is the wind turbines that have been established as a source of clean and environmentally friendly electrical energy. Crowning the high windswept ridges in a number of states, these wind farms are proving to have their environmental costs as well as benefits. Studies of Golden Eagle collisions with the blades of these turbines in Altamont Pass near San Francisco, California, have documented a surprisingly large number of mortalities—roughly forty per year. Similar problems have been documented with losses of Eurasian Griffon Vultures to wind turbines in Spain. While it might seem a relatively simple task for eagles and large vultures to avoid such structures, the death rates suggest

The two eaglets in an Arizona nest in 1971 enjoyed a diet consisting mainly of rabbits, and they fledged in May, much earlier than fledgings occur in Alaska. Adjacent Golden Eagle pairs in Arizona usually space nests about ten miles apart on cliffs in the foothills.

otherwise. Such collisions, together with losses to lead poisoning and a host of other miscellaneous causes of death, continue to challenge the overall health of Golden Eagle populations.

Golden Eagles are commonly regarded as birds of high mountains, but they are really much more typically birds of open country than of forested regions and are much more numerous nesting among low escarpments in the foothills of mountains than at high elevations. They characteristically place their nests on ledges of cliffs, although some populations nest in tall trees. The several active nests we have observed in Alaska, Arizona, and New Mexico have all been cliff sites and have been attended by adults that were thoroughly cautious about people. Only in the lower Sierra Nevada of California did we once encounter a pair that was very tolerant of human approach. This pair was also the only pair we have seen nesting in a tree, a twisted gray pine on a steep, south-facing slope.

The most interesting Golden Eagle nest we had a chance to observe was one we watched with Walter Spofford in Alaska in 1968. This nest was lodged in a cleft of a vertical flake of rock in a steep-sided ravine that cut into a hillside in the Alaska Range. Directly over the site was a den where wolves had gnawed on caribou bones, though we saw no wolves in the area when we watched the nest. The nest held a single chick, and we spent many days observing his development through the summer from a distant blind carefully concealed in brush. Fed on a steady diet of arctic ground squirrels, the chick gradually gained flight and prey-handling capacities, flapping his wings energetically as he stood in the nest, play-capturing already dead ground squirrels in the nest with stabs of his talons, and staring curiously at waterfowl on the ponds at the base of the ravine and at pikas on the slopes.

Another Golden Eagle nest we watched from a blind was situated on a rocky outcrop north of the Brooks Range on Alaska's North Slope. With no concealing vegetation in the area, our blind for this nest was a roofed-over

Golden Eagle

Incubating a single-egg clutch, a female Golden Eagle in the southern Sierra Nevada of California rests on an enormous stick nest in a gray pine.

pit sunk in the talus. One of the most northerly nests ever known for the species, it also held a single youngster developing vigorously on a steady diet of ground squirrels. The slopes of the outcrop were home for a large herd of Dall's sheep, but we saw no interactions between the eagles and sheep and found no evidence of lamb predation at the nest.

At still another nest we watched closely, a site in Arizona, the primary prey were rabbits, and here two young competed for food on a giant platform of yucca stalks and other debris evidently accumulated over a period of many years. Both young were fed good supplies of food and fledged successfully by early summer. They were on the wing much earlier in the year than the single youngsters in Alaska who barely had enough time to begin flying before the return of cold weather in late summer and early fall. The Alaskan youngsters were likely still dependent on their parents through the migration period. Indeed, Golden Eagles of the far north are often known to migrate in family groups.

For many years, Walter Spofford tracked a population of Golden Eagles nesting in northern New England and wintering in the southeastern states. This was an extremely small population, presumably because there were few large tracts of truly favorable hunting ground left in the northeastern states. In fact, these eagles seemed to be primarily dependent on bog habitats, feeding mainly on bitterns and herons, certainly an unusual diet for the species. Yet each year a number of Golden Eagles, presumably from this population and from eastern Canada, migrate south along the Appalachians, and at lookouts such as Hawk Mountain in Pennsylvania, Easterners still have a chance to see this primarily western species at close range. Despite relatively low productivity, the eastern population continues to hang on, demonstrating a surprising adaptability to continuing landscape changes.

In the western states and western Canada and Alaska, Golden Eagles continue to survive in much larger populations. Their total numbers in North America were estimated for the first time in the 1970s, and the count indicated perhaps as many as one hundred thousand birds—a total very similar to the numbers of Bald Eagles estimated in more recent years. More recent data for Golden Eagles suggest population stability in Canada and Alaska, but a spotty situation in the lower forty-eight states, with some areas showing recent increases, and others, especially various regions close to major urban centers, showing substantial declines.

Bald Eagle

Haliaeetus leucocephalus

Range of the Bald Eagle

■ Primary breeding range

--- Southern boundary of winter range

ON A WINDLESS MORNING, the horizon of Florida Bay can disappear in the distant haze, leaving the mangrove islands suspended motionless in a continuum of water and sky. The clouds above have exact counterparts below, but both seem equally insubstantial in a vast realm of salty air stretching to infinity. Only when a mullet slaps the water's surface, creating an expanding pocket of shimmering ripples that dissolves the lower clouds, does it become clear that there is some tangible reality to the scene and that the clouds below are the reflected images of those above.

Beneath the glassy surface of the bay, another realm lies hidden—a shallow realm of soft marl muds and endless rank beds of turtle grass. Here, marine plants combine dazzling light energy from the sun with carbon dioxide and other nutrients to form simple organic compounds—the basic foods that ultimately sustain the entire intricate web of interdependent organisms residing in the region. Without these subsurface pastures, the bay would be largely empty of inhabitants. In their presence, the bay has long been famed as a unique naturalists' paradise.

During the late 1960s and early 1970s when we lived in Florida, we often visited Florida Bay by small boat and were delighted with the variety of creatures found there. Fins of nurse sharks and porpoises creased the surface of the mangrove channels. Diamondback terrapins thrust their snouts into the air from island lagoons. Strange *Cassiopeia* jellyfish rested upside down on the soft mud bottom, displaying their flowerlike tentacles toward the surface, while scallops jetted from one resting place to another. Overhead, scattered flocks of Roseate Spoonbills, White Ibis, and Brown Pelicans beat paths across the sky, while Reddish Egrets and other small herons stalked the flats in pursuit of tiny killifishes. At night, crocodiles and Great White Herons took over the shallows, waiting for larger fish to move inshore to feed.

Historically, the mangrove islands of the bay also hosted substantial colonies of nesting Ospreys, and they have continued to host the southernmost breeding population of Bald Eagles known for United States. The eagles of the bay have traditionally preyed heavily on both fish and various fish-eating birds and waterfowl. As such, they have occupied a premier position in the food web of the bay and have reigned as the crowning avian residents of the region. Here, perhaps more than anywhere else, this species dominates its surroundings, matching in deeds what it claims by sublime appearances and fully earning its renown as the national symbol of our country.

During our boating excursions, we often had a chance to observe Bald Eagles among the northernmost mangrove islands of the bay. Most often we found the eagles perched conspicuously on weathered dead snags, where they patiently scanned their surroundings for promising foraging opportunities. Occasionally, however, we watched them in hunting attempts as they grabbed fish from the water's surface or pursued luckless waterfowl. The Bald Eagle is famous for its ability to force Ospreys to give up fish in midair, and several times we had a chance to see this exciting piratical spectacle. Each time, the eagle used aggressive swooping dives to challenge an Osprey carrying prey high above us. Burdened with his prospective meal, the unfortunate Osprey was unable to distance himself from his tormentor and finally dropped the fish in desperation. The eagle, sensing victory, now peeled over into a vertical dive of feather-scorching speed, often overtaking and grabbing the fish before it hit the water. Few wildlife encounters can match the drama of these aerial thefts.

Less well known is that around Osprey nests, the tables are often turned. Bald Eagles we watched intruding on nesting Ospreys in Florida

Bay had to summon all their acrobatic skills, including desperate sprints and barrel rolls, to avoid pummeling by this more agile species. Other inhabitants of the region, such as Common Crows, were also capable of driving off eagles that invaded their domains, as long as the eagles did not arrive with substantial initial advantages in altitude and speed. But the most thoroughly hostile greeting we have ever seen an eagle receive was bestowed on a bird that ventured too close to a nesting colony of Swallow-tailed Kites farther north in the Ten Thousand Islands. Mobbed by a whole flock of angry swooping assailants, the eagle left the area without delay. Despite a fully deserved reputation as monarch of the skies, the Bald Eagle bows to lesser species on occasion.

On their own turf, the eagles assert full authority unchallenged. Characteristically choosing the tallest trees available, they make no effort to hide their nests from view and instead rely on their imposing size and demeanor to intimidate intruders. Second only to the California Condor in size among the continent's raptors, the Bald Eagle sometimes exceeds twelve pounds in weight and displays a wingspread of more than seven-and-a-half feet. Adults are not really bald, but they can be recognized from long distances by their huge size and their magnificent white head and tail feathers, whereas immatures are mostly brown in coloration and lack white heads and tails until about five years old. Breeding is normally delayed until birds achieve full adult plumage, although younger birds occasionally attempt nestings that generally prove unsuccessful.

In the Florida Bay region, the tallest trees available for nesting are almost always modest-sized mangroves, and eagle nests rarely are more than thirty feet from the ground. While still providing a commanding view over the surrounding terrain, such low nests do not compare with the towering tree nests used by the species in other regions. Along the Chesapeake Bay, for example, nest trees have averaged more than ninety feet tall, and similar averages are known for Bald Eagle nest trees in Yellowstone National Park. On treeless islands of the Aleutians and on certain treeless islands off California, however, Bald Eagles usually nest on cliffs or right on the ground itself, making it clear that tall trees are not an obligatory nesting requirement for the species. The overall distribution of the Bald Eagle, while tied mainly to aquatic regions, is huge, and the species breeds in a great diversity of climates and habitat types.

Bald Eagle

Above: *Lesser creatures sometimes breach the supremacy of the Bald Eagle. We have seen nesting Swallow-tailed Kites and Ospreys drive off eagles with intimidating dives, and even crows sometimes succeed with such attacks.*

Bald Eagles begin their breeding cycles earlier than almost all other North American raptors. Some pairs in the Florida population are known to start egg laying as early as late October, and most have eggs by no later than December or January. Early breeding in this population may be timed in part to allow adults a good food supply of wintering waterbirds during reproduction. Egg laying comes much later in more northerly populations, but even on the Chesapeake Bay it commonly takes place in late February, when winter storms still occasionally blanket nests with snow. Alaskan Bald Eagles commonly commence incubation in April or May, a full half year after their Florida relatives.

Left: *In the late twentieth century, many of southern Florida's Bald Eagles constructed their nests in giant black mangroves that Hurricane Donna had killed in 1960. Despite the devastation caused by this awesome storm, it may have benefited the area's eagles and other wildlife by flushing large quantities of land-based nutrients into Florida Bay and other estuarine areas.*

An enormous expanse of sky, sea, and sun, Florida Bay is a unique wilderness. The bay's Bald Eagles, many nesting on isolated mangrove islets, survived the organochlorine pesticide era following World War II largely unscathed, while populations farther north nearly disappeared.

Bald Eagle

Bald Eagles normally attain fully white heads and tails around six years old and do not commonly breed until fully adult in coloration. Such prolonged maturation is common among the larger raptors and may reflect the time these birds take to become truly skilled in foraging and other crucial activities.

Near their nests, Bald Eagles most commonly vocalize with a series of coarse notes that is neither musical nor awe-inspiring but, nevertheless, leaves no doubt about the bird's displeasure.

In the great majority of cases, pairs lay a clutch of two eggs, and eggs usually hatch after thirty-five days of incubation. Nestling life generally lasts from eleven to twelve weeks but is quite variable in duration, and young usually associate with their parents for another one to two months after fledging, rarely making any prey captures on their own during the first month and a half after leaving the nest.

Like most large raptors, Bald Eagles are not the most lively birds at their nests, though their noble appearance largely makes up for the leisurely pace of events. At nests we have watched from Alaska to various parts of Florida, the dominant spirit has always been one of lethargy, occasionally punctuated by periods of restrained activity when one or the other of the parent birds has arrived with a fish or waterbird in its talons. Feedings of chicks are conducted calmly and deliberately, with none of the frantic haste seen in many smaller raptors.

The most characteristic vocalization of the Bald Eagle is a chattering call consisting of a series of seven or eight sputtering notes that sound painful to produce. Surprisingly unimpressive compared to the species' dramatic visual appearance, this vocalization seemingly lacks enough volume and character to intimidate an intruder by sound alone, and on first hearing, one is generally amazed to learn that this is all the species has to say in defense of its home, mate, or turf. Various ornithologists have described the call as "ridiculously weak and insignificant," or "weak in volume and trivial in

expression," but even if this might be true for human ears, impressions could be very different for other eagles.

Hunting efforts of the species are spasmodic, and most individuals spend long periods perched, apparently waiting for promising foraging opportunities to come to them. Nevertheless, when the right opportunities arise, Bald Eagles do not hesitate to gear into energetic efforts to seize victims. One adult we watched at a Florida nest commonly arrived nearly exhausted when he brought in prey, and he sat panting heavily on a snag before taking the prey the rest of the way to the nest.

Renowned as fish eaters, Bald Eagles are actually quite flexible in their diets, and like the Crested Caracara are one of the few raptor species that commonly take turtles. In Florida, the diamondback terrapin often finishes its career in an eagle nest. Bald Eagles do not normally capture fish in the deep plunging dives characteristic of Ospreys, but rather snatch them right at the water's surface in very shallow swoops. Birds and carrion also form very important parts of the diet, and in some regions the eagles turn heavily to mammals, such as rabbits, for food.

In California, Bald Eagles sometimes winter in the foraging range used historically by the California Condor, and during the mid-1980s, they sometimes fed on calf carcasses we put out for the condors. These Bald Eagles were much more sedate in behavior and much more tolerant of one another at carcasses than were the Golden Eagles feeding in the same region.

Bald Eagle

A nestling Bald Eagle with a mullet awaits the return of its parents in a Florida mangrove. Mullet commonly swim close to the surface, where they are vulnerable to capture by Ospreys and Bald Eagles. Other prey taken frequently in this region include diamondback terrapins, coots, various herons, and other water birds.

The use of rangeland habitats by Bald Eagles, while surprising to those accustomed to seeing the species only in aquatic settings, is actually quite common, especially in the western states.

At distances too great for us to see details of head color, immature Bald Eagles were the birds most easy to confuse with California Condors. General tail and wing proportions of the two species are quite similar and contrast with the more long-tailed appearance of the similar-sized Golden Eagle. Moreover, some immature Bald Eagles possess ragged white triangles on the undersurfaces of their wings—somewhat like those of condors. Only by counting the number of seconds it took distant birds to soar full circles in the sky could we reliably differentiate these two species. Bald Eagles normally took about twelve to fourteen seconds to complete a circle, while condors generally expended about sixteen seconds. These times were quite consistent and greatly exceeded the circling times of smaller raptors. Red-tailed Hawks, for example, usually circled in about eight seconds.

Perhaps the most impressive Bald Eagle spectacle to be seen today is the annual postbreeding gathering of thousands of individuals along the Chilkat River of southeastern Alaska. Drawn by the fall spawning runs of chum salmon, the eagles assemble to glean an easy living off a superabundant food supply. The salmon, their energies spent by the spawning process, die in windrows, and the eagles find it little challenge to procure all the food they could possibly consume. Wading into the shallows, they haul dead and moribund fish to shore on foot, then methodically rip them apart in an unhurried fashion.

With such an abundance of food, there is little need for intense aggression among the birds, though half-playful disputes erupt with some frequency. For the most part, the eagles perch amicably side by side on the gravel bars with no attempts at territorial defense. In favored locations, communal roosts often number many hundreds of birds. Similar, though smaller-scale gatherings of Bald Eagles are also known in coastal regions farther south in British Columbia and Washington State, as well as at certain winter trout-spawning areas along the Colorado River in Arizona, just as gatherings of California Condors were once common for the salmon runs along the Columbia River in Oregon.

In 1982, after much heated debate, the most crucial parts of Alaska's Chilkat River were set aside as a state Bald Eagle preserve. Prior to this step, controversy raged over alternative development plans for the area advocated by mining, lumbering, and fishing interests. Eventually, a consensus plan evolved that gave all interested parties, including the eagles, the prospect of long-term survival. In view of the huge numbers of eagles using the Chilkat, the development of a comprehensive preservation plan for this region was a major conservation achievement.

Another of the most gratifying chapters in Bald Eagle conservation was written by Charles Broley, a retired banker from Canada, who conducted a monumental study of the species in southwestern Florida. In 1939, at the age of fifty-eight, Broley arrived in the state to begin a banding program of nestling eagles that extended into the late 1950s. Overall, he ringed more than 1,200 individuals, with a maximum annual count of 150 in 1946. To do so, he was obliged to develop novel tree-climbing methods that allowed him to scramble up and around the overhung edges of some gigantic nests. Usually working alone, he learned how

With its single youngster looking on, an adult Bald Eagle brings food to its nest in south Florida. Eagles commonly use their nests year after year until either the nests or the supporting trees finally collapse under the weight of steadily increasing amounts of nesting material and debris.

to encourage fully grown nestlings to disengage their talons from his flesh, and he sometimes was faced with long chases through dense scrub vegetation to retrieve youngsters that fledged prematurely on his approach. These efforts, together with his natural history studies at nests, greatly expanded knowledge of the species' habits, revealing, for example, that each summer many immature Florida eagles migrate to the northeastern states and to southern Canada.

A naturalist who based his conclusions on experience in the field, Broley was the first to call attention to the declining fortunes of the Bald Eagle that began with the advent of organochlorine pesticides in 1947. His conservation efforts also led to the protection of many nests and had an important role in ending egg collecting of this species in the United States. His achievements, attained entirely as a private citizen, are an inspiring example of what one highly motivated person can accomplish when allowed considerable independence.

The Bald Eagle was one of the species most sorely stressed by chemical contamination during the organochlorine era following World War II. Reproduction dropped to near zero in many populations across the United States, and only arctic populations remained largely unaffected. In 1963 the total number of breeding pairs in the lower forty-eight states was estimated at just over four hundred (less than a tenth of the number found at present), and the species was classified as endangered in most of the lower forty-eight states in 1967. But with the banning of many organochlorine pesticides in the early 1970s, the species began a steady recovery and was largely out of danger by the 1990s. The overall prospects for the Bald Eagle continue to be favorable. The species has certainly been suffering local losses to housing developments and other forms of human encroachment, as well as attrition from illegal shooting, lead poisoning, and collisions, but the total number of Bald Eagles in the United States and Canada has continued to rise. In 1999 researchers estimated that one hundred thousand Bald Eagles inhabit North America.

Bald Eagle

Falcons and Caracaras

Gyrfalcon
Falco rusticolus

Range of the Gyrfalcon
■ Breeding
⋯⋯ Usual southern boundary of winter range

IT WAS LATE JUNE 1968 in the Alaska Range and still quite chilly, with temperatures consistently plunging well below freezing overnight. The day blustered with intermittent rainsqualls, and we wondered if we had brought enough clothing. Nevertheless, the very exercise of climbing from the valley floor to the distant Gyrfalcon cliff kept us quite warm, while the obviously fresh diggings of grizzly bears on all sides also helped keep our temperatures elevated. As we worked upward through the lingering snow patches and thickets of willow scrub, it was impossible not to wonder how soon we would run into one of these monsters. The terrain offered no refuge should a grizzly appear, and along the way were far too many swales and hollows where bears would have been invisible until we blundered upon them. Outside Alaska and Central Africa, few land areas remain on the planet where the sensation of being a totally vulnerable prey species is still inescapable.

We had only once before seen a Gyrfalcon, a wintering white-plumaged bird in upstate New York. But now, the American Ornithologists' Union meeting in Fairbanks had gotten us to Alaska, and we joined a post-conference party that was hiking to one of the few accessible eyries (cliff nests) of this rugged northern species. We were all keenly excited by the prospect of observing these birds at close range. The hike was a long one, but we could see the nest cliff from the start and our progress was rapid.

We approached up the back side of a ridge that broke out into the nest cliff at its end. As we finally crested the ridge at a point immediately opposite the nest cave, we quickly spotted one of the adult Gyrfalcons sitting on a barren knob about a hundred yards away, a dramatic silhouette against the glaciers descending to the valley below. On seeing us, the bird soon took flight, then made a pass overhead to disappear in the distance.

The terrain immediately surrounding the Gyrfalcon nest was just emerging from winter's grasp. Frigid snow patches alternated with dark talus slopes and rocky outcrops in all directions, and icy rain showers pelted us from low-hanging clouds. Yet as bitter and melancholy as conditions seemed, they were lush compared to what the same scene must have looked like two to three months earlier, when the Gyrfalcons had begun nesting. At that time, nearly the entire region must have been white, and about the only snow-free location would have been deep inside the cave that formed the eyrie itself. Gyrfalcons are often highly traditional in their use of specific nest sites, and this was a site known to have been active for decades.

Three well-grown nestlings stood in the eyrie entrance, with only a few patches of natal down showing on their fast-developing feathers. The nesting cycle was nearing completion, and soon enough these youngsters would be on the wing learning just how ptarmigan and ground squirrels react to Gyrfalcon shadows. Other than a few Rosy Finches and Snow Buntings, we saw few other birds in the immediate area, although Black-billed Magpies and Northern Shrikes frequented the valley below. Where the snows had melted, the low

Above: *The largest of the falcons, the Gyrfalcon is impressively swift in flight, though broader in wing, heavier in body, and less agile than the Peregrine Falcon.*

Left: *A fledgling Gyrfalcon awaits its parents' return on a prominence overlooking a wide reach of Alaska's North Slope. On the wing in early July 1987, this youngster still knew nothing about the process of capturing its own prey.*

At her nest in a crevice of a crumbling Alaskan cliff, a female Gyrfalcon in 1968 lands amid a frantic crescendo of screaming from her brood. The youngsters were close to fledging but still were many weeks from true independence.

vegetation was rapidly greening up, providing steadily increasing cover and food for the nesting activities of what species were present.

In the days that followed, we had a chance to return to the cliff to watch the nest closely from a tiny blind pitched on a narrow ledge nearby. The blind gave a clear view of the entrance of the eyrie, and the young were now old enough that essentially all their activities were in full view, although the cave faced north and received no direct sunlight through most of the day. The adults were surprisingly confident in coming to the nest despite the intrusion of a blind below them; they seemed not to recognize us as a major potential threat. We wondered if they might show a stronger response should a grizzly appear. Their nest was not so high on the cliff that it had secure protection from terrestrial predators, and we doubted that a grizzly would have much difficulty scrambling to the entrance or that it might pass up an opportunity to dine on young falcon flesh.

The eyrie was sufficiently accessible that ground squirrels, a frequent prey of the falcons, made repeated runs to the nest entrance to stare curiously at the youngsters within from a few feet away. Their stares were met by even more curious stares from the falcons. Did they recognize each other for what their true relationship soon would be? There was no sign, and it appeared that the nestlings still knew food only as something that their parents brought in, not as something they would ever have to capture themselves.

Visits of the adults to the nest were infrequent and brief, as the young were far beyond the stage when they needed brooding. We had much more

Lingering snow patches and fresh diggings of grizzly bears for peavine roots line the route to a Gyrfalcon eyrie (top right) in the mountains of central Alaska. The snow was disappearing fast by late June 1968, but the landscape must have been almost entirely white when the Gyrfalcons began their nesting cycle several months earlier.

opportunity to watch the behavior of the youngsters than of the adults. The nestlings were quiet for the most part, but when an adult appeared in the area, they began a tireless screaming, which rose in a frenzied crescendo as the parent bird shot in to land on the nest ledge. The bedlam did not cease until the parent left on another foraging expedition and the chicks sensed that the prospects of further immediate food had disappeared.

Both adults at the 1968 nest were of the gray phase, although Gyrfalcons come in a variety of color phases, usually classified as white, gray, and black, and in the early days of ornithology the birds of different phases were often considered separate species of Gyrfalcon. The records of many observers over the years, however, have revealed that the different color phases frequently interbreed and that they do not constitute separate species. Almost pure white birds are most common in northern Greenland and the eastern Arctic of North America, while most Gyrfalcons in Alaska are gray-phased. Nevertheless, all phases can be found, at least to some extent, in all major arctic regions.

Almost twenty years later, in July 1987, we had another opportunity to watch nesting Gyrfalcons, this time on the North Slope of Alaska far above the Arctic Circle. One nest we observed from a blind had apparently been constructed originally by Rough-legged Hawks or Common Ravens, and here, gray-phased Gyrfalcon adults were feeding a brood of four young a diet primarily of ptarmigan. Like the adults at the nest of 1968, the adults at this nest paid scant attention to us or our blind. Not nearly as agile as a pair of Peregrine Falcons that were nesting about a mile away, they were nevertheless impressively swift in flight, especially as they dove on a nearby pair of Rough-legged Hawks that strayed too close to them.

The young Gyrfalcons, as they left this nest, were also remarkably bold, regarding our close approach with only a few signs of initial fear, then apparent boredom once they had concluded we meant them no harm. Their true attentions were focused on the skies as they awaited the return of their parents with food. After fledging, young Gyrfalcons normally stay within two or three hundred yards of their nests for close to a week and remain fully dependent on their parents for more than a month.

At two other Gyrfalcon nests of 1987, young were farther into the post-fledging period by the time of our arrival and were covering respectable distances from the nest cliffs in their first exploratory flights out over the tundra. Not yet hunting on their own, they were still gaining the flight strength and agility that would ultimately give them the capacities to forage successfully. They spent most of their time perching, preening, and dealing with the clouds of mosquitoes that filled the air whenever the wind dropped below a moderate breeze. At times, they watched intently as Long-tailed Jaegers and Glaucous Gulls coursed over the rolling hills. From the nesting cliffs, the tundra was now in full flower, and far below, occasional moose and caribou browsed on willows and fireweed, while Dall's sheep kept to the steeper rocky slopes that allowed some refuge from attacks of wolves and other carnivores.

With large females sometimes weighing more than four and a half pounds and having a wingspread of more than five feet, the Gyrfalcon is the largest of all the falcons. It characteristically hunts in swift low flights, capturing prey by surprise, often right on the ground. In attack, the Gyrfalcon either immediately binds to the prey with its talons or delivers a stunning blow with its talons in passing, followed by a return to recover its insensate victim. The coup de grace is a quick bite to the neck at the base of the skull. The prey taken most commonly are terrestrial species such as ptarmigan and ground squirrels, but under conditions of scarcity of these prey, Gyrfalcons turn readily to other prey, such as seabirds and hares. Nevertheless, overall breeding productivity usually depends on the availability of ptarmigan, and in years of ptarmigan scarcity, few pairs breed.

Clutching a ptarmigan in his feet, a male Gyrfalcon approaches his nest, an old raven or rough-leg nest on a low cliff of Alaska's North Slope.

The female adult followed almost immediately, displacing the male to begin ripping apart the prey for the four youngsters.

In winter, many Gyrfalcons remain in the Arctic as long as food supplies permit, but some individuals, especially juveniles, move farther south, and like juvenile Snowy Owls sometimes reach the northern tier of states just south of Canada. In these southern wintering locations, the species often takes a great diversity of prey, ranging from other raptors to carrion.

While the Gyrfalcon is nowhere an abundant bird, it inhabits a realm, both in summer and in winter, that is mostly remote from civilization, and the species consequently enjoys a high degree of security from most of the stresses that threaten other raptor populations. The Gyrfalcon is not known to have suffered any significant impacts from the organochlorine era, and as far as information is available, it appears that its numbers are still as strong today as they ever were.

Available population estimates suggest that Alaska normally hosts perhaps five hundred pairs of Gyrfalcons, while Greenland may harbor as many as one thousand pairs. Many more occur across the Canadian Arctic. Iceland, where the Gyrfalcon is the national bird, normally hosts about three to four hundred pairs. The total population of this species, including both Old World and New World regions, has been estimated at fifteen thousand to seventeen thousand pairs.

Gyrfalcon

Peregrine Falcon
Falco peregrinus

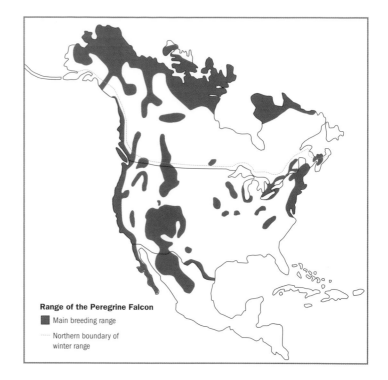

MUCH OF THE IMPRESSIVENESS of the Peregrine Falcon comes from its ability to subdue nimble and powerful avian prey. Few birds, unless they are very large or very small or are a species that never leaves cover, are safe from this raptor. Indeed, peregrines are among the very few birds of prey known to regularly capture swifts, surely among the most agile of all birds. Capable of executing astonishingly intricate maneuvers, the Peregrine Falcon is a true master of the air, fully worthy of its fame as a raptor of unequaled predatory abilities. From perches high above the surrounding terrain, it launches breathtaking stoops of incredible velocity as it attacks victims unfortunate enough to fly through its domain.

Aiding the peregrine in its aerial exploits are long, narrow wings and a body shape broadest about the shoulders and tapering smoothly to the tip of the tail. Females weigh as much as two to three pounds, although males are usually less than a pound and a half. The wingspread of the species normally

Range of the Peregrine Falcon
■ Main breeding range
⋯ Northern boundary of winter range

Viewed against the silt-choked Tanana River of central Alaska in 1968, an adult female Peregrine Falcon pauses before returning to her eggs. Extremely long toes adapt the peregrine for capturing elusive avian prey. In his early writings, John James Audubon called this species the Great-footed Hawk.

ranges between three and three-and-two-thirds feet. The peregrine is built for speed, and as a superlative predator of other birds, it enjoys a nearly worldwide distribution, thriving in a great variety of settings from arctic tundra to tropical rain forests. In North America, the species is best known as an inhabitant of canyons and cliffs, often bordering on open country or overlooking rivers.

Although it takes birds of many sorts, the peregrine is perhaps best known as a predator of waterbirds. And it was in its role as a slayer of ducks, befitting the old American name of Duck Hawk, that we first became closely familiar with the species. During the late 1960s and early 1970s, we frequently explored the bays, keys, and canals of the southern tip of the Florida peninsula in search of this species, sometimes in a small skiff, sometimes in a canoe. Wintering peregrines were concentrated in this region, attracted and sustained by the shoals of American Coots, Green-winged Teal, and Northern Pintails gathering in the shallow lakes and bays. The peregrines often perched in large dead mangrove snags with broad vistas of open marshes or water. From such vantage points they were able to survey their surroundings for potential prey, waiting patiently for the proper set of circumstances to allow successful hunts.

For the most part, the Peregrines did not attack ducks that were sitting on the water. The ducks appeared to know this and seemed extremely reluctant to take flight when a peregrine was in view. Thus, what appeared superficially to be a vast larder of waterbirds for the peregrines was apparently largely out of their reach, and only when potential prey were in the air, especially when they were unaware of the peregrines, did they become highly vulnerable.

Even in flight, a duck can often outdistance a pursuing peregrine. Or if the peregrine is gaining, the duck can sometimes escape by diving into the water. We once watched this tactic employed by a Lesser Scaup fleeing a peregrine on Florida's Whitewater Bay. Clearly unable to outfly his assailant, the duck finally gained safety by simply folding his wings and dropping like a stone, raising a plume of spray as he hit the surface just ahead of his pursuer.

Our boat sometimes provided the crucial advantage that a peregrine needed to catch its prey off guard. As we moved through the waterways, we often flushed waterfowl, who then became easy marks for attack because they concentrated their attention on escaping from us, only to place themselves in jeopardy from the rapidly reacting peregrines. Occasionally we even found peregrines that had gained a full appreciation of the predictable duck-flushing capacity of small boats and followed us high overhead for long distances, waiting for unsuspecting waterfowl to take to the air.

As fast as the peregrines are—their dives reputedly can reach two hundred miles per hour—they are not invincible and their intended prey can often elude them in level flight, where their cruising speed is more commonly about fifty miles per hour. We sometimes watched a peregrine making numerous successive chases of ducks completely without success. One such bird we watched for several hours finally gave up and circled high into the sky, beginning short forays in midair to take what appeared to be dragonflies that he ate on the wing.

One particularly skilled adult peregrine of the winter of 1969–70 gave us many exciting observations of its hunting capacities. This bird was nearly oblivious to our presence, and we were often able to watch it from distances of less than fifty feet without apparently disturbing it. Almost invariably, it used one of two different roost trees along the shore of Bear Lake, just off Florida Bay, and we could count on finding the bird on one of these roosts if we got to the area soon enough after first light.

Our most memorable encounter with this bird occurred shortly after dawn of February 28, 1970. This was an especially cold morning with fresh winds out of the north, and just as we arrived, we saw the peregrine take flight to overtake and capture a passing Green-winged Teal, dispatching his prey with a bite to the neck as he gripped it in his talons and flew back to a

The eyrie of 1968 consisted of nothing more than an overhung depression at the base of a rock band on a nearly vertical cliff. The eggs rested in a bare scrape of soil.

perch in a nearby snag. There, he began plucking feathers from the body of the teal in preparation for feeding on it. Suddenly, for no apparent reason, he became very alert and soon took off, carrying the prey in one foot beyond a line of low mangroves several hundred yards to the west. There, the peregrine inexplicably dropped the teal, although he soon returned to our vicinity, circling up and repeatedly calling *cack-cack-cack* with harsh agitation.

At last, we realized what was causing this puzzling behavior. An immature Bald Eagle came steaming across the lake from behind us and began coursing over the ground where the peregrine had dropped the teal. The eagle was obviously attempting to find the recently dispatched prey, while the peregrine cackled in dismay and harassed the eagle unmercifully. Unfortunately, about this time we drifted too close, and the eagle became aware of our presence and flew off into the distance, so we did not have a chance to see a natural conclusion to the incident. Nevertheless, the apparent attempt by the peregrine to hide its prey from the eagle was remarkable and suggested an astonishing level of foresight in the bird.

The Bear Lake peregrine was also remarkable in another respect. He was an *anatum* peregrine, at that time a race of the species that was close to extinction in the eastern states, apparently due mainly to direct mortality from Dieldrin poisoning and to the insidious eggshell-thinning effects of DDE, causing almost complete reproductive failure. Peregrine Falcons, together with a number of other bird- and fish-eating raptor species, were the species suffering the most from this chemical contamination, and *anatum* peregrines had disappeared from essentially all known nesting cliffs from the Mississippi Valley to the East Coast. The Bear Lake peregrine may well have been one of the last individuals from the breeding population in eastern Canada.

Fortunately, by the early 1970s the many detrimental effects of various organochlorine pesticides were becoming well documented, and these toxic chemicals were phased out of use both in the United States and in Canada. The recovery of the affected raptor species in North America since that time has been due mainly to the gradual decline in levels of these contaminants in their prey species, aided in the case of the peregrine by major reintroduction efforts in some regions.

Peregrine Falcon

Not all the peregrines we found wintering in Florida in the late 1960s and early 1970s were *anatum* peregrines. Many were arctic-breeding birds belonging to the race *tundrius*. As immatures, *tundrius* peregrines have very light sandy crowns to their heads, and as adults they characteristically show a very attractive light blue sheen to their crown, back, and wing feathers. Typical *anatum* peregrines from farther south have dark grayish black helmets and upperparts.

Both *anatum* and *tundrius* peregrines breed in Alaska, and this state was home for many of the last North American members of the species that were still producing some young at the height of the organochlorine era. There, in 1968, we visited a spectacular eyrie along a bend of the Tanana River with Walter Spofford, one of the first researchers involved with conservation of this species. This was the last known active peregrine nest along the Tanana, as even in this region of central Alaska pesticide contamination was heavily stressing the birds. At the nest site we were able to get an excellent appreciation of just what sort of habitat characteristics are favorable for the species. The peregrines were nesting high on a ledge of an escarpment overlooking a vast region of braided river flats, with the snow-covered Alaska Range looming in the distance and an abundance of both water and land birds in the near vicinity. The height of the cliffs and the unobstructed view gave the peregrines a crucial advantage over prey species in the area.

Clutch size of the Tanana pair was the three eggs typical for the region, although clutches of four eggs are predominant farther south in the lower states. The eggs were placed in a depressed hollow, or scrape, scratched in the earth by the feet of the birds and sheltered partially by an overhanging wall of rock. Despite the widespread pesticide contamination of the population, all three eggs hatched and the nest was successful in producing three apparently healthy chicks.

We have since seen peregrine eyries in a great many regions, ranging from Spain to Peru. Not all have been in regions with abundant waterbirds,

From the top of the nest cliff, a vast region of river flats extended toward the distant Alaska Range, giving the peregrines a superb vantage point from which to detect and capture prey.

but all have been in places with plentiful prey birds of one sort or another, and all have been characterized by topographic features that allowed the peregrines frequent opportunities to surprise their prey in vulnerable situations. Such places are not really all that common. Probably for this reason peregrines have never been, and presumably never will be, abundant birds, although they certainly achieve large enough populations in regions of relatively good habitat to qualify as locally common.

Broad black patches on the sides of their heads characterized the Peregrine Falcons of the historic anatum *race. This wintering individual habitually roosted on a dead mangrove bordering Bear Lake near Florida Bay in 1970 and often hunted prey that flew over the lake. Peregrines generally capture prey in flight and do best when they have the advantage of surprise or altitude.*

Above the torrents of the Sagavanirktok River of Alaska's North Slope, a tundrius *peregrine displays astonishingly agile aerial maneuvers in defending her nearby nest.* Tundrius *peregrines have much narrower black patches on the sides of the head than do* anatum *peregrines.*

In recent years, peregrines reintroduced in eastern states have often nested on ledges of skyscrapers and giant bridges in the hearts of some of North America's largest cities. These human-built surrogates for cliff-canyon topography have proved highly attractive to these raptors, very likely because of high populations of Rock Doves and other urban birds inhabiting the surrounding city environments. Many of these nesting areas have also had the virtue of low populations of Great Horned Owls, which constitute a very significant threat to nesting success of Peregrine Falcons in many natural settings. Variants on the skyscraper theme include peregrine nests atop grain elevators in the prairie states and atop abandoned lighthouses in other parts of the world. Aside from the opposition of some pigeon fanciers, modern urban peregrines have enjoyed widespread support from city residents, and few sights compare with a peregrine in hot pursuit of a luckless pigeon above the noisy traffic of city streets.

Perhaps the North American region with the most impressive population of Peregrine Falcons today is the Grand Canyon of the Colorado River in Arizona. A survey sponsored by the National Park Service in 1989 revealed a canyon population that may exceed a hundred and fifty pairs. Nesting in spectacular cliffs ranging from black Precambrian schists to brilliant red Paleozoic shales, sandstones, and limestones, these peregrines enjoy an abundant food supply that includes everything from clouds of Violet-green Swallows, White-throated Swifts, and bats, to shoals of waterfowl. Many of these species are ultimately dependent on the productivity of the Colorado River itself, which, as it continues to cut the cliffs and gorges of the region, simultaneously nourishes its inhabitants.

As part of the peregrine survey effort in the canyon during the spring of 1989, Noel joined a crew floating down the many rapids of the Inner Gorge, arriving each day at strategic observation points on sandy beaches and low bluffs. Here, it was possible to scan intently for glimpses of the falcons in late afternoon and early morning watches, before floating farther down canyon to the next set of observation points. Peregrines were sighted throughout the canyon, though clearly many must have been missed because of the steepness of the cliffs and the impossibility of examining more than a tiny fraction of the many nearby escarpments from any viewpoint. The enormous scale of the canyon dwarfs all efforts to explore it thoroughly or to arrive at a rigorously complete census of any of its inhabitants.

Our most memorable sighting of a peregrine in the Grand Canyon came many years earlier, however. During the mid-1970s when we were surveying the southwestern states for Common Black Hawks and Zone-tailed Hawks, we once stopped off to watch the dawn unfold from the canyon's South Rim. Our intention was to enjoy the progression of colors as the sun touched formation after formation from its path across the sky. But as we first reached the rim, there, hanging motionless in the breeze only a few yards out and a few yards up, was an adult male peregrine in perfect feather. A few long seconds passed, and the bird then slowly tipped over in a long slanting dive that took him steadily downward toward the very Inner Gorge of the canyon, past innumerable layers of muted colors, past majestic peaks and amphitheaters, past ages of geological time, to the earliest Precambrian rocks nearly a mile below and then finally out of sight. His journey, spanning the record of millions of years in the space of a few minutes, was silent and left us wondering if the bird could possibly have any knowledge of the geological epochs and successions of fossil life-forms he had traversed. From the bones of almost contemporary mastodons, ground sloths, and condors, back to dinosaur footprints, to trilobites, and finally to primitive algal remains, a major part of the earth's history had passed before both the peregrine and us, and as separate branches of evolution we had all journeyed back to our common origins in the earliest life on the planet.

Peregrine Falcon

Prairie Falcon
Falco mexicanus

COURSING LOW OVER THE TERRAIN with rapid wing beats and swift, purposeful flight, the Prairie Falcon leaves its intended victims little time for escape maneuvers or retreat into cover, and it usually captures prey by surprise at close range rather than by extended pursuit. A highly mobile and aggressive raptor with an overall tan coloration, black "armpits," a dark mustache, and long powerful wings, it ranges from one to two-and-a-half pounds in weight and is large enough to pose a substantial threat to medium-large prey such as various ground squirrels and meadowlarks. Its primary habitat is arid western canyons, grasslands, and deserts with scattered cliffs, and it covers huge areas in its daily search for food. Most of its kills result from chance encounters with vulnerable exposed prey.

With a range extending from northern Mexico to southern Canada and pretty much throughout the western United States, the Prairie Falcon enjoys a wide distribution, but it is quite unevenly spread within this range. Recent estimates suggest a total breeding population for the species of perhaps about five thousand to six thousand pairs, mostly in the Rocky Mountain states and Pacific Coast states. Many regions, however, have not yet been carefully surveyed for this species, especially in northern Mexico, and this total may grow to some extent when more complete data become available.

The Prairie Falcon is very similar to the peregrine in size and general flying skills, but it is much more inclined to come to the ground in hunting forays and is much more likely to take mammals as prey. Like the peregrine, the Prairie Falcon usually nests in high cliffs, though it is less restricted to regions with good waterfowl populations and often thrives in regions far from any sources of water whatsoever.

Prairie Falcons are especially abundant in certain regions of southern California, where the last historic wild California Condors nested. The condors suffered continual harassment from this species in several of their last nesting areas, and indeed, within one-and-a-half miles of one condor nest in 1984 we found no fewer than five nesting pairs of prairies simultaneously active.

One condor pair of 1980 had an especially hard time dealing with Prairie Falcons. This pair first appeared to be settling on a towering cliff with a variety of excellent nest caves, but a pair of prairies moved into the same cliff and soon began diving aggressively on the condors. The condors immediately moved to another site about a mile away, where they laid their egg. Unfortunately, another pair of prairies moved into this second cliff soon thereafter and chose a pothole site just two hundred feet or so from the condor cave, directly facing it from across a narrow ravine. The condors had no choice but to persevere, but they had a tough time through the reproductive cycle as they struggled to approach and leave their nest without being clobbered by the falcons.

The main challenge faced by the condors was penetrating the falcon-guarded airspace in front of their nest, but once they fought through the falcons and landed on the ground near their nest, they usually walked the rest of the way to the nest with head tucked and held low. Once, however, we saw one of the condors apparently forget the prairies in its final approach and walk upslope to its nest with head and neck held high. One of the prairies hit the condor hard and it tumbled head over heels for several yards.

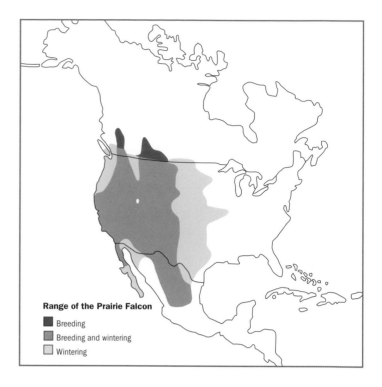

Range of the Prairie Falcon
- Breeding
- Breeding and wintering
- Wintering

On many occasions, a condor approaching this nest never even got close before it was forced to turn aside and flee down canyon, sometimes regurgitating mouthfuls of slimy food that cascaded to the ground as it attempted to lighten its load to escape the dives of its tormentors. Nevertheless, the condors always managed to get to their nest in the end, often by retreating to a safe distance, then sailing in very high over the nesting canyon and descending to their nest in long powerful stoops that the prairies could not prevent or significantly deflect.

Despite the harassment, the condors succeeded in fledging their young, as did the prairies. Moreover, in the balance, the presence of the prairies nesting nearby may actually have been very beneficial to the condors' efforts. The falcons were also highly aggressive to other large avian species, such as Golden Eagles and Common Ravens, which constitute strong threats to condor nests, and this condor pair was conspicuously free from threats from these other species while the prairies were active next door. In other nestings in subsequent years, the same pair of condors suffered incessant raven harassment resulting in the loss of two of their eggs, but these nestings were not characterized by nearby nesting prairies. While prairies have been much more tolerant of ravens than of other large avian species in most studies, they were highly aggressive to them in this region.

In any event, we were very grateful to the prairies nesting next to the 1980 condor nest. They always spotted the condors returning to their nest far sooner than we did, and by their angry cackles alerted us to imminent action at the condor nest. Fortunately, the prairies never showed the slightest inclination to capture the young condor chick, even though the falcon nest faced the condor nest directly and the chick was often left unguarded and in full view of the falcons.

Two years later, when we again studied the same condor pair nesting in the same canyon, we again watched an aggressive, though not as close, pair of prairies defending its nest area from all intruders. In this year, however, the risks of this behavior to the prairies themselves finally became clear. As witnessed by Dave Clendenen, one of our field collaborators, a Golden Eagle passing through the region responded to one of the prairies in the midst of an attack by reaching out with one of its massive talons, snatching the falcon in midair, and killing it instantly.

On her Colorado nest cliff, an adult female Prairie Falcon calls in alarm at intruders ranging from people to Golden Eagles.

The Prairie Falcons we watched in California fed heavily on ground squirrels and commuted long distances from their nest canyons to their foraging grounds. Despite intensive poisoning campaigns, ground squirrels were still an abundant species in the grasslands of the state, perhaps mainly because the squirrels thrive best in regions that are heavily grazed and where the height of vegetation is relatively low.

Prairie Falcons are also common in southern Arizona. A relatively accessible pair we studied in the Tucson Mountains in 1975 had chosen a very well protected cave that had evidently been used for many decades, possibly centuries, of nesting. The hardened white excrement dripping from the entrance was apparently inches thick in places and advertised the nest from many miles away. From a forty-foot-high tower blind, we had a view directly into the falcon eyrie with its four young, as well as a spectacular view of the surrounding terrain.

Down below the escarpment on the flats stretching off to the horizon were the saguaro cacti and palo verdes that typify well-vegetated Sonoran Desert. The birds most common nearby were Cactus Wrens, Gila Woodpeckers, and White-winged Doves. About the cliffs themselves flew Canyon Wrens and White-throated Swifts. Birds such as these formed most of the diet of the prairies during the days of observation, and the adults were highly successful in keeping their brood well fed. Nevertheless, in most regions Prairie Falcons tend to feed most heavily on mammals, and this emphasis was probably a critical factor in the much better survival of this species than the Peregrine Falcon through the organochlorine era.

Prairie Falcon

Above: *After concluding a feeding of her youngsters, the female prairie departs for another hunting expedition.*

Left: *Thick layers of hardened white excrement suggest that this Prairie Falcon eyrie in Arizona's Tucson Mountains has been used over many centuries.*

Our blind was especially well situated for observing the prey transfers between male and female adults. While the female did some hunting for the brood, she was more commonly in attendance in the nest vicinity and stood ready to receive what the male had captured. She fed most of what he supplied to her hungry youngsters, but she also satisfied much of her own needs from the same source.

Food transfers between the adults usually took place in midair, with the female surging up from below to snatch the prey from her mate's talons in a quick roll of impressive skill and timing. The male also occasionally brought food to the nest when the female was off hunting, but he did not stay to rip it apart for the young. His primary role was clearly hunting for the family, rather than tending the brood directly.

One of the most remarkable concentrations of Prairie Falcons known is found in the Snake River Canyon of southwestern Idaho. Here, 101

The male Prairie Falcon at the Arizona eyrie brought prey directly to the nest only when the female was off hunting and unavailable for food transfers. The male never fed the brood himself but simply left prey for the female to process when she returned.

Similar to the Peregrine Falcon in size and flight capacities, Prairie Falcons nevertheless concentrate more heavily on mammalian prey. In most regions, the species feeds on a staple of ground squirrels, varied with a diversity of open-country birds.

pairs were found occupying a forty-five-mile stretch of river in a study of 1972, and these pairs produced an astonishingly high average of 3.1 young per eyrie. A later study of eighty-one miles of the same river revealed an almost unbelievable total of 215 pairs, or close to one pair every third of a mile. Such densities far surpass those achieved by any known nesting population of the Peregrine Falcon, the most similar North American raptor in nesting habits.

Nevertheless, the foraging activities of the Snake River Prairie Falcons extend many miles away from the river, so that the actual home ranges of individual pairs are very large. Measurements of these home ranges have indicated an average size of about forty-six square miles, with some birds observed foraging as far as sixteen miles from their nests. Foraging ranges overlap broadly among adjacent pairs, and in practical terms it is unlikely, with ranges this large, that individuals could effectively defend exclusive foraging areas.

The Snake River Canyon is also a mecca for other raptor species, such as Golden Eagles and Red-tailed Hawks, and the overall density of nesting raptors here is very great. Nevertheless, it is not the region of highest known raptor diversity or density for North America. Much greater diversity and densities of raptors are known for Cave Creek Canyon in Arizona, for example, where a remarkable array of small owl species occurs together with many of the same diurnal raptor species found along the Snake River. The Snake River region, which hosts many more Prairie Falcons than Cave Creek Canyon, is in part incorporated into a National Conservation Area set aside specifically for birds of prey and administered by the Bureau of Land Management. This area represents a very fortunate juxtaposition of extensive favorable cliffs for nesting and extensive open-country foraging grounds. The Prairie Falcons of this region are thriving primarily on dense populations of Townsend's ground squirrels.

Much of the habitat occupied by the Prairie Falcon is arid, precipitous, and remote, giving considerable security from human influences. The dietary flexibility of the species further enhances its capacities to endure. Throughout its range, the Prairie Falcon remains a reasonably common species, and nothing indicates that it is presently having special difficulties in coping with the modern world.

Aplomado Falcon

Falco femoralis

THE APLOMADO FALCON is a long-tailed, long-legged, narrow-winged raptor with handsome black-and-chestnut bands across its breast and belly. Its name is derived from the Spanish word for "leadened," presumably referring to the gray coloration of the bird's back. Mainly tropical in distribution and occurring as far south as Argentina, the species once bred with some regularity in southern Arizona, New Mexico, and Texas, although it may never have been truly common in this region. Sightings and records of the species declined greatly by the early twentieth century, and until very recently, several decades had passed without an active nest being located north of the Mexican border. Despite much time spent in the southwestern United States from the late 1960s to the present, we only once have encountered an Aplomado Falcon in this region, a lone individual coursing over a wide reach of yucca grassland in southwestern New Mexico in early 1987.

In part, the virtual disappearance of the aplomado from the United States may have resulted from the overenthusiastic activities of early egg collectors. But it is a reasonable surmise that habitat degradation may have played a more important role. In the latter part of the nineteenth century, a combination of widespread drought and overgrazing devastated many of

Range of the Aplomado Falcon

☐ Present established year-round populations

☐ Area of release efforts

the lands just north of the Mexican border. Many of these regions have never fully recovered their former character, as has been particularly well documented for southern Arizona. Where aplomados still occur in Mexico and countries farther south, they are not restricted to virgin habitats, but

In defending her nest, the Veracruz female did not hesitate to strike blows at humans climbing the nest tree.

Above: *The male aplomado brings a small bird to the female to feed their young.*

Right: *After an unsuccessful hunt, a female Aplomado Falcon returns to her nest in Veracruz, Mexico, in 1978.*

they do appear to be restricted to regions with high prey densities and very specific habitat structures. The enormous habitat changes that occurred along the Mexican border around the turn of the twentieth century may well have destroyed the potential of many regions to support the species.

Once thought to be a predator primarily of reptiles, rodents, and various insects, the aplomado actually feeds mainly on birds, which has been well established by intensive studies initiated in Mexico by Dean Keddy-Hector of the Chihuahua Desert Research Institute during the 1970s. It also takes insects with some frequency, but by weight, insects form only a minor part of the diet. Like other bird-feeders, the aplomado exhibits a very strong size difference between sexes, with females weighing a little less than a pound and males averaging only 64 percent as heavy as females.

The means by which aplomados take birds include some unusual adaptations. In the spring of 1978, we joined Dean Keddy-Hector in the state of Veracruz in eastern Mexico to observe the hunting and nesting behavior of this species in some detail. We were greatly impressed with this falcon's specializations in dealing with its food supply and with the relationship of its hunting habits to its nesting habits.

Like other falcons, aplomados do not build their own nests, but instead occupy old nests of other species. The active nests we saw had mainly been constructed by White-tailed Kites and Roadside Hawks and were located in small groves of trees surrounded by largely open country. Around their nests, the aplomados were not exceptionally wary birds, and at one nest that we climbed to examine the nestlings, we found the female to be highly aggressive, cackling furiously and swooping in with reckless strafing runs, striking us repeatedly with her talons. Roughly the size and weight of a female Cooper's Hawk, she packed considerable power in her blows, and we kept our nest checks very brief to minimize the chances of injury, both to her and to us.

The nest of this female and her mate was placed in a small grove of acacias in the midst of a plowed cornfield and contained two chicks, a common brood size in the region. Both were only several days old and were feathered in the white down typical of young nestling falcons. Both were also

Aplomado Falcon

The Veracruz pair reared their young in an abandoned nest, probably built by White-tailed Kites, about twenty feet up a huisache. Despite pesticide contamination and severe eggshell thinning, the aplomados of Veracruz maintained reasonably normal productivity through the 1970s.

free of the warble fly maggots that are sometimes found infesting young of this species. The nest itself was a dilapidated old twig platform with barely enough cup left to hold the chicks. A pair of White-tailed Kites, perhaps the original owners of the nest, were breeding simultaneously in an adjacent patch of thorn-scrub woodland only a few hundred yards away, but we saw no interactions between the kites and aplomados.

We spent several days watching the hunting behavior of this pair of aplomados. Generally, the female brooded and fed the young and was in attendance at the nest, while the male perched in nearby exposed snaggy trees, waiting for prey to move into the open somewhere in the surroundings. Almost all hunts took place within five hundred yards of the nest, and almost always, the male hunted in full view of the female, an important behavior, as we soon learned.

Many of the male's forays were pursuits of flying insects. On these chases, he often followed an ascending path into the sky, followed at length by a return to his perch. But on one such hunt he took a route directly toward us and just above the ground that terminated as he suddenly swooped upward to snatch a large butterfly only a few feet in front of us. Until the last moment we had not seen the butterfly and instead thought that the male aplomado was intent on attacking us for unknown reasons. During our observations, none of the insect prey were taken to the female at the nest.

On other occasions, the male pursued small birds that chanced to leave cover to fly across the open fields near the nest. Some of these birds were

migrants heading for more northerly regions. Others were local residents. The male grabbed some victims immediately in tail chases. Most of these he soon took to the nest in decapitated condition for presentation to the female.

But some intended victims managed to duck back into brush before the male could reach them. On several such occasions we saw the female aplomado leave her nest and young to join the male in a cooperative follow-up. While the male hovered in the air over the tree or bush in which the prospective victim had taken refuge, the female flew right into the bush and hopped from branch to branch, pursuing the prey on foot until the latter finally took flight into the open again where it was an easy mark for capture by the male—a marvelous team effort.

The willingness of the falcons to enter the canopy of trees to chase after prey reminded us a bit of the behavior of Cooper's Hawks, and the long legs and very long tail of the aplomado show a strong resemblance to corresponding appendages of that species, perhaps aiding both raptors in balance at close quarters. It is also interesting that the female aplomado generally did the brush beating, rather than the relatively small male, although at first sight the male might seem better adapted to working through the cluttered branches. We suspect, however, that at least under some circumstances the male, with his greater agility, was perhaps a better choice to hover above, ready for the quick acceleration needed to capture the prey when it finally left cover.

In Keddy-Hector's overall studies of aplomados, the average success rate in capture attempts of birds was only 21 percent in solo hunts, as opposed to 45 percent in collaborative hunts of pair members. Further, the prey captured were often shared between the pair members. The enhanced success in hunting achieved by pairs may be one of the principal reasons that they commonly remain together in the nonbreeding season as well as the breeding season. Regardless of time of year, cooperative hunts are usually initiated by a sharp *chip* call, by which one bird alerts its mate to a hunting opportunity. What sounds like the same *chip* call is given by breeding males when they return to their nesting areas with food for their mates and young.

Interestingly, even during pair hunts, female aplomados tend to capture much larger prey birds than do their mates, so the advantages of females leaving their nests to join their mates in hunting not only include enhanced capture rates but also greater sizes of prey captured. In Keddy-Hector's overall observations, male Aplomado Falcons captured birds that averaged only 41 percent of the weight of the birds captured by females.

From what we saw of the hunting of the aplomado pairs, their habitat preferences made a great deal of sense. The critical requirements for breeding appear to be basically open-country habitat with an old stick nest of some raptor or corvid placed high in a tree or small grove offering a good view of the surroundings. Also apparently essential are relatively high numbers of prey birds placing themselves in vulnerable positions in the surroundings. The abundant North American migrants, together with conspicuously high populations of resident species, appeared to offer excellent food resources for the Mexican aplomados.

Overall, the Mexican aplomados appeared to be adapting relatively well to the habitat changes in the region, and may in fact have even been benefiting from the conversion of scrublands to pasturelands. Presumably, there may be some optimum balance between scrublands and pasturelands that maximizes prey supplies and hunting opportunities for the species, and long-term conservation of the aplomado in this region may well depend on determining what such a balance may consist of and working toward creating and maintaining it in selected areas.

In the United States, the Aplomado Falcon was once known as a bird of yucca grasslands and Gulf Coast prairies, and the prevalence of winter records north of the Mexican border suggests that the species was resident year-round in this region. Yucca grasslands and coastal prairies have by no means been wiped out in recent decades. In many regions, however, continuous stands of mesquite brush have invaded these habitats, making them impractical for aplomados to hunt because they provide too much cover for prey.

Like other bird-feeding raptors, the aplomado has also faced contamination with various organochlorines in its prey species. Alarmingly high levels of DDE contamination and severe eggshell thinning were documented for the species in coastal Mexico in the 1970s. Yet the population under study still showed quite good reproduction, and negative population effects of the contamination were not clear. In any event, the highlands of northern Mexico and adjacent areas

Near her nest in Tamaulipas, Mexico, in 2004, a female aplomado consumes a small bird provided by her mate.

in Arizona and New Mexico are one of the few regions where the Peregrine Falcon managed to hang on through the organochlorine era of the mid twentieth century without any programs to bolster wild populations with releases of captive-reared young. In more recent years, peregrines have become a common species once again in this region, and to the extent that populations of the aplomado may have faced stresses similar to those experienced by the peregrines, there are grounds for hope that aplomados may also have a relatively bright future in this same region.

The aplomado was classified as federally endangered in the United States and Mexico in 1986, largely on the basis of historic declines in the United States and evidence for severe pesticide contamination of birds in eastern Mexico. Overall population trends have not been carefully tracked in Mexico, however, and whether the species is any less abundant now than it was historically is speculative. In the United States, recent sightings and nesting records give tantalizing signs of an incipient recovery, but it is as yet too early to project that these trends will necessarily continue. Very recent nesting records for southern New Mexico may represent birds originating from a substantial population in north central Chihuahua, but whether habitat and prey populations are adequate for a fully successful recolonization of southern New Mexico remains to be seen. Deliberate efforts to reintroduce the species in southern Texas have also yielded a number of recent nestings, but long-term success here may likewise depend on hard-to-predict prey and habitat considerations.

Much may depend on land-use changes, both positive and negative, that may occur in the future. Many of the lands along the border with Mexico are still heavily degraded from brush invasion, overgrazing, and other factors, and the future of these lands is especially difficult to envision in the era of global warming and climate change now underway.

Aplomado Falcon

Merlin

Falco columbarius

IT WAS A FALL DAY OF THE EARLY 1960s in eastern Pennsylvania, and we were watching a small flock of migrant shorebirds working over the mudflats of the Tinicum Marshes. Among the foragers was a single individual of a species we had never seen before—our very first Stilt Sandpiper. With its image centered in the telescope at close range and with brilliant afternoon sunlight illuminating its feathers, we were easily able to confirm the bird's field marks. And just in time, it turned out. For suddenly, a Merlin appeared out of nowhere in the very center of the field of view and from the rear grabbed the very bird we had been scrutinizing before it had a chance to even consider flight. Without pausing, the Merlin carried off the sandpiper in its talons and disappeared in the distance. All this happened so quickly and unexpectedly, it took a few moments to be sure what species had made the kill. Regardless, we have rarely seen a prey capture by any raptor so vividly and closely, or had a first sighting of a new species terminated so abruptly.

As was obvious in this encounter, the flight of the Merlin is very direct, purposeful, and swift—much more so than the flight of the American Kestrel, the other small falcon of North America. Also obvious was the willingness of the Merlin to take prey on the ground, a trait also typical of Gyrfalcons and Prairie Falcons, but not normally seen in Peregrine Falcons or Aplomado Falcons, the other two North American falcons that focus on small- or medium-sized birds as prey. While Merlins, like American Kestrels, also take considerable numbers of insects, the primary dietary emphasis of this falcon is clearly on avian species, especially open-country birds such as various larks, sparrows, longspurs, and sandpipers.

Yet even though most of our observations of hunting Merlins have been made in marshes and open fields, we have also seen them hunting with some frequency over forested habitats—in particular, the mature rain forests of eastern Puerto Rico. There, during the early 1970s, we sometimes watched wintering individuals pursuing birds as large as Sharp-shinned Hawks that flew above the forest canopy. Merlins are also known to hunt over heavily wooded habitat in other regions, but although they sometimes perch within the canopy of trees, they rarely take prey in such locations. Presumably, their relatively long wings would be a risk in pursuing prey within cover.

Merlins lack the bold facial markings found in most other North American falcons. Both sexes tend to be heavily streaked with brown underneath, while adult males have bluish gray upperparts, and females and immatures have brownish upperparts. The tail is heavily banded in all ages and sexes and lacks the rusty coloration found in American Kestrels. With a two-foot wingspread, the species is very similar to the American Kestrel in linear dimensions, but it often weighs more than twice as much as that species, and is consequently a much more formidable predator.

Most of North American's Merlins breed in Canada and Alaska, dipping down into the northern tier of the lower United States in only a few regions. The species generally uses old stick nests of other relatively large birds, though in some regions it uses cliff ledges. Where neither cliffs nor old stick nests are available, it is known to nest with frequency right on the ground. Most Merlins begin breeding at two years of age, and eggs are most commonly laid in May. Clutch size averages slightly over four eggs, and these are incubated for about a month, with females doing by far the most incubation, although males cover eggs for short periods, mainly after passing food to females. The nestling period lasts about a month, and the adult male provides most of the food during this stage. Young fledge after about a month and remain dependent on their parents for several weeks thereafter.

The one Merlin nest we had a chance to observe closely was an old Black-billed Magpie nest in a spruce grove surrounded by tundra vegetation high in the Alaska Range. This nest contained only two eggs and was not successful. Neither of the eggs hatched after full incubation. We found this nest in 1968 at the height of the organochlorine era, and we were concerned that pesticide contamination might have been a factor in the failure. Merlins, because of their diet, were one of the species at potential risk, and the clutch size at the nest was unusually low, a potential sign of egg breakage and loss. To check the possibility of contamination with organochlorines, we were able to arrange for analysis of the eggs after it was clear that they were inviable. The eggs were indeed highly contaminated, though whether their failure to hatch could be definitely attributed to this cause was uncertain. In any event, it was discouraging to learn that even in a region as wild as this remote corner of Alaska, there was no escape from contamination. Much of the problem presumably stemmed from the fact that the Merlins were feeding heavily on migrant birds and from the fact that the Merlins themselves were migratory.

Later in 1968 we visited another nesting territory of Alaskan Merlins with Jerry Swartz of the University of Alaska. This territory was in the old gold-mining country of the mountains north of Fairbanks. Large old stick nests are almost nonexistent in this region, as it is north of the range limits of magpies, and this Merlin pair was one that habitually nested on the ground. We never found the actual nest site of 1968, however, because the brood had already fledged by the time of our arrival. Instead, we found five young Merlins still with wisps of down on their heads perched atop spruces in the area. Jerry was in the process of starting a captive breeding project with Merlins, and he was hoping to include young from this nest in the project. The fledglings showed no inclination to cooperate, however, and though they had just left the nest and could not fly well, they were able to stay just

Range of the Merlin
- Breeding
- Breeding and wintering
- Wintering

Right: *The male Merlin at a nest in the Alaska Range in 1968 was a capable predator of small birds, although the nest held only two eggs, a small clutch that suggested possible earlier egg loss.*

Merlin

Above: *The female Merlin lands on her nest tree after feeding on prey provided by the male.*

beyond our reach, even with a long-handled crab net. We got considerable exercise, but no success, in attempting to capture them.

We got even more exercise later in the day, when as we were hiking back to our vehicle we finally had a chance to experience the exact nightmare we had repeatedly envisioned in hiking to a Gyrfalcon nest earlier that same summer. For just as we got in sight of our vehicle, a full-grown grizzly bear suddenly appeared over a nearby hilltop running downhill at top speed directly toward us. A quick mental calculation, as we broke into a panic-stricken sprint ourselves, indicated that there was absolutely no way on earth that we could evade that bear. He was closing the distance to us rapidly, and there was not a scrap of nearby cover.

At moments like these, there is a strong tendency to give up and submit to the inevitable without a struggle. On sensing the futility of trying to escape, we soon stopped running and turned to face the overwhelming, oncoming threat. No time or even inclination for last profound thoughts. Just detached passive fascination with the certainty of our soon becoming bloody links in the arctic food web.

Left: *The nesting range of a Merlin pair in Alaska's White Mountains encompassed a broad reach of scattered spruces that petered out into open tundra near Eagle Summit.*

Prior to consuming an avian victim, an immature Merlin wintering in southern Chihuahua, Mexico, plucks and discards feathers from the carcass.

Unexpectedly, just as the bear was all but upon us, he too stopped running abruptly. For a moment he raised up and sniffed the air curiously, but then he immediately tore off in a new direction—away from us and down the valley. His departure was as rapid as his approach. Galloping over and through the dwarf willows and other brush as if they were no obstacles at all, he showed no signs of slowing down even as he finally disappeared over a last faraway hill.

Evidently, when we first saw the grizzly racing toward us, he was not actually aware of our presence, though there was no way for us to know this. Once he caught our scent, he was as frightened as we were and just as anxious to be somewhere else. The vision of that grizzly bounding down the valley, over rises and depressions, into the distance will always be linked in our minds with the futility of chasing fledgling Merlins from one side of a ravine to the other, in the dwindling hope that they might eventually tire enough to allow capture.

Breeding populations of the Merlin in the western United States and southern Canada experienced an unprecedented increase in the 1970s and 1980s, an increase that may have been fueled in part by recovery from the stresses of the pesticide era and in part by a remarkable spread of the species into urban environments, where it has proved capable of sustaining exceptionally high productivity. This invasion has been studied most closely by Lynn Oliphant in Saskatoon, Saskatchewan, where it immediately followed invasion of the same urban areas by American Crows and Black-billed Magpies. Both these species build stick nests of requisite properties for later use by Merlins, and the advent of these nest sites was most likely the crucial change allowing occupancy of the city habitats by breeding Merlins. In turn, the invasion of urban areas by crows and magpies was apparently due primarily to maturation

of ornamental spruce trees planted in residential areas; dense spruces offer favored nesting places for these birds. In the urban setting of Saskatoon, the Merlins have found excellent food supplies, especially House Sparrows and Bohemian Waxwings, and they have suffered only infrequent losses to nest predators.

Breeding Merlins have also been spreading into other urban areas in more recent years, especially in the northern Great Plains, but also along the coast of the Pacific Northwest and in Ontario. The urban invasion of Merlins has paralleled a similar invasion of urban areas in Scotland by European Sparrowhawks, an accipiter species similar to the Sharp-shinned Hawk. But whereas the Merlin's invasion can be attributed in large measure to a change in nest availability, the sparrowhawk invasion has apparently traced to other causes, since sparrowhawks build their own nests. Perhaps a progressively higher tolerance of our own species for raptors, evolving into interest and positive protection, has been an important component of the changes for both these species. Perhaps also important has been the increasing sponsorship of small prey birds by feeding programs of urban residents.

In any event, not all urban populations of raptors necessarily represent healthy and viable populations. While food supplies and nest sites may often be favorable in urban settings, these environments can at the same time offer major problems with collisions and electrocutions on power lines and with certain diseases carried by urban pigeons. The invasion of urban Tucson by Bay-winged Hawks and Cooper's Hawks has been characterized by both these kinds of problems, and whether these urban populations are fully self-sufficient or are maintained largely by immigration from other environments is a matter yet to be fully resolved.

American Kestrel

Falco sparverius

EANDERING MAINLY EAST TO WEST across the border between southern New Mexico and Arizona, Skeleton Canyon is a rugged gorge of sculpted red rocks cut into the western flank of the parched Peloncillo Mountains. The sides of this narrow canyon are too devoid of moisture to allow more than a limited cover of grasses, yuccas, and thornscrub, while the canyon bottom itself boasts only a modest scattering of emory oaks and sycamores nourished by an intermittently flowing stream. Despite considerable natural beauty, this is not a visually spectacular canyon on the scale of a Grand Canyon or a Zion Canyon. Nor is it a canyon blessed with a fauna and flora much different from what can be found in innumerable other dry canyons in the same general region.

It is, nevertheless, an extraordinary locality from the standpoint of turbulent human history. For it was here that the famous Clanton Gang waylaid pack trains of Mexican smugglers in the early 1880s; and it was here, in late 1886, that the renowned Apache leader, Geronimo, together with his remnant band of warriors, made his final surrender to General Miles of the U.S. Army after decades of violent conflict. So many desperados, American Indians, smugglers, and their beasts of burden met their ends in the canyon bottom that their lingering bleached bones gave rise to the modern name for the region.

The bones of Skeleton Canyon have long since disintegrated, and today the gorge has returned to the quietude it must once have enjoyed before Apaches and outlaws ever moved into the area. The occasional visitors to the canyon now are mostly unaware of the region's colorful past and find mainly lizards, snakes, grasshoppers, scorpions, and a host of other small creatures that have occupied the area for millennia. Ambushes and massacres are but a distant memory, and many years have passed since anything more violent than the monotonous languid ratcheting of cicadas has stirred the hot summer air of the canyon.

In this now thoroughly peaceful setting, we observed a nesting of one of the most pastoral of North America's raptors—the American Kestrel. Smaller than a Blue Jay and marked with bold patches of color, the kestrel is the most brilliant and most diminutive diurnal raptor on the continent. It is also one of North America's most prolific diurnal raptors, commonly laying clutches of four to six eggs and sometimes producing more than one brood per year. Alone among the falcons, it is a consistent hole-nester, most commonly occupying natural cavities or old woodpecker holes in trees but sometimes nesting in other assorted cavities, including holes in cliffs.

Kestrels are abundant in Skeleton Canyon, and at the time of our observations they were nesting mainly in cavities in the gnarled snags that line the main streambed. Less than a mile from the site of Geronimo's surrender, and almost exactly a century after that historic event, we spent a number of June days watching a natural cavity of a dying sycamore trunk that contained a vigorous brood of five young—four males and one female. Here we enjoyed watching the entire process of young kestrels making their first tentative explorations of the outside world.

Like the young of many other small hole-nesting birds, young kestrels are relatively noisy, apparently deriving considerable security against predators from the nature of their nest sites. The entrance to the Skeleton Canyon nest was an especially tight squeeze for the birds, and doubtless

A male American Kestrel perches aside his nest entrance in a dying sycamore in New Mexico's Skeleton Canyon. The male focused on lizards as prey, while his mate mainly brought grasshoppers to the five youngsters.

would have prevented entry of most of the birds' potential enemies, such as raccoons and ringtailed cats. From the protection of their nest hole, the young kestrels set up a clamor of anticipation each time they had any hints of the approach of one of their parents with food. Their tremulous triplet begging calls were easily audible from many yards away and continued for much of the day.

Both the male and female adults brought prey to the nest entrance, although the male sometimes passed prey to his mate instead of passing it directly to the brood. Strangely, the male adult, despite his smaller size than the female, seemed to be concentrating on relatively large lizards, while the female brought in endless meals of grasshoppers. Other prey included nestling birds, mice, and cicadas—altogether a smorgasbord of small creatures caught in surrounding open areas, most of which were quickly eaten by the youngsters.

The nest entrance was only large enough for one youngster to occupy at a time, but once this youngster received a prey item, he disappeared below and his position at the entrance was relinquished to another, so that

Two of the brood emerge from the Skeleton Canyon nest during the fledging process. The entrance was constricted and close to a honeybee hive, giving good protection from predators but causing difficulties in the fledglings' departure. All youngsters left the nest on the same day.

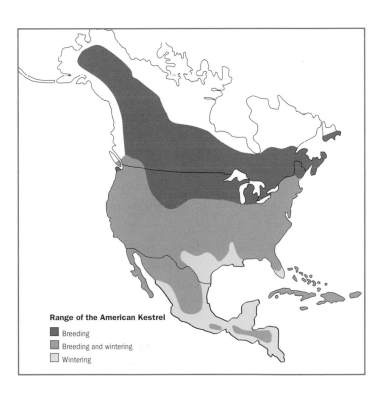

The adult female prepares to enter the Skeleton Canyon nest. The brown coloration of her wings contrasted with her mate's gray-blue wings.

Range of the American Kestrel

■ Breeding

■ Breeding and wintering

□ Wintering

food distribution appeared to be relatively equal among the nestlings. At first we were unsure how many young the nest held and we were reluctant to climb to the entrance to inspect them directly because the trunk also held a honeybee hive just a few feet away. But as time went by, we were able to recognize individual young by slight differences in facial feather patterns, and the number of males and females in the brood became clear.

Differences in the amount of down on the youngsters' heads suggested significant age differences among the nestlings. Nevertheless, the fledging process, which began June 8, seemed to infect all members of the brood more or less simultaneously, and their exits from the nest chamber followed one another rapidly. The first to leave the nest was one of the males, who struggled through the opening to perch on a broken branch base on top of the entrance in the early morning. Soon after, his only sister exited in a similar way. Both began short explorations of the vicinity of the nest entrance, scrambling from branch to branch and fully stretching their wings and bobbing their tails in the open air for the first time.

The third youngster to exit, however, was a relatively young male still with a considerable amount of down on his head. Though obviously excited and anxious to leave, he apparently lacked the full confidence to do it properly. He soon got his wings outside the hole but seemed reluctant to stand up on the nest lip, so he was trapped—unwilling to go the rest of the way out, yet unable to get back inside because his wings were caught awkwardly extended by the limited diameter of the entrance. This dilemma was no more frustrating to this bird than it was to the two youngsters left in the hole behind him. They now found their access to the outside and to food completely blocked. The impasse was only resolved when one of the males still inside the hole finally lifted

American Kestrel

the one stuck in the entrance up on his shoulders and forcibly launched him through the entrance to flutter uncertainly down into the branches below the hole.

The fledging process also seemed to excite the parent birds. They greatly increased their foraging rate, bringing twice as many prey to the nest on this day as they had on the previous day. The fledglings were indeed well attended through this crucial transition to outside existence.

Once the fledglings had left the hole, we were especially interested to observe how they handled the lizard prey that the adults were bringing them, because lizards are very tough-skinned animals that are difficult to dismember. Earlier we had once watched an adult kestrel give up in attempting to rip apart a horned lizard it had captured, and during 1971 we had witnessed numerous instances of young Cooper's Hawks at a nearby nest failing to rip apart lizards successfully and losing them over the side of the nest before managing to eat them.

The young kestrels at the Skeleton Canyon nest, however, solved the lizard ingestion problem in a very simple way—they swallowed the lizards whole and headfirst, including some comparatively large ones. Only once did we see the male adult bring a lizard so large that this was not possible, and he soon flew off with it, presumably to eat (or discard) it himself after the youngsters failed to ingest it.

Another kestrel population that concentrates on lizards for food is one that occupies the island of Culebra, east of Puerto Rico. On a trip to this island in 1974, we found individuals of this species seeming to occupy every clump of trees in the semi-open scrub of the lowlands—by far the densest population of kestrels we have ever encountered. Kestrels were both remarkably common and remarkably tame on this island, often allowing approach to within ten or fifteen feet. Nesting mainly in the hollows of large *Bucida* trees, this population seemed to have found the very essence of optimal kestrel habitat.

The American Kestrel is primarily a "sit-and-wait" predator that locates prey visually from exposed perches such as fence posts, dead snags, and utility wires. Most prey captures are made on the ground within fifty yards of

The American Kestrel lacks the extremely long toes of the bird-feeding falcons and accipiters, although it does take some birds as prey.

Like White-tailed Kites, American Kestrels often hover during hunting, inspecting the ground below for potential victims.

such perches, in direct descents from the perches. Where perches are scarce, however, kestrels often practice another hunting method—hover hunting. Facing into the wind and beating their wings rapidly, they remain nearly stationary in the sky, carefully inspecting the terrain below with their heads held low. When a potential meal is sighted, the bird descends to capture it in the same manner as when hunting from perches. Hover hunting is a much more conspicuous style of hunting than perch hunting, but studies have shown that it is not generally as successful as perch hunting. It is also much more expensive energetically. But where perches are absent and prey are abundant, it is still a profitable way for the species to hunt and is often the only way the species can successfully hunt many open habitats.

Like the Red-tailed Hawk, the American Kestrel has evolved into a great variety of color forms in different regions. All races of the species, however, show a very distinctive difference in coloration between males and females—and these differences are as obvious in juveniles as in adults. Males have conspicuous gray-blue wings, while the wings of females are basically rufous. The only other diurnal raptors of North America exhibiting obvious sexual color differences are Northern Harriers, Everglade Kites, Hook-billed Kites, Merlins, Sharp-shinned Hawks, and Cooper's Hawks. In most of these species, however, the sexual differences are not nearly so marked as they are in the kestrel. The sexual dimorphism in color pattern in these various species shows no obvious relationship with sexual size dimorphism, and no obvious simple behavioral or ecological characteristics bind these species together in ways that might explain why sexual differences in coloration might be adaptive for them and not for other species.

Another unusual feature of kestrel plumage is the presence of two dark spots on the back of the neck that look very much like eyes when the bird is viewed either from the rear or from the front when the head of the bird is bent over working on prey. Similar neck spots are present on Northern Pygmy Owls and Ferruginous Pygmy Owls, and there are even hints of such spots on the necks of Elf Owls. The possible function of neck eyespots has generated considerable speculation over the years, starting with an intriguing paper by William Clay of the University of Louisville, Kentucky, more than fifty years ago. Clay suggested that the spots might function mainly to deceive potential predators and prey as to which way a kestrel is facing.

Do the spots actually function deceptively? Such an effect could inhibit attacks by potential predators—predators that the kestrel might be unaware of and would otherwise be vulnerable to. This is an attractive idea and one that we once tested in a haphazard way with one such predator, the Cooper's Hawk. In studying nests of this accipiter in Arizona and New Mexico in 1970, we found that females almost invariably defended their nests by striking a climber from behind rather than by frontal assault. This observation led first of all to wearing a helmet when climbing nest trees. Later we painted conspicuous eyes on the back of the helmet to see if this might discourage attack. We saw no noticeable decline in the frequency of dives and blows, however, though it was hard to judge this in a rigorous way. Still, if eyespots of kestrels might even only momentarily slow down other raptors attempting to capture them, this could be enough of an effect to have led to the evolution of this coloration. The kestrel's habit of bobbing its head serves to make its neck eyespots especially realistic and "owlish" in appearance, and we are quite willing to admit that our painted helmet was not as deceptive a simulation.

The American Kestrel is generally a common species throughout its extensive range in North and South America and the West Indies. Missing only from the most arctic regions, it occupies a great variety of open and semi-open habitats, including many suburban and urban areas. It has adapted extremely well to disturbed areas and even nests frequently in cracks and crannies of buildings and in bird boxes put out for its use and the use of other species. In fact, the kestrel may well be the most abundant diurnal raptor on the continent. Estimates suggest well over a million pairs breeding in North America.

American Kestrel

Crested Caracara
Caracara cheriway

THE CRESTED CARACARA just barely reaches the United States, mainly in the cattle-ranching country of south-central Florida and southeastern Texas, and in the Sonoran Desert habitat of the Tohono O'Odham Indian Reservation of southwestern Arizona. Farther south, in a range extending from Mexico to Argentina, it is a widespread and common species in many open-country regions and is joined by several other caracara species of diverse habits. A distinctive race of the species, sometimes considered a full species, used to occur on the island of Socorro off western Mexico but is now extinct.

Weighing about two and a half pounds and sailing on wings about four feet in span, the Crested Caracara is a striking raptor with long yellow legs, naked bright-red cheeks, a large parrotlike yellow beak, a conspicuous white throat and neck, and a handsomely barred black-and-white breast. In many respects, its behavioral and physical characteristics represent a curious blend. Half-falcon and half-vulture, half-aerial and half-terrestrial, it seemingly combines the major features of several avian groups in one species. Like members of the family Accipitridae, for example, it builds substantial nests of twigs. Yet on anatomical grounds it is clearly a member of the family Falconidae, a group composed mainly of falcons, which do no nest building.

For us, the Crested Caracara will always be linked with the cabbage palm hammock prairies of Florida stretching to the west and north of Lake Okeechobee. These prairies, especially those bordering the Kissimmee River and Fisheating Creek, host not only a sizable population of caracaras but also a diversity of other avian species, all living in apparent harmony with traditional cattle-grazing operations. Burrowing Owls, Eastern Meadowlarks, Sandhill Cranes, various herons and ibis, Bald Eagles, Black Vultures, Turkey Vultures, and Red-tailed Hawks are common in open areas, while Wild Turkeys, Barred Owls, Red-shouldered Hawks, Pileated Woodpeckers, and Red-bellied Woodpeckers abound in the adjacent hammocks and cypress swamps.

During 1978 and 1979, when we lived in this region, we saw Crested Caracaras most commonly in relatively open areas, where they found much of their food on foot, striding along much in the manner of the Secretary Bird of Africa. The diet of this species is quite varied and ranges from carrion to all sorts of invertebrates and vertebrates. It is an opportunistic generalist, capable of taking advantage of ephemeral abundances of practically any animal food supplies it can manage to locate and capture.

Throwing its head backward and upside down, an adult Crested Caracara gives the peculiar rattling cry thought by some to be the source of the bird's name.

Like a variety of scavenging and partially scavenging birds, caracaras have only partially feathered heads. Caracaras often travel in pairs, but single birds are also common. Assemblages larger than family groups are infrequent.

Crested Caracara

Despite its striking appearance, the Crested Caracara is not always the easiest bird to find. In part, this results from the fact that the bird often forages on foot, obscured from sight by vegetation. In part, it apparently results from the skill with which the species has come to exploit human ecology. In many areas, caracaras have learned that they can make an easy living by foraging along the highways at daybreak, reaping the bounty of rabbits, armadillos, possums, and other vertebrates flattened by vehicles overnight. Since few people are out cruising the highways at first light, and since caracaras have mostly fed to repletion and retreated to favored roosts in the cabbage palms by the time that traffic really begins to build up, the birds are usually out of view when most observers would have a chance to see them. It is surprising how much more common the caracara suddenly becomes once you become aware of this daily pattern and start looking for the species at the proper time of day.

One pair we watched with some frequency in 1979 made regular dawn patrols of a several-mile stretch of U.S. Highway 27 west of Lake Okeechobee. Stroking rapidly along with strong wing beats, heads down, they had first choice of the assortment of overnight traffic victims. Local Turkey Vultures and Black Vultures were eager to feast on these victims as well, but because of their dependence on good soaring conditions, both these species normally began foraging later in the day. By then their choices were limited to leftovers from the caracaras and to more recently-killed prey.

During 1979 we maintained a feeding station of road-killed mammals out by our backyard chicken coop so that we could enjoy the company of the local scavengers. Black Vultures and Turkey Vultures were regular visitors, as were a pair of caracaras that, true to form, would arrive just at first light to see what the Snyders might have unaccountably discarded overnight. At these morning feasts, the caracaras normally dominated the other common scavengers in head-on confrontations, strutting erect about the carcasses and controlling the situation quite thoroughly.

During the spring these caracaras had a brood to feed, and we sometimes watched an adult ripping many small strips of meat from a carcass, laying them down one after another in a neat pile on the ground. When the pile had grown to the size of a small apple, the bird would carefully pick it up as a mass in its bill and head straight back to the nest about a mile away, returning for another load soon afterward.

In time, the caracara pair also brought their brood of two fledglings to the carcass dump, but four individuals are as many caracaras as we have ever seen together at one time in Florida. Larger aggregations, especially of immatures, are known for the species, however, and occasionally roosts of more than a hundred individuals have been documented. In Venezuela we have seen groups of more than a dozen individuals following a mowing machine to feast on the animals killed by the blades of the machinery.

In late winter of 1978 we observed the nesting activities of a pair of caracaras in a cabbage palm hammock near Florida's Fisheating Creek. When we first discovered the nest, the ground in the vicinity was littered with the shells of turtles that the pair had apparently brought in and fed upon earlier. At the nest itself, however, the only food fed to the young through the rest of the breeding cycle was unrecognizable pieces of meat, apparently carrion. The nest contained two young, the most common brood size for the species, and was built of innumerable fine twigs carefully woven and lodged among the bases of the fronds of a cabbage palm. Just underneath the nest were the compacted remains of another twig nest, very likely built by the same caracaras in a previous year.

From the blind we constructed in a nearby cabbage palm, we found the caracaras to be quite tolerant of our presence. They provisioned their young

Florida's Crested Caracaras often nest in the tops of cabbage palms. Unlike falcons (their close relatives) but like kites and hawks (their distant relatives), caracaras build substantial twig nests.

Crested Caracara

A pair of Crested Caracaras nested in this grove near Fisheating Creek in 1978. When first discovered, the site was strewn with the shells of numerous turtles the pair had apparently been eating. Later in the breeding cycle, the pair fed mainly on carrion.

Range of the Crested Caracara

◼ Breeding and wintering

Cranes and Crested Caracaras. In these nail-scarred palms, we strongly suspected we were looking at the signs of his past depredations on caracaras, since this is the one species that characteristically nests in cabbage palms and many caracaras still inhabit the region. Nevertheless, Wray Nicholson, another early egg collector on the prairie, is also reputed to have sometimes used nail ladders to ascend trees, and it is possible that he, rather than Charles Doe, may have built the ladders on these particular trees.

The extreme diversity of foods acceptable to the caracara has allowed the species to coexist in good numbers with people in many areas. Nevertheless, its continued survival in the United States may depend largely on the persistence of ranching as a livelihood in Florida and Texas. The species seems to be limited primarily to cattle country and cannot be expected to survive the continuing conversion of ranchlands to citrus orchards and housing developments. Like the Everglade Kite, the Crested Caracara faces a relatively uncertain future if the human population in the southern states continues to increase at the rate it has been.

The Florida caracara population, which has recently been classified as federally threatened, has been estimated to consist of only about 150 pairs and perhaps 150 to 200 immatures. Although this population has been reasonably stable in recent decades, little of the species' range is in any officially protected status. With Disney World and associated developments just to the north and rapidly expanding retirement communities in many locations near Lake Okeechobee, the prospects of this population seem precarious. Only a recently established 52,000-acre sanctuary in northern Okeechobee County offers any secure hope of permanent preservation of a representative sample of central Florida prairie. This sanctuary, a most significant achievement resulting largely from the persistent efforts of Rod Chandler, is nevertheless much too small by itself to sustain a viable caracara population, let alone viable populations of many other species.

Expanding the size of the Kissimmee Prairie Sanctuary to the point where it could serve to sustain a viable caracara population would have broad conservation value. Another bird that could benefit greatly from such a sanctuary is the Florida Sandhill Crane. Still another is a species of raptor that has been missing from our fauna for a couple hundred years—the King Vulture. Populations of this bird still occur in Central and South America, and the species evidently occurred in north-central Florida up until the time of the American Revolution, as was described in a remarkable firsthand account by an early American naturalist named William Bartram. Florida's King Vultures may have disappeared largely because local American Indian tribes sought these birds as a source of ceremonial feathers and because the birds apparently were very easy to approach and kill. Bartram's account of this species—he called it the Painted Vulture—is one of the most fascinating descriptions of early natural history in the New World. Though it has been discounted by some naturalists, his description of the species was so finely detailed and so close to the King Vultures of regions farther south that it seems clear that a geographic form of the King Vulture once existed in the region.

Given adequate protection from human depredations and given adequate amounts of suitable habitat, it seems quite plausible that the King Vulture could be reestablished in Florida, and in much the same habitats that caracaras presently use. The overall populations of scavenging birds on the Kissimmee Prairie are still impressive, and the region represents a potential long-term stronghold for such birds if it can be sufficiently protected before it is too late. Preservation of a truly viable prairie ecosystem for these and other species need not entail actual purchase of vast acreages if, through conservation easements or other equivalent means, land use can be permanently dedicated to practices no more intensive than traditional ranching. Nevertheless, time is very short for such actions before urban development will likely obliterate any chances for success.

with great frequency, apparently having an excellent food supply to exploit in the region. On one day we recorded no fewer than fifteen feeding trips of the adults to the nest, and the nestlings appeared to be receiving as much food as they could possibly consume.

At intervals during the nestling period, we weighed and measured the young to track their development and found that as they matured they became quite difficult to handle, attacking us with both their bills and talons. Such behavior is also typical of falcons, their close relatives, but is not normally observed in hawks, eagles, and kites, which characteristically defend themselves with their talons only.

Around the nest, the adults sometimes gave a startling display that is quite unlike anything we have seen in other North American raptors, though it is very reminiscent of displays given by European White Storks at their nests. In this display, the bird throws its head so far back that the top of its head touches its back and the head is upside down. Simultaneously the bird gives a rattling cry lasting a second or so, a cry thought by some to be the source of the name caracara. What specific meaning this display might have is not fully known, although it is most often seen in individuals disturbed around nest sites or in aggressive contexts around carcasses.

The most intriguing caracara nesting sites we have ever seen were on Florida's Kissimmee Prairie and were not in fact active nests, but trees that had held nests about a half century earlier. In 1979, we learned that one of the Kissimmee Prairie egg collectors of the 1920s, a fascinating individual named Charles Doe, usually climbed to nests by an unusual method. Instead of using standard climbing spikes, he pounded steps of nails up trees that held the nests. On learning this, we asked Rod Chandler of Okeechobee, a collaborator in our studies of Everglade Kites, if he recalled ever having seen nail ladders up trees on the prairie. Chandler had indeed seen such trees in the 1930s, and several days later he called to say that he had relocated a couple of these trees still standing.

The trees were cabbage palms, and when we went to see them, we found that the nail scars and in some cases the actual nails, giant rusty spikes, could still be seen marching up the trunks. The nail scars and nails in 1979 stopped short of the crowns of the cabbage palms by about fifteen feet, indicating the relatively modest amount of growth that the palms had put on in the previous five decades. Charles Doe had been an obsessive collector of the eggs of all birds, but he had a special fondness for the eggs of Sandhill

Crested Caracara

NOCTURNAL RAPTORS

Above: *An Elf Owl close to fledging eagerly awaits the arrival of a parent with a grasshopper. This strictly nocturnal species is highly migratory, appearing north of the Mexican border only during spring and summer.*

Left: *A fledgling Spotted Owl gazes at a sister butterfly in this pencil drawing by David Utterback. The artist and Noel witnessed this curious encounter during a summer 2003 visit to Scheelite Canyon in Arizona's Huachuca Mountains. The Spotted Owls of this canyon have delighted visitors for decades. The canyon is also one of the finest in the West for butterfly enthusiasts.*

Barn Owls

Barn Owl
Tyto alba

ONLY ONE BARN OWL SPECIES, usually referred to as simply the Barn Owl, or sometimes the Monkey-faced Owl, occurs in continental North America. As currently recognized, this species, *Tyto alba*, also occurs on all other continents of the world except Antarctica, rivaling the Peregrine Falcon in the breadth of its distribution, although unlike the peregrine, the Barn Owl does not range as far north as taiga and arctic regions. A renowned predator of small rodents, the Barn Owl often associates closely with human settlements and is generally valued highly for the benefits its dietary habits offer farmers and gardeners.

Generally weighing a little more than a pound, *Tyto alba* is a moderately large owl, and it occurs in many different color forms, from dark to light, in different regions. The North American and western European populations of the species are sufficiently white, particularly when viewed from below, that from a distance they can closely resemble Snowy Owls. Nevertheless, the chances of confusing Barn Owls with Snowy Owls are small under most field conditions. Barn Owls are almost completely nocturnal in activity and they roost in secluded locations during the day, while Snowy Owls are most often observed during the daytime and are characteristically found perching in wide-open regions. In addition, the overall ranges of the two species are largely separate, and the heart-shaped facial disk visible in the Barn Owl at close range is missing in the Snowy Owl. Snowy Owls generally invade only the northern fringes of the relatively low-latitude range of the Barn Owl, and they do so only irregularly and only in winter.

One other living barn owl species, *Tyto glaucops*, currently exists in the New World. This relatively dark creature, the Ashy-faced Owl, is similar in size to the Barn Owl, but it is limited to the island of Hispaniola in the West Indies, where it occurs together with *Tyto alba* and is reasonably common. In past geological epochs, the New World had a variety of additional barn owl species.

A mammal specialist that hunts open fields and deserts, both from flight and from perches, the Barn Owl of North America is best known as an inhabitant of abandoned buildings and other human structures, where it finds adequate shelter for roosting and raising its offspring. It also often roosts and nests in hollow trees and in caves in cliffs. On occasion it even uses horizontal burrows that it constructs itself in the walls of steep-sided earthen gullies, at least in part using its feet to scratch out the tunnels. Thus, the species is hardly limited to barns in its roosting and nesting habits, and it is far more adaptable in breeding than its name suggests.

In whatever protected nest sites it uses, the Barn Owl lays large clutches of white eggs—often ten or more—and sometimes rears two or more broods

Left: During the late 1960s and early 1970s, a Barn Owl pair regularly raised young in an old railroad cistern near our home in southeastern Arizona. Barn Owls differ from the typical owls in their heart-shaped facial disks and serrated middle claws. They are renowned for their abilities to capture prey in total darkness, using only their keen sense of hearing.

in the space of a year. Nestlings hatch asynchronously, normally two or three days apart, so that broods usually consist of youngsters differing greatly in size. This characteristic appears to allow efficient elimination of the smallest among them under conditions of food scarcity, but it also permits rearing of maximal-sized broods under conditions of food abundance.

Nestling Barn Owls are perhaps the strangest looking youngsters of any bird species on the planet. Decidedly satanic in appearance, they seem to be half smiling when one enters their lairs, but they soon express their displeasure with hissing vocalizations and bill snapping, swaying back and forth with their wings partly raised. Their heart-shaped facial disks are evident even long before feathers are emerging from their white natal down, and even at a young age their asymmetrical ear structures are in place. These structures are curious flaps of tissue positioned behind the eyes and in front of the ear openings. Higher on a bird's left side than on the right, and slanted differently on the two sides, these flaps significantly modify the bird's ability to hear sounds of differing frequency in its two ears, depending on how the bird's head is oriented toward a sound source. It takes close inspection of the chicks, however, to see these structures. In adults, the asymmetrical earflaps are covered with fine feathers of the facial disk so that they are completely invisible to the human eye unless these feathers are moved aside.

The function of ear asymmetry in the Barn Owl was the subject of some highly original graduate research conducted by Roger Payne at Cornell University in the late 1950s and early 1960s. In these studies, Payne was able to demonstrate that Barn Owl individuals could locate and capture rodents in the complete darkness of light-tight rooms even when their hunting perches were more than twenty feet away from the prey. Their success under such conditions depended entirely on their powerful ability to hear the sounds that the rodents made, both in moving about in leaves and in chewing on food. The owls clearly needed to have both ears unencumbered

Range of the Barn Owl

Breeding and wintering

Left: *Noel descends a ladder into the Barn Owls' cistern nest site in 1970. Centrally located in a broad expanse of grassland, the cistern was well situated for the owls' hunting activities. Unfortunately, the numerous fledgling skeletons in the site suggested that young birds had difficulty navigating the vertical entrance shaft, and the site appears to have been a "black hole" for owl reproduction.*

for accurate orientation to prey, because they made only unsuccessful capture attempts when one ear opening was blocked with a cotton plug. Furthermore their ability to locate prey in total darkness depended on the presence of high-frequency components in the sounds made by prey. In particular, the accuracy with which the owls captured loudspeakers broadcasting prey sounds was much worse when frequencies higher than 8500 cycles per second were removed from the sounds than when the full frequency spectrum was present.

The asymmetry of the earflaps of Barn Owls is apparently crucial for accurate orientation in the vertical plane. As we are all aware from personal experience, humans can use their symmetrical ears to detect the direction of a sound source in the horizontal plane with fair accuracy, but we have a very poor capacity for discriminating a sound source in front of us from one that is directly behind or telling how high above or below the horizon a sound source might be. Barn Owls do considerably better. In part by maximizing the intensity of sounds heard by both ears simultaneously, they

A full family portrait of the cistern-nesting owls in May 1970 included a light-colored male adult, a browner female adult, five downy nestlings of various sizes and ages, and one wood-rat prey.

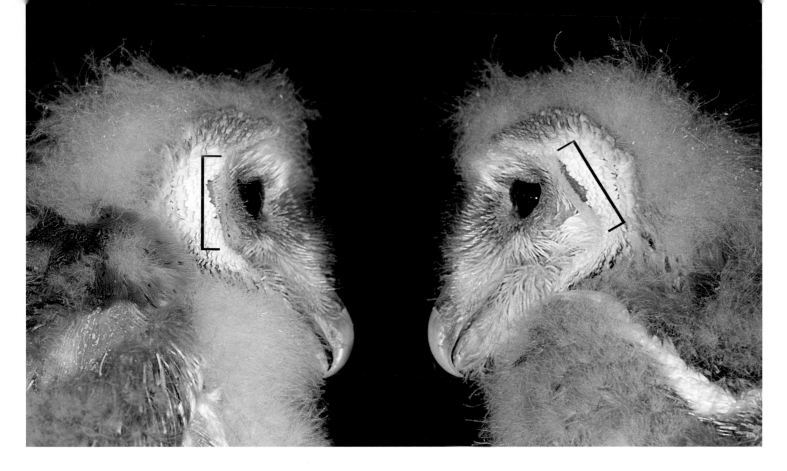

A close look at a nestling Barn Owl's facial disk reveals the asymmetric ear flaps behind the bird's eyes and in front of its ear openings. These flaps evidently allow the birds to fixate prey in the vertical plane by sound alone. Higher on the bird's left side than on the right and slanted at a different angle on the two sides (see brackets), these asymmetric structures are fully concealed by feathers in adults.

can very accurately orient themselves to directly face a sound source in both the horizontal and vertical planes. The asymmetry of their ears results in their hearing sounds above the horizontal much more strongly in one ear than in the other, and vice versa with sounds below the horizontal, and this is especially true for high-frequency sounds. When all sound frequencies are heard with equal and maximal intensity by both ears, the bird is directly facing the prey in both planes and can home in on prey by exactly maintaining this orientation in a capture approach. The Barn Owl's ability to fixate prey in the horizontal plane is also dependent on extraordinarily sensitive abilities of the species to detect slight differences in time of arrival of sounds at its two ears. Only when the owl directly faces a prospective prey and its two ears are exactly the same distance from the prospective prey do these differences in time of arrival disappear.

Roger Payne found that Barn Owls captured prey very differently in the light than in total darkness. In the light, the owls swiftly glided toward the prey with their feet tucked under their bodies, and only brought their feet forward in front of the bill to strike the prey at the last possible instant. In total darkness, they made slow flapping approaches with feet dangling and brought their talons forward in front of the bill much earlier. Their slow flapping flight likely minimized the chances of colliding catastrophically with objects in the way. Yet despite the slowness of their approach in total darkness, their angular accuracy in making a strike was generally within an astounding one degree in both the horizontal and vertical planes. Further, on the basis of sound alone, they were able to determine the direction in which a prey animal was moving and orient their talons to maximize the chances of contacting it in a pounce. They evidently had no way to determine distance to a prey from their perch locations in total darkness, but they seemed to know when to bring their feet forward in a capture attempt, possibly by sensing their closeness to the ground by tactile ground effects from their wing beats. Like the wing sounds of many other owls, the wing beats of the Barn Owl are notably quiet, especially in high-frequency sounds, a feature that likely disguises their approach to prey and simultaneously prevents their wing sounds from interfering with their ability to locate prey by sounds alone.

Other nocturnal owls, for example Saw-whet Owls, Great Gray Owls, and Long-eared Owls, also have asymmetrical ears and can also locate and capture prey in complete darkness. The asymmetry of their ears, however, is achieved by different anatomical structures than in the Barn Owl. In the Boreal Owl, for example, it is the skull shape of the bird, rather than its earflaps, that is grossly different from the right side to the left. Apparently the auditory skills of these other owls have evolved independently of, but in parallel to, the abilities of Barn Owls, achieving the same acoustical solution to the challenge of locating prey when there is no way to see it.

Still other owls such as Great Horned Owls, Northern Pygmy Owls, and Eastern Screech Owls lack any evident asymmetry in their ears, and experiments have failed to reveal any ability of these species to capture prey in total darkness. Yet these species hunt successfully under nocturnal conditions that are much too dim for humans to see anything clearly. Their ability to do this depends on the very large size of their eyes, and in fact, the eyes of all owl species are conspicuously well developed. In addition, the placement of their eyes, frontal and well apart, yields a high degree of binocular vision. Together, large eyes and binocular vision greatly aid in accurate prey location under dim light conditions, with or without the help of acoustic cues. Though some owl species are largely diurnal in their hunting habits, the great majority are also capable of nocturnal foraging, and many species concentrate their nocturnal efforts in the evening twilight hours and the hours just before dawn, when many prey species are active, when dim light prevails, and when keen vision is especially valuable.

Barn Owls are sufficiently skilled in locating food that under good conditions they are sometimes able to capture many more prey than are necessary to fulfill the needs of their families. During the incubation and early brooding

Storrs Olson and Fred Grady of the U.S. National Museum sift the rich fossil deposits of a limestone cave they christened Black Bone Cave in north-western Puerto Rico in 1976. The deposits were middens of pellets from the extinct barn owl of the island, Tyto cavatica, *and included bones of a variety of previously undescribed bird species dating as far back as 18,000 years ago.*

periods when males are the exclusive food providers, excess uneaten prey can accumulate in the nest chambers, and it is sometimes possible to find thirty to fifty small dead rodents scattered about in a single nest. One observer documented a phenomenal total of 189 uneaten prey in a Barn Owl nest in Michigan. As in other owl species, such larders of food presumably serve as reserves to tide families through periods of bad weather, when efficient hunting may not be possible.

Like other observers, we have also found prey larders in most active Barn Owl nests. One such nest we occasionally visited during the 1970s was in an old abandoned railroad cistern near our present home in the Chihuahuan Desert of southeastern Arizona. Made of cement, this structure had a constricted chimneylike entrance hole that widened abruptly into a large circular chamber mostly below ground level, and it often hosted a family of Barn Owls in the spring and summer. But in addition to living owls and larders of uneaten prey, this cistern also held the skeletons of a large number of deceased Barn Owls. Because these all proved to be skeletons of birds about fledging age, it appeared likely that over the years many of the birds reared in the site, lacking their parents' skills in flying and scrambling, were having difficulty navigating successfully up the smooth-sided chimney in the fledging process. Ultimately abandoned by their parents, they may well have starved to death within the nest chamber. As such, the nest site may well have been a "black hole" for Barn Owl reproduction despite the usual presence of larders of uneaten prey during the nestling phase.

The substrate on which these owls were nesting consisted largely of thousands of disintegrating pellets of fur and bones the owls had regurgitated over the years. These pellets formed a long-lasting record of the meals of many generations of Barn Owls, and had we analyzed them for what species were represented, we would have gained an excellent idea of overall diet of the species in this region. Such studies of Barn Owl pellets, conducted in various parts of the world, have given a tremendous amount of information

on the diet of this species. For example, a recent summary of five extensive North American studies, based on a total of more than a hundred thousand prey individuals in pellets, indicated that small mammals comprised between 87.3 and 99.9 percent of the species' diet, with only a small fraction of prey consisting of birds, reptiles, and insects.

Although we have never made studies of contemporary Barn Owl pellets, we once assisted such studies of the diet of the extinct Puerto Rican Barn Owl, *Tyto cavatica,* a species that evidently fed on both birds and mammals. Nesting in limestone caves in the northwestern reaches of the island during the Pleistocene, these owls created enormous middens of pellets under their nests. In some cases, these middens were still in place more than 18,000 years after their formation, based on radiocarbon dating, and the bones in different middens gave detailed information on a variety of topics in addition to the specifics of the species' diet in various time periods and locations.

The discovery of these deposits was made in the spring of 1976, when we participated in two expeditions to the Morovis region of Puerto Rico with Storrs Olson of the U.S. National Museum to locate fossil bird bones. We examined more than eighty caves in these efforts and found substantial fossil deposits in several that had not been completely dug out for bat-guano fertilizer by local farmers. At the time, we were conducting intensive studies of the endangered Puerto Rican Parrot, and our main interest in participating in the fossil-finding efforts was the possibility of obtaining materials that might help determine how long the Pearly-eyed Thrasher, a vexing enemy of the Puerto Rican Parrot, had been resident on the island.

The thrasher question was answered mainly by negation. Olson was unable to find bones of the pearly-eye in any of the materials collected, despite the fact that the pearly-eye today is frequently a cave nester, and in fact a pair was nesting right over one of the deposits at the time of our expeditions. Because the investigations yielded many tens of thousands of bones of numerous species of small birds and mammals, and because the thrasher falls within the size range of prey taken by barn owls, it seemed almost certain that bones of the pearly-eye would have been present if the species had been resident for any length of time on the island. The most reasonable explanation for the complete absence of thrasher bones is that the pearly-eye has been a relatively recent invader of Puerto Rico, something we had suspected from the poorly developed adaptations of the Puerto Rican Parrot to resist nest predation by the thrashers.

The middens of *Tyto cavatica* also yielded many other exciting finds. This extinct owl was evidently an accomplished predator of other birds, and a surprising number of species new to science turned up among the bones collected. Of particular interest were bones of a parakeet species that had been rumored to exist on Puerto Rico in bygone times and the bones of a distinctive species of burrowing owl, now extinct. But perhaps the most exciting finds were numerous bones of three species of hummingbird. Prior to these expeditions the fossil record for hummingbirds was virtually nonexistent.

Many of the bird species found in the middens were known or suspected to be birds of grassland habitats, such as Grasshopper Sparrows and the extinct burrowing owl. These species would have been completely out of place in the contemporary habitats surrounding the caves, which were entirely heavy forest except where recently cleared for agriculture. Thus, the fauna of the middens gave strong evidence that the climate of Puerto Rico was very different in the late Pleistocene—evidently a much drier place than in modern times.

Many of the discoveries resulting from the fossil owl nest studies on Puerto Rico were unexpected and of importance to the understanding of diverse biological questions. But had the owls nested in less well protected locations, the remains of their meals would have long disintegrated and this information would never have been gained. Because of its secretive nesting habits, Puerto Rico's extinct *Tyto cavatica* has left the modern world a priceless biological legacy.

A female Barn Owl in 2004 incubates a clutch of five eggs in the space between the first-floor ceiling and the second floor of an abandoned house in Arizona's Sulfur Springs Valley. Innumerable disintegrating pellets regurgitated in previous nestings littered the nest site.

Puerto Rico is not the only West Indian island to have had its own endemic species of barn owl during the Pleistocene. Fossil deposits have revealed that the islands of Cuba and Hispaniola once hosted several species of barn owls, including enormous forms that presumably once fed largely on the faunas of giant endemic rodents and ground sloths, some as large as beavers or small bears, that had developed on these islands in the absence of large mammalian carnivores. Many of the owls and large mammals on these islands, as on Puerto Rico, did not survive into historical times, perhaps mainly because of a change in climate of the West Indies to moister conditions that occurred near the end of the Pleistocene. Among the other species that disappeared from Cuba since the Pleistocene was a condor, possibly the same species that has been the focus of so much attention in California in recent years.

The Barn Owl of today continues to be a common species in many regions of the United States, but it has not been faring well in parts of the Midwest, apparently because of a scarcity of nest-sites in some areas and a scarcity of food in others. Experiments have shown that in regions of good food but poor nest-site availability, Barn Owl populations can be greatly increased by providing artificial nest boxes. Such results have been achieved, for example, in parts of Florida where sugarcane is grown in huge monocultures and rats are abundant in the fields. Barn Owls readily accept nest boxes, although boxes of considerable size are needed to accommodate the species' large broods (up to ten young). The reproductive potential of this species, considering its capacities for multiple brooding and large brood sizes, is one of the greatest among raptors of its size range, allowing very rapid population increases under good conditions.

The male adult Barn Owl arrives at the entrance of a New Mexico site in 2004 with a freshly killed wood rat for his two nestlings. The small brood size at this nest suggested poor food availability nearby.

Barn Owl

Eagle, Snowy, Wood, Eared, and Screech Owls

Great Horned Owl
Bubo virginianus

SOMETIMES REACHING FOUR POUNDS in weight, the Great Horned Owl averages only slightly lighter than the Snowy Owl and is a truly formidable predator known to have eaten Snowy Owls on occasion. Its massive and needle-sharp talons, backed by tenacious foot musculature, allow it to readily penetrate the soft tissues of its prey, and its grip can only be broken with the application of a surprisingly large amount of force. Armed with such weaponry, the Great Horned Owl enjoys one of the most diverse diets of any North American owl, and in most locations it occupies a premier position at the top of food chains for nocturnal avian species. It regularly captures species ranging in size from insects and mice to large waterfowl and herons, and it does not hesitate to take a variety of other birds of prey as victims. Raptor rehabilitators know that this species is exceedingly dangerous to handle and cannot be caged with any other birds—even eagles—without risking disastrous results.

The Great Horned Owl's ability to kill most any kind of small- to medium-sized bird is evidently well appreciated by other bird species, and like many other owls, horned owls are frequently the target of intense mobbing activities. Most commonly in these interactions, flocks of birds discovering an owl at roost will hop about in nearby branches giving raucous alarm vocalizations intermingled with occasional harassing attacks. For their part, the owls singled out for such attention rarely seem directly harmed by the insults and disturbance, and sometimes they do not even move from their perches or move only very short distances into denser cover, while their antagonists eventually wind down their harassing activities and drift away.

Except in cases where the mobsters are defending their nests or young, the reasons for their behavior are not obvious and have been long debated. Of the possibilities suggested, we favor the idea that one important value may be education. By means of such activities, experienced members of flocks may efficiently teach naive members, often their own offspring, the identity of their principal enemies and the degree of threat these enemies represent, without taking major risks in the process.

Owls are not the only targets of such mobbing activity. In fact, some of our best looks at mountain lions over the years have been of animals that we detected only because of intense mobbing activities of jays and robins following them as they walked through the forest. It pays to investigate groups of birds engaged in mobbing activities. This is often the best way

to obtain sightings not only of various owls but also of many other elusive, large predators. Additionally, on various occasions when we have followed mobbing birds to the sources of their dismay, we have found such targets as live snakes, a dead ringtail, and on three occasions, just clumps of feathers—evidently all that was left from a scene of predatory violence. On two of these latter occasions, birds returned for several days to mob the remains long after the predator had left the death scene.

The tendency of large hawks to attack Great Horned Owls that come near their nests is often highly advantageous for raptor studies. By tethering captive horned owls near nests of these species and surrounding them with mist nets or other traps, researchers can decoy in and capture the nest owners for marking and other examination purposes. For many years we had, under permit, a captive Great Horned Owl that we regularly used to capture nesting Northern Goshawks. Our tethered owl, McHooter, was missing one wing from a car collision and was hardly an enthusiastic participant in these efforts, usually freezing in a cryptic posture when placed in sight of the hawks. Nevertheless, he was struck by a goshawk only once, early in his career, and the hawks almost always confined their mobbing behavior to aggressive cackling and swoops close over his head. These close approaches allowed us to net numerous goshawks for banding and blood sampling.

Our ten years with McHooter gave us a glimpse into the mind of a Great Horned Owl, and our conclusion was that he was not exactly an intellectual powerhouse. Nonetheless, he had some interesting behaviors. When we supplied him with a whole *Neotoma* wood rat, he would invariably begin eating the head end first. Then, removing as little skin as possible, he progressed into the thorax to remove organs there. If he wasn't hungry enough to finish the prey, he would fold the skin neatly over the opening he

Range of the Great Horned Owl
◼ Breeding and wintering

Left: *Roosting in a low willow in southeastern Arizona's Chihuahuan desert, a Great Horned Owl awaits the onset of darkness. Mobbing flocks of small birds frequently harass such roosting owls, but although the owls sometimes move short distances, the attacks likely do not cause them any significant harm.*

An old Chihuahua Raven nest in southwestern New Mexico provides a home for a Great Horned Owl family. As in many other owl species, the adults' "horns" or "ears" are simply clumps of elongated feathers that have nothing to do with the birds' true ears. The facial disks of southwestern Great Horned Owls generally lack the orange tones typical of the species in the eastern states.

had made in the now headless carcass before caching it by jamming its front end against the wall in the corner of his cage. This effectively prevented the rest of the innards from drying out and discouraged flies from competing for his next meal. Even in summer, there were never fly eggs or larvae inside when we checked the tidy burrito-like package he had prepared, unless he failed to finish the meal within about twenty-four hours.

The Great Horned Owl has the largest range of any North American owl, and it is found essentially everywhere except in treeless arctic tundra, where it is replaced by its near relative, the Snowy Owl. Genetic studies indicate that these two species are sufficiently closely related that there would be good grounds for including them both in the genus *Bubo*. In fact, Great Horned Owls even have some tendency to resemble Snowy Owls in northerly regions, where an especially pale race of the species—*subarcticus*—occurs. Another pale race of the Great Horned Owl—*pallescens*—occurs in the deserts of the southwestern states, and altogether sixteen visually different races are generally recognized for this species, including several that occur in South America. Like the Red-tailed Hawk, the Great Horned Owl has extremely broad habitat tolerances, with a variety of plumages evidently adapted to local conditions, and these two

species are often considered closely allied in their ecology. Essentially the only region where Red-tailed Hawks occur and Great Horned Owls do not is on the larger islands of the West Indies, although fossils indicate that even larger strigid owls once occurred on both Cuba and Hispaniola.

Nest sites of the Great Horned Owl, like its choices in prey, are diverse, and we have seen the species breeding on cliff ledges, in old nests of various hawks, in old raven and crow nests, and in hollows in trees. In regions lacking large hollow snags, stick nests, or cliffs, the species even occasionally nests right on the ground. Great Horned Owls, especially females, are often highly aggressive in defending their nests from potential predators, and presumably this is one reason why they, like Snowy Owls, can often breed successfully in relatively accessible sites. In addition to beating off enemies with their formidable talons, we have sometimes seen them attempt to lure us away from their nests with convincing "broken-wing" acts, flopping about on the ground with their wings extended awkwardly, wailing piteously, but always keeping far enough away to avoid any real risks of capture. Such broken-wing displays to decoy predators away from nests or young are also seen commonly in a variety of other birds, ranging from various shorebirds to goatsuckers and many other owl species.

On the ground near her giant-yucca nest site in western New Mexico, a female Great Horned Owl wails and staggers about pathetically on the ground. Her remarkably realistic "wounded bird" or "broken-wing" act serves to lure predators away from the nest.

The Great Horned Owl begins breeding much earlier than most other raptors and commonly lays eggs in February or early March in the northern states and Canada. In Florida, eggs often appear as early as November or December. In northern localities, harsh winter storms are still frequent at the time of egg laying, and incubating females simply hunker down when foul weather materializes, sometimes winding up almost completely buried under snow in sites with no protection from the skies.

Adults are quite vocal around nests, giving a variety of calls, but the most familiar calls are a series of five to seven mildly syncopated and low-pitched hoots that are given by both sexes, often in response to each other and often in territorial contexts. Curiously, the pitch of the female's hoots is typically higher than the pitch of the male's hoots, despite the distinctly larger size of the female, a reversal of the usual inverse relationship of body size with pitch of vocalizations found in birds.

Clutch size for the Great Horned Owl averages the smallest for any North American owl, with the possible exception of the Barred Owl. The most common number of eggs is two in most regions and years, and single-egg clutches are not highly unusual. Although the species has a tendency to lay somewhat larger clutches in especially good foraging years and locations, with occasional clutches as large as five eggs documented, this tendency is nothing like what is seen routinely in Snowy Owls, Hawk Owls, and Short-eared Owls, where clutches of more than ten eggs are sometimes produced. The prey populations on which the Great Horned Owl depends are in general much more diverse and stable than the small rodent populations exploited heavily by these other species, and horned owls lack the wide-ranging nomadic tendencies of these other species.

Incubation takes about a month in horned owls, and youngsters do not become proficient in flight until about nine or ten weeks of age. After that point they still remain dependent on their parents for many weeks and commonly do not disperse from their natal territories until the fall of their hatching year. Thus, the full breeding cycle of the Great Horned Owl is the longest of any North American owl, and this may be the principal reason why these birds begin nesting so early in the year, even though this sometimes means risking addled eggs from harsh late-winter weather conditions. Such a long breeding cycle also means that a nesting pair with a brood of several fledglings can place considerable demands on the prey populations of the nesting territory for much of the year. In some cases the owl families may deplete these populations to such an extent that a nesting pair finds it advantageous to move to a different and better-stocked nesting territory the next year. Consistent with local prey depletion, reoccupancy of nest sites in the species is notably inconsistent; some sites are used repeatedly over the years, but many others are used only once or at irregular intervals.

Great Horned Owls commonly leave their roosts to begin hunting shortly after sunset, and they characteristically hunt from elevated perches, often in open fields and marshlands. In the deserts of southern Arizona, their hunting perches are often the tops of the same giant saguaros used by Bay-winged Hawks and Red-tailed Hawks for hunting during the day, and in regions where natural perches are scarce they readily hunt from the tops of telephone poles and billboards. From such strategic lookouts, they can carefully inspect their surroundings for potential victims, and they often launch attacks on much larger mammals and birds than most other raptors take. But although they have the abilities to subdue quite massive prey and have no hesitancy in attacking formidably noxious mammals such as various skunk species, they do sometimes make fatal mistakes. Records exist of individuals attempting to take large snakes and sometimes getting captured by the snakes instead—wrapped up in their coils and unable to escape.

Other individuals have come to grief in foolhardy attacks on porcupines. We once found a nearly immobile and moribund horned owl in southern

Great Horned Owl

Arizona whose breast and legs had been deeply skewered with multiple sharp spines of this mammal. We have also heard of other naturalists encountering porcupine-killed horned owls, and this well-armored mammal may actually be a fairly significant source of mortality for the species.

Other significant sources of mortality have been collisions with vehicles on highways, electrocutions on power poles, and shooting and trapping, especially associated with efforts to protect poultry. Losses to shooting and trapping continue, but they have progressively declined as the species has been given increasing legal protection in recent decades. In some years, many fledglings starve before reaching full independence, and it appears that the fledgling stage is an especially difficult one in the life cycle of this species.

Nevertheless, as a very widespread and frequently seen species, the Great Horned Owl is not known to be currently suffering major conservation threats from any source anywhere in its enormous range, although it has received very little monitoring for long-term population trends. More concern has been expressed about predatory impacts of the Great Horned Owl on other raptor species, for example Spotted Owls and Ospreys. It has also been a significant predator of adult and nestling Peregrine Falcons at their nest sites, apparently presenting a major resistance factor to reestablishment of the peregrine in many regions of the eastern states where this falcon was common prior to the organochlorine pesticide era.

Above: *Fledgling Great Horned Owls, such as this individual in the San Joaquin Valley foothills, depend on their parents for food for several months after leaving the nest. This fledgling's horn feathers are just emerging.*

Below: *Great Horned Owls raised two nestlings in an old crows' nest in upstate New York in 1967. The nest tree stood adjacent to an extensive snag-studded marsh that the adults used as their principal hunting grounds.*

Snowy Owl
Nyctea scandiaca

Range of the Snowy Owl

■ Breeding

--- Usual southern boundary
of winter range

A GHOSTLY, YET POWERFUL SPECIES of the most northerly treeless regions of Eurasia and North America, the Snowy Owl is the palest of the Strigiformes. Old male snowies are almost completely white, except for their eyes and bills, and although females and young birds are variably marked with dark bars and spots, they still appear largely white from any distance. The Snowy Owl is aptly named, and like the polar bear, it both symbolizes the frosty, windswept northlands and actually resembles them.

At least during the wintertime, the Snowy Owl shares its pale coloration with many other arctic birds and mammals, including various species of gulls, ptarmigan, and a most beautiful color phase of the Gyrfalcon. The close visual match of these creatures to surroundings that are covered with ice and snow helps camouflage them to both predators and prey, presumably aiding their survival in a most rigorous environment. Yet the Snowy Owl retains its white coloration even during the brief arctic summer, when the snows of

A wintering Snowy Owl at the Syracuse, New York, airport in 1966 blends with the weed stubble in a snowy field.

Snowy Owl

Near Barrow, Alaska, the northernmost settlement of the North American continent, a male Snowy Owl shares a tundra hilltop with a singing male Lapland Longspur. The longspurs bred with gusto in 2003, feasting on insects, but the owls mostly failed to reproduce, apparently due to a dearth of lemmings.

its tundra homeland disappear, whereas creatures such as various ptarmigan and arctic foxes change from white to a brownish hue and continue to match their surroundings closely. Against the soft-greens and browns of its summer habitat, the Snowy Owl is an extremely conspicuous bird, and it makes no effort to conceal itself in vegetation. One can hardly miss the species as it perches like a silver beacon on the low hillocks and promontories of its breeding grounds.

Part of the reason for retaining white coloration in summer may be that it would be difficult and stressful for a bird as large as a Snowy Owl to undergo a complete molt of its feathers twice a year. This may be especially true for flight feathers, which take months to regrow in large raptors and if molted too close together in time could severely compromise the flying abilities of the bird. Accordingly, most large raptors molt only a fraction of their flight feathers during a year, and individual flight feathers are often retained for two and sometimes even three years.

The seeming disadvantages of not matching surroundings during this season of continuous daylight may be less than one would think. The white

coloration may enable Snowy Owls to easily see each other at a distance during the breeding season. Further, when the species takes prey, the prey usually sees it against a cloudy or foggy sky, so that even in summer, white may still be the most adaptive color for surprising prey. Potential predators find the Snowy Owl a very difficult species to approach undetected regardless of the season, because the owl relies on hilltops for perches and nest sites. Since it can normally take to the air long before a potential predator can reach it, most predators probably soon learn not to bother trying. When predators do try to approach nests, however, the Snowy Owl is often a highly aggressive aerial antagonist, striking species as large as foxes, wolves, and humans with awesome talons that can force a hasty retreat. Characteristically attacking enemies from behind, the Snowy Owl likely can succeed regardless of its coloration.

The Snowy Owl is the heaviest owl in North America, with females averaging about five pounds and some females exceeding six-and-a-half pounds. Among the diurnal raptors, by comparison, only the eagles and the California Condor weigh more than this, and it is not surprising that Snowy Owls are sometimes

On their breeding grounds, Snowy Owls generally perch in conspicuous locations and can be seen from hundreds of yards away. Nevertheless, they are difficult to approach, as they keep a constant wary eye on their surroundings and usually take flight long before an observer gets close.

known to kill prey as large as geese. The species is renowned for its dependence on lemming populations, but it is actually very aggressive and adaptable in foraging. In some places it feeds heavily on hares or a variety of bird species, with females especially likely to take relatively large prey. Snowy Owls use a variety of hunting techniques, sometimes relying on perch hunting from high vantage points on the tundra, sometimes using hovering flight to prospect for victims, and sometimes actively pursuing avian prey in flight. Even when breeding, however, they usually spend the great majority of their time simply perched in locations that give them an expansive view of their surroundings, and for hours on end they often do not exert themselves beyond head movements to monitor their surroundings. They will physically defend their foraging territories from other Snowy Owls, but such encounters are infrequent. Most territorial defense is accomplished by deep hooting vocalizations that are especially frequent in males and carry for long distances across the tundra, stimulating other territorial snowies into responsive hooting.

Many of North America's Snowy Owls spend the winter on the Great Plains of Canada. Others, some of them regular migrants and some young birds, winter in the northernmost of the lower forty-eight states. Here they can be found occupying the closest thing to tundra that the region has to offer—large treeless fields and open spaces such as golf courses and airports. In fact, our very first collaborative field trip was a successful expedition to find this species at the Syracuse, New York, airport in the winter of 1966–67. As we learned on that trip, Snowy Owls perched on the snow-covered ground can be very hard to detect. The speckled pattern of dark spots commonly found on the bodies of females and immatures allows the birds to blend in remarkably well with a terrain of weed stubble. Nevertheless, wintering Snowy Owls also often perch on fence posts and other raised objects that make them quite visible from long distances.

The adaptations of Snowy Owls to their cold surroundings include dense feathering of the toes, which gives their legs the appearance of ending in puffy snowballs. The feathering of the Snowy Owl is in fact so dense that the species has been reported as having the second-lowest thermal conductance known for any bird, with insulation fully equivalent to the fur of an arctic fox. The species is very well prepared to deal with low temperatures and rarely is exposed to the high temperatures that many tropical and temperate raptors must tolerate. The core temperature of birds generally runs about 102 degrees Fahrenheit, so the insulating plumage of arctic species in winter has to allow them to maintain a heat gradient that can run as steep as 120 degrees Fahrenheit, or even more, over an inch or less of feathers.

The Snowy Owl is renowned for its irregular or nomadic movements, apparently a result of the fact that its prey often fluctuate wildly in abundance from time to time and place to place. Under conditions of summer food abundance, high densities of Snowy Owls congregate to breed in favorable sites and produce large clutches of eggs, sometimes fledging more than ten young per nest. Under poor food conditions, the birds generally disperse in search of better conditions, and many of the individuals that remain in marginal areas fail to breed altogether or produce only small clutches, many of which are abandoned in midseason. The Snowy Owl is a boom-or-bust

Snowy Owl

Old male Snowy Owls have nearly completely white feathers, exhibiting few of the dark spots of females and immatures.

species, adapted to move readily from place to place in search of favorable conditions. Such movements sometimes even take the species from the New World to the Old World, and with such extreme mobility it is no surprise that the species lacks definable geographic races.

The breeding season of Snowy Owls is relatively synchronized among pairs, with nearly all egg laying starting in late May or early June. The species is almost always monogamous, and, as is generally true in owls, female Snowy Owls perform all incubation of eggs. These are generally laid at two-day intervals, with incubation commencing with the first egg and usually lasting thirty-one to thirty-two days for each egg. Chicks likewise hatch at about two-day intervals, leading to a major spread of chick sizes and stages of development in nests with large clutches. At two to three weeks of age, youngsters leave their nests to wander about slopes in the near vicinity, but they do not gain real proficiency in flight until about seven weeks of age. They generally begin to hunt for themselves at about two months of age.

Nests of the Snowy Owl are little more than scrapes in the ground, characteristically placed on whatever hilltops or promontories are available in favorable foraging grounds. With repeated use and the accumulation of prey remains and fecal material, such locations sometimes become well-fertilized oases of green vegetation. From such locations, the incubating

or brooding females have a commanding view of their surroundings and any intruders that might appear in the distance. As with most raptors, males do most of the hunting during early stages of the breeding cycle, but unlike the males of many other raptor species, male Snowy Owls also take a major role in defending their nests from potential enemies. Because of the open nature of the habitat and the tendency of males to perch on hillocks comparable to their nest locations, they have a much higher probability of seeing approaching enemies than do the males of many other raptors, which are often completely out of sight of their nests during foraging activities.

Snowy Owls are sufficiently adept in repelling predators such as arctic foxes from their nesting areas that other bird species, for example eiders and geese, commonly seek out the vicinity of nesting Snowy Owls to make their own nests, apparently deriving valuable protection against the foxes in the process—a protection against predators similar to that apparently obtained by California Condors nesting close to highly aggressive Prairie Falcons or by Green Parakeets nesting close to Bat Falcons in Mexico. Evidently, for prey species that have some means of coping with the direct threats posed by predators such as Snowy Owls, it sometimes makes sense for them to associate discreetly with these predators and take advantage of their abilities to exclude other predators.

During takeoff, a Snowy Owl displays its heavily feathered legs and toes. The species is one of the best insulated of birds against heat loss.

The relationship of the Snowy Owl with the arctic fox is of special interest. In addition to effectively excluding this species from its nest sites, the Snowy Owls wintering in some northerly regions actually exploit the predatory capacities of the foxes and become strongly dependent on them for food. Researchers have observed the snowies becoming specialized thieves of the small mammals captured by the foxes, diving at foxes carrying prey and causing them to drop and give up their victims before having a chance to eat them, a relationship reminiscent of Bald Eagles stealing fish from Ospreys.

We long hoped for a chance to visit the Snowy Owl on its breeding grounds, and this finally became possible in the summer of 2003 with a short visit to Barrow, Alaska, the northernmost point of the North American continent and a location famed as the most accessible and reliable place to find the species in summer. Unfortunately, the year was a very poor one for lemmings—the third consecutive very poor year—and we encountered only nonbreeding owls during the visit. For the owls, as for other lemming predators of the region, including three species of jaegers, this was yet another year in which investments in breeding were largely avoided or soon terminated. With many poor food years in a row, biologists studying the wildlife of the region were raising concerns that something might be happening to disrupt the normally quite regular lemming cycles seen in the past, perhaps something related to general warming trends on the planet. Both the permafrost layer underneath the surface of the arctic tundra and the glaciers of Alaska have been steadily shrinking in recent years, with as yet unknown consequences for lemmings, Snowy Owls, and a host of other arctic creatures.

Despite such concerns, it was still an intriguing experience to observe this most spectacular raptor in its breeding habitat and to gain a first acquaintance with many other arctic creatures we had never seen before. The freshwater lakes in the vicinity of Barrow were still largely ice-covered in early July, and it was remarkable that many avian species were managing to breed successfully in spite of such harsh conditions.

While the Snowy Owls we located were not highly active, other species, including nesting Snow Buntings and Lapland Longspurs, were foraging at a dizzying rate on swarms of emerging arctic insects and were keeping their broods well fed. Even the Long-tailed Jaegers, which normally prey largely on the lemmings of the region, were mostly feeding on insects, gleaning them from the low vegetation on foot.

At the time of our visit, the pack ice had just recently retreated a short distance from the ocean shores, and temperatures still hovered just above freezing when the wind blew in from the ocean. In spite of the decidedly cool conditions, flowers were popping up everywhere on the tundra and the brown vegetation of the snow-free terrain was beginning to take on a greenish cast. The arctic growing season is extremely short, but once the snows melt, both the plants and animals of the region are highly evolved to race through their reproductive cycles in what time is left before bitter weather returns.

The Snowy Owl has been a traditional item of food for native arctic cultures of both the New and Old Worlds, and indeed Barrow, Alaska, was once the site of a village known as Ukpiagvik, which means "the place where we hunt Snowy Owls." The historical impact of such practices on Snowy Owl populations appears to have been significant in some regions, most notably northern Europe, but evidently it has never endangered the species as a whole. Human populations have generally been sparse in much of the breeding range of the species on the north coast of Alaska and in the arctic regions of Canada, Greenland, and Eurasia. The overall range still remains largely uninhabited by humans today. Nevertheless, the exploitation of energy reserves found in some northern locations has substantially increased human populations in a few regions, most notably in the Prudhoe Bay–Deadhorse region and in the region surrounding Barrow. Today, the economy of Barrow has shifted from subsistence hunting to the tapping of natural-gas reserves that lie underground in the vicinity, but considerable shooting of wildlife continues, including at least some shooting of Snowy Owls, and it remains to be seen how well the Snowy Owls of the region may fare in the face of the many influences that humans are now bringing to the arctic.

Snowy Owl

Great Gray Owl
Strix nebulosa

BY FAR THE LARGEST OWL of North America in external appearance, the Great Gray Owl exceeds all others in wing length, total body length, diameter of its facial disk, and many other dimensions. Yet the species weighs only half as much as a Snowy Owl and considerably less than a Great Horned Owl, and it normally takes much less formidable prey than are often taken by these visually smaller species. The size supremacy of the Great Gray Owl is basically an illusion, a facade of power created by a remarkably thick coat of loose feathers surrounding a deceptively modest-sized body underneath.

Nevertheless, no raptor is a more genuine and fitting symbol of the vast northern woodlands of North America. The great gray's thick coat of insulating feathers presumably functions mainly to provide superb protection against the cold temperatures of its normal habitat, and the species rarely strays far south of the boreal forests of Canada and Alaska. With the exception only of some populations in northern Minnesota and along the northern Sierra Nevada, Cascades, and Rocky Mountains of the western states, the Great Gray Owl drifts below the Canadian border only in occasional winters, presumably driven south by exceptionally poor foraging conditions farther north.

Like other owls of the remote northern forests, the great gray rarely encounters humans, and when it does, it typically exhibits little in the way of alarm or fear. Wintering great grays sometimes establish feeding territories on the fringes of northern cities of the United States where they often create a stir among local residents by perching conspicuously on fence posts and traffic signs as they hunt their usual prey of small mammals. When approached, these refugees from the north are often so unwary that they look the other way, even when one gets close enough to almost touch them. Observers patient enough to watch great grays hunting for any length of

Range of the Great Gray Owl

■ Usual breeding and wintering
■ Occasional winter invasions

Right: *A Great Gray Owl sits out a rain shower in a northwest Washington forest in December 2003. Great Gray Owls commonly hunt during the day but are fully capable of capturing victims under low light conditions.*

Great Gray Owl

This Great Gray Owl in Vancouver, British Columbia, captured two voles with a single pounce. In preparation for swallowing her victims, the bird spread apart the feathers adjacent to her bill.

time can see them make kills at very close range, acting as if they considered humanity no more threatening than the nearest clump of grass. Because of their unsuspicious nature, it is no surprise that wintering great grays commonly fall victim to collisions with passing vehicles as they hunt along highways. In bygone years, many were shot by curious gunners eager to obtain trophies proving their bravery and skill.

Great Gray Owls do most of their hunting from low perches, and they frequently forage during the daylight hours, most often in the early morning and late afternoon, although their powers of hearing fully equip them to hunt in darkness as well. Their auditory capacities are sufficiently acute that they routinely capture mammals beneath the surface of the snow, breaking through the crust with their talons to surprise victims that surely have had no warning of danger. Their plunges through the snow surface sometimes carry to depths as great as a foot and a half. On one occasion, a great gray was recorded successfully penetrating a crust strong enough to support the weight of a 175-pound person.

Great Gray Owls are efficient predators, typically capturing prey in a high percentage of their pounces. We once even observed a bird in British Columbia capture two voles simultaneously in a single pounce to the ground. Nevertheless, despite its hunting prowess, the great gray is nowhere truly abundant, and sightings of the species are always memorable occasions.

Our first opportunity to observe Great Gray Owls came on a June day in 1991 at a nest in eastern Idaho. The nest site was an irregular small cavity in the broken top of a Douglas fir snag, a site that demanded awkward contortions from the adult female as she brooded a single small youngster through the daylight hours. Only when temperatures had warmed sufficiently in the midafternoon did she temporarily leave the site for what appeared to be more comfortable surroundings on nearby perches.

The male great gray made an appearance but once during the day when he arrived with a small mammal, apparently a vole, which he passed to his brooding mate, who in turn ripped it apart for her chick. The female also went on one brief hunting trip of her own in the late afternoon, when she flew perhaps a hundred feet away to a low stump, from which she almost immediately dropped on another small mammal. Neither the male nor the female adult paid us any apparent attention as we sat perhaps fifty feet away from the nest without a blind or any other concealment.

Surprisingly, the owls' nest snag was also in use by another bird species— a pair of Mountain Bluebirds, who were nesting in a small hole just a couple feet below the owl nest and who repeatedly entered their own site without any challenge from the owls. Neither species appeared to be troubled by the presence of the other, and their close proximity was undoubtedly due to the absence of any other sizable snags with cavities suitable for nesting in the near vicinity. The whole area had been burned over in the recent past, and essentially all other nearby trees, mostly lodgepole pines, were both small and dead.

In addition to nesting in broken-off snags, many Great Gray Owls nest in abandoned stick nests of other raptors, especially Northern Goshawks and Red-tailed Hawks. Like most other owls and falcons, the great gray is not known to do any nest construction other than forming a shallow depression or scrape for eggs in whatever nest substrate it adopts. And although relying on ready-made sites allows the species to forego the time and energy investments entailed in nest construction, it usually precludes breeding in regions that have favorable food supplies but no suitable snags or stick nests nearby. Raptors such as Red-tailed Hawks and Goshawks are often common enough that great gray pairs may normally be able to find adequate sites for breeding, but the owls have no control over the quality of sites available and sometimes make do with sites that are cramped and very difficult to use. Great Gray Owls in some regions have readily accepted artificial stick-nest platforms in trees, suggesting true limitations in natural availability of nests for these populations.

Eggs of the great gray usually appear in April or May, and the usual clutch varies from two to three eggs in some locations and years to as high as four to five eggs in especially good years and locations. The variation in clutch size is much greater in this species than in other *Strix* owls and probably reflects much more variable prey populations for this species than for its congeners. Considering its relatively northerly range and the general tendency for large fluctuations in populations of small northerly rodents, this seems understandable. The great gray's very strong dietary focus on small mammals contrasts with the much more diversified diets of Barred Owls and Spotted Owls, despite the fact that the great gray is a larger species and one might think this would lead to a similar, if not greater, capacity to take fairly large vertebrates.

The strong fluctuations in its primary prey from year to year are also the presumed cause of periodic winter invasions of the northern United States. Perhaps the strongest such invasion in history was documented in Minnesota over the winter of 2004–05, when many hundreds of these birds appeared, attracting birders from all over the country. Although it is difficult to quantify exactly how many birds are present when they are not all concentrated in one place and when travel in many areas is difficult, reports for the state suggested that as many as two thousand individuals may have decided that Minnesota was a better place than Canada, at least temporarily.

Washington is another state that sees wintering Great Gray Owls in some years. In December 2003, we joined Jim Shiflett, a frequent associate of ours in parrot studies in Mexico, to watch several Great Gray Owls on winter territories near his home along the coast of that state. Though they do not appear every year, the individuals seen in coastal Washington likely originate from a region several hundred miles to the northeast in British Columbia. In fact, Shiflett and raptor researcher Bud Anderson have radio-tagged and tracked several of these birds as they made return trips to this region in the springtime.

On their wintering ranges, the Washington birds we observed occupied relatively small areas with good food supplies and abundant hunting perches and could be found on most days, regardless of the weather. We saw a number of successful prey captures, but most notably, no unsuccessful attempts. Evidently, the birds waited until the chances of success were very high before initiating a pounce. Prey taken, as best we could identify them, included several voles, a mole, a chickaree, and what appeared to be possibly a wood rat. Even during the day it seemed likely the birds were relying mainly on sound to locate prey, as the victims were all extracted from dense ground cover.

One bird we watched was hunting a small clearing in Stanley Park in nearby Vancouver, British Columbia. From the top of a young conifer, this bird endured several downpours of rain without budging from its perch. But when a small flock of crows arrived in the vicinity and noticed the owl, the latter flew immediately within the edge of the nearby forest where it perched low in a dense tree, waiting out the raucous mobbing harassment from the crows until they tired of the pastime and flew on. On their departure, the owl soon shook its feathers and returned directly to its former hunting perch on the edge of the clearing. Despite continuing periods of rain, the bird finally succeeded in capturing prey in a pounce preceded by intense scrutiny

A Great Gray Owl pair in eastern Idaho in 1991 situated their nest atop this broken-off Douglas fir snag.

of the prey's location about twenty feet from the owl's perch. Immediately after its meal it flew off out of sight into the dense forest, possibly seeking a more sheltered location for roosting.

The flight of the Great Gray Owl is relatively slow, but with regular deep, almost heronlike, wing beats. Because of the bird's low wing-loading, it is able to maneuver through cluttered forest habitats with surprising skill and agility. Some observers have described the flight as mothlike, but to our way of thinking it more closely resembles the highly maneuverable flight of a large bat. Further, the flight feathers of a great gray are quite soft and flexible, giving considerable protection from damage in striking branches at close quarters.

The feathering on the great gray's body, like that of some other far northern raptors, extends down to the toes. Feathers are sufficiently long and loose that the head of the bird sometimes seems to disappear completely when it preens the bases of its contour feathers. Concentric dark rings on the facial disk, together with bright yellow eyes, give the bird an intensely serious expression. From the side, the facial disk appears to be beautifully sculpted from a huge half dome of a head, with a ridge of raised feathers over the bill separating its two halves. The rim of the facial disk is attractively patterned in black and white, and below this the bird has a conspicuous, though narrow, white throat. The chest and belly are basically gray, with dark longitudinal streaking that changes to horizontal barring under the tail. Altogether, the Great Gray Owl is an exceedingly handsome raptor whose proportionately large head suggests profound Beethoven-like mental capacities. In visual appearance it far surpasses both of its close North American relatives in the genus *Strix*, the Barred Owl and the Spotted Owl.

Great Gray Owl

During preening, the head of a Great Gray Owl can fully disappear in its voluminous cloak of loose feathers. In external linear dimensions, the great gray is the largest North American owl, but it is surprisingly light-bodied and weighs only about half as much as the visually smaller Snowy Owl.

Nevertheless, it trails both of these other owls in the impressiveness of its vocalizations. In territorial contexts, both sexes of the great gray generally utter only a monotonous series of evenly spaced, low hoots—a much less flamboyant vocal display than the ringing territorial calls of its cousins. In addition, the maniacal caterwauling calls known for both Barred and Spotted Owls evidently have no close counterpart in the repertoire of the great gray, although the latter is known to give a variety of squeals during distraction displays. And while the great gray does have a variety of other calls, including an excited *chitter* given between sexes during food exchanges, these are mostly various short hoots and barks, many of them of low intensity.

The Great Gray Owl is the only North American *Strix* owl to be found also in the Old World, where it occupies similar habitat. The Barred Owl and the Spotted Owl are not found in far northerly regions, and their failure to exhibit populations in the Old World may primarily reflect the difficulties in dispersal between temperate regions of the two continents. Other members of the genus *Strix*, for example the Tawny Owl (*Strix aluco*) and Ural Owl (*Strix uralensis*), are found in temperate regions of Europe and Asia and correspondingly have not invaded temperate regions of the New World. They remain geographically separated sister species to the Barred and Spotted Owls of North America.

Left: *Tending just a single youngster, the adult female of the Idaho nest takes a break from brooding, while her nestling below surveys the outside world.*

Great Gray Owl

Barred Owl

Strix varia

"WHO COOKS FOR YOU, who cooks for you-all?" These powerful vocalizations resound unmistakably through the woodlands and are one of the best-known calls of any North American raptor species. Almost anyone who has spent any time at all in forests of the eastern United States has heard these distinctive calls and has known immediately that they must belong to some owl species, though not all have known that they belong to the Barred Owl. Deep and penetrating, the calls carry for long distances. In especially good locations, such as along many rivers in the South, one can stand in a single place and, sometimes, hear three or four pairs of owls uttering these calls simultaneously from their respective territories.

During courtship, the calls of the species become much more complicated and lengthy, often escalating into frenzies of manic hoots, hollers, and cackles that some observers have described as caterwauling or demonic laughter. Bouts of these unsettling vocalizations sometimes continue without letup for as long as a couple minutes and suggest twisted rituals of torture and evil appropriate for a grade Z horror movie. Presumably the vocalizations have mainly amorous connotations for the owls, but for humans they can contribute to widespread fears of dark, swampy woodlands.

Although it often vocalizes on cloudy afternoons, the Barred Owl is fundamentally a creature of the night, rarely venturing forth from its secluded roosts to seek food until after sundown. It is most active in the twilight hours of the evening and just before dawn, but it is another of the species with asymmetric ears that is apparently capable of taking prey in total darkness. Nevertheless, over a period of several midsummer days many years ago we once watched a recent fledgling Barred Owl foraging for grasshoppers in a fully sunlit field of upstate New York. The bird appeared normal and healthy, and it was actually quite successful in capturing prey, making an apparently easy living as a diurnal forager.

The usual nocturnal diet of the species includes a diversity of vertebrates common in woodland and woodland-edge habitats. Mammals, from small rodents to rabbits, and birds, from nestling

The huge old-growth cypresses of southwestern Florida's Corkscrew Sanctuary provide ideal nesting and roosting sites for Barred Owls. This sanctuary is also a traditional home for Short-tailed Hawks and Wood Storks.

An incubating female peers from her nest chamber in a cypress along Florida's Fisheating Creek in 1978.

passerines to grouse, are frequent fare. In wet regions, amphibians and reptiles are also frequently taken, and the species is even known to wade into shallow water to capture fish and crayfish. The owl is clearly adaptable in its feeding behavior and is a generalist, rather than a specialist, in its diet. While its overall main emphasis is on small mammals, it also takes a wide diversity of alternative prey, and mammals are not its most frequent prey in all localities. Prey are usually captured in descents to the ground from strategic perches, and are usually either swallowed whole, or first decapitated, with the head swallowed before the rest of the body.

Historically, the range of the Barred Owl was limited almost completely to regions east of the Great Plains in the United States and southern Canada, but in recent decades this range has expanded through the boreal forests of central Canada to the west coast of Canada and the northwestern United States. When the prominent early ornithologist Arthur Cleveland Bent wrote his historic account of the species in 1938, he mentioned only isolated records of Barred Owls as far west as Alberta. The species now occurs almost throughout British Columbia and has been spreading south through the mountains of Montana, Idaho, Washington, and Oregon to northern California. It is one of the

Barred Owl

few species of owls showing population increases or at least population stability in almost all regions of its range in recent decades, and unlike the Spotted Owl, with which it occurs in the northwestern states, it appears to do well in mature second-growth woodlands.

Bent's 1938 account of the Barred Owl described a number of nesting territories in New England that had been active over periods of several decades, and aside from the species' recent range expansion on the West Coast, it appears that the Barred Owl is one of the most sedentary of owl species, even in the face of major timbering operations and other disturbances. Bent himself repeatedly collected eggs from certain pairs, but they continued to lay in the same territories regardless. At one of these nests in a hollow tree in 1896, he almost met an early end, as he slipped in reaching for the eggs and wound up with his arm jammed in a narrow slit at the bottom of the cavity entrance. With nobody nearby to help him out of his predicament, he hung from the cavity by his arm for nearly a half hour before finally managing to rip his arm free, falling a considerable distance to the ground as he did so. Fortunately, although his arm was permanently damaged and thereafter allowed only minimal use of his writing hand, he lived on for more than another half century, surviving to nearly complete the first comprehensive compilation of the life histories of all the birds of North America. This monumental contribution is still a major source of information today, and it has been invaluable for all contemporary field ornithologists of North America.

Like other *Strix* owls, the Barred Owl nests mainly in large cavities in trees and in old stick nests of diurnal raptors. Most nests we have seen of the species have been natural cavities in trees, although we were once successful in getting a pair to adopt a nest box installed in a large tree in the Berkshires of western Massachusetts. Bent and other authors have also called attention to the close association of the species with the Red-shouldered Hawk, and to the fact that the owl has often been documented using the old nests of that species. In fact, there have even been cases of collectors finding fresh eggs of both these species together in the same nest where one had taken over the nest of the other in the same spring. Both these raptors are partial to swampy woodlands and feed on very similar prey, although they show very little overlap in the time of day that they forage. Like other observers, we too have found both species together in a variety of regions, from beech-maple forests of the northeastern states to mangrove forests of Florida. The similarities in the ecologies of these two species suggest that the Barred Owl may eventually come to occupy much of the range of the Red-shouldered Hawk in southern California, a region currently occupied by its sister species, the Spotted Owl.

Perhaps the most attractive and reliable habitat in which to find both Barred Owls and Red-shouldered Hawks is in the cypress swamps of the South. Here, Barred Owls often nest in giant hollow cypresses and roost on cypress limbs half-obscured with swaying gray curtains of Spanish moss. Bottomlands along rivers such as the Pocomoke in eastern Maryland, the Waccamaw in North Carolina, the Santee in South Carolina, and Fisheating Creek in Florida are well endowed with nesting pairs of this species, despite the fact that almost all of these cypress swamps have been extensively lumbered. Most lumbering operations, however, have removed only straight trees with solid cores,

Left: *Although Barred Owls are usually highly nocturnal, this recent fledgling near New York's Lake Champlain in the summer of 1960 had great success capturing grasshoppers in broad daylight.*

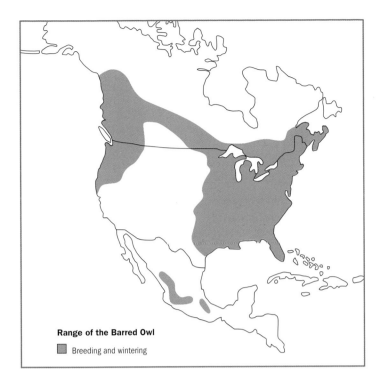

Range of the Barred Owl

■ Breeding and wintering

coloration may serve primarily to enhance the visibility of chicks and eggs to the parent birds, reducing the risks of accidental damage by missteps in the dark interiors of sheltered sites. Because owl eggs are normally laid in concealed sites well out of view of egg predators such as ravens and crows, because they are incubated very tenaciously by adult females, and because incubation usually begins with the laying of the first egg, there would presumably be no appreciable advantage and very likely only disadvantages in having eggs that were camouflaged.

Less apparent is the reason why the Barred Owls have completely dark irises, an eye coloration shared only with Barn Owls, Spotted Owls, and Flammulated Owls among the North American owls. All other North American Strigiformes have conspicuously yellowish eyes, which in some species almost seem to glow from within. For example, the Great Gray Owl, a very close relative of the Barred and Spotted Owls, has bright yellow eyes, as do most owls of the genera *Otus*, *Asio*, and *Aegolius*. The adaptive forces producing these differing eye colorations have not yet been clearly identified, and it is well to consider if the dark-eyed species, for example, share features in their ecology or behavior that might provide clues to the significance of their eye coloration. The wide taxonomic spread represented by the four dark-eyed species mentioned above, and the yellow eye coloration of many of their close relatives, suggest that the former may not simply have received their dark eye coloration by common descent, or if they have, the most interesting question may be why so many different evolutionary lines of owls have independently adopted yellow eyes.

Dark eye coloration seems unrelated to body size, as these four species range from small to moderately large, and it likewise seems unrelated to gross habitat preferences or diet, as the four species occupy habitats ranging from open grasslands to dense woodlands and have diets ranging from insects to mammals and other vertebrates. One feature they do all share is a quite thorough commitment to nocturnal foraging, although other species that are equally and in some cases even more nocturnal in habits have yellow eyes. Three of the four species are relatively dark and cryptic in feather coloration, while the Barred Owl is conspicuously light colored overall, so this appears to be another unpromising linkage. Conceivably, eye coloration could relate to a variety of physiological constraints or aspects of communication with potential enemies or kin, but no simple correlation seems to provide a consistent and plausible explanation.

The fact that many owl species with conspicuous yellow eyes also have a cryptic posture in which they compress their plumage, raise their ear tufts (if they have them), and close their eyes almost completely suggests that bright yellow eye coloration may have some function outweighing the advantages of being cryptic in at least some contexts. Nevertheless, the cryptic posture with eyes kept closed is also highly developed in the Flammulated Owl, which lacks yellow eyes. Finding a satisfactory overall explanation for eye colors of owls may require some novel hypotheses.

leaving many twisted and hollow old cypresses in place. Many of these large old trees offer relatively good potential as nest sites. The conspicuous abundance of Barred Owls and many woodpecker species is one reason why we have always been uneasy with the hypothesis that certain species no longer found in these swamps, such as the Carolina Parakeet, have been lost because of the destruction of suitable cavity nest sites.

With a usual weight of about one-and-a-half to two pounds, the Barred Owl is one of the largest owls of North America, and like other owls of its genus it lacks earlike feather tufts on top of the head, a characteristic that immediately distinguishes all the *Strix* species from some other large owls found in the same regions, namely the Great Horned Owl and the Long-eared Owl. The Barred Owl's low pitched vocalizations follow the usual trend for large owls, though the correlation of body size with depth of vocalizations does have some exceptions. Perhaps most notably, the Flammulated Owl, a very small species, has surprisingly deep vocalizations that can lead one to believe a much larger species is calling nearby. The Barred Owl also provides a reasonably good fit to other general correlations that have been noted with body size. For example, length of the incubation period (about a month) and length of the nestling period till fledging (about ten weeks) tend to be relatively long in the species.

Like the Spotted Owl, the Barred Owl commonly lays clutches of two or three eggs, and like the eggs of other owls, the eggs of these species are white and relatively rounded in shape. White eggs and chicks are characteristic of most cavity-nesting birds, and this

Left: *This sleeping Barred Owl rested in low mangroves at the southernmost tip of the Florida Peninsula near Cape Sable in 1971.*

Barred Owl

Spotted Owl

Strix occidentalis

The Spotted Owl is the smallest of the *Strix* owls found in North America, but at about one-and-a-third pounds in weight it still qualifies as a large owl. Its name reflects the white spots found on its head, back, and underparts, which differ from the barring and streaking found on the otherwise quite similar Barred Owl. Basically a western counterpart to the Barred Owl, the Spotted Owl has a range extending from extreme southwestern Canada south through mountainous country to the Sierra Madre of central and northern Mexico.

Like other members of its genus, the Spotted Owl is often found in heavy timber, and in fact its fundamental dependence on such habitat in the northwestern United States led to a major conflict between conservationists and the timber industry in the last quarter of the twentieth century. At issue was the basic question of how much old-growth timber should be preserved in perpetuity on public lands. Research starting in the 1970s revealed that the long history of cutting old-growth woodlands in the region was severely affecting the fortunes of the owl. Under terms of the Endangered Species Act and the National Forest Management Act, the federal government had a responsibility to prevent the extinction of this and other associated species, and on this basis conservationists challenged the right of the government to continue its long-standing timbering practices.

The conflict over conservation of the Spotted Owl became a series of bitter legal battles that received major national attention in the press, with contending parties highly polarized against each other. Although matters are still not completely resolved, the federal government finally came up with a compromise plan in 1994 that has so far proved viable in the courts. This plan, called the Northwest Forest Plan, established a chain of large-scale reserves of mature and near-mature forests free from timber harvest within federal forestlands in Washington, Oregon, and northern California. At the same time, other federal lands were left subject to continued timber harvest. The Northwest Forest Plan represented a fundamental shift of priorities within the U.S. Forest Service and the Bureau of Land Management from an overwhelming emphasis on commercial exploitation of forest resources to a much more diversified emphasis that explicitly recognized general wildlife

Above: *High in southern Arizona's Huachuca Mountains in 1998, a female Spotted Owl brings a Whiskered Owl prey to a nestling that had fallen from its original nursery atop a dead pine snag. While still very small, this youngster evidently tumbled to the earth during an attack by a goshawk. His sibling was eaten by the hawk.*

Right: *The female parent stood close guard over the grounded nestling, ready to challenge any terrestrial predators that might appear.*

conservation values as crucially important. The Spotted Owl was a central focus in this evolution of priorities, and in the process the species became the subject of far more research than has been conducted with any other owl on the continent.

The blitz of Spotted Owl research, which continues today, has covered many aspects of the species' ecology and has revealed that habitat destruction is not the only threat the species faces. The closely related Barred Owl, a larger species, has been invading the northwestern range of the Spotted Owl from the northeast in recent decades, and evidence suggests that it is a superior competitor to the Spotted Owl, with a potential for displacing the latter from many areas. In addition, hybridization of the two species has been documented in several instances, and if it proves frequent enough, the final result could be a complete amalgamation of the two species into a single species. On the other hand, if hybrids prove significantly inferior to either parental species, natural selection could lead to an ultimate sharpening of ecological differences between the species, with hybridization declining in frequency and importance. Thus, it is quite uncertain what may happen as a result of interactions between the two species, and it is possible that outcomes may vary geographically. In any event, the Spotted Owl could be lost in much of its range quite independent of the effects of cutting old-growth woodlands, and it is presently difficult to predict how well it will survive as a distinct species into the future.

Regardless of future developments in the Northwest, Spotted Owls are presently still relatively common in much of southern California and in other southwestern states south into the Sierra Madre of Mexico—including many regions where the forests are limited to very steep slopes and where timbering practices have not been quite as uniformly thorough as in the northwestern states. These also are regions where Barred Owls have yet to put in an appearance. It is in these more southerly regions where we have become familiar with the species, often running into it in our survey work with other raptor species and the Thick-billed Parrot. The Spotted Owl was a regular resident of some of the nesting areas of the California Condor, which we studied in the 1980s, and it is still a regular inhabitant of many of the canyons of Arizona, where we have studied a number of forest raptors over the years. While one would hesitate to describe it as truly abundant anywhere, the Spotted Owl is a species that continues to be regularly dispersed in the right sort of habitat—moist well-wooded forests at mid-to-high elevations. In the Southwest, as in the Northwest, the species is quite easy to detect because of its penetrating territorial vocalizations—sort of an incomplete version of the "who cooks for you" calls of the Barred Owl.

In the mountainous region just north of Los Angeles, we found the California subspecies of the Spotted Owl nesting in cool, shady stringers of pine growing in narrow, dark, slotlike canyons—tiny pockets of good habitat separated from similar habitat in adjacent canyons by wide expanses of hot, dry chaparral and rock. In structure, this habitat mimics many logged areas. Similarly, in Arizona and Mexico the Mexican subspecies of the Spotted Owl appears to be doing well in relatively small patches of forest in narrow canyons with a northerly exposure. In many areas of the Southwest, timber harvesting is not practiced because it has yet to prove economical. In fact, wildfires are currently more of a threat to these montane habitats than is logging. The region has become extremely vulnerable to catastrophic fires as a result of a hundred years of fire suppression, combined with the effects of widespread cattle grazing and long-standing drought. Each year

Left: A week after we discovered the grounded nestling, he was still alive, though he had moved to the sheltered hollow of a nearby fallen log. This nestling eventually fledged successfully despite the region's many terrestrial predators, ranging from raccoons and coatis to bears and mountain lions.

Spotted Owl

In the years following the successful fledging of their 1998 youngster, the Huachuca Spotted Owls moved to nest atop a similar conifer snag about 150 yards distant.

thousands of acres of Spotted Owl habitat, including numerous known territories, go up in smoke.

One place where we have frequently encountered the species during field surveys is the Huachuca Mountains of southern Arizona, right on the Mexican border. Here, Spotted Owl pairs occupy several of the canyons descending from high elevations, and in fact the pair traditionally occupying lower Scheelite Canyon on Fort Huachuca may be the best-known pair of this species anywhere in the country. Seemingly well habituated to people, this pair is easily accessible for birders and other nature enthusiasts, and visitors may well have seen it on the great majority of days in recent years.

Another pair in the Huachucas is a pair we almost passed right by in 1998. We were searching for nesting accipiters in a high-elevation ravine shortly after dawn on an early June day, and as we moved up canyon we noticed a large bird

fluttering up from the ground at the base of a pine snag about a hundred feet away along a small tributary drainage. The bird proved to be a Spotted Owl, and in fact it had been attending a very small white-downed nestling in the litter at the base of the snag. Our first thought was that it was amazing that the owls would have chosen to nest completely exposed to terrestrial predators on the ground. But further examination suggested instead that this was a chick that had tumbled from its original nest location at the top of the broken-off snag and had somehow survived a fall of close to twenty-five feet.

Putting aside our survey activities for a few hours, we sat down near the earthbound chick to see what might develop, and in no time at all the female adult returned to the chick, this time carrying in her bill what appeared to be the carcass of a Whiskered Owl, which she proceeded to feed to the chick. This feeding was followed by her retrieval some time later of the carcass of a small cottontail rabbit that had been cached on the ground on a steep slope overlooking the nest snag. Before these observations, we had been unaware of any tendency for Spotted Owls to be active in daylight hours.

Considering the local abundance of terrestrial predators—ranging from coatis and ringtailed cats to bobcats, mountain lions, and black bears—we had little hope for the survival of this owl chick. Nevertheless, when we revisited the nesting grove a week later, the chick was still alive and well and had gained considerable size and weight. It had also moved from its exposed position at the base of the nest snag to a nearby hollow in a fallen log, where it was not as conspicuous as before.

We later learned that the same nest had been discovered earlier by Russell Duncan during his extensive survey work on Spotted Owls for the U.S. Forest Service and Fort Huachuca throughout southeastern Arizona. Duncan had documented that the nest originally had two chicks. But judging from remains he found in the vicinity, the second chick had been lost to goshawk predation, and the surviving chick may well have fallen to the ground during the attack. Despite the fall and despite its subsequent vulnerability to terrestrial predators, the surviving chick eventually made it to fledging.

Since 1998 we have found Spotted Owls nesting in the same grove in several additional years, and although they have not reused the snag from which the nestling apparently fell in 1998, they have used another very similar broken-off snag only about 150 yards away. One year, however, Northern Goshawks used this grove for nesting, and we were not able to find an active owl nest. Nevertheless, the following year, when the goshawks were no longer present, the owls were back nesting in the grove. It may be that Spotted Owls and Northern Goshawks find it difficult to coexist very close together, and it is possible the owls were obliged to move elsewhere while the goshawks were active in the area. As another possibility, the goshawks could have killed one or more of the resident adult owls, and the owls occupying the grove the following year could have been a new pair. The Spotted Owl, despite its classification as a threatened species, is a much more common species in southern Arizona than the Northern Goshawk, although both generally use the same type of habitat.

In addition to nesting in broken-off snags, the Spotted Owls of Arizona and New Mexico often nest in potholes of cliffs or use old stick nests of goshawks and other hawks. Some nests have been found atop witches'-broom (tangles of branches caused by fungi) and in duff that accumulates at the bases of branches in many conifers. With so many different types of possible nest sites, finding Spotted Owl nests is often challenging, especially because the birds often leave few signs of activity, such as whitewash or feathers shed in the vicinity. Nevertheless, the species has a quite strong tendency to use specific sites repeatedly, so once nests are located, there is a good chance they will continue to be active for many years.

We have also regularly found territorial pairs of Spotted Owls in both the eastern and western Sierra Madre of Mexico. In Mexico the species often occurs in proximity to nesting aggregations of Maroon-fronted Parrots and Thick-billed Parrots, the species that have been the primary targets of our survey work. All these species are associated with well-developed coniferous forests, and all three species are of conservation concern as indicator species of ecosystem viability. In Maroon-fronted Parrot habitat in the eastern Sierra Madre, Spotted Owls are often associated with nest sites in precipitous cactus-clad cliffs, but in the western regions where Thick-billed Parrots occur, cliffs are uncommon, and the owls are mostly found in more gentle terrain, nesting mostly in snags and old stick nests.

Like most other owls, Spotted Owls produce only a single brood per year, and egg laying, though dependent on elevation, usually takes place in March or April. The most usual clutch size for the species is two or three eggs, with

Range of the Spotted Owl

▨ Breeding and wintering

occasional examples of single-egg or four-egg clutches. Nevertheless, the average production of fledged young per pair has been quite low, generally less than a single youngster, so the species is clearly dependent on high survival of adults to maintain population stability. Young generally fledge in late May or June and remain dependent on their parents through the summer months. Recent fledglings, although quite similar to adults in plumage, can be recognized easily by the white triangular tips to their tail feathers. Adults have rounded tail tips lacking the conspicuous white edgings.

Like the Barred Owl, the Spotted Owl takes a variety of vertebrates and invertebrates as prey, including everything from insects to medium-sized mammals and birds. Flying squirrels are an especially frequent prey in northern portions of the range, while wood rats become predominant farther south. Prey are most usually captured by still-hunting from strategic perches, and the prevalence of good hunting perches is an important characteristic affecting the adequacy of various habitats for the species. It's not enough that prey be abundant in the range of any raptor species. They also have to be vulnerable to capture, and for perch-hunting species like the Spotted Owl, trees of the proper characteristics are essential in allowing efficient detection and approaches to prey. While the Spotted Owl can take some prey species characteristic of open-field habitats, this is generally only possible along the edges of such habitats, and extensive clear-cut areas are difficult for the species to use. Thus, the importance of forests to Spotted Owls involves many aspects of the species' biology, ranging from nest sites and prey populations to hunting methods.

Both the northwestern subspecies of the Spotted Owl (*Strix occidentalis caurina*) and the Mexican subspecies (*Strix occidentalis lucida*), including populations in Arizona and New Mexico, are currently classified as threatened under the federal Endangered Species Act, while the California subspecies (*Strix occidentalis occidentalis*) is not so listed. The conflicts entailed in conserving this species, like the conflicts inherent in preserving the Ferruginous Pygmy Owl in Arizona, have been among the most severe tests yet to arise for the Endangered Species Act. Whether or not the act will survive in effective form in the future, we believe it has actually worked quite well for the Spotted Owl, producing a fundamental change in government land management practices that ultimately promises to be highly beneficial for multitudes of species beyond Spotted Owls, including our own species.

Spotted Owl

Short-eared Owl
Asio flammeus

ROWING STEADILY THROUGH THE AIR with deep, floppy wing beats, the Short-eared Owl shares its world closely with the Northern Harrier. Both species average a little less than a pound in weight and primarily occupy marshlands and grasslands at high latitudes. Both normally hunt from flight close to the ground, taking mammals and birds unlucky enough to reveal their presence at the wrong moment. Both species also do much of their hunting during daylight hours, although both are quite reliant on sounds given by their prey, and both have an excellent ability to locate prey by sound alone.

Nevertheless, in places where we have had a chance to watch both harriers and short-ears hunting the same areas simultaneously, the two have foraged in different ways. The short-ears have seemed far more nervous and high-strung, repeatedly cartwheeling to the ground to make speculative pounces that have only now and then resulted in successful captures. Harriers have made far fewer capture attempts in the same lengths of time and have seemed far more

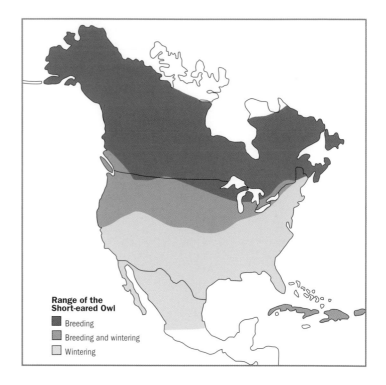

Range of the Short-eared Owl

- Breeding
- Breeding and wintering
- Wintering

Above: *A female Short-eared Owl in 2004 covers her eggs and young on the edge of a southern Idaho marsh. Incubating females, often nearly invisible from even just a few feet away, do not normally flush until almost stepped on.*

Left: *The black wrist marks of a foraging Short-eared Owl make an excellent field mark for identification of the species. Females tend to be darker overall than males, but this characteristic works better for distinguishing males from females within pairs than for sexing isolated individuals.*

cautious and discriminating in committing themselves to serious efforts to grab prey. In line with the very active hunting behavior of the short-ear, laboratory measurements suggest that this species has a considerably higher metabolic rate than the rates found in other medium-sized owls.

With both short-ears and harriers hunting the same areas and both frequently taking small mammals as prey, it is not surprising that they sometimes act aggressively toward each other. Yet in our observations, the short-ears have been far more aggressive to other short-ears, and likewise the harriers have been far more aggressive to their own kind. Wintering short-ears that we watched hunting the marshes of coastal Washington in late 2003 had very clearly defined feeding territories defended with vigorous chases whenever other short-ears transgressed their boundaries. When challenged, an intruder usually fled quickly, and the victor, on expelling an intruder, sometimes gave an audible wing-clap display in midair, banging its wing tips together rapidly and repeatedly beneath its body, as if applauding its own performance.

The wintering harriers of the Washington marshes were as vigorous as the short-ears in maintaining territories free of other members of their own species, but for the most part they allowed short-ears to pass through their defended areas without challenge. The short-ears similarly ignored the harriers in their domains on most, but not all, occasions. It is tempting to speculate that the relatively low level of aggression seen between harriers and short-ears might in some way have reflected a lesser degree of competition for food between these species than within the species, but whether this was actually true was not easy to confirm. From a distance we were usually unable to identify just which prey the two species were capturing, and although the periods of activity of the two species showed differences, with short-ears foraging mainly in late afternoon on into the nighttime and harriers foraging throughout the daylight hours, such differences in timing do not necessarily imply the two species were feeding on significantly different prey populations.

Short-eared Owl

The Short-eared Owl is a very widely distributed species, found in open habitats in both the Old and New Worlds. In part, its huge range likely reflects its considerable powers of dispersal, aided by its long wings and low wing-loading. The flight of the short-ear is especially buoyant for an owl, and the species is sometimes even seen soaring, an efficient mode of travel not normally available to strictly nocturnal species. Sightings of short-ears have been recorded hundreds of miles from land over the oceans, and the species has managed to colonize a variety of distant islands such as the Galapagos, the Hawaiian Islands, Iceland, and many of the West Indies. In addition, it occurs in many disjunct regions of both North and South America and throughout much of Europe and Asia. Though not quite as widely distributed around the planet as the Barn Owl, it is clearly one of the most cosmopolitan of raptors.

Under most conditions, the ear tufts of the Short-eared Owl are invisible, and they are normally raised into view only when the owl is perched and concealing itself cryptically in vegetation. Nevertheless, if not by its ears, the species is easily recognizable by its moderate size, manner of flight, and the conspicuous black wrist marks and wing tips on the largely white undersides of its wings. Its topsides are largely brown mottled with white, and its yellow eyes can sometimes be extremely conspicuous. Females tend to have darker underparts than males, making it possible to determine the sex of the partners of breeding pairs from a distance.

The short-ear is not commonly found in wooded areas, although it belongs to a genus of owls with other members that are often associated with woodlands or woodland edges. The short-ear, however, does sometimes form communal roosts in conifer stands, and in fact, our very first good look at the species was in a mixed winter roost of this species with Long-eared Owls in a conifer grove near Syracuse, New York, in the late 1960s. Nevertheless, at least when the ground is not covered with snow, Short-eared Owls most often form communal roosts on the ground in the open country where they forage—roosts that, like the communal roosts of Northern Harriers, may have a variety of purposes for the species.

Short-ears in most regions exhibit dramatic swings in abundance from year to year, largely correlated with major fluctuations in abundance of their main prey of small rodents, especially voles. Whereas the owls may be present and breeding in great numbers when prey are abundant, when prey populations crash, the owls readily move long distances in search of better food supplies and settle in different areas, leaving their former homes empty of the species. Overall, the short-ear is a relatively nomadic species that is dependent on its well-developed powers of flight to find regions of good food supplies.

Some coastal regions, however, offer reliably abundant colonial seabirds as prey, and here, the short-ear populations tend to be relatively stable from year to year. In early 2005 we had a chance to watch the short-ears traditionally associated with seabirds on Genovesa Island, one of the Galapagos Islands off the coast of Ecuador. Here, the owls were making an easy living by cropping victims from a colony of thousands of Wedge-rumped and Band-rumped Petrels that were nesting in crevices of the weathering lava rock making up the island. In one morning within an hour's time, we watched a single owl consume two of these petrels, one on the ground out in the open under a leafless tree and one that the owl carried to a habitual perch strewn with seabird feathers inside a cave near the colony. Exceedingly tame, this bird showed no alarm at human approach

Left: *A Short-eared Owl on Alaska's North Slope rests in low willows between foraging flights. The short-ears we observed here in 2004 struggled to locate prey and rarely even attempted pounces, despite hours of cruising over the tundra.*

Short-eared Owl

One newly hatched nestling and four eggs formed the contents of the Idaho short-ear nest. Short-eared Owls typically lay their eggs on a pad of grasses believed to be assembled by the owls, although most owl species lack such nest-building behavior.

within ten feet when working on its first victim, but eventually took flight when harassed by an impetuous Galapagos Mockingbird evidently intent on stealing food scraps. Short-eared Owls fortunate enough to be able to exploit such superabundant food supplies as seabird colonies have to invest very little of their daily activities in foraging, and the Galapagos birds we watched exhibited virtually none of the methodical speculative coursing over the landscape that one normally expects of the species. In capturing prey, the owls had little more to do than to fly directly over to the nearest nesting crevices of the petrels, where they quickly procured vulnerable individuals.

Nests we have seen of the short-ear have been shallow hollows on the ground's surface minimally lined with grass stems, mostly situated in open grassland and marsh habitats. One site in southern Idaho in 2004 was located on a ridge in the middle of a stubblefield, and the landowner, a committed farmer-conservationist, had first flushed the bird while plowing the field. The short-ears continued to attend their nest faithfully, despite the fact that the immediate nest surroundings had become a small island of stubble in a sea of bare earth. When we visited the site on May 25, it contained five small young and two eggs not yet hatched. The female sat tight and was very difficult to see, despite the plowed surroundings, for she was so well camouflaged against the background of remaining weed stubble. The nest appeared to be doing well, with vigorous youngsters and with unconsumed prey on the nest rim.

Another short-ear nest we found on the same day in a marsh roughly fifteen miles away contained a single newly hatched chick and four eggs.

This nest was likewise very difficult to see even from a short distance, again because the female was so well camouflaged and sat so tightly. We were not able to revisit this site until nearly a month later, and by that time the young were gone, evidently dispersed from the nest, although we flushed one adult about a hundred feet away and found remains of one unhatched egg about six feet from the nest. Nestling short-ears generally leave their nests at about two weeks of age, and although they cannot yet fly, they can walk and scrabble about, and presumably become much safer from predators by dispersing into nearby vegetation. A substantial accumulation of pellets and droppings in the nest location suggested that the nesting effort was likely succeeding, although we had no practical way to determine how many young were still surviving. The offspring would still have been too young to be flying.

Timing of breeding was more advanced in another marsh about a hundred miles farther north near Idaho Falls. Here, a day earlier, we had found a brood of short-ears that had reached the flying stage. Prey populations in this particular marsh, judging from the comparatively rapid success of hunting attempts of the short-ears, were much stronger than in the case of the marsh nest in southern Idaho, and the presumably superior prey populations offered a plausible explanation for earlier breeding of the short-ears in this location.

Still another population of short-ears we observed in 2004—on the north slope of Alaska—appeared to be foregoing breeding altogether. Here, we watched individuals failing to locate prey in hours of hunting effort in mid-June, and it was questionable that the birds were even finding enough food to survive, let alone breed. Like the Snowy Owls we observed in 2003, this arctic population appeared to be suffering major stress from depressed lemming populations. It would be very difficult to say, however, whether such stress might indicate a long-term and widespread trend or only a temporary and local difficulty.

Because of its erratic use of range and tremendous population fluctuations in many locations, the short-ear has been a difficult species to monitor in any rigorous way. Nevertheless, a strong consensus exists that the species has declined appreciably in the northeastern states and in certain western locations, as well. Presumably, pervasive declines have traced largely to habitat changes such as drainage of marshes and conversion of grazing lands into cropland. Researchers in some regions, however, have suggested that nest-box efforts to increase Barn Owl populations may have adversely affected short-ear populations by increasing competition for food supplies.

A Short-eared Owl on the island of Genovesa in the Galapagos guards its storm petrel prey from a Galapagos Mockingbird moving in from the rear. The owl soon took flight with the petrel in its talons. The short-ears on this island enjoy such an abundant food supply of colonial seabirds that they spend little time foraging.

Short-eared Owl

Long-eared Owl
Asio otus

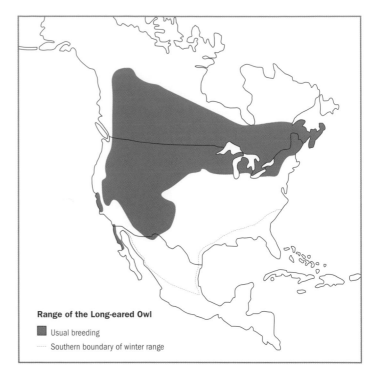

Range of the Long-eared Owl
- Usual breeding
- Southern boundary of winter range

LIKE THE SHORT-EARED OWL, the Long-eared Owl is a medium-large species that characteristically hunts from low flapping flight, forages mostly in open grassland habitats, and relies mainly on its ears to find prey. But unlike the short-ear, it is nearly exclusively nocturnal in its hunting activities so that its presence in a region is often unsuspected by all except dedicated owl enthusiasts. Only in some far northerly regions, such as Finland, are Long-eared Owls known to forage commonly during daylight, at least in the summer months when they have little choice about the matter. In flight, Long-eared Owls tend to cruise with much shallower wing beats than are seen in the short-ears, and they rarely raise their wings high above their bodies. When seen perched in a dense conifer roost or at the nest, the long-ear is much darker than the short-ear, with much longer, earlike feathers on top of the head, and with an attractive orange facial disk. Its overall expression seems to be one of permanent surprise.

A female Long-eared Owl in 1967 broods her four young in an old crow's nest. Located in a white pine in upstate New York, this site may have represented a second nesting attempt for a pair that had earlier nested unsuccessfully in a broken-off snag a quarter mile distant.

Voles were evidently the primary food for the young long-ears in 1967.

The owl species most closely resembling the long-ear in appearance in North America is the Great Horned Owl, which likewise has well-developed ears on top of the head and an orange facial disk in most regions. However, Great Horned Owls are considerably larger than long-ears and their "horns" are set distinctly farther apart than the "ears" of a long-ear. Further, the hunting behavior and vocalizations of these two species bear little resemblance to one another. Great Horned Owls characteristically hunt from perches, not from steady buoyant flight over the terrain, and they often take much larger prey than the long-ears do.

The primary prey of the Long-eared Owl are various small rodents, especially voles, although the species also takes a few small birds (generally less than about 4 percent of the diet). Once captured, mammalian prey are normally killed with a bite to the head and are normally swallowed whole, though they are sometimes eviscerated first. The wings of small birds are generally removed and discarded before their bodies are ingested, judging from remains in pellets cast after meals. The proportion of birds in the diet is considerably higher in Europe than in North America.

In its North American nesting distribution, the long-ear is primarily a bird of southern Canada and the northern United States, although it breeds south to the Mexican border in the far western states. Most of the encounters we have had with breeding pairs have been in the arid Southwest. In the years we were intensively studying accipiters in Arizona and New Mexico, we found a long-ear pair or two in most years, commonly nesting in old Cooper's Hawk nests. But these pairs were relatively few, and we never found long-ear nesting activity in the same location for two years in succession. So even though there were winter roosts that the species tended to occupy with some consistency in the region, the locations of their nests were very difficult to predict.

Arizona and New Mexico, however, are at the southern fringe of the long-ear's breeding range in North America, and in some other regions the species has been more habitual in its use of nesting areas. Repeated use of specific nesting areas has been typical of long-ears in Europe, where the species is generally considered a permanent resident in its breeding areas and where some particular nest sites have been occupied for many years.

Long-eared Owl

Within a few days of this photograph, these youngsters abandoned their nest to scramble about in nearby branches and trees. True flight came weeks later.

The differences in patterns of occupancy found in different regions may be related mainly to patterns of prey abundance and prey fluctuations. In locations where prey supplies are especially marginal and changeable over the years, the owls have little opportunity to become sedentary.

Most often, the long-ears breed in old stick nests built by medium-sized diurnal raptors or corvids. In many regions the species commonly occupies old crow's nests, and in the western states nests contructed by Black-billed Magpies, Common Ravens, or Cooper's Hawks are also frequent choices. The nests chosen are generally in well-wooded areas, or at least in patches of

trees; long-ears rarely use old stick nests in isolated trees surrounded by open country. Nevertheless, most nests are within easy commuting distance of the open-field habitat most commonly hunted by the species. Often the nests are situated in dense groves of conifers, but the nests we found in Arizona and New Mexico were mostly in oaks, and one long-ear nest we found in southeastern Idaho in 1981 was located in an extensive aspen grove. Other observers have reported nests in many other species of tree.

The very first long-ear nest we ever located, however, was not a stick nest and was an unusual site for the species—a hollow in a broken-off snag. We stumbled on this site in upstate New York in March 1967 during

The nesting location for the 1967 long-ears was characteristic for the species—a dense grove of trees next to open-field foraging habitat.

our occasional checking of a Saw-whet Owl cavity we had discovered in a woodlot of mixed conifers and deciduous trees. The saw-whet site was an old woodpecker hole about thirty feet up in a dead snag near the middle of the woodlot. One day in early spring we decided to stay into the evening to observe owl activities around the site. Unexpectedly, what we found was that the snag was not only a center for saw-whet activities, but also was a focus for a pair of Long-eared Owls. The latter were associated with the very top of the snag and were giving a variety of strange vocalizations as they flew about in the vicinity. But these activities turned out not to be very persistent, and for whatever reasons, the long-ears abandoned their nesting attempt in the snag after laying a single white egg in its hollow top.

After realizing that the long-ears had abandoned the snag site, we decided to search surrounding areas to see if they had renested in some other site nearby. We soon located another active nest perhaps a third of a mile away across a fallow field, and although we cannot be certain it was the same pair, this seems likely. This second nest was a much more typical choice for the species—a sturdy old crow's nest in a dense grove of white pines—and this nesting effort carried through successfully. During late May and early June we spent a number of nights watching and photographing the owls at this nest, which by then included a brood of four healthy youngsters being fed a diet largely of voles.

The activities at the white-pine nest followed the typical pattern for raptors, with one bird, presumably the female, remaining in close attendance during the early nesting stages, while her mate foraged for food. The return of the male to the nest area was often associated with wing claps like those of Barn Owls and Short-eared Owls, but claps near the long-ear nest were usually given singly rather than as a series. In the dark, moonless conditions, however, we were never able to establish exactly what the function of the claps was or whether the claps were given by just a single adult or by both. In other studies of the long-ear, wing claps have been given in a great variety of contexts, and by either sex, making it likely that the claps can serve multiple

functions. Documented contexts have ranged from courtship display in males to advertisement of nest choices by females to flushing of prey from cover during foraging. Whatever their function may have been during our observations, the wing claps around the white-pine nest, together with the weird moaning vocalizations given by the birds in the nest vicinity, created an eerie soundscape for the birds' activities.

As has been reported for other long-ear pairs and some other owl species using open nests, for example the *Strix* owls, the youngsters in the white-pine nest left their nest for good while they were still largely downy and long before they were capable of flight. Their dispersal was on foot through the dense network of branches leading into surrounding trees, and they soon became very hard to find. Presumably, the trouble we had in locating them at this stage was representative of the difficulties that natural predators of the chicks would have had in finding and cleaning out the entire brood, and increased safety of the brood may well be the underlying reason for such early dispersal. Young long-ears usually desert their nests at about three weeks of age, but they do not commonly take their first real flights until about two weeks later.

In addition, Idaho studies by Helen Ulmschneider of Boise State University have revealed that females commonly desert their broods when the youngsters reach an age of about six-and-a-half to eight weeks, leaving their mates to carry on alone in feeding the youngsters for another two or three weeks. Because multiple brooding is not well documented in the species, it does not appear that this mate desertion functions as it does in the Everglade Kite—that is, allowing the deserting bird an opportunity to immediately begin a new nesting cycle with a new mate. But presumably, such behavior at least indicates that a single adult can readily care for a full brood at this stage.

Although banding and recovery studies reveal that the Long-eared Owl is often relatively nomadic over its lifetime, this is one of the owl species in which at least some individuals of some populations make southward

Long-eared Owl

An eastern Idaho long-ear pair in 1981 reared their young in an old crow's nest in an extensive aspen grove. The "ears" of a Long-eared Owl sit much closer together than the "horns" of a Great Horned Owl.

migrations in the fall and return migrations in the spring. At least in relatively northerly populations, fledglings of the year commonly head south in October, while most adults of these populations head south in November. Most movements north in spring occur in April. Migration normally takes place at night, and researchers in Minnesota have directly observed migrating birds flying at altitudes of about a hundred to a hundred and fifty feet above the ground, starting right after sunset. Unlike diurnal raptors, who can often soar in thermal air masses during migration, the long-ears characteristically migrate with flapping flight. The high energy costs of migrating with flapping flight are presumably minimized by the light wing-loading of the species

On their wintering grounds, long-ears often form communal daytime roosts, sometimes in the company of Short-eared Owls and often in dense groves of conifers. While the functions of these roosts have been speculative, marking studies have shown that the individuals making up specific roosts often change considerably from year to year. Often, roosts appear to be made up of multiple families of long-ears, including their recent fledglings, and

the fledglings of different families seem to intermix quite fluidly. Roosts sometimes contain as many as a hundred individuals, although totals anywhere from a few birds up to a couple dozen are more usual.

Because of its frequent unpredictable movements from year to year, the long-ear is a difficult bird to census comprehensively, and no rigorous estimates of total numbers in North America exist. Nevertheless, general population declines of the species have been documented in at least some areas—for example California, Minnesota, New Jersey, and some other eastern states— while populations have apparently been relatively stable in most western states. In Europe, recent population estimates suggest about three thousand to ten thousand pairs in the United Kingdom, five thousand to seven thousand pairs in the Netherlands, one thousand to ten thousand pairs in France, and perhaps ten thousand pairs in Sweden. These estimates suggest relatively good numbers in many areas that are far from pristine. Evidently, the species can do quite well in modified habitats as long as appropriate nest sites and nesting groves remain available and prey supplies remain healthy and huntable.

Eastern Screech Owl
Otus asio

T HE MOST FAMILIAR VOCALIZATION of the Eastern Screech Owl sounds nothing like a screech, but is a long tremulous call descending in pitch, much like a ghostly whinny. One of the most mellow and intriguing sounds of the night, this call is heard most commonly during the summer and fall, and its quavering, melancholic quality generally evokes a mood of pensive sadness in a human listener. Emanating mysteriously from the woodlands, the call has a strong capacity to transport the listener back in time to childhood days of wonder in exploring the natural world. Almost every resident of rural and suburban regions in the eastern states has heard this call as a youngster, and the screech owl is generally one of the first bird species that easterners learn to identify by voice alone.

Both sexes of Eastern Screech Owls give the descending tremulous call, and its most usual function appears to be territorial advertisement and defense. The species also has other vocalizations, and in fact it does screech on occasion, as well as hoot, bark, rasp, chuckle-rattle, and bill-clap. Nevertheless, the descending tremulous call is by far the most commonly heard vocalization and appears to be one of the most important calls in aggressive contexts. As sad as the call may sound to humans, it is doubtful that the owls experience anything like the same emotions on hearing it.

Range of the Eastern Screech Owl

▇ Breeding and wintering

For many years the screech owl of the western states was considered to be the same species as the screech owl of the eastern states, but in 1983 the American Ornithologists' Union officially divided this single species into two species, the Eastern and Western Screech Owls, based largely on

In a partly fallen cabbage-palm trunk in central Florida, a roosting Eastern Screech Owl catches the morning sun at the entrance of an old Pileated Woodpecker cavity.

An Eastern Screech Owl in central Montana roosts in dense vegetation near her nest. A member of the subspecies maxwelliae, *an especially large and pale form of the species, this individual was of the typical gray phase predominant in westerly populations.*

behavioral research in Texas by Joe Marshall, a preeminent authority on the biology of small owls. Although very similar in appearance and ecology, these two species differ significantly in vocalizations. The characteristic descending tremulous call of the Eastern Screech Owl is missing from the vocabulary of the Western Screech Owl, and the latter species has a very distinctive, accelerating bouncing-ball call that is not found in the Eastern Screech Owl. These two calls appear to be roughly comparable in function in the lives of the respective species. Eastern and Western Screech Owls overlap somewhat in range, primarily in the western Great Plains, but with only occasional hybridization between them.

Usually weighing only slightly more than a third of a pound, the Eastern Screech Owl is one of the smaller owls of North America. It exhibits two distinct color phases that occur in all ages and both sexes: a red (actually rufous) phase and a gray phase, with no intermediates. No other North American owl has such conspicuously different color morphs, although considerable variability in color is found in a few other species. In the Eastern Screech Owl, the gray phase is the most common overall, but rufous-phased birds are the majority in a midlatitude region extending from Arkansas to Georgia and north to coastal New York. Fewer than 15 percent of individuals are rufous along the western fringe of the species' range in Texas, and essentially all the Western Screech Owls that are found even farther west are gray in overall coloration. Measurements suggest higher metabolic rates in red than in gray screech owls, and it appears that the rufous morph may be best adapted to warm, wet environments, while the gray phase is best adapted to cold, dry regions. Overall, more females than males are rufous, possibly mainly for metabolic reasons. Among our earliest childhood memories of the Eastern Screech Owl was a beautiful red-phased individual with a broken wing that Noel once had as a captive in eastern Pennsylvania. Possibly the victim of a nighttime collision with a car, this bird readily accepted the mice that were trapped for it, but its wing injury was much too serious for the bird ever to recover an ability to fly or to be a candidate for release back to the wild.

Many years later we found another red-phased Eastern Screech Owl injured by a collision. Sitting in the middle of a central Florida highway in obviously stunned condition, this owl had evidently suffered severe neurological damage, and like a windup toy, it slowly rotated its head 180 degrees from one side to the other, snapping its head back to the starting point to repeat the same process over and over again. We took the bird home to begin a rehabilitation effort, and here it became known, inevitably, as "Lighthouse." Although Lighthouse did not appear to be fully conscious at first, we were able to get cockroaches and other insects into its stomach by force-feeding. Over a period of weeks, the head rotations gradually subsided, and eventually they ceased completely. Soon thereafter the owl resumed its ability to fly, land, and catch insects, and we were able to release it back to the wild in apparently fully recovered condition.

The diet of the Eastern Screech Owl is one of the most varied of any North American owl. Foods include all manner of terrestrial and aquatic vertebrates and invertebrates, from earthworms, insects, and crayfish to mammals, reptiles, and birds, and probably because of its highly generalized tolerances, both for food and habitat types, the species is very widely distributed within its range. It relies primarily on vision in its hunting endeavors and captures most prey in descents to the ground from perches.

Because of its strongly nocturnal habits, the Eastern Screech Owl is not often seen, but the species is nonetheless a common inhabitant of just about all wooded habitats, including old orchards and highly modified suburban and urban parks and backyards. A permanent resident throughout its range, it occurs in nearly all parts of the eastern and midwestern states except most of Maine, northern parts of Vermont and New Hampshire, and northern

regions of Minnesota, Wisconsin, and Michigan. In Mexico it is largely limited to the northeastern lowland regions of Coahuila, Nuevo Leon, and Tamaulipas, while in Canada it is largely limited to extreme southern Quebec, Ontario, Manitoba, and Saskatchewan.

Intensive long-term study of the Eastern Screech Owls of Texas by Fred Gehlbach of Baylor University has revealed a wealth of information on many aspects of the natural history of the species. It is normally monogamous, with lifelong pair bonds, although a small minority of males have multiple mates under conditions of high population density and abundant food. Nests of the species are usually natural cavities in trees, often apples, oaks, and cottonwoods, and in central Texas close to a third are in old woodpecker holes. The species does not normally adopt sites in the vicinity of nests of the Great Horned Owl, a known predator of the species, but sometimes uses sites close to the nests of other diurnal raptors and owls. Adjacent pairs of the species sometimes nest as close together as a hundred feet. The owl commonly uses old Northern Flicker holes as nests but often faces competition for sites with the flickers, with European Starlings, and with fox squirrels, all of which are sometimes capable of displacing the owls. Preferred nest sites are relatively deep and roomy inside, but with small entrances that presumably reduce the chances of relatively large predators being able to enter.

Clutch size of the owl in various regions generally averages about four eggs. Clutches are incubated solely by females, as in other owl species, with incubation usually starting with the laying of the first egg and continuing for about a month. Males shoulder essentially the entire role of provisioning females and nestlings with food up until the mid-nestling stage, when the nestlings no longer need constant brooding and the females become free to forage on their own. Nestlings are in the nest for about twenty-eight days and normally depart from the nest in the same order in which they hatch. After fledging they remain dependent on their parents for another eight to ten weeks.

Food for the nestlings, as for adults, ranges from insects to a variety of mammals and birds. The adult female dismembers prey for the nestlings during the early nestling stages. Curiously, in addition to bringing in food, Gehlbach has documented adults bringing in small living blind snakes (*Leptotyphlops dulcis*), which are not killed and dismembered for the young but are allowed to burrow in the nest litter. These snakes pose no threats to the nestlings, and instead they apparently form a symbiotic relationship with the young owls, consuming ant and fly larvae also found in the nest litter. These actions may help reduce insect competition for prey cached in the nests and may also reduce attacks of the fly larvae on the nestling owls. Preliminary evidence suggests that the snakes may contribute positively to breeding success of the owls.

The studies by Gehlbach and others indicate a very wide range in breeding success among Eastern Screech Owls, with the success rate in different populations running between 32 percent and 69 percent. In central Texas, pairs nesting in suburban habitats have tended to be much more successful than pairs nesting in rural habitats, largely because of better food supplies in suburban areas and much higher rates of nest predation in rural habitats. Identified predators of nests in the region include black rat snakes, opossums, raccoons, and ringtails. Overall, 12 percent of suburban nests have suffered loss to predators, while a whopping 62 percent have been depredated in rural areas.

Nest success rates have not been uniformly distributed across the owl populations, and some females have been much more successful than others. In fact, Gehlbach's data for Texas indicate that half the production of young comes from just 16 percent of the females in suburban regions and from just 13 percent of the females in rural regions. Similar strong differences among females in production of young, with just a few birds responsible for most of the birds of the next generation, have also been seen in other raptor species.

The Montana screech owls nested in a natural cavity of a cottonwood along the Yellowstone River. Roughly thirty feet from the ground, the entrance on the underside of the trunk was well shielded from the rains that pounded the area during our observations.

The Montana screech owls fed their young a diet almost entirely of large caterpillars. The adults captured these at such a rapid rate that a bird arriving with food often was blocked from the nest interior by its mate already feeding chicks inside.

In 2004 we had an opportunity to watch a nest of Eastern Screech Owls in the most northwesterly portion of the species' range in central Montana. Here, a pair of gray-phased individuals under study by Helen Carlson of Billings was nesting high in a natural cavity of a cottonwood in a city park along the Yellowstone River. The screech owls of this region belong to the race *maxwelliae*, which is an especially large and pale race of the species, conspicuously larger than the screech owls of the eastern states. The pair fed its youngsters a diet that appeared to be almost exclusively large caterpillars. In the early evenings, the adults provisioned their nest at a surprisingly frequent rate—roughly a feeding every two minutes—and we wondered if their success in finding prey so frequently may have been related in part to the relative brightness of the night skies in the region resulting from nearby city lights. Considering the large size of the caterpillars taken, the youngsters were very well cared for, indeed. The adults were completely silent during the nights of observation. By day they roosted nearby in dense deciduous trees.

The Eastern Screech Owl appears to be doing well in the modern world, perhaps in significant part because of its adaptability to suburban habitats, which have been increasing substantially in recent decades. Frequent breeding of the species in backyard trees with large hollow limbs, however, leads not uncommonly to nestling owls being delivered to raptor rehabilitation centers when nest trees are trimmed or cut during yard maintenance. Although the species does appear to go through local population cycles of alternating abundance and scarcity over periods of a few years, it remains one of the most abundant raptor species to be found in eastern North America overall. The species adapts well to artificial nest boxes, although it continues to depend largely on natural nest sites in most regions. In its body size, it is well suited to use old nests of the widespread and abundant Northern Flicker.

Western Screech Owl

Otus kennicottii

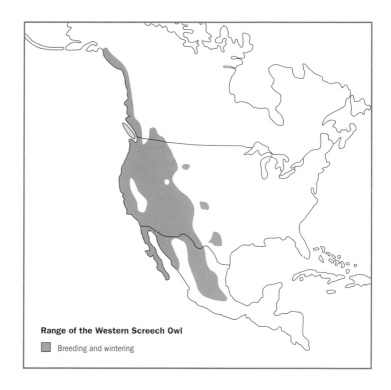

Range of the Western Screech Owl

▨ Breeding and wintering

THE WESTERN SCREECH OWL is probably the most abundant small owl in its overall range, although this is not true in all parts of its range, and the species is not usually encountered with anything like the frequency typical of its larger cousin, the Great Horned Owl. In many high-elevation mountainous regions of the west, Western Screech Owls are much less abundant than Flammulated and Saw-whet Owls, and at low elevations along the Mexican border the species is not nearly as common as the Elf Owl. Still, within its entire range, extending north to south from southern Alaska and Canada to Central Mexico, and west to east from the Pacific Ocean to the Great Plains, low-elevation habitats are much more prevalent than high-elevation habitats, and the Western Screech Owl is usually the most numerous owl at low to middle elevations, where it typically occupies a great variety of wooded zones.

The Western Screech Owl closely resembles the gray phase of the Eastern Screech Owl, both in size and coloration, and its soft gray plumage marked with black streaks and bars is a close match to bark in color and pattern, often allowing individuals to hide in plain sight without detection. Behavior as well as plumage aids in this deception. When an individual is closely approached, it usually adopts a concealment posture, with its eyes slitted, elongated ear tufts stretched tall, and body compressed against a tree trunk. Once danger has passed, the eyes open more widely, and the body posture changes back to a more normal, rounded shape. To find the species, it is often productive to hike narrow canyons and dry washes, closely inspecting the entrances of all cavities in cottonwoods and sycamores. With a little effort and luck, a Western Screech Owl can often be spotted just after a chilly winter night, when individuals commonly come to the entrances of their roost cavities to catch the morning sun.

Western Screech Owls nest in a wide diversity of situations, ranging from riparian areas in desert canyons to urban parks and backyard trees. The species frequently adopts standard nest boxes and other artificial sites, including odd nooks in barns and outbuildings, irrigation pipes, and holes in cement-block walls. Its preferred nest-entrance diameter is about three inches, and several of our nest boxes that were originally intended and sized for bluebirds ended up being adopted by the owls after the entrances had been enlarged to about this size by squirrels or wintering Northern Flickers. Western Screech Owls don't normally use the small cavities produced by species such as Acorn or Hairy Woodpeckers unless the openings have been enlarged. The natural sites the species nests in are most commonly old flicker holes or natural tree cavities formed by decay.

One pair adopted a nest box we put up eight feet from the ground on the wall of a small storage building next to our home in southeastern Arizona. These owls persisted in using the site for several years, and this gave us the opportunity to watch them at close range. One bird used the box for roosting in the winter as well as nesting in the spring, and both members of the pair became very accustomed to our presence, allowing us to walk within several feet without putting them to flight. The presumed female often sat with her face in the entrance, looking sleepy-eyed and watching our goings-on a few feet below. She soon learned to accept the dead mice we occasionally provided on perches nearby, and perhaps partly in consequence of the food bounty, laid exceptionally large clutches of five eggs in two consecutive years, fledging all young successfully. Clutch size in the species is most often three or four eggs in this region.

The female even tolerated being misted by a garden hose as we watered plants in the vicinity on scorching-hot days. Her response was limited to slowly blinking one eye, then the other, as the cooling droplets rolled from her facial feathers. But on one afternoon while Helen was watching the female, the relaxed demeanor of the bird changed suddenly. She leaned far out of the nest entrance and glared intently at the ground a short distance away. Following the owl's gaze, Helen spotted a small diamondback rattlesnake crawling toward the building where the nest box hung. The snake was quickly removed and the owl resumed her relaxed pose in the nest entrance.

Nest-site investigations by the owls began in January, and we could sit in lawn chairs to watch as night deepened and two dark shadows materialized and moved into the vicinity. The owls were quite vocal in the early breeding season, giving their bouncing ball call (a call that accelerates in pulse like a tennis ball bouncing to rest), as well as other calls during visits to the nest. Soon the owls were incubating, and once the eggs hatched after about a month of incubation, we began to appreciate just how active these owls are by day as well as by night. During the day, the male owl was often perched in a favorite shrub just a few yards away from the nest. He was far from somnolent, however, and would suddenly disappear, then just as suddenly reappear with freshly killed prey in midmorning. We had put up a horizontal section of hollow sycamore limb in a nearby mesquite for them to use as a roost and food-cache site, and it often contained stored prey, including species such as a Wilson's Warbler, an oriole, towhees, and various rodents. These meals commonly arrived and vanished during the day as the adult owls continued to feed their young. One of the more common prey types exploited by the owls was kangaroo rats, and we sometimes found the adults standing on these mammals during the day. Later, we found many of their uneaten tails in the nest box.

The nest box the owls adopted was actually quite small for a brood of five young, and in 2003, as the young began to fill up and fall out of the space available, Helen moved a couple of the young into a spacious second box mounted nearby. The adults quickly adapted to the extra nursery and obligingly continued to feed all five young, even though they were now in two locations. With much more space available, the youngsters had an opportunity for more wing exercise prior to fledging, and this may have aided the fledging process.

Fledging is one of the most risky transitions in most birds' lives. Naive youngsters are often incapable of effective defense or escape, and their clumsy

Probably the most abundant and widespread small owl of the western states, the Western Screech Owl thrives in low-elevation wooded canyons and washes but is less common at higher elevations.

Eagle, Snowy, Wood, Eared, and Screech Owls   264

The color pattern of Western Screech Owls camouflages them well when the birds roost among mesquite trunks and limbs. Often the most successful way to locate this species during the day is to investigate flocks of small birds engaged in excited mobbing behavior.

Western Screech Owl

Young screech owls become visible at their nest entrances just prior to fledging, but entrances often have room for only one or two youngsters. Members of larger broods continually trade places at the entrance.

movements are an open invitation to sharp-eyed predators, such as various hawks. Judging from the rank odor of well-used owl nests, fledgling owls may also be quite conspicuous to odor-oriented predators, such as snakes and various mammals. Thus, no matter how still and well-hidden fledglings remain, they face a time of life when survival depends heavily on good luck as well as the vigilance of their parents in heading off encounters with accomplished enemies. Adult screech owls stay close to their young after fledging and become highly defensive when approached too closely.

At fledging, Western Screech Owls look more like overgrown fur balls than owls, with fuzzy heads and a generally unfinished look. In our observations, fledging usually took place halfway through May and was quite synchronized among nest mates, with all fledging on the same night, despite obvious differences in age and development among brood mates. For a couple of days after fledging, the brood remained pretty much where they first landed in nearby mesquite trees. After that, they assembled for several additional days, roosting with one of the adults, in a dense juniper about fifty feet from the nest box. During the day, all five could be found perched within a yard and a half of each other and sometimes sitting in pairs pressed close together.

Within a week, however, they moved farther from the nest and eventually became impossible to find in the thick desert brush, although their single-note contact calls sounded all night from the darkness within a hundred yards of the house. Then several weeks later, in early July, they all reappeared at night, hunting in the backyard and catching insects attracted to the house lights. By this time their rudimentary "horns" (tufts of feathers above their true ears) were beginning to develop, and they were starting to look like real owls. We had an active Elf Owl nest nearby, and the brood of Western Screech Owls moved in on the Elf Owl nest tree to feed at the light we had

An adult pauses with a partially eaten kangaroo-rat prey a few feet from her nest log on our shed wall in 2003. Adults brought prey to the nest during both the night and the day, and all prey observed were vertebrates.

hung there to attract insects, but the Elf Owls, only one-third the weight of the screech owls, drove them back in short order, not allowing them to approach closer than fifty feet.

Soon afterward, the brood was no more to be seen, and the adults were once again roosting by day on the ridge beam of our barn or on top of an old thrasher nest under the rafters of our house. The wintering adults rarely flushed from their roosts, but they were occasionally discovered by local Cactus Wrens, who proceeded to mob them mercilessly. Pellets collected under their fall and winter roosts indicated that the owls were continuing to find some insects but were also frequently taking mice.

Like the Eastern Screech Owl, the Western Screech Owl hunts prey primarily by sight and most prey captures occur in descents to the ground from perches. Diets of the two species are very similar and include practically all animal groups of small to moderate size—insects, crayfish, earthworms, whip-scorpions, shrews, mice, and small birds. Nevertheless, in our experience the emphasis on small vertebrates has been marked in the Western Screech Owls of the Southwest and sets these birds apart from all other small owls of the region except Northern and Ferruginous Pygmy Owls. Elf, Flammulated, and Whiskered Screech Owls are all quite insectivorous in their habits, at least during the breeding season.

Western Screech Owls are sustaining vigorous populations in most portions of the species' range, and the adaptability of this owl to disturbed habitats appears to be similar to that found in the Eastern Screech Owl. Nevertheless, there is some evidence of local declines in the northwestern states where Barred Owls have recently invaded, possibly because of predation by the larger species on the smaller. In the southwestern states, the Western Screech Owl is a characteristic bird of the desert canyons, where it occurs together with Elf and Great Horned Owls. Its very generalized feeding habits, tolerance of dry habitats, and tolerance for many habitat disturbances give the species a favorable potential for long-term survival.

Western Screech Owl

Whiskered Screech Owl

Otus trichopsis

THE WHISKERED SCREECH OWL, also known as just the Whiskered Owl, is so similar in appearance to the Western Screech Owl that the two species are very difficult to tell apart in regions where they both occur. The Whiskered Owl averages smaller than the Western Screech Owl, but the size difference between the two is too small to be obvious unless the two species are seen side by side. And although Whiskered Owls tend to nest at higher elevations than Western Screech Owls, the two species overlap quite extensively in nesting locations, so elevation is not a trustworthy means for their identification.

By far the most reliable way to distinguish the two species is by their vocalizations. Unfortunately, vocalizations are frequent only during the breeding season, leaving field identifications problematic during much of the year. The two species do have small differences in eye color (yellowish in Western Screech Owls and slightly more orangish in Whiskered Owls), bill color (more greenish in Whiskered Owls), and throat color (normally buffy in the Whiskered Owl and gray in the Western Screech Owl), but these characteristics are too subtle and difficult to perceive under many field conditions to allow routine conclusive identifications. The name Whiskered Owl is derived from distinctive fine plume extensions on feathers of the facial disk visible at very close range, but these plumes are exceedingly difficult to see in the field, and similar, but shorter, plumes occur in the Western Screech Owl. Aside from vocalizations, the characteristic we have found to be most useful overall in separating the species is the color of the throat.

The Whiskered Screech Owl is one of the most sought-after species for birders who visit southeastern Arizona or southwestern New Mexico, because this is the only region where the species can be found north of the Mexican border. In contrast, the Western Screech Owl is found pretty much throughout the far western states north as far as southern Alaska. In Mexico, both species occur widely, but their ranges overlap only partially, with Western Screech Owls often found in riparian areas of the desert flatlands while Whiskered Owls are pretty much restricted to mixed conifer, oak,

and sycamore forests in mountainous terrain. The range of the Whiskered Owl includes both the eastern and western Sierra Madre of Mexico, and the species is also found farther south in the mountains of Guatemala and Nicaragua. A rufous phase of the Whiskered Owl occurs in Central America but is not known for the species in Arizona and New Mexico.

Despite their similarities in size and appearance and the fact that they are often found nesting nearby to one another, Whiskered and Western Screech Owls are significantly different in their feeding habits and ecology, at least during the breeding season. The Western Screech Owl is quite fond of small vertebrates, and usually takes arthropods in lesser quantities, while the reverse is true for the Whiskered Owl. Diet data are scarce for both species, however, especially in winter, and it is possible that both focus heavily on small vertebrates in that season. Owls that are arthropod specialists, such as Elf and Flammulated Owls, migrate out of the southwestern United States in winter, presumably because of the generally low availability of insects. Whiskered Owls are evidently nonmigratory in the same region, suggesting that their diet may shift seasonally from an emphasis on arthropods to other prey.

In hunting behavior, the Whiskered Owl is quite similar to other screech owls, making most prey captures in descents from perches to the ground or to the surfaces of vegetation. Prey are first grabbed in the talons, but once immobilized are often transported in the bill. When perched, the owls commonly hold large prey in one foot and use the bill to tear pieces off for ingestion.

In southeastern Arizona, the Whiskered Screech Owl is one of the commonest raptors in its preferred habitat, which ranges mainly from about 5,000 to 6,000 feet in elevation. Here, it can be found quite readily in the spring by tracking down the location of a calling bird. Its most easily recognizable vocalizations include a syncopated "Morse code" hooting and a fairly rapid series of hoots that tends to drop slightly in pitch toward the end. Both these call types are usually readily distinguished from the single or double hoots of Flammulated Owls, the long series of steady hoots of Northern Saw-whet Owls, the irregular hoots of Northern Pygmy Owls, the accelerating bouncing-ball hoots of Western Screech Owls, and the excited chatter of Elf Owls found in the same regions. Whiskered Owl calls are also completely different from the distinctive deep hoots of Spotted Owls, Long-eared Owls, and Great Horned Owls, and the harsh rasps of the Barn Owls found in some of the same canyons. Those seeking to find and identify the various members of the diverse assemblages of owls found in the borderland canyons must become familiar with the main vocalizations of all these various species. It's not all that difficult, although one sometimes encounters secondary and aberrant vocalizations of various species that can only be identified by tracking down the calling individuals visually.

In good habitat one can find a pair of Whiskered Screech Owls every few hundred yards along the canyon bottoms. In a census that Helen coordinated of the raptors of the Cave Creek Canyon region in the Chiricahua Mountains between 2002 and 2004, we located no fewer than thirty-four Whiskered Owl territories in approximately eleven linear miles of canyon bottom, or an average of one territory every third of a mile. Whiskered Owls were one of the most abundant raptors in the canyon, although they were not as dense as Elf Owls at low elevations. Altogether, we documented an average of 4.15 raptor territories per square kilometer of the Cave Creek drainage basin

Right: *Only at close range and under favorable lighting conditions is it possible to see the fine whiskerlike feather extensions growing from the facial disk of the Whiskered Screech Owl. These whiskers, which gave the bird its common name, are so hard to see that they are usually useless as a field mark, making the species difficult to separate from the Western Screech Owl, except by its distinctive vocalizations.*

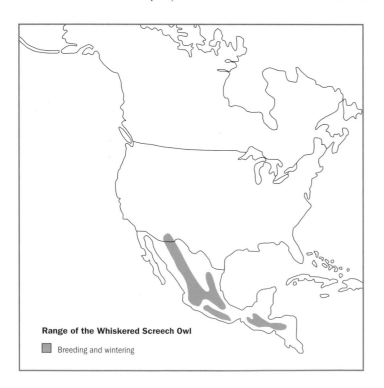

Range of the Whiskered Screech Owl

■ Breeding and wintering

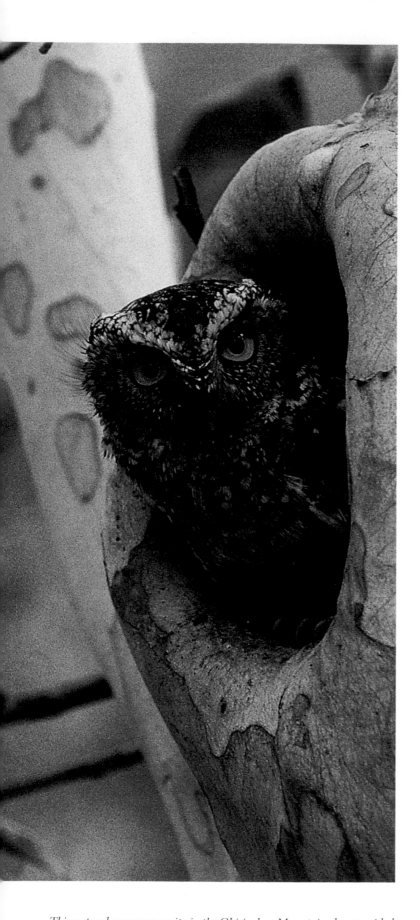

This natural sycamore cavity in the Chiricahua Mountains has provided a traditional nest hole for Whiskered Screech Owls, although Northern Saw-whet Owls took over the site in one recent year. The female owl nesting here in 2003 exhibits an alert posture, with conspicuous yellow eyes wide open and "ears" flattened on the top of her head.

Perceiving danger, an owl can rapidly transform its appearance from an alert to a cryptic posture in which the eyes close to slits and the ears shoot up to disguise its head and body shape.

Right: *Like the young of many other owl species, Whiskered Screech Owls usually leave the nest long before they can fly, scrambling about the ground and climbing small saplings on foot, almost like parrots.*

Whiskered Screech Owl

(including slopes to the highest peaks), an astonishing density that exceeds the renowned density of raptors in the Snake River Birds of Prey National Conservation Area in Idaho by a factor of approximately 3.8. Other raptor species that were frequent in the survey were Elf Owls (thirty-two territories), Northern Pygmy Owls (seventeen territories), Western Screech Owls (seventeen territories), and Flammulated Owls (seven territories). Overall, small owls comprised 65 percent of the territorial raptors and a significant fraction of the bird communities in the canyon.

Less intensive survey work in other canyons in the region suggests that the remarkable density of raptors in Cave Creek Canyon is typical for the "Sky Islands" region of southeastern Arizona and southwestern New Mexico, and it is clear that raptors are especially abundant and diverse in this region. A total of thirteen species of owls and twenty-seven species of diurnal raptors are found regularly in this region, the most recent arrival being the Short-tailed Hawk, which began breeding in the Chiricahuas and Huachucas in 1998.

The Whiskered Owls of southeastern Arizona nest most commonly in natural cavities of the sycamores that line the canyon bottoms. Most of these are cavities in living trees produced by branch breakage and subsequent decay, although some are old nest holes of Northern Flickers. Use of old woodpecker holes is much more common in Flammulated and Elf Owls, and indeed the Elf Owl in many riparian areas is almost a complete specialist in old cavities of Acorn Woodpeckers. Whiskered Owls are too large to use old Acorn Woodpecker nests unless they have been enlarged by the activities of squirrels or other agents, and they have shown very little interest in artificial nest boxes in locations where these have been provided. Whiskered Owls appear to prefer cavities roughly twenty-five feet from the ground that are situated in relatively open flying space. The choice of relatively high and open sites may primarily reflect flight considerations, but it could also reflect a tendency to avoid the sites most easily reached by snakes and other terrestrial predators.

As in most small owls, female Whiskered Owls perform all incubation of eggs while their mates provide essentially all food for the pair and their young up until the stage when brooding of young is no longer necessary. During the daytime, males typically roost either in cavities or in sheltered locations next to tree trunks near their nests, sometimes on perches only three or four feet from the ground. Females begin roosting in nest cavities several days before egg laying begins, and the termination of their roosting in these cavities often appears to be controlled by the disappearance of enough space in the cavities to simultaneously accommodate both the females and their rapidly growing youngsters.

Clutch size of the Whiskered Owl averages about three eggs. Eggs are generally laid in early May, with young fledging in late June or early July. Young generally leave the nest well before they can fly, often jumping to the ground, scrambling about the underbrush, and using their bills and feet like parrots to ascend into saplings. After leaving their natal cavities, the young Whiskered Owls remain dependent on their parents for food until they become competent in flight and in capturing prey, usually more than a month later. During this period, family groups move progressively through

Whiskered Screech Owls often nest in relatively high natural cavities surrounded by open air space.

the parental territories, sometimes returning to the immediate nest vicinity after a week or two, but youngsters do not normally reenter their nests once they have left them.

As a very local resident in North America, the Whiskered Owl has shown some considerable population fluctuations over recent decades, although it has generally been one of the most abundant raptors in its preferred habitat. It appears the species may have expanded into the Peloncillo Mountains of southwestern New Mexico only in relatively recent years. Trends toward planetary warming in recent decades suggest that a further range expansion to the north could occur in the future. Habitats similar to those currently occupied exist in the Graham Mountains, a little farther north in Arizona, and these mountains seemingly could become an additional region to be colonized by the species under the proper circumstances. The population in the Chiricahua Mountains appears highly productive and potentially could serve as a source population for such an expansion. Nevertheless, if warming trends in the region are accompanied by increasing drought conditions, the range of the Whiskered Owl could well contract, rather than expand, in the decades ahead. Since the 1980s, droughts have been frequent in the Southwest, and recent studies suggest that reproduction in the species is highly responsive to the amount of winter rainfall, so its status in the future may well depend on more climatic variables than just ambient temperatures.

Flammulated Owl
Otus flammeolus

THE FLAMMULATED OWL IS ONE of the least familiar of the North American raptors. Although a common resident during the summer in montane habitats of the western United States, extreme southwestern Canada, and northwestern Mexico, this tiny insectivore, only two ounces in weight, is hard to glimpse at any season and virtually disappears in winter. It is presumed to migrate largely to southern Mexico and Guatemala, but with few records of migration and winter activities, little is known about what migration routes it takes or where it spends the winter. Further, the Flammulated Owl's natural history during the summer has received relatively little attention in most regions, so that many aspects of its overall basic breeding biology and demography have yet to be established. What is known about the species is in many respects surprising and unusual.

The descriptive common name "flammulated" and scientific name *flammeolus* are derived from the Latin word for flame-colored, referring to the rusty coloration found in patches on the species' facial disk and elsewhere on its body. The Flammulated Owl is currently placed in the genus *Otus*, but available information suggests that it is a highly atypical member of this genus, especially because of its low-pitched vocalizations, relatively low clutch size, and dark eye coloration, but also because of its presumed long migrations and nearly exclusive reliance on arthropods for food. Genetic studies indicate that it has no close relatives among the owls of North America or elsewhere, and it probably deserves to be placed in its own exclusive genus. The genus name *Psoloscops* has been suggested as a replacement for *Otus* in the species' scientific name. Meanwhile, genetic studies of the relationships of other North American *Otus* owls have suggested that they are only distantly related to the *Otus* owls of the Old World and should probably also be removed from the genus and placed in a new genus, *Megascops*.

The Flammulated Owl was first recognized as a distinct species in 1859—a relatively late date in the history of descriptive North American ornithology. Following recognition, it was considered a very rare species for many decades, but this probably was because of its thoroughly nocturnal and inconspicuous habits, not because it was actually few in numbers. Very likely, the Flammulated Owl has always been a common species in its preferred habitat of open montane coniferous forests, but until surveys became based on an understanding of its vocalizations, it simply escaped the notice of most naturalists.

The most typical vocalization of the Flammulated Owl is a low-pitched single or double hoot that can be confused only with the hoot of the much larger Long-eared Owl. This hoot is deceptively difficult to locate and often sounds as though it is much farther away than it actually is. Under ideal conditions the hoot can be heard from as far as a half mile away, but it is usually quite soft even when the observer is much closer to the bird. A vocalizing bird generally sits in dense vegetation close to the trunk of a tree, often quite high up, and can be very difficult to see even

once the source tree is found. The low pitch of the hoot seems incongruous for a species that is not much bigger than an Elf Owl.

Other vocalizations known for the species include a soft catlike mewing or moaning call given by females soliciting food from their mates. Through much of the breeding cycle, the birds are very quiet around their nests, and a persistently calling Flammulated Owl is very often an unmated male in search of a partner.

The diet of the Flammulated Owl is so thoroughly committed to insects and other arthropods that reports of it taking mice and other small vertebrates have been commonly discounted as misidentifications of the owl species or other assorted errors. Most of these reports have been based on findings of the remains of small vertebrates in Flammulated Owl nests, and skeptics have argued that the presence of such remains does not conclusively prove that the nest owners took the vertebrates as prey, since there are other means by which the remains could have wound up in the nests. Nevertheless, the occasional findings of vertebrate remains in stomachs of wild Flammulated

Motionless at the entrance of an old woodpecker hole in a sycamore snag nearly fifty feet from the ground, a Flammulated Owl is difficult to distinguish from the surrounding bark surface. This cavity in southeastern Arizona was just eight feet above an active Northern Pygmy Owl nest in the same snag.

Above: *During bill-to-bill food transfers, owls of many species close their eyes, presumably to reduce the chances of injury by the sharp bills of their feeding partners.*

Owls are much harder to dismiss in the same fashion, and from such data it appears that this species, like the Elf Owl, may indeed take vertebrate prey occasionally, in spite of a quite single-minded focus on arthropods. A captive juvenile Flammulated Owl we once reared for release—a youngster not yet flying competently that had been picked up by a hiker—readily ate mice parts when these were offered and exhibited no signs of indigestion, so we know of no compelling reasons to believe that small vertebrates are completely unsuitable as prey for the species. At the same time, direct observations of these owls capturing prey, observations of prey deliveries at nests, stomach analyses, and the seasonal migration habits of the species suggest a very strong dietary reliance on arthropods, a commitment also reflected in the relatively late breeding cycle of the species.

Flammulated Owls do not commonly lay eggs until late May or June, with some clutches not started until early July, and with some nests still holding young in August. Thus, the breeding season of this species is even later than that of the Elf Owl, the other North American owl with an almost exclusive diet of arthropods, and is quite similar to the breeding season of the Mississippi Kite, another insect specialist. The tardiness of the Flammulated Owl relative to the Elf Owl seems reasonable in view of the higher elevations occupied by Flammulated Owls. Despite their relatively short nesting cycles, roughly a month and a half from egg laying to fledging, neither species starts breeding early enough in the calendar year to allow more than a single brood per breeding season.

Clutch size of the Flammulated Owl is almost always two or three eggs—fewer eggs on average than other *Otus* owls, and even fewer than the most common clutch size of the Elf Owl, which is three eggs. While recent intensive studies have indicated high nest success, with 82 percent to

Right: *A Flammulated Owl pair we watched intensively in Arizona's Chiricahua Mountains in 2004 nested in what was probably an old Hairy Woodpecker hole near the top of a slender oak snag. The male adult disappeared early in the nestling period, most likely the victim of some predator, leaving the female to shoulder all foraging duties. At this distance from landing, the female's eyes are still wide open, while the nestling's eyes are already shut in anticipation of a food transfer.*

Close to fledging, the nestling spent most early evenings at the nest entrance, and the female adult no longer entered the cavity with any frequency.

87 percent of nests yielding at least one young, the low clutch size limits wild populations to fairly low productivity that can be balanced only by good survival of free-flying birds. Judging from the overall stability of wild populations, survival must be relatively good despite the long migrations believed typical of the species. Studies of marked adults have also shown a high degree of fidelity in the use of breeding territories from year to year.

A consensus exists that the most usual summer habitat occupied by the Flammulated Owl is relatively open ponderosa-pine or Douglas-fir forests at high elevations. Nevertheless, most of our encounters with the species in southern Arizona have been in another sort of habitat—multistoried riparian woodlands with a heavy proportion of oaks at moderate elevations. Here, the Flammulated Owl occurs at variable densities in areas also occupied by Western Screech Owls, Whiskered Screech Owls, Northern Pygmy Owls, and Elf Owls, though it tends to overlap the Elf Owl (its closest ecological counterpart species) to only a limited spatial extent.

The Flammulated Owl nests we have found have appeared to have been almost exclusively old flicker or Hairy Woodpecker holes in sycamores and oaks. Extremely camouflaged in coloration, the Flammulated Owl looks like an extension of the surrounding bark surface when it appears at its nest entrance. Usually, it closes its eyes almost completely, and the camouflage is still further enhanced by barklike ear tufts, although these are not nearly as long as in other *Otus* owls and are often not raised substantially.

The absence of a large and fully developed facial disk and possession of fairly noisy wing beats suggest that the Flammulated Owl may depend mainly on vision in its hunting behavior. The species characteristically hunts from strategic perches, and most of its insect prey are gleaned from the surfaces of vegetation, from tree trunks, or from the ground in sallies from these perches. Foraging is quite strictly nocturnal, and although prey captures occur throughout the night, they are generally most concentrated in the early evening and just before dawn, as in many other owl species. Relative to other small owls, the Flammulated Owl has quite long wings, a characteristic to be expected in a long-distance migrant.

One nest of the species that we watched in 2004 in the Chiricahua Mountains of Arizona was about fifteen feet up in a dead stub of an Arizona white oak, in what was probably an old Hairy Woodpecker hole. The female, as in other owl species, was the primary attendant at the nest, and through the late incubation and early nestling periods in late June, the male generally brought in an insect food item about once every five minutes in the early evening, passing the item to the female at the nest entrance. But unexpectedly, just at the stage when the female began to leave the brood for short foraging expeditions of her own, the male of the pair disappeared, most likely lost to some predator. The female continued to care for the brood on her own, but initially with far less frequent feeding trips than her mate had provided, because she also continued to brood the nestlings intermittently.

Three days later, however, she was averaging a feeding trip to the nest every three minutes in the early evening, and in subsequent days this quickly increased to a feeding every two minutes. These rates greatly exceeded the provisioning rate of her mate before his disappearance, but despite the frequent feedings, one of the two young whose voices we could hear from the ground perished in the nest shortly thereafter of unknown causes. The female eventually fledged a single youngster successfully, despite the loss of her mate.

Fledging of the single surviving nestling began under peculiar circumstances at about 1:00 a.m. on July 19. The process appeared to be triggered, at least in part, by the invasion of the nest stub by a hairy black caterpillar roughly two inches long. This creature had first appeared about an hour and a half earlier, crawling up the bark surface around the nest hole and going inside for about a minute. The young Flammulated Owl was down at the bottom of the hole at

Range of the Flammulated Owl
- Breeding
- Breeding and wintering
- Wintering

that time and we saw no evidence that the two species had yet interacted. But shortly after midnight the caterpillar again entered the nest hole, this time for five minutes. The young owl rushed quickly to the entrance and back down at 12:14 a.m., and at 12:17 it reappeared at the entrance, vigorously shaking its head in apparent great discomfort, very likely suffering from contact with the hairs or chemical defenses of the caterpillar. The caterpillar then emerged, apparently unharmed, at 12:18 but continued to crawl about the vicinity for at least another hour. Shortly after another close brush of the owl with the caterpillar at the nest entrance at 12:55, the youngster reversed himself on the nest entrance, for the first time facing into the cavity, and soon began vigorously flapping his stubby, half-developed wings, clinging to the entrance with his talons. Within five minutes he had begun to climb up the outside of the nest stub to the very top of the stub, flapping his wings in a frenzy as he went. The caterpillar soon followed, whether by accident or design. The female adult, meanwhile, hovered over the chick's head, hooting continuously in excitement.

Finally, at 1:18 a.m., after several more bouts of vigorous flapping, the young owl took to the air in a very unproductive first flight that ended about six feet from the ground in an oak immediately adjacent to the nest stub. Here, the youngster was quickly fed by the adult female as the two called continuously to each other, but on trying to climb higher in the oak, the fledgling lost his grip on the branches, hung momentarily upside-down from one branch, and came fluttering to the ground. We quickly tried placing the youngster on the limbs of small nearby saplings, but he always fell immediately to the earth again, so we pulled back to watch developments from a distance without causing further interference.

Now the young owl began moving quite rapidly across the ground on foot. He was a comical and very unbirdlike sight, a round gray fuzzball on hairy legs as he scrambled up lichen-covered boulders and over dry leaves that made his progress clearly audible. Like a newborn fawn gaining strength by the minute, he seemed at first impossibly weak for the task of hiking across the rugged terrain, but he soon began using wing action to help him, at first in jumps of six inches, then eighteen inches, then six feet from one rock to the next.

In short spurts, not always in the same direction, the chick progressed about seventy-five to a hundred feet across boulders and stumps until he finally encountered an eight-inch-diameter oak tree sixty feet from the nest stub. Here, he began an ascent of the trunk in much the same flapping manner

Flammulated Owl

A large arctiid moth caterpillar, believed to be Hemihyalea edwardsii, invaded the nest site shortly before midnight of July 18–19, evidently stimulating the single chick to fledge prematurely.

After several contacts with the caterpillar, the owl began to exit the nest hole, first reversing himself to face inward with his body outside the cavity.

Still hanging from the entrance, the youngster engaged in several brief bouts of vigorous wing exercise, then began a climb to the top of the stub, flapping his half-grown wings continuously.

From the top of the nest stub, the youngster soon made his first clumsy flight—two feet forward and nine feet down—coming to rest in the lower branches of an adjacent oak, from which he fell to the ground almost immediately. On the ground, the youngster began a long half-flapping trudge across the forest floor, finally ending with his ascent of another oak trunk about sixty feet from the nest tree.

Throughout the travels of the youngster on his fledging night, the adult female remained in close attendance. In the oak he ascended sixty feet from the nest tree, the female fed him numerous times on a small branch fourteen or fifteen feet from the ground.

in which he had climbed the top of the nest stub earlier. He first came to rest on a broken-off branch base about fifteen feet from the ground, where the female fed him several times before he began climbing again, eventually coming to rest in a crotch just below the top of the tree about twenty five feet from the ground. This became his roost at daybreak, and here, on his first day free of the nest, he sat stoically, with eyes closed, through a midday monsoon rain and hailstorm that turned the landscape white for a short period. In the next evening, the adult female resumed feedings of the youngster in his treetop location, as he excitedly exercised his wings and moved from branch to branch.

Both on the night of fledging and subsequently, the female adult quite obviously tracked her youngster's movements by homing in on the begging rasps that he gave in response to her typical hoots. From the time he first started ascending his roost oak on the night of fledging until dawn of the next day, he received a total of fifteen feeding visits from the adult. The latter then finally went off to roost an hour before sunrise at some unknown location as the morning sky began to brighten.

Although the fledging of the youngster may have been slightly premature, thanks to invasion of the nest by a large caterpillar, young Flammulated Owls usually do leave the nest before achieving true competence in flight, a situation also typical of many other owl species. Their survival immediately after fledging depends on their abilities to climb back up into trees to safety when they fall to the ground, and they seem to have remarkably good climbing abilities, clinging tenaciously to tree trunks with their talons and powering themselves upward with their partly grown wings. All seemed to come out well for the young Flammulated Owl we watched on his night of fledging, despite the seemingly desperate nature of his struggles.

Cause of the death of the other chick in the nest remains a mystery. Starvation seems highly unlikely, as feeding rates at the nest were twice as great when this chick was still alive as the rates that immediately followed its death, and this suggests strongly that both chicks were being well fed. It's pure speculation, but the encounter with the caterpillar we watched on fledging night at least raises the possibility that an earlier encounter with a noxious or toxic arthropod, such as a scorpion, could have been involved. On several occasions before fledging, the surviving youngster gave what sounded like loud chitters of pain after accepting a prey item from the female, suggesting that he might have been bitten or stung by a still-living food item. Perhaps such encounters are occasionally fatal. The caterpillar species that invaded the nest on fledging night (a larva of a large arctiid moth) was not an individual brought to the nest by the female and was not a prey type we had ever seen the adults bring to the nest in three weeks of nightly observations, although we saw other individuals of this species in the vicinity. It may well be a species normally avoided by the owls because of its noxious properties.

Although it is a relatively little-known species that is easy to overlook, the Flammulated Owl does not appear to face severe conservation difficulties. Because of its frequent association with mature coniferous forests, it is considered sensitive to timbering practices, but the species does not appear to have any special demands for virgin forests and has survived in many regions that have been selectively logged. The Flammulated Owl is a creature of forested areas, but as long as enough forest persists to maintain good overall insect populations and the presence of cavity-creating birds such as Hairy Woodpeckers and Northern Flickers, the owl seems to do quite well. It apparently prefers relatively open forests and does less well in regions with dense dog-hair thickets of regenerating conifers, possibly because of reduced food availability in the latter sort of habitat.

Flammulated Owl

Burrowing, Boreal, Saw-whet, Hawk, Pygmy, and Elf Owls

Burrowing Owl

Athene cunicularia or
Speotyto cunicularia

AS ITS COMMON NAME SUGGESTS, the Burrowing Owl is renowned for its habit of nesting underground. The burrows it uses often originate as tunnels dug by tortoises or by various grassland mammals, such as prairie dogs, ground squirrels, and kangaroo rats. But in many cases, particularly in Florida, the owls construct the burrows themselves, loosening up soil with their bills and vigorously ejecting it from the tunnels with powerful kicks of their feet. Pairs in Florida have been known to create complete nesting burrows ten feet long in just two days.

Less well known is the fact that burrow construction also occurs occasionally in other species of owls. The Barn Owl sometimes creates horizontal tunnels in dirt banks for nesting, and similar nest sites were reported historically for Short-eared Owls in the Aleutian Islands. While owls are generally regarded as birds that do no nest building, there are some outstanding exceptions, and most owl species at least scrape out depressions in their nest substrates to hold their eggs.

Underground nesting in the Burrowing Owl can be viewed as an adaptation that has helped allow the species to occupy vast areas of favorable grassland feeding habitat, where typical owl nesting sites in old stick nests or cavities in trees and cliffs are very scarce. The species occurs in open areas throughout most of North and South America, and populations are also known for some islands in the West Indies.

Only two other North American Owls have adopted ground nesting as standard behavior, the Snowy Owl and the Short-eared Owl, and these likewise are owls of open grasslands or tundra. But the usual nests of both these other species are hollows or scrapes in the surface of the ground, not burrows. Both these species are much larger than the Burrowing Owl and are presumably better fitted to defending exposed ground nests from potential predators.

The underground nests of the Burrowing Owl provide considerable protection against weather stress, especially temperature extremes, as well as effective refuge against attacks by large raptors. Nevertheless, these burrows still remain vulnerable to attacks by certain terrestrial predators, such as badgers, weasels, and ferrets, and the species exhibits a number of adaptations that can be viewed as potential defenses against these predators. For example, Burrowing Owls frequently gather materials such as fragments of cow dung to line their nest tunnels and chambers. Such

Left: *With his head rotated directly backward, a Florida Burrowing Owl in 1968 guards the entrance of his nest tunnel. When constructing a burrow from scratch, these birds use their bills and feet to loosen the soil and then kick it out the entrance. They sometimes complete a ten-foot-long burrow in just a few days.*

materials may function to disguise the odor of active nests or repel some potential predators from the nests.

Another defense is a startling vocalization sounding like the rattle of an angry rattlesnake that nestling Burrowing Owls emit when their homesites are disturbed. Rattlesnakes do occupy burrows on occasion, and the owl's call is so realistic that it causes involuntary withdrawal responses in most humans and perhaps other species as well. It has also led to a persistent folklore that Burrowing Owls and rattlesnakes are bound together by some sort of unholy alliance.

Another adaptation is very conscientious nest guarding by males while their mates incubate eggs or brood young. Males often hunt right from the burrow entrance, and when they go elsewhere on foraging expeditions they are rarely gone for long. Males also are unusually large relative to their mates for an owl species, usually exceeding females in both wing and tail length.

Another apparent adaptation that very likely often prevents predators from trapping females in their burrows is the birds' ability to rapidly exit when they hear vocalizations of their mates. We once spent an evening in a subterranean blind constructed by Bill Courser for his graduate studies at the University of South Florida. With our faces just inches away from an incubating female owl, who was visible through a glass plate under infrared, we were impressed by how quiet the sound environment was underground and by how instantaneously the female disappeared up the burrow when she heard the calls of her mate outside. One moment she was placidly incubating, the next she had vanished to the burrow entrance, without any perceptible reaction time in between.

The potential vulnerability of burrow-nesting birds to entrapment by terrestrial mammals is well illustrated by the Bahama Parrots of Abaco

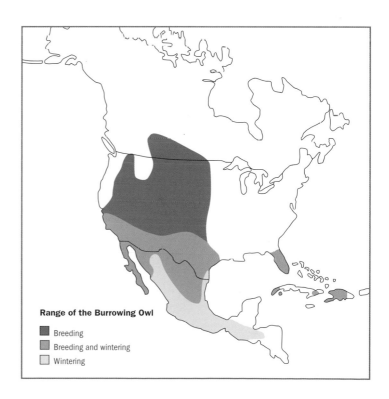

Range of the Burrowing Owl

■ Breeding
■ Breeding and wintering
□ Wintering

Fledgling Burrowing Owls retain an association with their nest burrows even after they can fly. This nest in northern Chihuahua, Mexico, occupied a central position in a large colony of black-tailed prairie dogs and may well have originated as a prairie-dog burrow.

Island. Like the Burrowing Owl, these parrots have adopted the unusual habit of nesting in underground chambers, although they are not capable of rapid running on the ground and have to climb laboriously in and out of their nest sites, which are vertical solution holes in limestone bedrock. Their nesting habits posed no risks from terrestrial predators before feral house cats became established on the island. Now, however, nesting parrots are lost with some frequency to cats that discover their nest sites, as Rosemarie Gnam of the City University of New York has carefully documented in her thorough studies of the species. Feral cats have also succeeded in killing Burrowing Owls on occasion.

The burrows of Burrowing Owls also are vulnerable to collapse during excessive rainfall or when large mammals trample the ground above. One nest we watched in 2004 suffered partial collapse just at the time of fledging of its three young, but the family quickly moved to another burrow about a hundred feet away, and both parents and young showed no difficulties in transferring their allegiance to this site. From nearby fence posts the adults closely guarded the youngsters and made occasional forays to capture nearby terrestrial insects and snakes, while the youngsters began inquisitive exploration of the surroundings near their new nest, mostly on foot, but sometimes taking to the air to

attempt their own landings on fence posts—sometimes on sites already occupied by their parents.

For many years the Burrowing Owl had the attractive scientific name *Speotyto cunicularia*, which literally means "mining cave owl," but the species is sufficiently closely related to Old World owls in the genus *Athene* (named after the Greek goddess of wisdom) that it is now more commonly regarded as *Athene cunicularia*. Certain other species in *Athene* are known to run about on the ground, but none are as consistently terrestrial as the Burrowing Owl, and although the Little Owl (*Athene noctua*) occasionally nests in low cavities in banks in arid regions, it is hardly a habitual underground nester. This would seem to provide some grounds for retaining the genus *Speotyto* for the Burrowing Owl, but whether the Burrowing Owl will ultimately come to rest in *Athene* or *Speotyto* remains to be seen. In direct genetic measurements made so far, the Burrowing Owl has been sufficiently distant from *Athene noctua* to justify its residence in a separate genus—a magnitude of separation comparable to the genetic distances found between other owl genera. Nevertheless, no hard-and-fast rules exist for determining when species belong in the same or different genera, and the sizes of generic realms are notoriously inconsistent in the classification of birds.

In the western states, the fortunes of the Burrowing Owl have been closely tied to the fortunes of the prairie dogs that once occurred in enormous underground colonies in short-grass prairies. Although Burrowing Owls in the West do use burrows created by other terrestrial mammals and have at least some capacity to create their own burrows, they have also shown a strong and positive association with prairie dogs. This association may be based both on the presence of ready-made burrows and on the enhanced detection of terrestrial and aerial predators made possible because the prairie dogs give loud alarm calls on the approach of such enemies. The owls clearly settle preferentially in active dog towns, as opposed to inactive towns, and their nesting success has often been considerably greater in central parts of active towns than in peripheral regions.

Unfortunately, in many regions of the western states, prairie dogs have been the target of massive extermination campaigns by ranchers who believe that the dogs compete for forage with livestock and that their burrows pose threats of leg injury to livestock. Rigorous data to back up such judgments have been few, however. Furthermore, livestock and native herbivores such as bison often show obvious preferences for grazing on prairie dog towns, which is likely a direct result of the greater nutritional content of the immature forage that results from the dogs' cropping activities. Indeed, the prairie dogs

The black-tailed prairie dog functions as a keystone species with enormous importance to many other vertebrates. Burrowing Owls in the western states show a strong affinity for prairie-dog colonies. They often nest in old dog burrows and tend to have enhanced nesting success in central portions of the colonies. Unfortunately, prairie dogs have been exterminated throughout most of the western states, and Burrowing Owls have suffered as a consequence.

An adult male Burrowing Owl in Arizona's Sulfur Springs Valley arrives at his nest mound with cattle-dung nesting material soon to be carried into the burrow in his bill. In addition to enlarging preexisting burrows and sometimes constructing complete burrows from scratch, Burrowing Owls generally line their nests with all sorts of rubble and trash.

Burrowing Owl

With eyes nearly closed, possibly in anticipation of potential contact with defensive secretions or sharp spines, a Burrowing Owl works on a scarab beetle captured near the nest. Most scarab beetles do not have noxious secretions, although many other beetles of similar appearance do.

help maintain these regions as grassland by their steady consumption of the forage surrounding their burrows.

Regardless of the overall impact of prairie dogs on cattle grazing, Burrowing Owls have declined severely where the dogs have been exterminated, and for this and other reasons the species is believed to be in progressive decline in most parts of its range. Gone are the days when locations such as the Sulfur Springs Valley in Arizona and the Animas Valley in New Mexico hosted colonies of prairie dogs that stretched for many dozens of miles and early residents reported difficulties sleeping because of the incessant calling of Burrowing Owls.

Fortunately, efforts to reverse long-standing traditions of antagonism to prairie dogs have had success in some areas, and black-tailed prairie dogs have been reintroduced in some regions where they were earlier exterminated. Interestingly, where these reintroductions efforts have been carried out, for example, on the Gray Ranch of southwestern New Mexico, Burrowing Owls have moved into the newly established prairie-dog colonies almost instantaneously.

Prairie-dog towns also represent an important habitat for other raptors besides Burrowing Owls, for example, Golden Eagles and Ferruginous Hawks, which prey on the dogs. The dogs are also a crucial food supply for the endangered black-footed ferret, which came within a hairsbreadth of extinction several decades ago. Conservation of prairie-dog towns represents a crucial component in conserving major prairie ecosystems, and where dog towns have been lost, they can be reconstructed. Prairies complete with bison, prairie dogs, black-footed ferrets, prairie chickens, and a host of other species represent the original highly productive ecosystems to be found on the Great Plains, and in most cases they represent a much more stable land use of the region than other alternatives.

Despite the overall population decline of the Burrowing Owl, the species has exhibited an ability to breed in some disturbed suburban habitats—in particular, vacant lots, golf courses, airports, and other similar locations. An apparent range expansion of the species in recent decades in Florida, for example, may be due largely to occupancy of such habitats. Unfortunately, many of these habitats are ephemeral, offering little in the way of long-term security for the birds. And although the species also commonly occupies pasturelands (often highly degraded pasturelands), these too are steadily being converted to other land uses in many regions. The housing developments and citrus orchards that have replaced many open habitats in Florida offer little appropriate habitat for the species in the long run, and the overall decline in the Burrowing Owl throughout its North American range is very likely due mainly to progressive loss of suitable habitat.

The Burrowing Owl is a fairly small species, weighing about a third of a pound, and it lacks the conspicuous ear tufts found in similar-sized screech owls. Its upperparts are largely brown in color with numerous white spots, while its underparts are largely buffy white with broad brown bars. On the ground, it can be quite comical in appearance, frequently bobbing its head down and up in apparent curiosity and often running rapidly from one place to another on its long legs. In the air, it commonly flies only short distances and progresses with an undulating flight reminiscent of many woodpeckers.

The Sulfur Springs male enters his burrow to feed a sun spider (solpugid) to his mate or young. Arthropods form the major part of the species' diet, although Burrowing Owls also occasionally take vertebrates such as small snakes.

Its vocalizations are diverse and include calls that are given in territorial advertisement, mating, and alarm.

Yet despite its terrestrial habits and preference for grasslands that are uncluttered with any widespread intrusions of shrubs, the Burrowing Owl does make extensive use of elevated perches, such as mounds, stumps, and fence posts—both for launching hunting forays and for general vigilance around nests. In a visit to southwestern Brazil in late 2002, we watched a population of Burrowing Owls make frequent use of the earthen termite mounds, often five or six feet tall, that dot the grassland landscape. In this region of Aplomado Falcons, White-tailed Hawks, giant anteaters, maned wolves, and Blue and Gold Macaws, we found greater densities of Burrowing Owls than we have seen anywhere in North America, with many pairs and nests often visible from single locations. The owls of this region were colored much more intensely than their North American counterparts, with ruddy plumage apparently derived from contact with the deep-red soils in which they were nesting. The termite mounds on which they often perched were also a deep maroon color, probably likewise derived from the soil colors.

The Brazilian termite mounds were also host to another dazzling natural spectacle. At the start of the rainy season in October and November when the termites form aerial mating swarms, their mounds often become homes for bioluminescent click-beetle larvae. At night the surfaces of the mounds glow with innumerable motionless points of light, transforming the mounds into ghostly earthen statues. Evidently, the click-beetle larvae are predators of the termites, but how their luminescence functions in their biology is not clear. Perhaps it acts as a lure for the termites, or perhaps more likely it is primarily a signal to other predators, such as Burrowing Owls, that the larvae themselves are distasteful or poisonous. Burrowing Owls are indeed mainly insectivorous, and if the larvae were not chemically noxious, the owls presumably could wipe them out in short order.

In the vicinity of their burrows, Burrowing Owls are usually quite conspicuous during the daylight hours, not because of conspicuous coloration (they are actually quite cryptic except for their white throats and bright yellow eyes), but because they tend to perch on conspicuous objects. But whether they are primarily nocturnal or diurnal in their foraging behavior has been the subject of some debate. It appears that the species is variable in this regard by locality and season, with a heavy emphasis on daytime foraging and diurnal prey such as grasshoppers in some regions and on nocturnal insects and foraging in other regions. Evidently, the species adapts to whatever period of the day or night offers the most favorable local foraging conditions during the season in question. With the disappearance of most insects in the wintertime, the Burrowing Owl in the western states is highly migratory and mostly spends the colder months in Mexico.

Burrowing Owl

Boreal Owl
Aegolius funereus

Range of the Boreal Owl
▢ Breeding and wintering

THE BOREAL OWL IS ONE OF the more mysterious owls of North America, although it is not uncommon in its native northern habitat and readily uses artificial nest boxes for breeding when they are provided. A relatively small species, it is roughly the size of an Eastern or Western Screech Owl, but the boreal averages slightly lower in weight and lacks the earlike feather tufts of these better-known species. In addition, the boreal differs markedly from the various screech owls in body proportions and facial pattern. Most notably, for its size it has an unusually large head, perhaps functioning to maximize the sound-gathering capacity of its facial disk in auditory detection of prey. Moreover, its head size and raised white eyebrows give the species a decidedly surprised appearance, quite unlike the much less conspicuous facial patterns of screech owls. Like the screech owls, however, the boreal is strongly nocturnal in its habits—much more nocturnal than the Great Gray Owls and Northern Hawk Owls that are also found in the same northerly regions—and this combined with the remoteness of its haunts largely explains why the species is so seldom seen.

Like the Great Gray Owl and Northern Hawk Owl, the Boreal Owl inhabits forests of spruce, fir, aspen, and birch in Canada and Alaska. All three species also occur in similar northerly habitats in Eurasia. But what was unknown until very recent decades is the fact that the Boreal Owl also occurs in high mountain forests far to the south of these regions. In North America the species can be found breeding in the Rocky Mountains as far south as northern New Mexico, and in Europe it breeds as far south as the Pyrenees separating France and Spain. It is very doubtful that these southerly locations represent recent expansions of the owl's breeding range and much more likely that the species was previously overlooked in these regions. Knowledge of the species' distinctive vocalizations has been the key to discovering new populations.

In North America the Boreal Owl was formerly known as Richardson's Owl, and in Eurasia it is still most commonly known as Tengmalm's Owl. Other names used at times for the species include Funereal Owl and Arctic Saw-whet Owl. This plethora of common names complicates matters for those interested in tracking down the historic literature on the species, but in fact the literature on the North American populations is not extensive because the species has been so little studied on this continent until very recently. Studies of the species have been much more abundant in the Old World.

Among the most informative North American studies have been those conducted in Colorado and elsewhere by Greg and Patricia Hayward of the University of Wyoming. Another of the informative ongoing studies is an investigation of breeding habits of the species in the Anchorage region of Alaska by Ted Swem of the U.S. Fish and Wildlife Service. In 2003 and 2004, we observed the nesting activities of several Boreal Owl families in Swem's study area, spending several nights watching the provisioning activities of adults and the fledging activities of youngsters in an extensive deciduous-coniferous forest. These were the first close observations we had ever made of the species' behavior, and we found the boreal to be another charismatic northern owl with a strong dependence on small mammals for food and almost no fear of humanity.

In 2003, our observations took place at the time of the summer solstice, and although the Anchorage region is far below the Arctic Circle, the skies never became fully dark in the vicinity of the nest observed. Because of this,

The coastal forests of spruce, birch, and aspen near Anchorage, Alaska, provide excellent habitat for Boreal Owls, Northern Saw-whet Owls, moose, and Bald Eagles. One pair of Boreal Owls under intensive study by Ted Swem in 2003 fledged three young from a nest box on this birch.

An adult in another forested tract near Anchorage in 2004 arrives with prey to nourish its brood. Well-developed facial disks and highly asymmetric ears permit Boreal Owls to locate prey by sound alone, and the owls under observation were active only in the darkest hours of the night.

we were able to see the activities of the adults reasonably well, despite the fact that their activities were almost completely compressed into the hours between midnight and 2:30 a.m. Despite the brevity of this active period, both adults made repeated trips to the nest with prey, evidently bringing in enough food to supply the daily requirements of their brood.

The nest site the pair used was a plywood box mounted about twenty-five feet from the ground on the main trunk of one of the largest birch trees in the forest. The three young in the nest were close to fledging, and one or more of them occupied the entrance almost continually in the darker hours, while they anxiously awaited the return of their parents with food.

One of the two adults normally vocalized on returning to the nest and foraged consistently to the east of the nest site. The other adult, who was generally silent, consistently arrived from the west. Both were apparently foraging at considerable distances from the nest, and after trips to the nest, both flew back toward their respective foraging areas at surprisingly fast speeds, maneuvering skillfully through the cluttered branches of the forest. On the night of the summer solstice, we observed nine trips to the nest by

the adults in just three hours: five by one bird, and four by the other. The prey we could see well enough to identify were all small rodents. Though we saw none of the prey captures, these prey were almost surely the victims of hunts from low perches, the typical foraging method used by the species.

On the same night, the first of the three young fledged from the nest at 12:30 a.m. in a modest flight of about two feet to a nearby branch. Once free of the nest, the youngster continued to scramble along the branch to the outer limits of the nest tree, and a quarter hour after its first flight, it took a much more ambitious flight to another tree, losing a bit of altitude in the process. After this point the bird was lost from view from our observation point for several hours, although we heard it continue to give begging calls nearby. It was still relatively close to the nest at sunrise, and during the full daylight that followed we saw it take several more flights from tree to tree that were surprisingly skillful and did not involve a loss of altitude.

Through the following night there were still two young Boreal Owls in the nest when rain persuaded us to end observations at about 2:30 in the morning. The first fledgling was still within a hundred feet of the nest at that

Boreal Owl

In preparation for flying the final leg to its nest, a Boreal Owl transfers prey from feet to bill, allowing an unencumbered landing at the nest entrance and efficient passing of food to the young.

In profile, the Boreal Owl appears conspicuously large-headed. The species' vocalizations sound much like the winnowing aerial sounds of snipe, and both of these bird species often occur in the same regions.

point, but when we returned at 10:00 p.m. the next evening, it had moved off a considerable distance and we found that a second young had fledged and was sitting on a branch against the trunk of a tree about ten feet from the nest. That night both fledged young worked progressively farther from the nest, and by daylight the next day, one was about a hundred and fifty yards from the nest while the other had managed to get about thirty yards from the nest. The third youngster was still in the nest. Like the first fledgling, the second flew moderately well from tree to tree and gave intermittent begging calls, which appeared to allow the adults to find it efficiently.

Quite unlike their parents in appearance, the youngsters at this stage looked like uniform chocolate-colored balls of fluff. At rest they characteristically perched on small branches right against the main trunks of trees. Both fledglings persistently worked their way east after leaving the nest, the direction from which the vocalizing parent arrived with food, but whether the youngsters headed this direction in anticipation of the arrival of food or due to some other factor was not clear.

The forest where the Boreal Owl families were based was also home for a variety of other northern residents. We repeatedly saw and heard Bald Eagles vocalizing and sailing past overhead and we often heard the characteristic winnowing sound of snipe in the sky—a sound that is very similar to the rapidly pulsed territorial call of the Boreal Owl. At one point, a Northern Goshawk came careening past one of the nests, and on another occasion a gray fox walked right by our observation point as we sat on the forest floor. During the darker hours there were also occasional startling calls from marmots who were occupying the edge of a nearby meadow. Moreover, on one night shortly after feedings were over

A fledgling in 2003 roosts against a spruce trunk about thirty yards from its nest after a night of scrambling and short flights through the forest canopy.

and owl activities had quieted down, the stillness of the scene was interrupted by the sounds of a huge creature thrashing through the forest not far away. We lacked any means of defense, so we awaited developments with some uneasiness. The animal continued to get steadily closer, and before long it emerged from the brush in the dim light. But instead of some giant carnivore, it was a cow moose, apparently as nervous about blundering into us as we had been about attracting its attention. All parties—owl fledglings, moose, and humans—inspected each other without making any desperate attempts to flee or attack, and the moose soon stumbled onward, leaving us to contemplate how rewarding it might be to get some solid sleep far from further wildlife encounters.

For the most part, Boreal Owls are year-round residents of their nesting territories, and regular migratory behavior appears to be absent in the species. In years when prey populations drop severely, however, the owls exhibit nomadism and sometimes settle in new regions to breed, with females tending to be considerably more nomadic than males. Boreal females normally lay clutches of three or four eggs in April or May. Young are usually in the nest in May and early June and fledge after about a month of development, usually by late June. Independence is usually achieved between three and six weeks after fledging, with both adults attending the young after fledging.

Interestingly, Greg and Patricia Hayward have documented a strong tendency for Boreal Owls not to use the same cavity nest site two years in succession, a tendency we have also seen in California Condors but apparently not a tendency for many other cavity nesters, including many owl species. One potential advantage of frequent changes of nest sites may be that the owls can reduce the risks of parasite buildups in nests over the years. Frequent changes in nest sites may also allow the owls more flexibility in tracking geographic changes in prey abundance than if the owls practiced more traditional use of nest sites.

Another interesting aspect of Boreal Owl behavior that has emerged from a number of telemetry studies is the strong tendency of the species to change

Boreal Owl

A Boreal Owl peers from its nest hole high in a cottonwood in Canada's Yukon Territory in 1968. When just its head is visible, a Boreal Owl is easy to confuse with a Hawk Owl, although Hawk Owls rarely occupy such natural cavities.

its daytime roost sites from one day to the next, commonly moving more than a kilometer between successive roosts and commonly roosting far from its nests. Except for females tending eggs or small young, the species characteristically roosts in sheltered sites in the branches of trees, rather than in natural cavities, and individuals may simply choose the nearest suitable site they happen to be adjacent to on termination of their last foraging flights for the night. In contrast, many other owl species have favored regular daytime roosting spots to which they return with some consistency, and under which substantial piles of regurgitated pellets and whitewash (excrement) accumulate. The absence of consistent roosting locations in the Boreal Owl adds to the difficulty of finding this species, and despite considerable searching we were unable to locate any daytime roosting locations for any of the birds nesting near Anchorage. Frequent changes of roosting locations may have no more significance than avoiding the energy costs of commuting back and forth to a regular roost, but they may also prevent the buildup of odor cues in specific sites that could increase the risks of predation to roosting birds.

With much of its habitat still remote and little modified, the Boreal Owl, like the Northern Hawk Owl, faces a relatively favorable future in North America, at least in the near term. The boreal's apparent preference for mature forests, however, poses some potential conflicts with the timber industry, especially if logging activities destroy a high percentage of suitable nest sites. Under natural conditions, the Boreal Owl most commonly uses old nests created originally by Northern Flickers and Pileated Woodpeckers, so the boreal is dependent on habitats remaining favorable for these species, as well.

Where timbering has been especially thorough in Scandinavia, however, the Boreal Owl has adapted well to nest boxes and in fact has become almost totally dependent on them. The same potential exists for heavily lumbered regions in North America. Nevertheless, conservation through nest boxes presupposes a perpetual obligation to provide and maintain boxes, and thus it is not as reliable or favorable a means of species preservation as maintaining large tracts of fully suitable habitat.

Northern
Saw-whet Owl

Aegolius acadicus

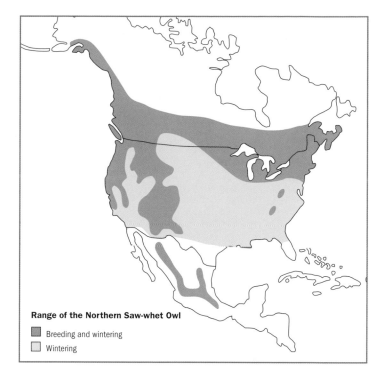

Range of the Northern Saw-whet Owl

■ Breeding and wintering

□ Wintering

A CONSPICUOUSLY LARGE-EYED species with a peculiar common name, the Northern Saw-whet Owl is a tiny raptor not much bigger than a Northern Pygmy Owl. It is distinctly smaller than its congener, the Boreal Owl, and generally occurs in more southerly regions than that species, although the ranges and habitat preferences of the two species overlap considerably. Its common name is generally assumed to be derived from the peculiar rasping vocalizations it sometimes gives that sound like someone sharpening a large metal saw with a file. These calls are not the only vocalizations in the species' repertoire, however, and more commonly, saw-whets are heard delivering a long series of repetitive hoots that apparently serve primarily as territorial advertisement calls. These hoots have much the

Fledgling Northern Saw-whet Owls are perhaps the most attractively colored young owls found in North America. These youngsters were roosting together about three feet from the ground at a mid-elevation of Mount Pinos, California, in July 1972. The nest they came from was probably nearby, but we failed to locate it.

An adult saw-whet roosting in upstate New York in the early spring of 1967 allowed close approach without exhibiting any signs of alarm. This species sometimes responds to whistled imitations of its calls by landing on the person doing the whistling.

quality of Northern Pygmy Owl hooting calls, although they are generally given in steady sequences, not as the paired or irregularly spaced hoots typical of that species. Saw-whets often respond to whistled imitations of their hooting calls, and they sometimes even attempt to land on the whistler in their apparent eagerness to challenge what they presumably perceive are other saw-whets intruding on their territories.

The saw-whet owl is a highly nocturnal species that is closely associated with forests, where it commonly hunts quite close to the ground. Like some other highly nocturnal forest owls, the saw-whet is much more common than is generally realized. The range of the species, including wintering areas, spans essentially all wooded regions of the United States and southern Canada, except for most of Florida and southern Texas. We have also encountered saw-whets in both the eastern and western Sierra Madre of Mexico.

In Mexico, saw-whets occupy the same high-elevation forests as the Thick-billed and Maroon-fronted Parrots and can sometimes be found nesting in close proximity to these species. For an extreme example, we were shown a single aspen snag in western Chihuahua during the summer of 2002 that was in simultaneous use by three pairs of Thick-billed Parrots, one pair of saw-whet owls, and a honeybee hive, each in different cavities—apparently all old Northern Flicker holes. A scene of almost constant avian and hymenopteran activity, this snag had been located by Javier Cruz-Nieto and Diana Venegas-Holguín, two of our long-term collaborators in Mexican parrot studies. Unfortunately, the snag later became the scene of considerable mammalian activity as well, and of the avian residents, only the saw-whets, which finished nesting by midsummer, were successful in fledging their young. All the parrot nests were still active with eggs or small young in August, but by early September, the ground in the vicinity of the snag was paved with piles of feathers of destroyed parrot nestlings, and none of the parrot nests was still active. All were apparently the victims of ringtailed cat predation. Notably, none of these nest sites was in use by parrots the following year, although Thick-billed Parrots commonly use the same nest holes year after year when nesting is successful.

As the history of this snag well illustrates, small cavity-nesting birds are hardly immune to the threat of predation, despite a general perception among naturalists that cavity nests are relatively safe nest sites. While cavity nests may enjoy considerable protection against predators that are too large to fit through the entrances and are incapable of enlarging the entrances sufficiently to allow entry (for example, various species of large raptorial birds), these nests are highly vulnerable to those predators that are small enough to easily pass through the entrances. The various small owl species that use old flicker holes as nest sites are at the mercy of various arboreal snakes and ringtailed cats in southerly regions and pine martens in more northerly regions. Not only are nestlings of many small owl species effectively doomed if these predators discover their nests, but also the female adults in attendance at the nests through the incubation and brooding periods are likewise at risk if they do not get out of their nests before such predators get to the cavity entrances.

The primary defense that an incubating or brooding female has against entrapment in her nest cavity is a finely tuned sensitivity to the sounds a predator makes in climbing the nest tree. Many small owls, including the saw-whet, are very quick to look out of their nest holes or exit their nest holes when one merely scratches the bark lightly at the base of their nest trees.

Unfortunately, many nest predators are highly persistent and difficult for hole-nesters to deter. We once watched a large indigo snake foraging in the canopy of a tree in eastern Tamaulipas, Mexico. It systematically crawled out each major limb of the tree poking its head into each and every cavity it encountered, until it had investigated the entire tree. All the while, a flock of noisy

Saw-whets near Anchorage, Alaska, use nesting habitat similar to that of Boreal Owls, and the two species often occupy adjacent territories.

Brown Jays excitedly mobbed the snake, but their actions had no perceptible influence on the snake's activities. On another occasion we watched a large gopher snake in northern Arizona swallowing nestling after nestling as it worked its way systematically from one Cliff Swallow nest to another in a colony situated on the underside of a rocky ledge. The excited vocalizing and milling about of the adult swallows provided no evident discouragement for the snake. At another site in Arizona, we came upon a gopher snake in the act of cleaning out an Elf Owl nest high in a sycamore. One adult owl was perched nearby, helpless to prevent the attack.

The importance of arboreal snakes as predators of nesting birds is not to be underestimated. They are a major force affecting the nesting success of many species and causing the evolution of a variety of defenses. Some species, for example various tropical orioles, caciques, and oropendulas, build their nests at the ends of long dangling branch tips that are difficult for snakes

Near its nest in the Anchorage region in 2004, a saw-whet pauses briefly on a birch limb before taking prey to its brood.

the advantages in safety from predators offered by roosting outside cavities.

In 2004 we had the opportunity to watch nesting activities of both Northern Saw-whet Owls and closely related Boreal Owls in the coastal forests of Alaska near Anchorage. Here, in a population under study by Ted Swem of the U.S. Fish and Wildlife Service, the two species were roughly synchronous in breeding, were feeding on similar prey, and were using very similar habitats, often quite close to one another. Their personalities, however, were rather different. The large Boreal Owls were relatively measured in their movements and frequently perched for a minute or two near their nests before entering them with prey. The saw-whets were much more active and mobile, rarely sitting for more than a few seconds in any one spot. The saw-whets also tended to be more vocal around the nest as they brought in prey, giving rising inflection calls grading into long series of hoots similar to their typical territorial calls but softer. And while the boreals also often gave rising inflection calls as they approached their nests, they only occasionally gave their typical rapidly pulsed territorial calls.

Fledgling saw-whet owls are perhaps the most attractive of all fledgling North American owls, with chocolate covering much of the upperparts, face, and chest, with a tawny belly, and with distinctive white eyebrow and whisker marks. Fledgling Boreal Owls are quite similar but lack the tawny belly. In both species, adults are much lighter colored than juveniles and are characterized by brown upperparts spotted with white, together with white underparts marked with rusty or brown streaking on the breast and belly. Weighing only

Vigilant against terrestrial predators such as ring-tailed cats and large squirrels, a female saw-whet in Arizona's Chiricahua Mountains rests at her nest entrance in an old Northern Flicker hole high in a Douglas-fir snag. Youngsters in this nest did not fledge until August 2005 and may have been a second brood of the year.

to reach. For cavity-nesting species, the options for defense are limited. Nevertheless, significant reductions in snake predation can be achieved by nesting preferentially in regions where snakes are uncommon or by nesting in sites that snakes have difficulty climbing, for example cavities in trees that are too smooth-barked for snakes to ascend. The heavy use of smooth-trunked gumbo limbo trees for nesting by many tropical birds may be primarily an adaptation to escape snake predation. Other bird species, such as the Thick-billed Parrots and Northern Saw-whet Owls of Mexico, apparently achieve considerable protection from snakes by nesting in high-elevation coniferous forests, where arboreal snakes capable of taking them are too rare to present major threats. In addition, saw-whet owls nesting in the primary breeding range of the species in the northern United States and southern Canada are far enough north to be largely free of predation threats by arboreal snakes.

The roost sites chosen by various bird species also vary in their vulnerability to predators. Perhaps largely because of the risks of entrapment, Northern Saw-whet Owls are not known to roost in cavity sites when they are not nesting. Instead, their roost sites tend to be relatively dense tangles of branches, often close to the main trunks of conifers, where it may be difficult for many large predators to reach them, but from which they can escape in a variety of directions if necessary. For both the Northern Saw-whet Owl and its close relative, the Boreal Owl, the potential advantages of roosting in cavities—namely, thermal conservation and shelter from snow and rain—appear to be overwhelmed by

about a sixth of a pound, the saw-whet is one of the smallest owls, and it is also usually one of the least wary, perhaps in part because it rarely encounters people in its preferred densely forested habitat.

The diet of the Northern Saw-whet Owl is heavily slanted toward deer mice, in keeping with the association of the owl with forested areas, although it also commonly takes other small mammals, such as shrews and voles, and it occasionally takes small birds, especially during migration seasons of the prey. Despite the very small size of the owl, insects are a relatively unimportant part of the diet—less than I percent of prey individuals in a great variety of studies. Like the Boreal Owl, the saw-whet appears to be a quite thorough specialist on vertebrate prey. Also like the boreal, the saw-whet relies heavily on hearing to locate prey, which is perhaps not surprising in view of the preference both these species have for relatively dark, forested habitats.

The Northern Saw-whet Owl, although not a conspicuous species, is not known to be in conservation trouble anywhere in its range. Progressive timbering of its forested habitats has undoubtedly reduced populations in some regions, especially through destruction of potential nest snags, but the overall status of the species appears to be robust. A recent conservative population estimate for the species suggests a total of perhaps one hundred thousand to three hundred thousand individuals.

A recently fledged Northern Hawk Owl near Fort Nelson, British Columbia, in 1968 vocalizes insistently to solicit food from its parents.

Another fledgling in the same brood, possibly the recipient of the last feeding, exhibits more passive behavior.

Gray Owl, which often shares the same habitat, the hawk owl rarely uses old stick nests of other birds.

Most Northern Hawk Owls lay eggs in April or May. Clutch size for the species varies from three to thirteen eggs, with an average of about six or seven eggs, apparently dependent in significant measure on prey availability. Young hatch after about four weeks' incubation. In another four weeks, they generally leave the nest, although they usually cannot maintain level flight at this age and still are considerably shy of adults in weight and wing length. After fledging, they remain dependent on their parents in the nesting territory for another month or two, during which they finish growth and feather development and develop hunting skills. As in almost all other owls, only one brood is possible in a breeding season.

In five summer trips in different years to northwestern Canada and Alaska, we encountered Northern Hawk Owls in only two years, despite covering hundreds of miles of appropriate habitat in each year. Our luck was best in 1968, when we found multiple individuals, including one nesting family, but these birds were widely scattered in the endless sweep of boreal forest in the region, and even in that year we were impressed by how scarce the species was overall. In other years our success has been much worse, despite examination

of the tops of innumerable roadside spruce trees for the characteristic shape of the species. The ratio of spruce trees to observable hawk owls must generally run hundreds of millions to one.

Our first encounter with the species was along the Alaska Highway near Fort Nelson in northern British Columbia. Here, in early June 1968, we found a family of recently fledged youngsters together with their parents in an open field with scattered skeletons of dead birches and other trees. The fledglings were not yet highly mobile and mostly just perched in the tops of snags, giving repeated begging screams and exhibiting no interest in hunting for themselves. The nest from which they had originated was surely close by and was very likely the top of one of the many broken-off snags in the area, but it was not obvious which snag was the source of the brood.

The adults, meanwhile, hunted from high perches in the vicinity, mostly staring intently at the ground and sometimes uttering soft and squeaky, high-frequency vocalizations that seemed like they might be aimed at attracting rodents to reveal themselves for capture. Luring prey, however, is not the only possible explanation for these sounds, and we saw no prey captures. Nevertheless, the adults seemed focused entirely on their hunting responsibilities and were apparently oblivious to our presence, even allowing us to walk right underneath them without this appearing to disrupt their

Left: *Perched atop a dead spruce along the Alaskan Highway of the Yukon Territory, a Northern Hawk Owl surveys its surroundings for potential prey.*

Northern Hawk Owl

concentration to any significant extent. Occasionally, they changed hunting perches by flying fast and low over the ground and suddenly swooping up to some new vantage point, where they immediately resumed intent scanning of the ground.

In hunting from perches, the hawk owls characteristically jerked their tails upward almost vertically at irregular intervals; then allowed their tails to descend at a slower pace. This tail-cocking habit is of unknown significance, but it makes the birds quite conspicuous from a distance and may function mainly in signaling other hawk owls of the presence and location of individuals. Tail cocking is most frequent right after a bird lands on a new perch, and it is repeated only occasionally thereafter. Similar tail-cocking behavior is known in pygmy owls under conditions of excitement, and it is one of the pieces of information suggesting a close evolutionary tie of the hawk owl to the pygmy owls. Nevertheless, similar tail cocking is also characteristic of another completely unrelated raptor, the White-tailed Kite, so it appears possible that independent evolution of the trait might also have occurred several times among owls and that hawk and pygmy owls are not necessarily closely related because they share the trait.

Later during 1968, we had two other sightings of hawk owls farther to the northwest, and these likewise were very approachable birds in fairly open boreal forest, perched in the tops of snags. A fourth apparent sighting of the species during the same summer—a bird peering out of an apparent nest cavity in a high cottonwood—turned out on careful examination to be not a Northern Hawk Owl, but a Boreal Owl. The head-coloration patterns of these two species are very similar, with dark edgings to their facial disks, a black patch under the bill, and yellow eyes, and it is relatively easy to confuse the two if only the head of the bird is in view. Nevertheless, the spotting and streaking of the upper-breast feathers of the bird were visible enough to clearly identify it as a Boreal Owl and not a hawk owl, which has barred upper-breast feathers.

Although the Northern Hawk Owl is a highly erratic and nomadic species with a sparse overall population, no good evidence suggests that it is threatened or endangered. In fact, its willingness to occupy cutover tracts of forest suggest it may even benefit from certain types of timbering operations. While it appears to be largely limited to boreal forests in its distribution, these forests comprise a substantial fraction of the land area of Canada and Alaska, and for the most part these habitats remain intact. The Northern Hawk Owl may always be a species that is exceedingly hard to find, but unless it proves susceptible to some unforeseen global catastrophe, its prospects for long-term survival seem reasonably favorable.

A perch-hunting hawk owl usually adopts a near-horizontal posture more typical of hawks or shrikes than of owls.

At irregular intervals, perch-hunting hawk owls cock their tails briefly to near vertical, making them conspicuous from a distance. The function of this behavior is unknown.

Northern Pygmy Owl
Glaucidium gnoma

DESPITE ITS TINY SIZE—not much larger than an Elf Owl—the Northern Pygmy Owl is a formidable predator of vertebrates, a fact that explains why small- and medium-sized birds frequently respond to the irregularly pulsed hooting calls of this owl with vigorous mobbing behavior. By imitating these calls, naturalists are often successful in arousing small birds in the bush to declare themselves and come in close for identification and observations.

Pygmy owls, to be sure, are also known to take many insects in their daily activities, but the dozen or so prey deliveries we have seen at nests included only mice, lizards, and small birds. It appears that the species is heavily reliant on such relatively large prey for breeding. Wintering pygmy owls are also renowned for their fondness for vertebrate prey and are quite commonly seen capturing small passerines around bird-feeding stations. Pygmy owls often kill prey that are nearly as heavy as they are, and in some cases they have been documented taking birds that are considerably heavier, for example, quail. A quail represents several times as much food as a pygmy owl normally eats in a day, and it presumably can suffice to keep an owl satiated for several days if fully consumed in a number of successive meals. Pound for pound, the Northern Pygmy Owl bows to no other raptor in its ferocity and willingness to capture challenging prey. Historical accounts frequently condemned the species as a "bloodthirsty killer" or "fiend."

The Northern Pygmy Owl does nearly all of its hunting during the early morning and evening hours near dawn and dusk, and correspondingly, prey deliveries we have seen at nests have been confined almost entirely to these periods. The species is a classic sit-and-wait predator that perches in strategic locations until a potential victim places itself in a vulnerable position, whereupon the owl goes for it in a rapid and direct approach with talons and bill. Vision, rather than sound, is apparently the main modality it uses in homing in on prey. The pygmy owl lacks the well-developed facial disks and asymmetric ears of sound-hunting raptors, and its flight is

A pair of Northern Pygmy Owls in 2002 nested in this cavity, probably an old Northern Flicker hole, in a living sycamore. Nearly thirty-five feet from the ground, the site was located at about 5,500 feet elevation in Arizona's Chiricahua Mountains.

The relatively large diameter of the cavity entrance left the nest vulnerable to entry by mammalian predators, and indeed a nocturnal predator later destroyed the nesting female and her brood.

Northern Pygmy Owl

much more noisy than that of the sound-hunting raptors, although its eyes are relatively large and presumably keen. The genus name of the species, *Glaucidium*, is derived from the Greek word for "gleaming," a reference to its piercing yellow eyes. Curiously, the species even has an extra set of dark "eyes" (eyelike markings) on the back of its neck, much like the neck eyespots found on the American Kestrel, and potentially serving a similar purpose of deterring predators approaching from the rear. Such neck eyespots are also found on other species of *Glaucidium* owls.

Like many other small owls, Northern Pygmy Owls frequently use abandoned woodpecker holes as nest sites. They are not known to adopt artificial nest boxes. Eggs are generally laid in April or May and the usual clutch size appears to be four or five eggs. Incubation has been reported at about twenty-eight days, and young remain in the nest about twenty-three days, but the length of the dependency period after fledging has not been comprehensively studied. Youngsters tend to hatch and fledge quite close together in time, suggesting that full incubation does not commence until late in the egg-laying period.

In June 2002, we watched the activities at a nest in southeastern Arizona, where Northern Pygmy Owls commonly choose holes in tall canyon-bottom trees. About forty feet from the ground in the main trunk of a living sycamore tree, this was a nest we found by hearing the birds vocalize in the vicinity and by searching for nearby tree cavities. When we imitated the hooting calls of the species, the head of the presumed female promptly appeared at the entrance of the most promising cavity we had found.

Like many raptors, the adult female at this nest performed all the incubation duties and brooding of small young while her mate foraged for food. The prey we saw the male deliver to the female were entirely tree lizards and mice. When he arrived in the nest area with food during incubation, he summoned his mate with characteristic repeated double hoots interspersed irregularly with single hoots. She answered immediately with a soft twittering call sounding much like an extremely weak Hairy Woodpecker, then exited the nest to receive the prey and returned a few minutes later.

When hatching of the young commenced on June 8, the same division of labor between adults continued, but now the female appeared more reluctant to leave the nest hole, and the male commonly flew to the entrance to pass prey to the female. Sadly, on June 11, when we arrived at our blind in the early morning, expecting to gain more prey data for the pair, the male was calling continuously. He repeatedly flew to the nest entrance with a tree lizard in his bill, but no female appeared from within to receive the prey, and we heard no twittering calls. He eventually just dumped the lizard in the nest hole from the entrance and returned to foraging, apparently concluding his mate was off somewhere else. But after seeing this same pattern repeat through the morning, we became steadily more worried that something had happened to both the female and her brood. Sure enough, on the ground under the nest hole we found one detached wing from the female and some scattered feathers, and the nest hole was empty of any chicks when we climbed to inspect it. Many more of the female's feathers were lodged in a crotch of the nest tree below the nest hole. Her career as a bloodthirsty predator had evidently been terminated overnight by an even more bloodthirsty predator.

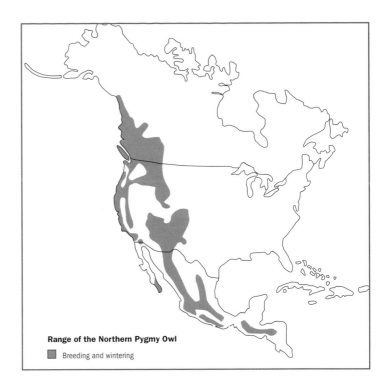

Range of the Northern Pygmy Owl

■ Breeding and wintering

Though we were unable to find any conclusive evidence of the identity of her killer, we strongly suspected from the nature and location of her remains that she might have been the victim of a ringtailed cat, a nocturnal species common in the area with a strong appetite for cavity-nesting birds. We had earlier run into repeated cases of predation by this species on nesting Thick-billed Parrots in a variety of locations. Moreover, the diameter of the entrance to the nest hole chosen by the owls was substantially larger than necessary and more than adequate to allow entry by a ringtail. The male owl may well have been elsewhere at the time of the predation event and failed to witness it. He continued to call in the

Above: *The probable predator of the female and nestlings was a ring-tailed cat. The relatively large entrances to old flicker holes do not exclude this slender predator, and on several occasions we have encountered cases of ring-tails preying on Thick-billed Parrots nesting in old flicker holes.*

Left: *The male pygmy owl provisioned the nest largely with mice and lizards such as this tree lizard.*

Northern Pygmy Owl

On the morning after his mate was killed on the nest, the male flew repeatedly to the nest entrance when the female did not respond to his food calls. Here, he simply dumped his prey items inside without entering the cavity.

vicinity of the nest through the rest of the day after the night of the female's destruction, but after that, we saw and heard no more of him.

At another pygmy owl nest in a sycamore snag the following year, we again watched a male that often caught lizards for food, although we made only brief observations of the activities of this pair. The snag chosen by the pair was also a home for a Flammulated Owl, and in fact the day we first examined the snag—May 9—the Flammulated Owl was occupying the hole ultimately used by the pygmy owls. But by the following night, the pygmy owls had taken over the site, and the Flammulated Owl had moved to another old woodpecker hole in the snag, eight feet above the hole it had lost.

The pygmy owls were initially quite aggressive to the Flammulated Owl, but both species continued to occupy the snag for at least another three weeks, after which the Flammulated Owl disappeared. It was never clear whether or not the Flammulated Owl had a mate and was initiating nesting, but the pygmy owls went on to conduct nesting activities in their hole. The snag was much too rotten and dangerous to climb to allow a direct inspection of the Flammulated Owl hole for clues about this bird's breeding status and why it disappeared. Neither were there any clues to be found on the ground below.

The Northern Pygmy Owl shows considerable geographic variation in the pulsing of its hooting calls, and this has led some researchers to suggest that the populations of different regions may represent a cluster of very similar species, rather than just a single species. Conclusive supporting data for splitting up the species have yet to be assembled, however, and strong geographic variations in vocalizations do occur within many bona fide bird species. For the present, at least, the ornithological world still recognizes just one Northern Pygmy Owl, although the matter is still under debate, and the trend in recent decades has been toward splitting many single species into multiple species.

Northern Pygmy Owls, like American Kestrels and Ferruginous Pygmy Owls, bear dark eyespots on the back of their heads that may function in deceiving onlookers as to the directions the birds are facing. Similar spots are also found to a lesser extent on Elf Owls.

The hooting calls of the Northern Pygmy Owl have a nebulous ventriloquial quality and are often maddeningly difficult to trace to the calling bird. In part, this difficulty arises from the fact that the bird often calls from the entrance of a tree cavity, and when it perches in the entrance and fills it up with its camouflaged body, the cavity seems to disappear. Until all tree trunks in the vicinity are closely examined with binoculars, the calls seem to be coming from everywhere and nowhere simultaneously.

In overall coloration, the Northern Pygmy Owl is basically brown with white spots and streaks and with a brown tail barred with white bands. Enhancing its camouflaged appearance, the species also has a concealment posture, in which body feathers are compressed and earlike tufts of feathers appear on its head. These "ears," however, are not composed of feathers longer than adjacent feathers, as is true of many other owls, but are simply clumps of feathers that are not compressed along with adjacent feathers.

Also unlike many other owl species, pygmy owls keep their eyes wide open when adopting a concealment posture.

Within North America, the range of the Northern Pygmy Owl, as the species is currently recognized, is limited largely to mountainous regions of the western states and provinces. Although not highly migratory, Northern Pygmy Owls are known to move to lower elevations during winter. The species can be found from extreme southeastern Alaska, British Columbia, and Alberta south through the Rocky Mountains, Cascades, and Sierra Nevada of the United States to the Sierra Madre of Mexico, and from thence, farther south to the mountains of Honduras and Guatemala. It is a relatively common resident of conifer and mixed conifer-deciduous forests, but it characteristically occurs in much lower densities than species such as Elf Owls and Whiskered Owls, probably reflecting its different feeding habits. Flocking and communal roosting are not known to occur in the species. In relatively southerly regions, the Northern Pygmy Owl tends to be replaced at low elevations by the Ferruginous Pygmy Owl and various other tropical pygmy owls.

Northern Pygmy Owl

Ferruginous Pygmy Owl
Glaucidium brasilianum

Range of the Ferruginous Pygmy Owl

■ Breeding and wintering

THE FERRUGINOUS PYGMY OWL, as its name suggests, tends to be much more rusty in overall coloration than the Northern Pygmy Owl. It is a lower-elevation counterpart to the Northern Pygmy Owl and has a much more southerly distribution in North America. The two species can also be easily distinguished by voice—rapid, steady hooting in the Ferruginous Pygmy Owl and slower, irregular hooting in the Northern Pygmy Owl. But otherwise, the two species are quite similar in size, diet, and various aspects of behavior. Both take many vertebrates as prey, hunt frequently during the daytime, and generally nest in old woodpecker holes at about the same time of year. Moreover, both exhibit dark eyespots on the back of the neck that may be important in deceiving onlookers about which way the owl is facing.

The U.S. range of the Ferruginous Pygmy Owl is limited to extreme southern Arizona and extreme southern Texas, although south of the border the species also occurs commonly in many lowland regions all the way down to Argentina. In South America, where the species was first described (in Brazil), it occurs in a great diversity of habitats, ranging from moist tropical lowlands to arid thorn scrub. In North America, its limited distribution suggests that it may be excluded from northerly regions primarily by competition with the Northern Pygmy Owl. As far as is known, the species is a year-round resident throughout its range and exhibits no migrations. In much of its range it is apparently the commonest species of owl.

Ferruginous Pygmy Owls vary in coloration. Most typically, they are heavily streaked underneath and possess conspicuous white eyebrows, as seen in this breeding female in 2004 in Tamaulipas, Mexico. A featherless brood patch on her breast allows maximal skin contact for warming of her eggs and nestlings.

Habitats occupied in the United States include low-elevation riparian woodlands and saguaro deserts in Arizona and mesquite-oak dominated woodlands in Texas. The species normally occurs from sea level to about 4,000 feet elevation, and thus it is often found together with Elf Owls, Western Screech Owls, and Great Horned Owls in Arizona, but it normally does not interact with Whiskered Owls, Flammulated Owls, Northern Saw-whet Owls, or Northern Pygmy Owls. In southern Texas it occurs with Eastern Screech Owls and Great Horned Owls. Like the Elf Owl, the Ferruginous Pygmy Owl is renowned for nesting in old woodpecker holes in saguaro cacti, where this plant occurs, but it readily uses natural cavities in other species of tree in regions where saguaros do not occur.

The diet of the Ferruginous Pygmy Owl is very similar to that of the Northern Pygmy Owl, with both species often taking relatively large prey, some up to the size of quail. Studies in both Texas and Arizona suggest a special fondness for reptiles among vertebrate prey, but a great diversity of sizes and types of prey are taken overall. With symmetrical ears and relatively noisy flight, the species is not adapted for locating prey by sound in total darkness, and it makes most captures in the dim light of evening and early morning, apparently using vision as its primary sensory modality.

The Ferruginous Pygmy Owls of Texas comprise the largest population in the United States and have been under intensive study by Glenn Proudfoot of Texas A&M University. His nesting observations indicate a normal clutch of two to five eggs and a fairly high nest success rate, with young fledging from about 76 percent of nesting attempts in nest boxes and 64 percent of attempts in natural cavities. Most nestling losses have apparently been due to predators such as raccoons and snakes, and it appears that the threats of nest predation may explain a preference of the species for nest holes with small entrances—ranging from only 1.7 to 2.3 inches in diameter. Renesting after failure has been common in the population, but birds produce only a single brood per breeding season, likely necessitated by a period of dependence of young on adults after fledging that usually lasts for about two months.

Our own experiences with Ferruginous Pygmy Owls have been limited to a ranch in coastal Tamaulipas, Mexico, about two hundred miles south of the Texas border. Here, in the early 1990s and again in 2004, we found the species in company with Blue-crowned Motmots, Bat Falcons, Aplomado Falcons, Collared Forest Falcons, Gray Hawks, Roadside Hawks, and Crested Caracaras, a decidedly tropical assemblage. The habitat on the ranch is a mixture of woodlands and rich pastures, and we found the owls in forest-edge woodlands, where they evidently were feeding heavily on small lizards.

As in other regions, the Ferruginous Pygmy Owls on the ranch in Tamaulipas were highly variable in coloration, with some individuals basically grayish brown in tone and others quite rufous overall. Some individuals had conspicuous white eyebrows, while the eyebrows of others were hardly distinguishable from surrounding rufous feathers. Underparts of various individuals ranged from white heavily streaked with rufous to largely rufous with scattered white patches. On breeding females we could often see a conspicuous brood patch lacking feathers in the central breast region.

A nest we watched closely in 2004 was attended by a highly aggressive pair. The nest was located about thirty feet up in a cavity of a large fig tree and was a scene of frequent interactions between the owls and other species, in part because the tree was loaded with fruit at the time and was drawing in a stream of fruit-eating birds and mammals. Most prominent among these were Altamira Orioles, Black-hooded Orioles, and Golden-fronted Woodpeckers, but other less frequent visitors included Brown Jays, Plain Chachalacas, Masked Tityras, Green Parakeets, coatis, and a jet-black species of squirrel. In addition, the tree had several large cavities that were under periodic investigation for nesting by Muscovy and Black-bellied Whistling Ducks. Whenever any of these visitors got too close to the owl nest, they were subject to harassing dives

Another nearby Ferruginous Pygmy Owl, photographed in 1991, exhibited a different streaking pattern underneath, and barely visible light eyebrows.

by the owls, although only one—a coati—appeared to have any suspicions that the owls might be defending something worth checking out. Fortunately, the positioning of the owl nest on the underside of a wide trunk prevented this well-known predator of nestling birds from gaining access, and it soon gave up in its efforts. Interestingly, the owl nest was in a cavity produced by branch breakage and subsequent heart rot, not in an old woodpecker nest, although in most studies the majority of Ferruginous Pygmy Owl nests, like those of the Northern Pygmy Owl, have been old woodpecker nests.

The resident owls were also highly aggressive in defending their nest tree against other Ferruginous Pygmy Owls. Another pair habitually vocalized from a clump of trees just to the west of the fig tree, and on one occasion during our stay, members of the two pairs met on a horizontal limb of a tree not far away in a battle that involved birds grabbing each other's bills and grappling with each other for a full half minute. The density of Ferruginous Pygmy Owls on the ranch was sufficiently high that pairs appeared to stimulate one another into frequent vocalizing, and we were often able to hear individuals from distances approaching a half mile.

At one time, the Ferruginous Pygmy Owl was also a common resident of west-central Arizona as far north as the Phoenix region, and south to the Mexican border. It has declined substantially in Arizona during the past century, however, disappearing from essentially all regions except suburban Tucson and a few other southerly areas. The species has also declined in Texas, although it still remains locally common in some areas. In 1997, the U.S. Fish and Wildlife Service designated the Arizona population as endangered.

Nevertheless, the precise causes of decline of the species have not been rigorously established. The fact that the remnant Ferruginous Pygmy Owls of Arizona are found partly in suburban areas that are not pristine raises questions about whether it is habitat modification that has produced the decline. Recent studies suggest the species is relatively tolerant of many forms of human disturbance. Unfortunately, the bird was never studied intensively during the major portion of its decline, and in the absence of a comprehensive database, it is difficult to reconstruct crucial demographic events of the past.

In the absence of comprehensive information on causes of decline, the U.S. Fish and Wildlife Service has had little choice but to protect remaining habitats where the species still occurs. Unfortunately, the efforts to protect suburban riparian habitats of the Ferruginous Pygmy

Ferruginous Pygmy Owl

Above: *A male Ferruginous Pygmy Owl, at his nest entrance in a fig tree, displays the alternating dark and rusty tail bars characteristic of this species. In the Northern Pygmy Owl, tail bars are white and black, and the white bars are much narrower than the rusty bars of the Ferruginous Pygmy Owl.*

Left: *From the entrance and near the entrance, the owls aggressively guarded their nest from various other species. The nest site's location on the underside of a slanting fig trunk protected it both from the rain and from certain potential predators, including a coati that unsuccessfully attempted to gain access from the topside of the trunk.*

Owl in the Tucson region have not surprisingly led to strong resentment in some quarters against the Endangered Species Act itself. This owl does not appear to be endangered as a whole species, so some conservationists have questioned whether efforts to conserve the species in Arizona should take precedence over efforts to aid other species that are clearly endangered throughout their ranges. Issues such as these have made the Ferruginous Pygmy Owl, like the Spotted Owl, a crucial test species of the operational viability of the U.S. Endangered Species Act. One can only hope that current intensive research on the species may lead rapidly to a clear understanding of the factors currently limiting the abundance of the species in Arizona, so that conservation efforts can be focused on the true limiting factors of importance today, whether they be habitat related or otherwise and whether or not they be the same factors that caused the historic decline.

Right: *At the time of nesting, the nest tree was fruiting heavily and attracted a procession of fruit-eating birds and mammals, as well as Muscovy Ducks and Black-bellied Whistling Ducks seeking cavity nest sites.*

Ferruginous Pygmy Owl

Elf Owl

Micrathene whitneyi

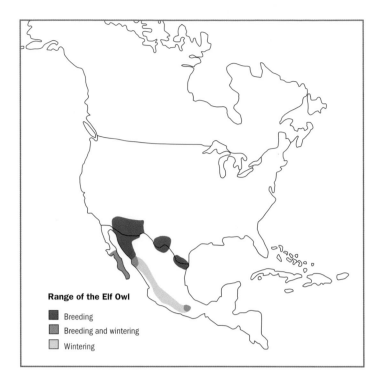

Range of the Elf Owl

- ■ Breeding
- ■ Breeding and wintering
- ■ Wintering

The world's smallest raptor, the Elf Owl averages less than one-and-a-half ounces in weight and is no bigger than a large sparrow. A denizen of the warm southwestern borderlands, the species is a renowned inhabitant of the giant saguaro cactus forests of Arizona's Sonoran Desert. But in fact, Elf Owls are also abundant in habitats completely lacking saguaros—especially sycamore-lined montane canyon bottoms at low to medium elevations. Indeed, the partial association of the species with saguaro cacti is easy to overemphasize and may be fairly recent in Arizona. The giant saguaro did not arrive in the owl's current desert habitat until about eight thousand years ago.

The North American breeding range of the Elf Owl stretches from the Colorado River in the west to southern Texas in the east, and in optimal canyon-bottom habitats the species reaches densities as high as sixteen pairs per linear mile. Thus, although often overlooked because of its nocturnal habits, this species is one of the commoner southwestern birds, and it is surely the most common owl to be found within most portions of its range.

A mighty mite of a hunter, the Elf Owl has tiny toes ending in curved, needle-sharp claws that can exert a surprisingly powerful grip. It rarely misses in attempts to capture food. Almost entirely insectivorous, it is nonetheless a scrappy and pugnacious protector of its interests and will vigorously harass potential nest predators far larger than itself, sometimes even including humans.

Like other small owls, the Elf Owl is a hole nester, but unlike many other owls, it almost never uses cavities formed naturally by death and decay of tree limbs. Instead, it relies mainly on holes originally excavated by woodpeckers. In the giant cacti of the Sonoran Desert, Gila Woodpeckers and Gilded Flickers create most of these holes. In montane riparian forests, the Elf Owl prefers cavities made by Acorn, Arizona, and Hairy Woodpeckers. Occasionally, Elf Owls will also use holes that Ladder-backed Woodpeckers carve in agave stalks and fence posts.

Nests are commonly used repeatedly over the years and several have become famous among birders visiting the Southwest. These include cavities in utility poles at the Rio Grande Village campground in Big Bend National Park in Texas and at the Santa Rita Lodge in Madera Canyon near Tucson, Arizona. Lights and people do not appear to faze Elf Owls, and indeed they will carry out their nesting activities under full artificial illumination.

The population of Elf Owls in the United States is migratory. Through the winter season, the riparian forests of the borderlands are mostly quiet at night except for the rustlings of rodents, the trills of screech owls, and the occasional hoots of a Great Horned Owl. But suddenly on a warm night in mid-March, the woods erupt with the tootling and cackling calls of not one, but dozens of Elf Owls signaling their presence in the dark. This chorus of multiple calling birds lasts only a few nights, but its synchrony suggests an unseen wave of migrants traveling together. Indeed, transient flocks of Elf Owls have occasionally been observed resting by day along migration routes.

Within a week of spring arrival, the density of calling birds decreases as residents disperse and settle into territories where they remain for the rest of the breeding season. Low-elevation habitats are occupied sooner than higher sites, and the onset of egg laying is likewise staggered by elevation, a reflection of earlier seasonal abundance of arthropods at lower and warmer elevations.

Elf Owls are most vocal on moonlit nights, especially when setting up territories. Their calls are quite different from the sounds of other owls and have sometimes been described as puppylike barks or elfin shrieks and laughter. Males give a multi-note chatter song to advertise their presence at nest cavities. The quality of this song varies from soothing to manic—its intensity possibly keyed to the reactions of potential mates or competitors. Once pairs are formed, partners keep in contact with each other around nests with soft descending *peew* calls.

The birds also have an alarm call—a sharp *yip* given singly or in a series and often in response to disturbance. Sometimes they give *yips* to sounds such as a slamming screen door or a barking dog, or to the menacing silhouette of a larger owl. Both males and females give *yips*, and the owls are always alert to intruders in the early breeding season, responding no matter whether the intruder is another Elf Owl, a potential mammalian predator, or a human playing a tape or giving a whistled imitation of the owl. They react especially strongly to other owls in their territories, both with alarm calls and mobbing behavior.

For more than a decade Elf Owls have nested in our backyard in rural southeastern Arizona. In 2003 and 2004 they used a wooden nest box that we had mounted fifteen feet up on the limb of a sycamore and had fitted with a removable back. Once the chicks were large enough to no longer need brooding, we replaced the back with a glass plate during nighttime observation periods so that we could watch feedings inside the box from an outside blind erected atop scaffolding. The adults and youngsters exhibited no problems in accepting temporary insertion of the glass plate in the nest box, and it became possible to study directly how the parents distributed food among their nestlings and how the nestlings interacted with one another. With the success of these observations, we modified the nest box even further in 2005, fitting it with a tiny infrared spy cam and microphone and leaving the wooden back permanently in place. With this arrangement, we were able to watch an entire breeding cycle inside the box via a cable

Right: *After wintering in Mexico, Arizona's Elf Owls return to their breeding grounds in early spring—many weeks before egg laying. This habit allows them to secure optimal nest holes before many of the other cavity-nesting birds arrive in the region.*

Adults typically hunt from low perches, from which they make short flights to grab insects and other arthropods on the ground and low vegetation.

television hookup to our living room, tracking and recording activities day and night from a camera viewpoint inside the box that looked down at the nest bottom from above the box entrance.

By March 11, the video camera had been trained on an empty expanse of sawdust nest bottom for several days, when suddenly in the predawn hours a male Elf Owl landed in the bottom of the box. Apparently unaccompanied by a mate, he nervously inspected the premises, then retired to roost elsewhere during the day. After this initial visit, he was invisible and silent for almost a week as a cold spell gripped Arizona, but suddenly one warm night as he sat near the entrance giving his chatter call, we heard a second owl's faint voice and the male became instantly frantic as he backed into the cavity and called till a female joined him inside in a crashing flurry of wings and beaks. From detailed markings on the faces of the two birds, they appeared to be the same pair that had occupied the site in previous years.

For the next month, the female roosted sporadically in the cavity during the day, racing up to the entrance whenever an intruder poked an inquiring head inside. Day roosting in a hole prior to egg laying affords the owls the crucial opportunity to defend the site against prospecting nest competitors such as woodpeckers, wrens, flycatchers, and House Sparrows. Thus, the presence of the female quite clearly prevented occupancy of the nest box by a singing male Bewick's Wren that arrived carrying grass and sticks in his bill, but soon gave up. At other cavities originally excavated by Acorn Woodpeckers, we have seen the owls evict the original cavity owners in prolonged battles, forcing the woodpeckers to excavate additional cavities to conduct their own nesting activities. Elf Owls are one of the earliest migrants to return to their nesting areas, even though they do not normally lay eggs for another six to eight weeks. The long delay between early-spring arrival and late-spring egg laying may reflect the importance of being able to

In usual hunting forays, the owl swoops past and grabs prey in its feet without landing.

claim optimal nest sites before other cavity-nesting species commence their breeding seasons.

Throughout the nesting cycle, the male Elf Owl generally remained near his nest box by day, but finding his roosts was difficult. Those we found were only about a yard off the ground in thick tangles of vegetation. We once witnessed a vigorous battle between the male and a much larger Curve-billed Thrasher that discovered him in his day roost. After a half-dozen noisy clashes, the Elf Owl fled the roost tree and dove into even denser brush to escape further attack, but he was back in his roost tree by nightfall. Although Elf Owls pose no real threat of predation to other birds, they often trigger mobbing by passerines, who probably do not differentiate them from other owl species, especially Northern Pygmy Owls and Western Screech Owls, which are indeed significant bird predators.

Activity at the nest generally began about twenty minutes after sunset, while it was still light enough for the human eye to see colors. Prior to egg laying, one owl entered the nest and called back and forth to its nearby mate before both birds moved away from the nest tree for a period of feeding, often close to the ground. After feeding, they returned to the nest area and the male entered the nest hole, his voice fading and becoming muffled as he descended inside the entrance. When the female also entered, he exploded out of the hole to perch nearby and call. The notes of the chatter song flowed steadily, soft and bubbling, at a rate of about four notes per second as the pair conducted nest site inspections.

As egg laying approached, the female remained within the nest box most of the day and night, making only brief excursions abroad. From inside the nest she gave a soft *peew* call about every two or three seconds all night long, while the male hunted at a leisurely pace, bringing her an insect every ten minutes or so. We recorded three of her four egg layings on videotape, and each took place at midday. Prior to each, the female exhibited an increasing respiration rate and bouts of panting, and the egg was laid after a series of popping vocalizations that synchronized with her body movements. Each egg was laid from a standing position and hit the substrate with an audible sound. The interval between eggs was in each case about three days.

Like the females of some other small owl species, the female Elf Owl did not begin full incubation with the laying of her first egg but did start to warm the clutch inconsistently before it was complete. Steady and consistent incubation began only with the laying of her fourth and final egg. As a result, the eggs did not all hatch simultaneously, nor did they hatch at the three-day intervals at which they were laid. The first three hatched at about one-day intervals and the last egg hatched two-and-a-half days after the third egg. The incubation period of the last egg was twenty-four days, but the duration of incubation was hard to calculate for the first three eggs because incubation was only partial for these eggs at the start.

Elf Owl

During early nestling stages, adults often remove the stingers before taking scorpion prey to the nest.

In late nestling stages, adults often bring in scorpions with their stingers intact.

Once the chicks had hatched and began rapid growth, the pace of feedings quickly rose to about one prey delivery every minute or two in the early evening, but this rate varied greatly over the course of a night, typically subsiding to one prey delivery every three minutes, then one every five minutes as the youngsters reached satiation. By 11:00 p.m., the adults often just sat resting on their hunting perches for an hour or more while their progeny, packed with food, digested the many prey they had received.

The last chick to hatch, however, was at a major disadvantage in getting food. The adult birds made no special efforts to feed it, and because it was nearly three days behind the third chick in growth, it was much smaller in size than all its siblings and could not reach high enough to compete effectively for the meals available. In all nestings we watched closely, the last-hatched chick remained much smaller in size than its siblings throughout the nestling period. Sometimes it got enough food to survive and fledge, but sometimes it did not. If it made it to the stage when its siblings fledged, it then enjoyed a period of relative food abundance as the only bird left in the nest, and rapidly gained weight to fledge successfully—but it did not always survive to this stage.

Once the chicks were old enough to no longer need brooding, both the male and female adults hunted for prey. Feeding visits of the adults to the nest were brief and rapid. Holding food in its bill, an adult descended the hole headfirst, with its wings jammed against the nest walls and its talons either gripping the walls or sometimes closed in a ball to avoid injuring the chicks as it stood on top of them. The insect prize vanished instantly down the opening throat of whichever youngster first got to the adult, and it appeared clear that food transfers proceeded more by touch than by vision.

With wings partly extended against the nest walls, an adult descends headfirst inside its nest hole, carrying a spider prey.

Several hours into the evening, chicks have mostly fed to repletion, and adults have difficulty finding takers for food items. Both adult and larval moths make frequent fare.

The adults were already carrying insects when they first showed up from their day roosts in the early evening. They seemed to hunt for the first hour in well-lit areas over open ground at the edge of a nearby dry wash and gravel driveway. After full darkness, an hour after sunset, they moved to hunt near artificial lights, where they took moths, June bugs, and other insects attracted to the lights. They often perched within a few yards of our brightly lit house windows and called loudly enough to be heard indoors above conversation and music, even audible at times to friends on the other end of the phone line in a distant state.

But more commonly they took advantage of an electric light we installed under their nest site. Here, they hunted from perches two to five feet above the ground, choosing bare horizontal twigs about three-eighths of an inch in diameter in locations where a dense wall of mesquite or blackbrush was at their backs and extended a bit overhead. Several favorite perches were used repeatedly, including ones we provided deliberately, and the ground beneath became littered with discarded moth wings after a night of heavy use. The owls were easily observed from just outside the immediate circle

of light, and they hunted without hesitation among whatever observers had assembled, sometimes snatching crickets just inches from our feet. Watching the Snyders' owl feeder became a popular pastime in our local community.

The adults appeared to hunt mainly, if not completely, by sight. We ourselves could often see a cricket walking along the ground that was not visible to an owl, and the owl never made a hunting strike until the cricket emerged into a visible position. Crickets were grabbed in a swoop without landing on the prey, while moths, walking sticks, and katydids were snatched from leaves and the undersides of limbs, sometimes in a near-vertical strike from below. Some insects were taken in flight. Most were taken from within four yards of where the owl sat, usually closer. Large insects such as crickets, June bugs, katydids, and grasshoppers were apparently favored over the many small moths and other small insects in view that batted about the light or crawled on the ground below. Every large sphingid (hawk moth) that appeared was chased.

When an insect was captured, the owl returned to a perch to process it before taking the food to the nest. When the nestlings were still small, the

Elf Owl

Elf Owls prey almost exclusively on arthropods, but at nests we sometimes saw the adults provision their chicks with wormlike blind snakes.

level of the nest box. Their flying capacities at this stage were clearly superior to those seen in fledglings of many other owl species, which characteristically leave the nest long before they have fully developed wings.

Once all young had fledged they became almost undetectable. Most begging calls stopped, although in one instance a fledgling did reveal itself by begging calls just at dusk. It was perched in a dense shrub a hundred and fifty feet from the nest tree, and as we approached it, both adults gave alarm calls and moved to the front of the bush to confront us. Taking the hint, we backed off and left the birds to their business. After each year's brood fledged, we tried by day and night to relocate fledglings, but we rarely succeeded. The parent birds, in contrast, seemed to have no difficulty tracking their youngsters' movements.

Elf Owl reproduction is timed so that chicks fledge in early summer, when large prey insects are becoming abundant with the arrival of summer rains. The fledglings perfect their hunting skills unseen and unheard. Once they are capable of hunting on their own, they have no need to advertise their presence, and neither they, nor their parents, are responsive to taped or whistled calls. They seem to simply melt away into the concealing darkness.

By early fall, the rains taper off, the nights cool down, and the Elf Owls slip away unnoticed on fall migration to their wintering grounds in Mexico, a transition quite unlike their very noisy and public arrival in spring. The nest sycamore behind our house soon sheds its leaves and once or twice each winter bears a light dusting of snow. Yet soon enough, and long before the tree again leafs out, we know the Elf Owls will return, as focused as ever on turning moth meat into a new generation of one of the most fascinating birds of prey found anywhere.

As the smallest raptor of North America, the Elf Owl is by no means the least successful, and it seems to be thriving in most portions of its range. Only the population along the Colorado River in eastern California has been known to be having major difficulties—evidently because of massive habitat change. Populations across other regions of the desert Southwest appear to be vigorous. A few threats loom: recent invasions of exotic weed species in the Sonoran Desert fuel unnaturally hot wildfires that may ultimately change the distribution of saguaro cacti; and Elf Owls sometimes do not seem to persist well in urbanized areas, even when native trees and nest sites are carefully preserved. It may be that this tiny and confiding bird is relatively vulnerable to house cats or collisions with automobile traffic, perching near the ground and hunting as it does around house lights. Its other favored habitat—sycamore riparian canyon bottoms—is mostly under national forest ownership and is seemingly well conserved for the future. Here, the species appears as abundant now as it ever was.

As a highly migratory species focused on nocturnal invertebrate prey and making hundreds of feeding trips to its nest each night, the Elf Owl holds little in common, other than hole-nesting, with the majestic California Condor, the largest of North America's birds of prey and the first species discussed in this book. Nevertheless, these two species and the other fifty-one raptor species of North America are all miracles in their own right and are fully worthy of our continuing concerns. One can only hope that all raptors of the continent, with their diverse lifestyles and adaptations, may survive the many stresses that the future may hold and that their native habitats can endure despite the enormous environmental changes that are taking place. The prehistoric cave painters of the world had their symbolic priorities right. Raptors are among the most magnificent of all living organisms. A world without them would be profoundly sad and diminished.

adults stripped prey of spiny legs, stiff wings, and potentially dangerous mouthparts and stingers before taking the prey to the nest. But later on, these parts were not removed. Thus, scorpions had their stingers removed at first but were later fed whole to the chicks.

Insects were often visibly still alive as they were passed to chicks, the gangling legs of a katydid sometimes slowly waving good-bye on the way down the throat of a youngster. The adults often ate large moths themselves, swallowing them tail first with the head still attached. The moths' points of bright orange eye-shine still glowed like coals as they disappeared from view. We did not see the owls catch vertebrate prey, but we did watch them bring two small blind snakes to the nest, and we found the remains of an earless lizard in the nest.

As the time of fledging approached in late June, the young began to appear at the entrance of the nest, anticipating the arrival of adults with food. From there, their rasping food cries carried for long distances, and indeed, nests are especially easy to locate at this stage by these vocalizations. In 2004, fledging of the entire brood occurred over a period of more than a week, and the first fledging we witnessed looked almost accidental. The chicks had been changing places at the entrance every few minutes with much struggling and complaining. The oldest chick was leaning out of the entrance, evidently looking for a returning parent, when another chick shoved so hard from behind that the one in the entrance toppled forward, splayed its wings briefly over the face of the nest, and then flopped too far over, losing its balance and parachuting away to land about fifty feet from the nest tree. Both adults immediately swung in behind the fledgling like jets giving a fighter escort to a cargo plane. For weeks the adults had been very quiet, but now both began a chorus of alarm *yips* and chatter songs, creating a racket we had not heard since the nest-investigation stage in early April. The young still in the nest box reacted to the chorus by scuttling back down into the cavity and going silent. Meanwhile, the fledgling young gave only a few begging rasps before likewise falling silent for the rest of our observation time—another three hours. Perhaps the adults' chorus was a mechanism to silence the fledgling to keep it hidden from other nocturnal predators.

Other fledgings were clearly by choice. In two cases observed well, the chicks launched from the entrance with no preliminary indications that they were about to fly, and they landed in the nest tree a few feet away at about the

Suggested Further Readings

In the first edition of this book, we presented a moderately extensive bibliography of suggested further readings on various species. Since that time much more comprehensive and complete bibliographies have been assembled for the various raptor accounts to be found in the Birds of North America series edited by Alan Poole and Frank Gill. We highly recommend these accounts to the reader as an initial entry point into the vast literature on North America's birds of prey. In addition to the Birds of North America accounts, however, we wish to call the reader's attention to a number of general accounts of raptors that have special importance and significance. These references are as follows:

A fledgling Burrowing Owl exhibits long legs well adapted for running and digging but almost completely lacking the dense feathering found on the legs of most owls.

Amadon, D., J. Bull, J. T. Marshall, and B. F. King. 1988. Hawks and owls of the world, a distributional and taxonomic list. Proceedings of the Western Foundation of Vertebrate Zoology, vol. 3, no. 4: 295–357.

Beebe, F. L. 1974. *Field studies of the falconiformes of British Columbia*. British Columbia Provincial Museum Occasional Papers, No. 17.

Bendire, C. E. 1892. *Life histories of North American birds*. U.S. National Museum Special Bulletin I.

Bent, A. C. 1937–1938. *Life histories of North American birds of prey*, parts 1 and 2. U.S. National Museum Bulletins 167 and 170.

Broun, M. 1949. *Hawks aloft: The story of Hawk Mountain*. New York: Dodd, Mead Company.

Brown, L., and D. Amadon. 1968. *Eagles, hawks, and falcons of the world*. New York: McGraw–Hill.

Burton, J. A., ed. 1973. *Owls of the world: Their evolution, structure, and ecology*. New York: Dutton.

Cade, T. J. 1982. *The falcons of the world*. Ithaca, NY: Cornell University Press.

Chancellor, R. D., ed. 1977. *World conference on birds of prey*, Vienna, 1–3 October 1975, report of proceedings. International Council for Bird Preservation (ICBP).

Clark, R. J., D. G. Smith, and L. H. Kelso. 1978. *Working bibliography of owls of the world*. Washington, DC: National Wildlife Federation.

Clark, W. S., and B. K. Wheeler. 1987. *A field guide to hawks. North America*. Boston: Houghton Mifflin.

Craighead, J. J., and F. C. Craighead, Jr. 1956. *Hawks, owls, and wildlife*. Harrisburg, PA: Stackpole.

Cramp, S., and K. E. L. Simmons, eds. 1980. *Hawks to bustards. The birds of the western Palearctic*, vol. 2. New York: Oxford University Press.

Duncan, J. R. 2003. *Owls of the world: Their lives, behavior and survival*. Buffalo, NY: Firefly Books.

Duncan, J. R., D. H. Johnson, and T. H. Nicholls. 1997. *Biology and conservation of owls of the Northern Hemisphere*. Second international symposium, North Central Forest Experiment Station, St. Paul, MN. USDA Forest Service General Technical Report NC–190.

Dunne, P., D. Sibley, and C. Sutton. 1987. *Hawks in flight*. Boston: Houghton Mifflin.

Garcelon, D. K., and G. W. Roemer, eds. 1988. *Proceedings of the international symposium on raptor reintroduction, 1985*. Institute for Wildlife Studies, Arcata, CA.

Glinski, R. L., ed. 1998. *The raptors of Arizona*. Tucson: University of Arizona Press.

Hamerstrom, F. N., Jr., B. E. Harrell, and R. R. Olendorff, eds. 1974. *Management of raptors*. Raptor Research Report No. 2. Proceedings from the conference on raptor conservation techniques, Fort Collins, CO, 22–24 March, 1973.

Johnsgard, P. A. 1990. *Hawks, eagles, and falcons of North America*. Washington, DC: Smithsonian Institution Press.

Johnsgard, P. A. 2002. *Owls, biology and natural history*, second edition. Washington, DC: Smithsonian Institution Press.

König, D., F. Weick, and J. H. Becking. 1999. *Owls: A guide to the owls of the world*. New Haven, CT: Yale University Press.

Ladd, W. N., and P. E. Schempf, eds. 1982. *A symposium and workshop on raptor management and biology in Alaska and western Canada*. Anchorage, AK: US Fish & Wildlife Service.

Meyburg, R. U., and R. D. Chancellor, eds. 1989. *Raptors in the modern world*. Proceedings of the third world conference on birds of prey and owls, Eilat, Israel, 22–27 March 1987.

Millsap, B. 1981. *Distributional status of falconiforms in west-central Arizona: With notes on ecology, reproductive success, and management*. U.S.D.I. Bureau of Land Management Technical Note 355.

Murphy, J. R., C. M. White, and B. E. Harrell, eds. 1975. *Population studies of raptors*. Raptor Research Report No. 3. Proceedings from the conference on raptor conservation techniques, Fort Collins, CO, 22–24 March, 1973.

National Wildlife Federation. 1988. *Proceedings of the southwest raptor management symposium and workshop*. Scientific and Technical Series No. 11.

———. 1989. *Proceedings of the western raptor management symposium and workshop*. Scientific and Technical Series No. 12.

———. 1989. *Proceedings of the northeast raptor management symposium and workshop*. Scientific and Technical Series No. 13.

Nero, R. W., R. J. Clark, R. J. Knapton, and R. H. Hamre. 1987. *Biology and conservation of northern forest owls: Symposium proceedings*. Rocky Mountain Forest and Range Experiment Station, Fort Collins, CO. U.S.D.A. Forest Service General Technical Report RM–142.

Newton, I. 1979. *Population ecology of raptors*. Berkhamsted, England: Poyser.

Newton, I., ed. 1990. *Birds of prey*. New York: Facts on File.

Newton, I., and R. D. Chancellor, eds. 1985. *Conservation studies on raptors*. ICBP Technical Publication No. 5. Washington, DC: Smithsonian Books.

Olendorff, R. R. 1971. *Falconiform reproduction: A review*. Part 1. The pre–nestling period. Raptor Research Report No. 1.

Olendorff, R. R. 1973. *The ecology of nesting birds of prey of northeastern Colorado*. Technical Report No. 211, Grassland Biome, U.S. International Biological Program.

Olendorff, R., and S. Olendorff. 1968–1970. *An extensive bibliography of falconry, eagles, hawks, falcons*, parts 1–3. Published privately.

Palmer, R. S., ed. 1988. *Diurnal raptors*, parts 1–2. Handbook of North American birds, vols. 4–5, New Haven, CT: Yale University Press.

Senner, S. E., C. M. White, and J. R. Parrish. 1986. *Raptor conservation in the next 50 years*. Raptor Research Report No. 5. Proceedings of a conference held at Hawk Mountain Sanctuary, Kempton, PA, 14 October, 1984.

Voous, K. H. 1988. *Owls of the northern hemisphere*. Cambridge, MA: MIT Press.

Walker, L. W. 1974. *The book of owls*. New York: Knopf.

Wheeler, B. K., and W. S. Clark. 1995. *A photographic guide to North American raptors*. London: Academic Press.

Wilbur, S. R., and J. A. Jackson, eds. 1983. *Vulture biology and management*. Berkeley: University of California Press.

Yaffee, S. L. 1994. *The wisdom of the Spotted Owl: Policy lessons for a new century*. Washington, DC: Island Press.

Index

Accipiters, 87–103
Accipiter cooperii, See Cooper's Hawk
Accipiter gentilis, See Northern Goshawk
Accipiter striatus, See Sharp-shinned Hawk
Accipitridae, 17, 18, see also Buteos, Eagles,
    and Kites
Aegolius acadicus, See Northern
    Saw-whet Owl
Aegolius funereus, See Boreal Owl
American Kestrel, 158, 202–205, 295, 301, 303
    Appearance, 205
    Eggs, 202
    Fledgling, 203, 204
    Habitat, 202
    Hunting, 204
    Neck spots, 205
    Nest, 202, 203
    Population, 205
    Prey, 202, 204
    Range and map, 203, 205
    Young, 202, 204
Anatum peregrine, 185, 186
Apache Goshawk, 27, 90, 93
Aplomado Falcon, 12, 193–197
    Appearance, 193
    Breeding, 196
    Diet, 194
    Habitat, 193, 194, 197
    Hunting, 194, 196, 197
    Nest, 193, 194, 196, 197
    Pesticides, 196, 197
    Population, 193, 197
    Prey, 197
    Range and map, 193
Aquila chrysaetos, See Golden Eagle
Arboreal snakes, 293
Archbold Biological Station, 125
Arctic fox, 228, 229
Arctic Saw-whet Owl, *See* Boreal Owl
Ashy-faced Owl, 215
Asio flammeus, See Short-eared Owl
Asio otus, See Long-eared Owl
Asturina nitida, See Gray Hawk
Athene cunicularia, See Burrowing Owl
Athene noctua, See Little Owl
Audubon, John James, 40, 184
Backstanding, 157
Bald Eagle, 152, 172–179, 185
    Alaskan, 175
    Appearance, 173, 176, 178
    Breeding, 173, 175
    Conservation, 178
    Diet, 177
    Eggs, 175, 177
    Fledgling, 177
    Hunting, 173, 177
    Nest, 173, 175, 177–179
    Pesticides, 179
    Population, 179
    Prey, 177, 178
    Range and map, 173
    Vocalization, 177
Band-rumped Petrel, 251
Barn Owl, 158, 215–219, 241, 253, 257,
    268, 281
    Appearance, 215
    Diet, 218
    Ear asymmetry, 215–217
    Eggs, 215
    Habitat, 215
    Hunting, 215–217
    Nest, 215, 216, 218
    Nestling, 215
    Population, 219

Prey, 217, 218
    Puerto Rican, 218, 219
    Range and map, 215
Barred Owl, 27, 223, 233, 235–242, 245, 267
    and Red-shouldered Hawk, 239
    Appearance, 241
    Asymmetric ears, 236
    Diet, 236, 237
    Eggs, 239, 241
    Fledgling, 239
    Habitat, 236, 239, 241
    Nest, 239
    Population, 239
    Prey, 237
    Range and map, 237, 241
    Vocalizations, 236
Bat Falcon, 228
Bay-winged (Harris's) Hawk, 116, 155–159, 201
    Appearance, 157
    Backstanding, 157
    Breeding, 157–159
    Diet, 157, 158
    Fledgling, 155, 157, 159
    Group hunting, 157, 158
    Habitat, 155, 157, 159
    Hunting, 155, 157
    Nest, 155, 157–159
    Polyandry and polygyny, 157
    Population, 159
    Prey, 155, 157, 158
    Range map, 155
    Size dimorphism, 158
Bear Lake peregrine, 185
Beissinger, Steve, 58, 59, 61
Bendire, Ben, 148, 149
Black-shouldered Kite, 54
Black Vulture, 45–49
    Aegypius monachus, 45
    and Turkey Vultures, 47, 48
    Appearance, 45, 48, 49
    Eggs, 47
    Fledgling, 47, 48
    Flight, 48, 49
    Foraging/scavenging, 45, 47–49
    Habitat, 47, 48
    Nest, 45, 47
    Predators, 47
    Range and map, 45, 49
    Urohidrosis, 49
    Vocalizations, 48
Blind snakes, 261, 314
Boreal Owl, 217, 286–291, 294
    Appearance, 286, 287
    Breeding, 286
    Conservation, 290
    Eggs, 289
    Fledgling, 287–289
    Habitat, 286, 290
    Migration, 289
    Nest, 286, 287
    Other names, 286
    Population, 289
    Prey, 288
    Range and map, 286
    Vocalizations, 288
Broad-winged Hawk, 43, 105–108, 114, 127
    Aerial displays, 106
    Appearance, 105
    Breeding, 107
    Diet, 105
    Eggs, 107
    Fledgling, 107
    Habitat, 105, 106
    Hunting, 106

Migration, 105–107
    Nest, 105, 107
    Pesticides, 107
    Population, 107, 108
    Puerto Rican, 108
    Range map, 105
    Vocalization, 105
Broley, Charles, 178, 179
Bubo virginianus, See Great Horned Owl
Burrowing, 281, 282
Burrowing Owl, 281–285
    and prairie dogs, 283, 284
    Appearance, 284, 285
    Breeding, 284
    Conservation, 284
    Fledgling, 282
    Foraging, 285
    Habitat, 281, 284, 285
    Hunting, 281, 285
    Population, 284
    Range and map, 281, 284
    Urban, 284
    Vocalizations, 281, 285
Buteos, 105–159
Buteo ablonotatus, See Zone-tailed Hawk
Buteo Albicaudatus, See White-tailed Hawk
Buteogallus anthracinus, See Common
    Black Hawk
Buteo brachyurus, See Short-tailed Hawk
Buteo Harlani, See Red-tailed Hawk
Buteo jamaicensis, See, Red-tailed Hawk
Buteo lagopus, See Rough-legged Hawk
Buteo lineatus, See Red-shouldered Hawk
Buteo platypterus, See Broad-winged Hawk
Buteo regalis, See Ferruginous Hawk
Buteo swainsoni, See Swainson's Hawk
California Condor, 21, 29–39, 163, 167, 173,
    177, 178, 188, 228, 245, 289
    Appearance, 29
    Breeding, 29, 35, 37–39
    Conservation, 29, 31, 33, 37, 38
    Diet, 37
    Egg, 33, 35, 38
    Fledgling, 35, 38, 39
    Flight, 33, 39
    Flight-feather pattern, 33, 35
    Habitat, 29
    Hunting, 37
    Nest, 29, 30, 33, 38
    Pesticides, 31, 37
    Population, 29, 31, 33, 35, 37–39
    Range map, 29
Camouflage, 263, 265
Caracara cheriway, See Crested Caracara
    Elf Owl, 205
Carrion, 169
Cathartes aura, See Turkey Vulture
Cave Creek Canyon, 192, 268, 272
Chandler, Rod, 25, 58, 60, 211
Chihuahua Desert Research Institute, 194
Chiricahua Mountains, 27, 124, 268, 272,
    274, 277, 299
Chondrohierax uncinatus,
    See Hook-billed Kite
Circus cyaneus, See Northern Harrier
Classifications, 15–19
Color phases, 139
Common Black Hawk, 23, 119, 121, 150–154
    and Turkey Vulture, 150
    and Zone-tailed Hawk, 150, 152
    Appearance, 150
    Breeding, 150
    Conservation, 154
    Diet, 150, 152, 154

Eggs, 152
Fledgling, 152
Habitat, 150
Hunting, 150
Migration, 150, 152
Nest, 152
Population, 150, 152, 154
Prey, 152
Range and map, 150
Vocalizations, 150, 152
Common Raven, 45, 188
Conservation, 11, 12
Cooper's Hawk, 90, 92–98, 116, 149, 158,
194, 196, 201, 204, 205
Appearance, 96, 97
Breeding, 96, 97
Cannibalism, 97
Diet, 96
Eggs, 97, 98
Fledgling, 98
Gundlach's Hawk, 97
Human predation, 98
Hunting, 97
Migration, 97
Nest, 94
Pesticides, 94, 96
Population, 94, 96
Prey, 94, 96, 97
Range map, 94
Corcovado National Park, 150, 154
Corkscrew Swamp Sanctuary, 124, 236
Corygyps atratu, See Black Vulture
Cottonwood, 119–121
Crab Hawk, See Common Black Hawk
Crested Caracara, 24, 25, 143, 158, 177,
206–211
Appearance, 206, 207
Breeding, 208
Conservation, 211
Diet, 206
Egg collectors, 211
Foraging, 208
Groups, 208
Nest, 206, 208, 211
Population, 211
Range and map, 206, 211
Vocalization, 206, 211
Young, 211
Dawson, Jim, 157 159
Duck Hawk, See Peregrine Falcon
Eagles, 161–179
Ear asymmetry, 215–217, 236
Eastern Screech Owl, 217, 259–262, 267
Appearance, 261
Breeding, 261
Conservation, 262
Diet, 262
Eggs, 261
Fledgling, 261
Maxwelliae, 260, 262
Nest, 262
Range and map, 259, 261
Urban, 262
Vocalizations, 259, 261
Eastern Wood Pewee, 105
Egg collectors, 211
Elanoides fortificatus,
See Swallow-tailed Kite
Elanus caeruleus, See Black-shouldered Kite
Elanus leucurus, See White-tailed Kite
Elf Owl, 15, 213, 268, 274, 308–314
Appearance, 308
Breeding, 308
Eggs, 308, 311
Habitat, 308, 314
Hunting, 310, 312, 313
Migration, 308, 314
Nest, 308, 310–312
Population, 308
Prey, 312–314
Range and map, 308, 314
Vocalizations, 308, 311

Young, 312–314
Endangered Species Act, 31, 242, 247, 307
Eurasian Griffon Vultures, 170
European Sparrowhawk, 116, 201
Everglade Kite, 55–61, 158, 159, 161, 205, 211, 257
Appearance, 55
Breeding, 59
Conservation, 57
Desertion of mates, 59, 60
Diet, 57, 61
Florida apple snails, 57–61
Foraging, 57, 59
Hunting, 59
Nest, 57–60
Population, 57, 59, 61
Prey, 60, 61
Range map, 55
Everglades National Park, 55, 57–61, 74, 113,
124, 126, 128, 161
Eye color, 241
Faconidae, 18, 19, see also Falcons
Falco columbarius, See Merlin
Falco Femoralis, See Alpomado Falcon
Falco mexicanus, See Prairie Falcon
Falco peregrinus, See Peregrine Falcon
Falco rusticolus, See Gyrfalcon
Falco sparverius, See American Kestrel
Falcons, 181–205
Families, 17–19
Ferruginous Hawk, 139–142, 284
and Humans, 142
Appearance, 139
Diet, 139
Eggs, 140
Habitat, 139
Hunting, 140, 141
Migration, 140
Nest, 139–141
Prey, 140–142
Range and map, 139, 142
Young, 140
Ferruginous Pygmy Owl, 205, 247, 303–307
Appearance, 304, 305, 307
Conservation, 307
Diet, 304, 305
Eggs, 305
Habitat, 305
Hunting, 304, 305
Neck eyespots, 304
Nest, 305, 307
Population, 305, 307
Prey, 304, 305
Range and map, 304
Vocalizations, 304
Fisheating Creek, 124, 206, 210, 237, 239
Flammulated Owl, 241, 273–279, 303
Appearance, 273
Breeding, 273
Breeding, 274, 277
Conservation, 279
Diet, 273
Eggs, 274
Fledgling, 276–279
Habitat, 273, 277
Hunting, 277
Migration, 273
Nest, 277
Population, 279
Prey, 274
Range map, 277
Vocalizations, 273
Fledging, 263, 267
Florida apple snail (Pomacea paludosa),
57–61
Florida Sandhill Crane, 211
Funereal Owl, See Boreal Owl
Glaucidium brasilianum, See Ferruginous
Pygmy Owl
Glaucidium gnoma, See Northern Pygmy Owl
Glinski, Rich, 23, 71, 120, 147, 150
Golden Eagle, 167–172, 177, 178, 188, 189,
192, 284

and Carrion, 169
Appearance, 167
Fledgling, 167, 171
Habitat, 171
Hunting of, 170
Hunting, 167
Migration, 172
Nest, 169, 170–172
Population, 170, 172
Prey, 167, 169
Range map, 167
Gray Hawk, 114, 118–121, 154
and Cottonwoods, 119–121
Appearance, 118, 121
Breeding, 121
Diet, 120
Eggs, 120
Fledgling, 120
Habitat, 119–121
Hunting, 120, 121
Migration, 120
Nest, 119–121
Population, 118, 119
Prey, 120
Range map, 118
Vocalizations, 121
Great Gray Owl, 217, 230–235, 241
and humans, 230, 231
Appearance, 230, 233, 235
Diet, 233
Eggs, 233
Flight, 233
Habitat, 230, 235
Hunting, 230, 231, 233
Nest, 231, 233
Prey, 230, 231, 233
Range and map, 230, 235
Vocalizations, 235
Great Horned Owl, 187, 217, 230, 214,
221–224, 255, 261, 268
Aggressiveness, 221
Appearance, 222
Breeding, 222, 223
Conservation, 224
Diet, 221
Eggs, 223
Fledgling, 224
Habitat, 222
Hunting, 221, 223, 224
Nest, 222–224
Pallescens, 222
Population, 224
Prey, 221–223
Range and map, 221, 222
Subarcticus, 222
Vocalizations, 223
Wounded decoy, 222, 223
Greater Yellow-headed Vulture, 147
Great-footed Hawk, See Peregrine Falcon
Gurney's Buzzard, 143
Gymnogyps californianus, See
California Condor
Gyrfalcon, 132, 134, 138, 181–183, 198,
200, 225
Appearance, 181, 183
Fledgling, 181–183
Hunting, 183
Nest, 181–183
Population, 183
Prey, 182
Range and map, 181, 183
Haliaeetus leucocephalus, See Bald Eagle
Harris's Hawk, See Bay-winged Hawk
Hawk Mountain, Pennsylvania, 21, 94, 96,
106–108, 138, 172
Hawk Owls, 223, 290
Hayward, Greg and Patricia, 286, 289
Hook-billed Kite, 62–67, 205
Appearance, 62–65, 67
Conservation, 67
Diet, 64, 67
Fledgling, 65

Habitat, 65
Mollusks, 62, 63
Nest, 63, 64
Population, 65, 67
Prey, 62, 65
Range and map, 62, 63
Vocalizations, 62, 64
Huachuca Mountains, 13, 213, 242, 246
Ictinia mississippiensis, See Mississippi Kite
Ivory-billed Woodpecker, 125, 126
Keddy-Hector, Dean, 194, 196, 197
King Vulture, 211
Kissimmee Prairire Sanctuary, 211
Kites, 51–79
Koford, Carl, 29, 31, 38
Laguna Atascosa National Wildlife
    Refuge, 143
Lake Okeechobee, 55, 59–61, 79, 124,
    206, 208
Lapland Longspur, 226, 229
Lemmings, 227, 253
Leptotyphlops dulcis, See Blind snakes
Little Owl, 282
Long-eared Owl, 217, 241, 254–258, 268
    and Great Horned Owl, 255
    Appearance, 254, 255
    Diet, 255, 257
    Flight, 254
    Foraging, 254
    Habitat, 254, 256
    Hunting, 254
    Migration, 257, 258
    Nest, 254–256, 258
    Population, 258
    Prey, 255, 256
    Range and map, 254, 255
    Vocalizations, 257
    Wing claps, 257
    Young, 256–258
Long-tailed Jaeger, 229
Loquillo Mountains, 105, 108, 110, 111
Mader, Bill, 157–159
Merlin, 15, 116, 198–201, 205
    Appearance, 198
    Breeding, 198, 201
    Diet, 198
    Eggs, 198
    Fledgling, 198, 201
    Flight, 198
    Habitat, 201
    Hunting, 198
    Nest, 198, 200
    Pesticides, 198, 201
    Population, 201
    Prey, 198, 201
    Range and map, 198
    Urban habitat, 201
Mexican Goshawk, See Gray Hawk
Micrathene whitneyi, See Elf Owl
Mississippi Kite, 68–73, 127, 274
    Appearance, 68
    Breeding, 70, 71
    Diet, 68
    Eggs, 70, 71
    Flight, 68, 73
    Foraging, 70
    Habitat, 68
    Hunting, 68
    Migration, 71
    Nest, 70
    Population, 73
    Prey, 68
    Range and map, 68, 71, 73
    Vocalizations, 70
Monkey-faced Owl, See Barn Owl
Montezuma Quail, 87, 89
National Audubon Society, 25, 33, 37
National Forest Management Act, 242
Neck eyespots, 205, 301, 303, 304
Nicholson, Donald J., 57, 161
Northern Flicker, 261, 272
Northern Goshawk, 87–93, 221–233, 247

and Montezuma Quail, 87, 89
    Appearance, 87
    Breeding, 89
    Diet, 90
    Eggs, 87, 90
    Fledgling, 89, 92
    Flying, 87
    Greenery collection, 92
    Habitat, 87, 93
    Hunting, 87, 89, 93
    Nest, 87, 90, 92
    Population, 93
    Prey, 87
    Range map, 87
    Vocalization, 89
Northern Harrier, 81–85, 205, 248
    And Tree Swallows, 81, 82, 84
    Appearance, 81
    Breeding, 84
    Conservation, 85
    Defense, 85
    Facial disk, 81
    Habitat, 85
    Hunting, 81, 82, 84
    Nesting, 81, 82
    Polygamy, 84
    Range map, 81
    Roosting, 84
    Sky-dancing, 84
    Vocalizations, 85
    Wintering, 81
Northern Hawk Owl, 295–298
    Appearance, 298
    Eggs, 297
    Facial disks, 295
    Fledgling, 297
    Habitat, 295, 297
    Hunting, 295, 297, 298
    Population, 298
    Prey, 295
    Range and map, 295
    Size dimorphism, 295
    Tail-cocking, 298
    Vocalization, 297
Northern Pygmy Owl, 11, 217, 268, 299–305
    Appearance, 299, 301, 303
    Breeding, 299
    Eggs, 301
    Fledgling, 301
    Hunting, 299
    Neck eyespots, 301, 303
    Nest, 299, 301, 303
    Predator, 301
    Prey, 301
    Range and map, 301, 303
    Vocalizations, 299, 303
Northern Saw-whet Owl, 268, 291–298
    Appearance, 294
    Defense, 293, 294
    Diet, 294
    Fledgling, 294
    Habitat, 291
    Nest, 293
    Population, 294
    Predators, 293
    Range and map, 291, 293
    Vocalizations, 291–293
Nyctea scandiaca, See Snowy Owl
Ogden, John, 33, 161
Osprey, 53, 127, 161–165, 173, 175, 177,
    178, 224
    Appearance, 161, 163, 164
    Breeding, 163
    Diet, 161
    Eggs, 163, 164
    Fledgling, 163
    Flight, 163
    Habitat, 161
    Hunting, 163–165
    Migration, 161, 163, 164
    Nest, 161, 163–165
    Pesticides, 164

Population, 164, 165
    Prey, 161
    Range map, 161
    Vocalization, 163, 165
Otus asio, See Eastern Screech Owl
Otus flammeolus, See Flammulated Owl
Otus trichopsis, See Whiskered Screech Owl
Owls, 21, 215–314
Pandion haliaetus, See Osprey
Pandionidae, 18, see also Osprey
Parabuteo unicinctus, See Bay-winged Hawk
Patagonia Sonita Creek Reserve, 121
Patuxent Wildlife Research Center, 117
Payne, Roger, 215, 217
Pearly-eyed Thrasher, 218
Peregrine Falcon, 116, 127, 132, 134, 146,
    181, 183–187, 197
    Anatum peregrine, 185–187
    Appearance, 184, 185, 187
    Breed, 186
    Duck Hawk, 185
    Eggs, 185, 186
    Great-footed Hawk, 184
    Habitat, 185, 186
    Hunting, 184–186
    Nest, 185, 186
    Population, 185
    Prey, 184, 185
    Range and map, 184, 186
    Speed, 185
    Tundrius peregrines, 186, 187
Pileated Woodpecker, 125, 126
Plumbeous Kite, 73
Prairie dogs, 283, 284
Prairie Falcon, 188–192, 198, 228
    Appearance, 188, 192
    Breeding, 191
    Diet, 189, 192
    Fledgling, 188
    Habitat, 188, 189, 192
    Hunting, 188, 191
    Nest, 188, 191
    Population, 188, 192
    Prey, 191
    Range and map, 188, 192
Puerto Rican Parrot, 109, 110, 218
Pygmy Owl, 205, 298
Red-backed Buzzard, 143
Red-shouldered Hawk, 27, 114–117, 121,
    124, 158, 239
    Appearance, 114, 115
    Broad-winged Hawk, similarity to,
        114, 115
    Conservation, 117
    Diet, 114
    Gray Hawk, similarity to, 114
    Habitat, 114–116
    Nest, 116
    Population, 116
    Range map, 114
    Vocalization, 115
Red-tailed Hawk, 93, 109–113, 120, 124, 127,
    139, 192, 222, 232, 233
    Albinism, 113
    Appearance, 109–112
    Breeding, 110
    Diet, 111
    Eggs, 110
    Habitat, 109, 113
    "Harlan's Hawk", 111–113
    Hunting, 110
    Nest, 110, 111
    Pesticides, 113
    Population, 111, 113
    Prey, 112
    Range and map, 109, 111
    Vocalizations, 110
Richardson's Owl, See Boreal Owl
Ridgway's Hawk, 115, 121
Roadside Hawk, 121
Rostrhamus sociabilis, See Everglade Kite
Rough-legged Hawk, 132–138, 139

Appearance, 134, 136, 138
Breeding, 134, 136
Diet, 134
Habitat, 132
Hunting, 138
Migration, 136
Nest, 135, 136
Prey, 134
Range map, 132
Young, 138
San Pedro National Conservation Area,
121, 154
Santa Cruz River, 119–121
Saw-whet Owl, 217, 257
Scheelite Canyon, 213
Schnell, Jay, 152, 154
Secretary Bird, 206
Sespe Condor Sanctuary, 29–31, 35, 38
Sharp-shinned Hawk, 8, 92, 99–103, 127,
158, 198, 201, 205
Appearance, 100–102
Breeding, 101, 102
Diet, 100, 101, 103
Eggs, 100, 101
Fledgling, 102, 103
Habitat, 99
Hunting, 99, 101
Nest, 101
Pesticides, 103
Population, 102, 103
Predation, 103
Puerto Rican, 99, 102, 103
Range map, 99
Vocalizations, 100
Short-eared Owl, 223, 248–253, 257, 281
Aggression, 249
and lemmings, 253
and Northern Harrier, 248, 249
Appearance, 249, 251
Breeding, 253
Eggs, 252
Flight, 251
Foraging, 252
Habitat, 251, 253
Hunting, 248, 249, 251, 253
Nest, 249, 252, 253
Population, 251, 253
Prey, 249, 251, 253
Range and map, 248, 251, 253
Short-tailed Hawk, 106, 122–126, 139, 143
Appearance, 122, 124–126
Diet, 126
Habitat, 122
Hunting, 124, 126
Nest, 124, 125
Population, 126
Prey, 124
Range map, 122
Size dimorphism, 124
Young, 125
Silt Sandpiper, 198
Size dimorphism, 295
Sky-dancing, 84
Smith, Tom, 63, 64
Snail Kite, See Everglade Kite
Snake River Birds of Prey National
Conservation, 272
Snake River Canyon, 191, 192
Snow Bunting, 229
Snowy Owl, 221, 222, 225–230, 281
and Arctic Fox, 228, 229
and lemmings, 227, 229
Appearance, 225–228
As food, 229
Breeding, 227–229
Defense, 227, 228
Eggs, 228
Foraging, 227, 229
Habitat, 226, 229
Hunting, 226, 227

Migration, 227
Movement, 227, 228
Nest, 228, 229
Population, 229
Prey, 226, 227
Range and map, 225, 229
Speotyto cunicularia, See Burrowing Owl
Spofford, Walter, 169, 172
Spotted Owl, 13, 213, 224, 233, 235, 239,
241–247, 268
Appearance, 242, 247
Breeding, 247
California subspecies, 247
Conservation, 242, 245, 247
Fledgling, 247
Habitat, 242, 245–247
Hunting, 247
Mexican subspecies, 247
Nest, 242, 245–247
Northwestern subspecies, 247
Prey, 242, 247
Range and map, 242, 247
Vocalizations, 245
Strigidae, 19, see also Owls
Strix nebulosa, See Great Gray Owl
Strix occidentalis caurina, See Spotted Owl,
Northwestern
Strix occidentalis lucida, See Spotted Owl,
Mexican
Strix occidentalis occidentalis, See
Spotted Owl, California
Strix occidentalis, See Spotted Owl
Strix varia, See Barred Owl
Surnia ulula, See Northern Hawk Owl
Swainson's Hawk, 43, 127–131, 139
Appearance, 128, 130
Breeding, 128, 130, 131
Conservation, 131
Diet, 128, 130
Eggs, 130
Habitat, 127, 131
Hunting, 127, 128
Migration, 127
Nest, 128
Population, 127, 131
Prey, 128, 130, 131
Range map, 127
Young, 130
Swallow-tailed Kite, 43, 74–79, 92, 127
Appearance, 74
Breeding, 74, 77, 78
Conservation, 79
Eggs, 77
Fruit feeding, 79
Habitat, 74, 79
Migration, 79
Nest defense, 79
Nest, 74, 75, 77
Population, 74, 79
Prey, 77, 79
Range and map, 74
Vocalization, 77, 79
Young, 74, 77, 79
Swem, Ted, 286, 294
Tail-cocking, 298
Tawny Owl, 235
Tengmalm's Owl, See Boreal Owl
Teratornis incredibilis, 45
Thick-billed Parrot, 93, 245, 247
Tree Swallows, 81, 82, 84
Tundrius peregrines, 186
Turkey Vulture, 40–44, 127, 146, 147
Appearance, 40, 41, 44
Breeding, 44
Conservation, 44
Diet, 41
Eggs, 44
Fledgling, 44
Foraging/scavenging, 40, 44
Migration, 42–44

Nest, 43
Population, 44
Prey, 41
Range and map, 40, 42, 43
Smell, 40, 41
Spread-wing display, 40
Tyto alba, See Barn Owl
Tyto cavatica, 218
Tyto glaucops, 215
Tytonidae, 19, see also Owls
Ulmschneider, Helen, 257
Underground nesting, 281, 282
Ural Owl, 235
Urohidrosis, 49
Vultures, 29–49
Vulturidae, 17, see also Vultures
Wedge-rumped Petrel, 251
Western Screech Owl, 259, 261, 263–268
Appearance, 263
Breeding, 263
Eggs, 263
Fledgling, 263, 267
Habitat, 267
Hunting, 267
Nest, 263, 267
Population, 263, 267
Prey, 263, 267
Range and map, 263
Whiskered Screech Owl, 242, 246, 268–272
and Western Screech Owl, 268
Appearance, 268, 270
Diet, 268
Eggs, 272
Habitat, 268, 272
Hunting, 268
Nest, 268, 270, 272
Population, 272
Ranges and map, 268
Vocalizations, 268
White-tailed Hawk, 138, 139, 143–145
Appearance, 143, 144
Breeding, 145
Eggs, 145
Fledgling, 145
Habitat, 145
Hunting, 143, 144
Nest, 144, 145
Population, 145
Prey, 144
Range map, 143
Vocalizations, 144
White-tailed Kite, 51–54, 158, 298
Appearance, 51, 53
Breeding, 53
Diet, 51
Fledgling, 52, 54
Hunting, 51, 53, 54
Nest, 51, 52, 54
Population, 51
Prey, 53, 54
Range and map, 51
Vocalizations, 53, 54
Wiley, Jim and Beth, 105, 116, 117, 158
Wind turbines, 170
Wing claps, 257
Wounded decoy, 222, 223
Yellowstone National Park, 173
Yellowstone River, 262
Zone-tailed Hawk, 18, 120, 127, 136, 146–149
and Turkey Vultures, 146, 147, 149
Appearance, 146, 149
Breeding, 148
Conservation, 149
Diet, 146
Eggs, 148, 149
Hunt, 146–148
Mimicry, 147
Nest, 147, 148
Prey, 146, 147
Range map, 146

About the Authors

The professional careers of Noel and Helen Snyder have been devoted mainly to field conservation studies of various endangered birds, with special emphasis on the Puerto Rican Parrot, the Thick-billed Parrot, the Florida Everglade Kite, and the California Condor. The Snyders have also worked with other wildlife species, however, and have devoted considerable time to writing and music. Noel earned simultaneous bachelor's degrees in music (majoring in cello) at the Curtis Institute of Music and in biology at Swarthmore College, and he completed a Ph.D. in evolutionary biology at Cornell University in 1966, working with aquatic snails. Helen completed her bachelor's degree in biology at Oberlin College and was also pursuing graduate studies at Cornell when they began their long-standing collaborations.

The Snyders' field efforts have included behavioral and ecological studies of many raptor species, resulting in numerous scientific papers. In 1972, they joined the Endangered Wildlife Research program of the U.S. Fish and Wildlife Service and the U.S. Forest Service to conduct research on the Puerto Rican Parrot, and this effort was followed by studies of other endangered birds for the federal government and the National Audubon Society. For work on the Puerto Rican Parrot and California Condor, Noel received the William Brewster Award of the American Ornithologists' Union, a distinguished achievement award from the Society for Conservation Biology, and the Conservation Medal of the Zoological Society of San Diego.

From the late 1980s to the present, the Snyders have been based in southern Arizona, where they have conducted research on Northern Goshawks, Thick-billed Parrots, and various owl species. These activities have been interspersed with participation in research and conservation training programs focused on parrots in Jamaica, St. Lucia, and Mexico for Wildlife Preservation Trust International. They played an important role in recent successful efforts to ensure the protection of Cave Creek Canyon of the Chiricahua Mountains from mining development and have spent considerable recent energies aiding campaigns to preserve important montane habitats in Mexico.